Building Windows 8.1 Apps from the Ground Up

Emanuele Garofalo

Antonio Liccardi

Michele Aponte

Apress·

Building Windows 8.1 Apps from the Ground Up

ISBN-13 (pbk): 978-1-4302-4701-2

ISBN-13 (electronic): 978-1-4302-4702-9

President and Publisher: Paul Manning
Lead Editor: Ewan Buckingham
Technical Reviewer: Fabio Claudio Ferracchiati
Editorial Board: Steve Anglin, Mark Beckner, Ewan Buckingham, Gary Cornell, Louise Corrigan, James T. DeWolf, Jonathan Gennick, Jonathan Hassell, Robert Hutchinson, Michelle Lowman, James Markham, Matthew Moodie, Jeff Olson, Jeffrey Pepper, Douglas Pundick, Ben Renow-Clarke, Dominic Shakeshaft, Gwenan Spearing, Matt Wade, Steve Weiss
Coordinating Editor: Anamika Panchoo
Copy Editors: Mary Behr, Nancy Sixsmith
Compositor: SPi Global
Indexer: SPi Global
Artist: SPi Global
Cover Designer: Anna Ishchenko

Distributed to the book trade worldwide by Springer Science+Business Media New York, 233 Spring Street, 6th Floor, New York, NY 10013. Phone 1-800-SPRINGER, fax (201) 348-4505, e-mail orders-ny@springer-sbm.com, or visit www.springeronline.com. Apress Media, LLC is a California LLC and the sole member (owner) is Springer Science + Business Media Finance Inc (SSBM Finance Inc). SSBM Finance Inc is a Delaware corporation.

For information on translations, please e-mail rights@apress.com, or visit www.apress.com.

Apress and friends of ED books may be purchased in bulk for academic, corporate, or promotional use. eBook versions and licenses are also available for most titles. For more information, reference our Special Bulk Sales–eBook Licensing web page at www.apress.com/bulk-sales.

Any source code or other supplementary materials referenced by the author in this text is available to readers at www.apress.com. For detailed information about how to locate your book's source code, go to www.apress.com/source-code/.

Contents at a Glance

Contents

About the Authors

Emanuele Garofalo is a solution architect who specializes in development for the .NET Framework. He is an active member of the DotNetCampania user group community. He is also speaker at technical conferences on the subject of XAML and C# technologies.

Emanuele's previous book, Windows Phone 7 Recipes, was also published by Apress. He is currently employed by E-Fil s.r.l.

Antonio Liccardi works as chief technology officer, senior consultant, and trainer at BC Soft s.r.l., an Italian software development company.

Antonio is both the cofounder of and regular speaker at the DotNetCampania user group community (`http://www.dotnetcampania.org`). He is an accredited MCP, MCSD, MCST IT, and OCA.

Michele Aponte is cofounder and chairman of the DotNetCampania user group community (`http://www.dotnetcampania.org`), for which he organizes technical events covering Microsoft technologies in the Campania. He is cofounder and CEO of Blexin Srls (`http://www.blexin.com`), for which he develops applications for Microsoft platforms.

Michele is an MCP, MCTS, MCPD, and MCT, and has been a Microsoft MVP for ASP.NET and IIS since January 2011.

About the Technical Reviewer

Fabio Claudio Ferrachiati is a senior consultant and a senior analyst/developer using Microsoft technologies. He works for Brain Force (http://www.brainforce.com) in its Italian branch (http://www.brainforce.it). Fabio is a Microsoft Certified Solution Developer for .NET, a Microsoft Certified Application Developer for .NET, a Microsoft Certified Professional, and a prolific author and technical reviewer. Over the past 10 years, he's written articles for Italian and international magazines and coauthored more than 10 books on a variety of computer topics.

CHAPTER 1

■ ■ ■

Introduction to Windows 8.1

This chapter introduces you to Windows 8.1 and Windows Store apps, starting with the history of Windows, including a discussion on the evolution of user interfaces (UIs) from the textual interfaces up to modern gestures on multitouch devices. After we've refreshed your memory and highlighted the concepts of modern UIs, you'll be ready to understand what's under the hood of Windows 8.1. You will look at the Immersive apps and learn the philosophy behind the Windows Store apps' UI and how it has influenced the development of Windows 8.1 to give you the knowledge to create user-centric applications. Obviously, having knowledge without the tools to implement it doesn't make much sense; so during this introduction, we'll also show you the developer environment that you need to use to develop applications for Windows 8.1.

Once Upon a Time in Windows

This section introduces you to the history of Windows versions, starting from version 1.0 up to Windows 8.1. We'll list improvements introduced by Microsoft version to version, and we'll follow the upgrade path made to the concept of the UI, starting from its introduction up to the new Windows 8.1 UI.

From Windows 1.0 to 3.1

Once upon a time, everything had a text interface; then along came the mouse and everything changed. Microsoft's first OS was MS-DOS, which was a simple command parser. This type of interface couldn't be called a GUI and certainly did not encourage less-technical users to use a computer. To compensate, in 1983 Microsoft announced the Windows project (code name *Interface Manager*).

After 2 years, Microsoft released the first version of Windows (1.0), which many still think was simply a graphical interface for MS-DOS, but the executables that ran under this release were significantly different by format. Instead, Windows 1.0 was a complete system ready to work with multitasking, which offered the possibility to swap between various applications without having to close them. This was different from MS-DOS because it was a monotasking operating system (OS). Looking at Windows 1.0 as a real OS is still an error; more properly, it was a graphical environment hosting applications that ran on it.

The use of hand-eye coordination in UIs was the real turning point in User Experience (UX) because users were catapulted from pure text interfaces made of long sequences of key combinations to the ability to access software commands—and into a world of menu bars, scrollbars, and "windows."

Two years later, Microsoft released Windows 2.0, designed to support Intel 286 processors. Shortly afterward, when Intel released the 386 processor, Windows/386 supported the functionality of extended memory that this processor was offering. With this release, the first software companies began to produce software for Windows. These apps were the first signs of the success of the Microsoft OS, supported by the fact that computers became "personal" (becoming part of everyday office employees' lives).

The real breakthrough in the world of personal computers came in 1990, when versions 3.0 and 3.1 of Windows were released in rapid sequence (see Figure 1-1). These two versions of the OS from Redmond sold 10 million copies in the first 2 years and decreed the dominance of Microsoft in the world of personal computers. The main features of the 3.x releases were 16-color graphics; Program Manager; File Manager; and Print Manager, enriched by features that are included in the multimedia upgrade kits that comprised a CD-ROM drive and a sound card.

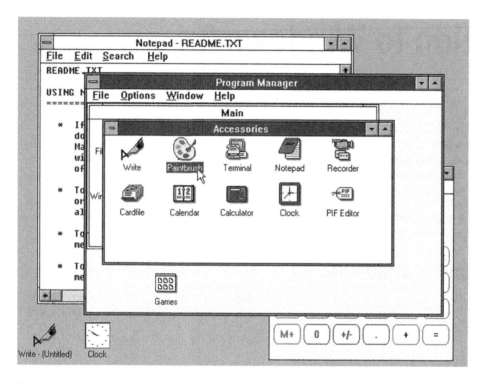

Figure 1-1. *Windows 3.0 interface*

In addition to the features that Microsoft has introduced for users since version 3.0, the story got interesting for developers with a new version of the Windows SDK that simplified software development. The PCs entered peoples' homes as well as their workplaces, so there was a need for software capable of supporting users in their small daily tasks. With version 3.11 for Workgroups, Windows added support for peer-to-peer networks and domains, casting PCs as an integral part of the structures of client/server networks that emerged.

Windows 95 to 2000

The growing interest by the community of developers and dizzying sales led Microsoft to invest in what would become the father of its own modern OS: Windows 95, a consumer-oriented OS. Among the various improvements for users were context menus; built-in Internet support, which was gradually becoming more widespread in the world; Plug and Play capabilities to easily install hardware; and a taskbar with a button named Start (see Figure 1-2), from which the user has access to virtually any element of the OS. Considering the whole of Windows 95, you can guess that the key to its success lay in the simplicity of use for nontechnical users, a concept that became crucial in the evolution of computing.

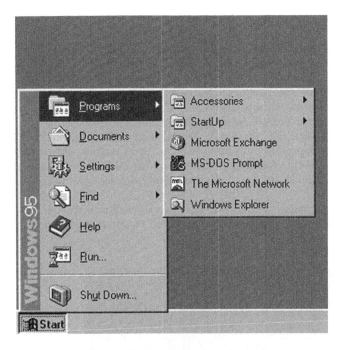

Figure 1-2. *Taskbar with Start button*

The next step in the evolution of Microsoft's OS was the Memphis project known as Windows 98, which introduced several new features such as USB, support for DVD, and the Fat32 file system. But its main feature was the integration of Internet Explorer (IE) with the shell of the OS. This enabled another feature, Active Desktop, which allowed users to view and access HTML contents directly from the desktop.

The same features were also present in Windows Millennium Edition (ME), a version that has enjoyed little fame because it differed from Windows 98 only by multimedia features. The most publicized change from Windows 98 was that it didn't include real mode MS-DOS; it included a MS-DOS virtual machine (VM). Windows ME was intended to be an update of Windows 98 instead of a new version; it supported domestic use with multimedia capabilities, providing software such as Windows Media Player 7 and Windows Movie Maker.

■ **Note** The integration of IE some years later would cost Microsoft a legal battle with the European Commission on charges of abuse of dominant position.

Windows ME was probably the most unstable version of Microsoft's OSs; Windows 2000, often abbreviated as W2K, replaced it. It was an OS based on Windows NT, thought to work with advanced network capabilities; ready to be used as a client in professional version; and used as a server with Server, Advanced Server, and Datacenter Server versions.

Windows 2000 was the link that joined the desktop to enterprise versions of the Microsoft OS, merging in the NT line of OSs some features from the Windows 9x branch, such as Windows Desktop Update, Outlook Express, and others. Among the more interesting features for the consumer market was the support for NTFS (a file system that manages the allocation of blocks in a more intelligent manner to avoid waste of space and allows users to easily manage security settings files by using different features). Another interesting enhancement was made to Windows Explorer, which allows users to customize the way folders look and behave. Unfortunately, this feature paved the way for malicious scripts and other form of infection.

From Windows XP to Windows Vista

In 2000, Microsoft merged the team members of project Neptune, a new consumer version of Windows built on Windows NT, into the team working on Windows Odyssey, an upgrade for Windows 2000 for business purposes. This new team worked on a project named Whistler. In the 2001 Microsoft release, Project Whistler was better known as Windows XP (eXPerience). After the experiment to reunite the desktop and server versions in a single product, Microsoft resumed the usual conduct, dividing them again into two separate lines.

For the server version, the next release was Windows Server 2003; but for the desktop version, there was the launch of Windows XP, still the longest-running OS from Microsoft. Windows XP came with a new fresh UI, improved by many visual effects, which the OS decide to use or not depending on system resources. All the explorer windows contained a sidebar window, Common Tasks, including the Open Documents folder or Images folder or Access to Network. From a technical point of view, Windows XP included GDI+, a sort of facade responsible for drawing lines and curves, and rendering fonts.

The taskbar supported the grouping of windows (see Figure 1-3). Many enhancements were included in the new version of the kernel, touching Power Management, Memory Management, I/O Subsystem, Logon, Registry, and much more.

Figure 1-3. *Grouping windows in the taskbar*

Microsoft released three service packs for Windows XP:

- *Service Pack 1*: Released in September 2002, it contained a lot of security and stability fixes, and offered support for hard drives larger than 137 GB.

- *Service Pack 2*: Released in August 2004, it contained other security fixes, such as support for Wi-Fi Protected Access (WPA) encryption for Wi-Fi and enhancements for Windows Firewall.

- *Service Pack 3*: Released in April 2008, side by side with other security fixes, it introduced support for SHA-2 signatures in X.509 certificates and descriptive security options in Group Policy.

Five years after the release of Windows XP (in 2007), Microsoft announced the next version of Windows that was code-named Longhorn and better known as Windows Vista. From a nontechnical point of view, the most important updates in this version were the following:

- Windows Aero (which stood for authentic, energetic, reflective and open) was the new version of the Windows UI, intended to be cleaner, including glass-like effects that applied to window borders.

- Another interesting feature was Windows Flip 3d, which arranged the preview of all opened windows in a sort of carousel. Always referring to the preview effect, with Aero you could point to a Windows taskbar button to display a preview of the window (or windows, when grouped).

- The Start menu was changed, again losing the label and showing the Windows orb (see Figure 1-4), and showed a text box to search inside the computer for applications, files, and mail; and to run applications by just writing the name. Another significant change was the disappearance of the All Programs item, replaced with the entry Programs.

Figure 1-4. Windows Vista Start button

- Even Windows Explorer was changed in this version. The task panel was removed, and a new panel contained the favorite folders and the Details pane, which displayed information about the selected item. The address bar was modified, showing breadcrumbs about the current path that allowed users to click everywhere on the hierarchy to rapidly change the folder instead of pressing the Back button.

The technical aspects that changed in this version related largely to the core of the OS, in which audio, print, networking, and display subsystems changed.

Windows supported IPv6 for all network devices installed and the Link Local Multicast Name Resolution (LLMNR) protocol to resolve hostnames on networks without a DNS server.

Windows Vista had a rewritten audio stack that ran at user level, thus increasing the stability of the system. Every application that needed to use the audio needed to start a session using the Windows Audio Session API (WASAPI) that worked in two ways:

- *Exclusive mode (DMA)*: Played only one stream from one application; was particularly efficient for applications that needed to output compressed audio such as Dolby Digital or DTS.

- *Shared mode*: Audio streams were rendered by the application, the global audio engine mixed the streams, and then the streams were rendered on the audio device.

Starting with this version of Windows was fully integrated support for speech recognition, which no longer required the installation of Office and was improved to command the computer through voice by using the Microsoft Speech API 5.3 and Speech Recognizer 8.

The print subsystem was rewritten to conform to the XML Paper Specification (XPS) and the Windows Presentation Foundation (WPF). These two technologies repaired the defects of the graphics device interface (GDI), improving the Color Management by adding support for a resolution-independent, vector-based, paged document format.

For programmers, it was the first version of Windows to use WPF to improve the UI, still retaining compatibility with Windows Forms and previous versions of the .NET Framework. For the uninitiated, WPF also made its first appearance with XAML, an XML dialect for designing graphical user interfaces (GUIs) that were used in this technology, in Silverlight, and in Silverlight for Windows Phone.

Windows 7

We have now discussed 23 years of Windows history, and the user experience has been at the center of the improvements introduced by Microsoft (which always considered the need to improve purely technical aspects to reduce the gap that arose with other OSs of the new generation). First, Microsoft focused on time spent to boot up the system. Until Windows 7, when you installed a service or a program that started with the OS, it meant that even unused services consumed resources that might otherwise be helpful to enable the system to run rapidly. For this reason, in Windows 7 you can set a service to start delayed in order to speed up the boot.

The taskbar has been modified in several ways: it is 10 pixels taller than in previous versions to allow touch capabilities, and the user can pin the application to the bar (this feature replaces the old Quick Launch bar).

Another interesting feature is support for *multitouch*, which refers to the capability of a touch device (touchpad, touchscreen, and so on) to recognize more than one point of contact on the surface.

The advent of multitouch devices shows endless horizons of evolution to developers and users; gestures are some of them.

Following is a list of the most common gestures (see the examples in Figures 1-5 to 1-12):

- *Tap*: Single or double touch (single tap, double tap).

- *Double finger tap*: Tap with two fingers at the same time, taking care to keep the target in the middle.

- *Panning with inertia*: Drag one or two fingers up and down.

- *Press and tap*: Press with a finger and tap using another finger.

- *Pinch and stretch*: Make a pinching motion with your fingers or move them apart.

- *Rotate*: Can be done in two ways: moving two fingers in opposing directions, or holding a finger and moving around another.

- *Press and hold*: Press and wait a range of time (can vary between systems) and then release.

- *Flick*: Swipe your finger quickly in a direction.

- *Drag*: Drag one finger left or right.

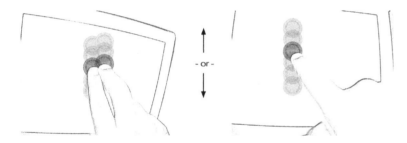

Figure 1-5. *Panning with inertia*

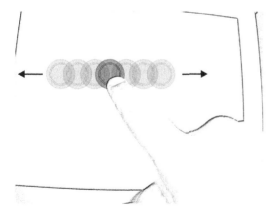

Figure 1-6. *Drag*

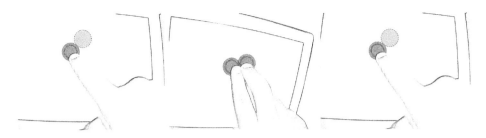

Figure 1-7. *Press and tap*

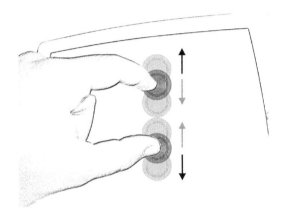

Figure 1-8. *Pinch*

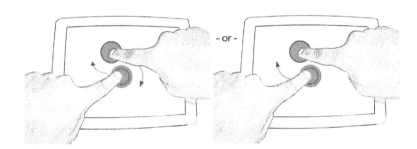

Figure 1-9. *Rotate*

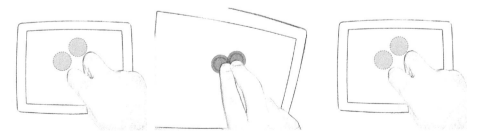

Figure 1-10. *Double finger tap*

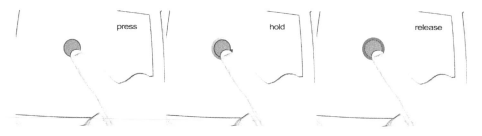

Figure 1-11. *Press and hold*

Figure 1-12. *Flick*

Not everyone knows that some of these gestures are implemented in the Windows 7 UI. For example, you can use press and hold or press and tap instead of right-click, zoom in and out using pinch and stretch, and rotate items using the rotate gesture.

With Windows 7, we conclude the history of Microsoft OSs and the most important features that have characterized their existence. You'll now learn about the important features that are part of the OS known as Windows 8.

Windows 8

The cardinal principle of Windows 8 is the adoption of the Microsoft Design Style UI, which was introduced with Windows Phone and can be summarized in a few words: "Bring the immediacy of the signs we see every day in the metropolis in a UI with tiles containing simple icons (minimal) that allow the user to understand, in a very intuitive way, what functionality is being accessed." Of course, these few words do not describe completely what is behind the idea of Microsoft Design Style (the code name for the Windows Store apps UI), but we need only to introduce it to explain what's new in Windows 8 (we will cover it in depth in the next section).

The feedback received regarding the Microsoft Design Style UI on Windows Phone inspired the idea to standardize the interface of various platforms, giving end users the same User Experience (UX) moving from one device type to another (e.g., phone, tablet, PC, or TV).

As we did with other OSs, we will examine the features of Windows 8 so you can compare it with other versions.

A first point of comparison is the disappearance of the Start button from the taskbar (as you can see in Figure 1-13). To be precise, it disappeared only visually, but conceptually it has been replaced by the Start screen that includes a mosaic of tiles (just like Windows Phone). We will discuss functionality from a technical point of view later in the book.

Figure 1-13. *Windows 7 application bar*

Tiles are a dynamic representation of applications. If your application doesn't update the tile, it can be defined as "static" and operates as a link used to launch the application to which it refers; whereas a "dynamic tile" acts both as a link and as a summary of the actual state of the application.

The startup screen is the heart of the new UI concept that was created for the new OS. At first, many accused Windows 8 of being too tablet-oriented or more generally touch-oriented. It can probably look like this with the use of tiles that don't seem to look like the classic menu and are made to have everything at users' fingertips.

But consider the Microsoft point of view: to meet the new needs imposed by the modern era. Users are increasingly accustomed to using touch devices, children grow up already learning to perform gestures on tablets, and it doesn't make sense to invest in a direction that isn't related to new trends. The use of tiles responds to requests from users to stay connected with the information they need. For a comprehensive assessment, we must also put ourselves in the shoes of those who don't use touch devices. For these users, Windows 8 retains all the stability of Windows 7 and (minimizing the concept) replaces the classic Start menu with the new Start screen, which will work both as a dashboard and as a menu to launch applications.

The new Windows Store app interface has also changed the login/lock screen, which now includes information such as date, time, pending notifications (only from a limited number of applications), and support for Picture Password (a sequence of gestures to be performed on an image for faster access on touch devices).

More great news about Windows 8 is the presence of IE. Now in its tenth version with a new Microsoft Design Style interface, it is ready for touchscreen, with full support for HTML5 and CSS3 to reduce the need of external plug-ins (which means "No plug-in, no external applications"). All apps come from the Windows Store (we will talk about that in the last chapter, which is dedicated to application publishing).

Windows 8 will resolve the problem linked to procedures (more or less complex) in order to put a Windows self-consistent installation within a USB stick. For Windows-To-Go enterprise users (who sign the enterprise license), it will create images of the PC and write them on a USB stick, so they can start the OS from any computer without compromising corporate security.

Windows 8.1

Windows 8.1, a.k.a. Blue, is the evolution of Windows 8. Based on feedback received from customers, Microsoft made many improvements. First, two new sizes of app tiles are available: one of 70 x 70 pixels and one of 310 x 310 pixels. Because both sizes are square shapes, we cannot continue to reference the 150 x 150 pixels tile as a square tile. From this version of Windows, the tiles sizes are named as follows:

- Small tile: square 70 x 70 px

- Medium tile: square 150 x 150 px

- Wide tile: wide 310 x 150 px

- Large tile square 310 x 310 px

These new tile sizes allow the user to customize the Start screen, showing more tiles or more information. And, keeping an eye on the customization, from this version of Windows, the user can choose to have a slideshow as the background of the lock screen.

Keeping our focus on the UX, we cannot forget to talk about the reintroduction of the Start button. In the first release of Windows 8, many users missed the Start button because they were used to it as the entry point for everything. With Windows 8.1, Microsoft integrates a new kind of Start button.

Clicking it with the primary button of your mouse (the left button if you are right-handed) will move you to the Start screen. Otherwise, with the right-click a contextual menu appears, as shown in Figure 1-14, that allows you to quickly access a list of system shortcuts, including the shutdown menu, (which was omitted in the first release and disappointed many users). The second update that will make Windows 8.1 similar to older versions of Windows is the Boot to Desktop feature that lets users boot directly to the desktop instead of the Start screen.

Figure 1-14. *Contextual menu on the Start button*

Another interesting feature is the introduction of aggregated search, which allows users to search on Bing, the Internet, apps, and locally all at once, which improves the user experience.

There are other enhancements that Microsoft groups under the "bring-your-own-device" category that helps users to rapidly associate resources with the OS. For example, the NFC Tap-to-Pair printing feature lets the user configure a printer by simply reading the NFC tag of the printer from the NFC sensor of the device; Windows will do everything else. Because users want to avoid the use of cables, Windows 8.1 introduced the support of Wi-Fi direct printing that allows a peer-to-peer connection to a Wi-Fi printer, avoiding the need for an access point. To avoid the use of wires, Microsoft introduced native support to Miracast Wireless Display that lets users use compatible devices as a remote display. Not many compatible devices are currently available because this is an extremely new standard, but we think that the Xbox One will surely be compatible.

Speaking of mobility enhancements, there is expanded support for a wider range of VPN clients, VPN auto-triggered connections, and tethering.

Finally, Windows 8.1 has the eleventh version of IE, which is faster than previous versions, even with many tabs on the Start page; and supports the SPDY protocol. The immersive version can now keep up to 100 tabs open instead of 10 and allows multiple instances.

Thinking in Metro: Fundamentals of the Windows Store App UI

This chapter will introduce the philosophy behind the new interface in the Windows 8 Store app, starting with different sources of inspiration and ending with the guidelines that a developer should follow.

What Is the Microsoft Design Style?

Microsoft Design Style is the code name for a new set of concepts that Microsoft has introduced in the Windows Phone interface. The aim is to make the UI cleaner, more intuitive, and faster.

Figure 1-15 shows an example of the Windows Phone Start screen.

Figure 1-15. *Windows Phone Start screen*

The screen is formed by squared elements called *hubs*, each of which is *alive*: every hub can display *real-time* notification and images.

Before Windows Phone, some of the distinct elements of the Microsoft Design Style were actually already present in a few Microsoft products such as Encarta 95, MSN 2.0, Windows Media Center, and Zune (see Figure 1-16).

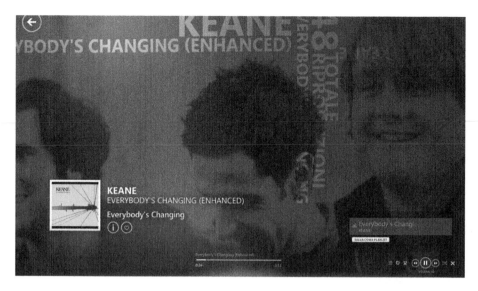

Figure 1-16. *Zune UI (Wikipedia)*

This new kind of interface garnered much approval from customers, and Microsoft decided to use the same guidelines as a starting point for the Windows 8 UI. But what exactly are these concepts?

Origin of the Microsoft Design Style UI Design Language

The Microsoft Design Style UI is inspired by many sources. First are the signs that can be found in public transport systems. In fact, Microsoft designers declared that the King County Metro transit system in Seattle was one of the sources for the Microsoft Design Style because of its simplicity of providing information (see Figure 1-17).

Figure 1-17. *King County Metro signage (Wikipedia)*

Microsoft Design Style is influenced by three concepts:

- Modern design
- International typographic style
- Motion design

The next sections provide details of each concept.

Modern Design

What do Windows Store apps have to do with modern design? To understand the reason why they are connected, we have to figure out where modern design comes from.

One of the main sources of inspiration of modern design was the *Bauhaus* school, which opened in Germany in 1919. The main principle of this school was to combine craftsmanship and the fine arts. All the works were characterized by the absence of adornments to show the matter properties to emphasize the pursuit of a balance between functionality, rationality, and technique.

All the Bauhaus ideas came from the historical context that preceded the period when the school was created (see Figure 1-18). We are talking about the second half of the nineteenth century, in which the effect of the Industrial Revolution, starting from the changes on every aspect of daily life, was spread all over the world.

Figure 1-18. *The Bauhaus building in Dessau*

The progress that was made until today in every field of human knowledge has changed the ways we live our lives. Today, thanks to communication and travel, we feel more connected to each other.

For this reason, modern design fits very well in the Microsoft Design Style conception:

> *"Artisans were stills using yesterday's design thinking"——Moreau (Designing Metro Style: Principles and Personality; Build Conference 2011).*

We need the essential, we need something that is direct, and we need something that is present in our age.

International Typographic Style

Also known as *Swiss style*, the International Typographic Style is a graphic design developed in Switzerland in the 1950s. It was actually created in the 1920s in Russia, Germany, and the Netherlands, but only Swiss graphic designers were capable of expressing these principles in their work.

The main focus was the pursuit of simplicity, readability, and cleanliness. Craftspeople paid a lot of attention to keeping their works essential by preferring typography, content layout, or images to the use of texture and illustration.

Some of the concepts behind the Swiss design are the widespread use of whitespace and geometrical organization of the elements (thanks to the use of a grid system). In Figure 1-19, which shows a Helvetica format example, the typography is the strong point because it enables messages expressed in simple and clean ways. The use of hierarchy in the text also helps to organize information. And all that is not essential is removed.

Figure 1-19. *An example of Swiss design based on a Helvetica font (Wikipedia)*

The way Swiss design expresses a message is so straightforward that today it is usually used in airport and metro signs (see Figure 1-20).

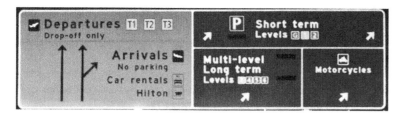

Figure 1-20. *Melbourne Airport signs (Wikipedia)*

Motion Design

Another source of inspiration for Microsoft Design Style is the use of design applied to cinematography. Many films use a mixture of sounds, images, and typography to express *motion*. Some examples can be seen in the opening credits by Saul Bass in the films *Anatomy of a Murder, North by Northwest,* and *Ocean's Eleven.*

You can also find good examples in Steven Spielberg's film *Catch Me if You Can* or in YouTube videos about kinetic typography such as *Where Good Ideas Come From* (by Steven Johnson).

Microsoft Design Style Principles

All the previously discussed concepts about Microsoft Design Style are the fundamentals of the five principles that every developer has to follow when designing apps.

Principle 1: Show Pride in Craftsmanship

Details are important and user experience is, too. When a developer has to design an application, he or she has to consider these aspects. It's important to organize the space in the UI to achieve balance, hierarchy, simplicity, and clarity. It helps to use a grid in which the objects can be laid (see Figure 1-21). Remember that creating software is an art, but creating a good UI is an art, too. Only if both are perfect will you have good software!

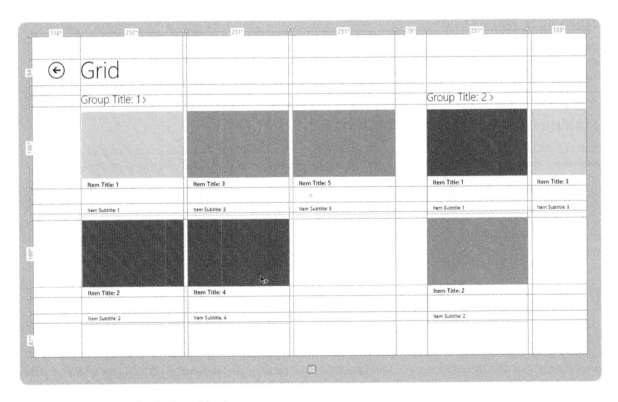

Figure 1-21. An example of using grid to lay text

Principle 2: Be Fast and Fluid

Life is always in motion. Whenever a person needs to use a device, he or she wants a simple, comprehensive, and responsive interface. An application must be intuitive, and a user must be carried away by its UI (maybe by using animations). Most of the modern devices are touch-based. The Microsoft Windows 8 development team has put lots of effort into studying how people interact with a touch-based UI. Developers need to be aware of this.

Principle 3: Authentically Digital

We live in a digital era, which means that *we are always connected.* Social networks, blogs, and cloud services have one thing in common: sharing information. All that matters today is information. And this is why typography is important. People need to share their everyday lives, and they need to do it in a modern way by using images, colors, motion, and typography.

Principle 4: Do More with Less

People need to see only what they are interested in. Content is the heart of the experience. There's no need to always see bars, buttons, and icons. Interfaces must be direct and essential, and users want to explore the content by dipping into it.

Principle 5: Win as One

Embrace the Microsoft Design Style spirit. It is an entire ecosystem that your app can use to work, communicate, and provide control to users. Fit into the UI model and you'll be sure that users will love your applications. You can integrate a set of built-in *contracts* to add features to your app.

Making Great Windows Store Apps

How can developers use all this information to create their applications? First, a developer must have all the knowledge about the Windows 8 application life cycle. Then, by following Microsoft Design Style principles and maybe with the help of a designer, he or she has to create a UI focused on the content. No chrome, nothing unnecessary—just a clean and direct layout; well organized; and based on the use of images, colors, and typography.

Applications have to be touch. It's important to understand how users interact with devices: by touching the screen, using gestures, and with their fingers. A developer could use what is already available; there are built-in controls and contracts that help to create full Windows Store apps. Last but not least, he or she shouldn't be limited to these principles! They are good starting points, but it's up to them to use them and reinvent them.

Platform and Tools

Developing the Windows 8.1 Store app requires the installation of Visual Studio 2013 (VS2013), which is available in full and express editions. The main differences are the price and the auxiliary tools: the Express Edition is free and contains all available tools for Windows 8.1 application development; the full edition (professional or ultimate) also provides tools not directly connected with Windows 8.1. All the examples in this book use the Express Edition, but the code and procedures can be applied to all the major Visual Studio editions.

You can install VS2013 on Windows 8 or previous versions of Windows without restrictions, but if you don't choose Windows 8.1, you can't develop the Windows 8.1 Store app. We'll use Windows 8.1 for the book examples and we advise you to do the same, even in a VM.

When you are developing your application, you should pay attention to the user experience provided by the UI, following the Windows Store app guidelines for Windows 8.1. Visual Studio might not the best tool for this requirement because the designer provided for managing the UI isn't as user-friendly for this scope. In fact, Blend for Visual Studio is more appropriate to design the user experience of your application, with an environment specifically created for the designer who hides the UI code generation behind a collection of graphical designers.

Installing the Tools

You can download Visual Studio 2013 Express for Windows 8.1 from the Microsoft site: http://go.microsoft.com/?linkid=9832256. When the download is complete, click winexpress_full.exe, agree to the license terms and conditions, and click the Install button. Don't interrupt the Internet connection because the installation program must download the components for the installation process (see Figure 1-22).

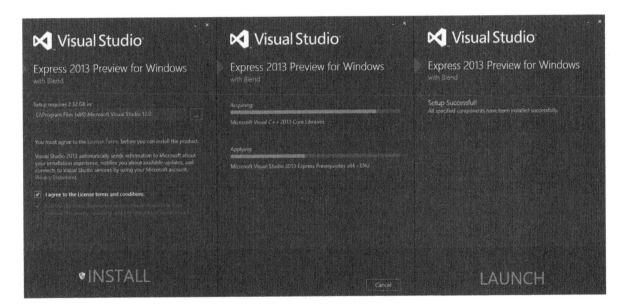

Figure 1-22. *Installation process*

If the Express Edition of VS2013 for Windows is free, it requires a valid product key that can be generated automatically by using a Windows Live account and following the steps suggested by the installation process (see Figure 1-23).

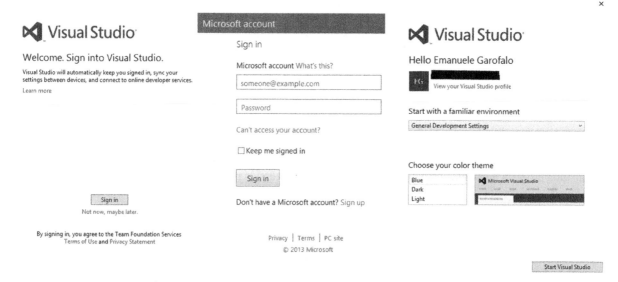

Figure 1-23. *VS2013 for Windows 8 activation process*

The last step is to acquire the developer license for Windows Store development. It is absolutely free (at the moment) and requires only a Windows Live account (see Figure 1-24).

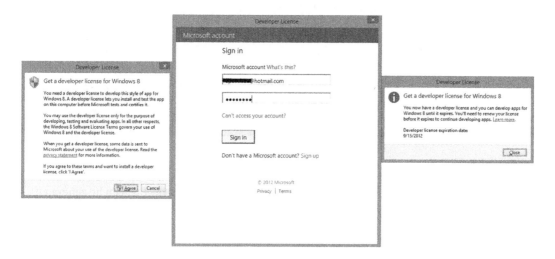

Figure 1-24. *VS2013 for Windows 8 environment*

At the end of the installation process, you can launch Visual Studio, which shows an environment that is completely new compared with previous versions (see Figure 1-25), all in Microsoft Design Style. If you use Visual Studio for the first time, don't panic; it's quite simple to start with this environment.

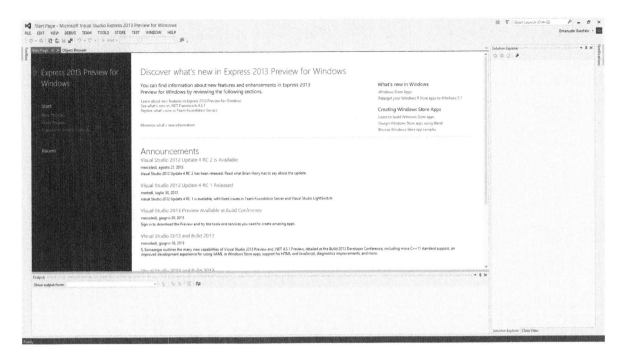

Figure 1-25. *Visual Studio 2013 for Windows*

There are five functional areas:

- *Main menu* (context sensitive): Area for all the commands available for the current view

- *Command bar* (context sensitive): Area of the main and most-used commands for the current view

- *Toolbar* (context sensitive): Area with all the tools for the current view

- *Working area*: Area with the code editors and/or the available designers

- *Solution Explorer*: Area in which you can explore the application structure

First, you have to create a new project with the New Project dialog box by clicking the New Project menu item of the File menu, clicking the new project icon on the command bar, or using the Ctrl+Shift+N shortcut.

In this wizard, you can choose a starter template (Grid App in this example), a name for the project (FirstApp, in this case), the location for the project files, and a solution name (by default, the same as the project name). Click OK and wait for the project creation (see Figure 1-26).

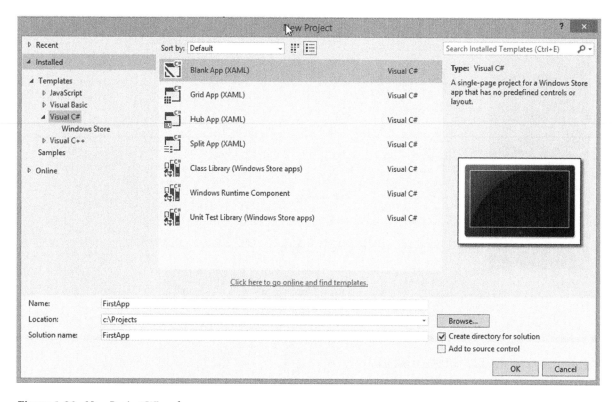

Figure 1-26. *New Project Wizard*

Starting Your Application in the Simulator

In the next chapters, you will analyze the code created by the template. At this time, try to launch the empty application that was created. Starting from VS2012 (and even in VS2013), we have more control over the environment that we want to use to test our app because the Play button (the F5 shortcut if you use the C# key configuration) is a combo box button (see Figure 1-27).

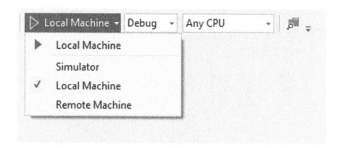

Figure 1-27. *Starting application options*

You can choose to launch the current project in the following:

- *Local Machine*: Launches the current project directly on the OS.

- *Simulator*: Runs the application on a Windows 8.1 tablet Simulator. This is the best choice if the current hardware doesn't support touch or other device capabilities, and you want to simulate them.

- *Remote Machine*: Launches the application on an external device connected to the current device. This is the best choice if you can try the application on real hardware.

For example, choose Simulator and click the Play button (or press F5). Visual Studio launches the Simulator (see Figure 1-28): a complete environment that tests all the capabilities offered from Windows 8.1 and the major devices available for the market. Look at this simulation environment. The Simulator creates a terminal server connection to your OS. This is very cool because if you use Simulator for tests, touch, or GPS, you can do it in your Windows 8 configuration!

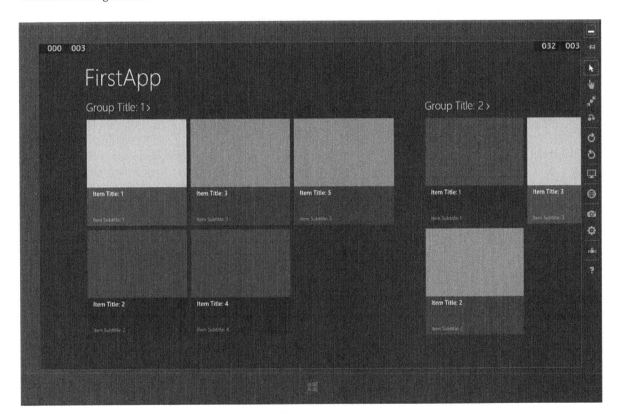

Figure 1-28. *Windows 8 Simulator*

The Simulator has a command bar on the right for changing the environment settings; these functionalities are introduced in Table 1-1.

Table 1-1. *Simulator Commands*

Mouse Mode	The Simulator input type is a mouse pointer.
Touch Mode	The Simulator input type is touch–mode simulated with the mouse.
Touch Emulation Pinch/Zoom	The Simulator input is the touch combo for pinch and zoom operations.
Touch Emulation Rotate	The Simulator input is the touch rotation combo.
Rotate Simulator Clockwise 90 Degrees	Rotates the Simulator screen 90 degrees clockwise.
Rotate Simulator Counterclockwise 90 Degrees	Rotates the Simulator screen 90 degrees counterclockwise.
Change Resolution	Changes the resolution used by the Simulator. Possible values are these: 7" 1920 x 1200px 7.5" 1440 x 1080px 10.6" 1024 x 768px 10.6" 1366 x 768px 10.6" 1920 x 1080px 10.6" 2560 x 1440px 12" 1280 x 800pxu 23" 1920 x 1080px 27" 2560 x 1440px
Set Location	Allows you to send geographic coordinates to a device as a GPS device. During first use, the device requires the authorization for GPS device configuration that wants administrator privileges. Manually set the latitude (degrees), longitude (degrees), altitude (meters), and error radius (meters) with a simple form (see Figure 1-29).
Capture Screenshot	Allows you to create a picture shoot of the Simulator content in the location indicated into screenshot settings.
Screenshot Setting	Allows you to change settings for the Capture Screenshot command via a pop-up menu: • Save the screenshot as a file or in the Clipboard • Quickly access the folder that contains the saved screenshots • Change where on HD the screenshots must be stored
Change Network Properties	Access the Set Network Properties dialog box shown in Figure 1-30. Here you can set Network functionality such as to see if the connection is near the data limit or whether the connection has roaming enabled or not. This allows you to test your app against various scenarios.
Help	Opens the online help site for the Simulator.

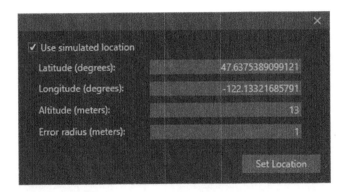

Figure 1-29. *Set location authorization form and set location form*

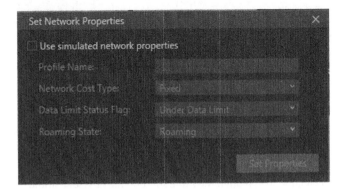

Figure 1-30. *Set Network Properties dialog box*

On the bottom you can see the windows button for switching between the immersive desktop and the last opened application. If the Simulator has the focus, the keyboard commands are captured from the Simulator, and you can also use the windows button on your keyboard or all the keyboard shortcuts available for Windows 8.

To close the Simulator, press the right mouse button and choose the Exit menu item from the contextual menu; the `Minimize` command obviously does not close the Simulator.

Blending for Microsoft Visual Studio 2013

If you are a designer, a user experience designer, or a developer who is creating the UI of an app, you probably prefer to use tools specifically made for this type of task to simplify your work. For this purpose, Microsoft has the Expression Studio suite, which is a component of the suite called Blend (see Figure 1-31).

Figure 1-31. *Blend for Visual Studio 2013*

When it created Expression Studio, Microsoft wanted not only to create a suite for graphic users but also to create an environment to include graphics users in the team. In fact, Blend can open the same solution file of Visual Studio and share the code with it as the same source control server application, as Team Foundation Server, and directly launch the application with the classical F5 button. The idea is that the user experience designer is part of the team in all aspects of the developing process.

You can also create a new project directly with Blend by selecting the classical menu item File ➤ New Project and choosing your preferred options for the project creation (see Figure 1-32). If this is your first time working with Blend and you are a developer, remember that this tool is for designer users, and all the operations should be done with the graphical designer or the available palettes. You also can edit the HTML or the XAML directly. If you are a designer, you will feel at home with the Blend UI because it is in line with the most famous Adobe tools. Note that starting from VS2012 and so on to the 2013 XAML designer has been improved with many components in the past available only with Blend, so if you are a developer and you don't want other software, you can use the new designer and be happy.

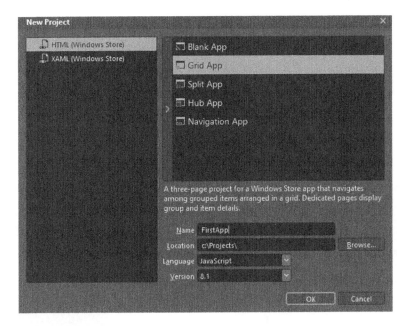

Figure 1-32. *New Project Blend Wizard*

Blend is made of five main components (shown in Figure 1-33):

- *Menus*: Area in which you can manage the project and have access to all application settings
- *Tools Panel*: Contains all available tools to modify applications
- *Main Panels*: Show all available main panels for projects
- *Artboard*: Area in which you can design applications
- *Additional Panel*: Area in which you can see all the other available panels with the current kind of project

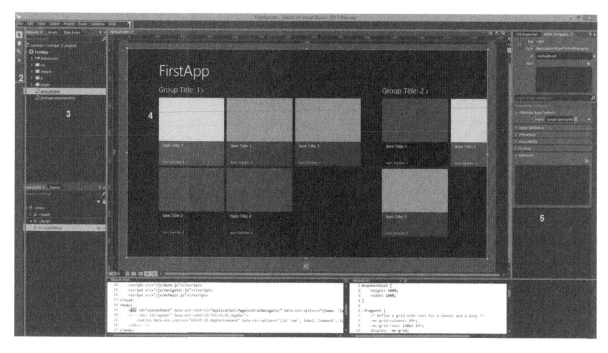

Figure 1-33. *Five main Blend components*

Begin with the Tools Panel (shown in Figure 1-34), which provides these elements for interacting with the environment:

- *Selection Tools*: Composed of the first two buttons with the arrow icons; used to select and the direct the selection of designer elements

- *View Tools*: Composed of the button with the hand and the magnifying glass; used for panning and zooming actions

- *Asset Tools*: Used for fast access to the Assets Panel (explained later)

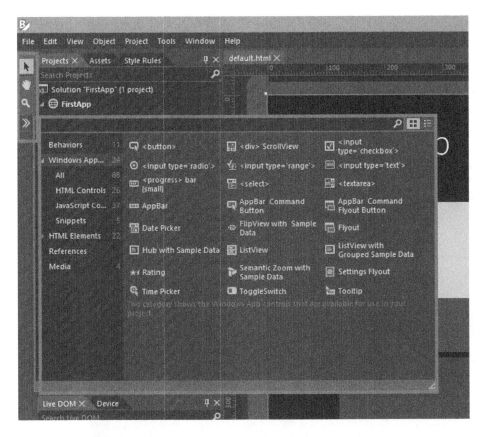

Figure 1-34. *Tools Panel*

The area called Main Panels (see Figure 1-35) includes the most important panels in the UI design process:

- *Projects Panel*: Area in which all the files that compose applications are managed

- *Assets Panel*: Area in which all the available controls for the current project type can be found

- *Platform Panel*: Area for selecting all the platform settings such as resolution, available views (landscape, filled, snapped, portrait), deploy target (local machine or Simulator), and other options

Figure 1-35. *Main Panels*

Other panels appear in this area, but they're specific to project type. For example, the *Styles Panel* is for the CSS file managing of HTML Windows 8 applications, and the *States Panel* is for XAML Windows 8 application visual states managing (explained in Chapter 5).

Now we focus our attention on the *Artboard* (shown in Figure 1-36), which is the core of the environment. On the top left (see element 1 in Figure 1-36), you can see the tabs of the current opened views; the current view is shown in light gray in the designer. If you hover over these tabs, you can see the complete path of the files. Click once to change the current view. On the top right (element 2 of Figure 1-36), if you are in design mode and you have to choose HTML for your project, you see three buttons: the first shows the designer in full screen for helping you with element positioning and manipulation, the second alerts you about errors in the current file (hover with the mouse for the errors detail), and the third refreshes the designer.

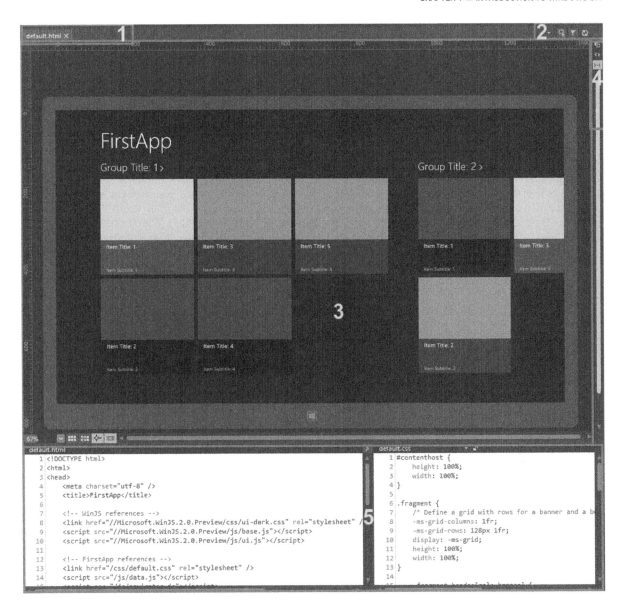

Figure 1-36. *Artboard area*

With the buttons on the middle right (see element 4 of Figure 1-36), you can choose whether the middle area must show the graphical designer (element 3 of Figure 1-36), the code editors (element 5 of Figure 1-36) or both (splitting them). As shown in Figure 1-36, if you use HTML 5 for your project, the code editor shows you HTML and the corresponding CSS elements.

The term *Additional Panels* means all the secondary panels shown, by default, on the right area of the Blend UI. One of them is the *Properties Panel* that shows the properties of the current selection (or multiselection), and its content is specific for the project type.

Conclusions

Window 8.1 introduces many improvements based on the WinRT and WinJS libraries, enabling you to create beautiful Windows Store apps by using the Microsoft Design Style principles. This kind of app, also known as an *immersive app*, opens new horizons of learning. These horizons are ready for desktop developers who come from WPF, Silverlight, or simply from the Web because immersive apps can be designed with XAML or HTML. When you work with XAML, you can write code using managed languages such as VB.NET and C#, or with C++. If you work with HTML, you know a lot of JavaScript; the good news is that you can use your knowledge to inject code in your application.

Of course, if you want to write a Windows Store app, you must know what Microsoft Design Language is. Indeed, this is the code name of the new UI introduced by Microsoft that resembles metropolitan signs, allowing you to design your application with an intuitive look that helps users quickly find and access available functionalities.

The time of writing code in Notepad is certainly over, so in order to be productive, you must know which tools you will need to use when you write a Windows Store app. The first tool is Visual Studio 2013 (VS2013), which you can get (in the Express Edition) from this link: `http://go.microsoft.com/?linkid=9832256`. With VS2013, you can start creating apps for the Windows Store using one of many templates included and choosing your preferred language.

This chapter gave you basic information about the philosophy and tools for Windows 8.1 Store app development. Of course, you cannot start developing without a concrete introduction to the life cycle of the Windows Design Style app or an introduction to the numerous possibilities that WinRT and WinJS offer that enable you to exploit all the capabilities of this OS.

Come with us now to Chapter 2, in which we introduce you to the Windows Runtime environment.

CHAPTER 2

■ ■ ■

Windows Runtime Environment

After giving you a complete introduction to the basic principles of Windows Store apps and the related tools that you need to develop an application, we now want to explore the environment and tell you about the new platform architecture and its components. The following list shows the key concepts you need to know before writing a new application:

- *Communication*: An introduction to Windows Runtime (WinRT) application programming interfaces (APIs) that enable your applications to communicate with external sources

- *Data*: An introduction to all the APIs that allow applications to store and retrieve data

- *Graphics*: Classes that you can instantiate to draw something on your application

- *Media*: Classes that help you play video and audio in your applications

- *Devices and printers*: The support of Windows 8 for devices such as Camera, GPS, Printers, and much more

Windows 8 Platform

Looking toward the future, Windows has been redesigned with a new set of core services shared between the classic desktop applications and the new immersive Windows Store apps. Some of the main problems of Windows operating systems (OSs) were end user problems with installing, uninstalling, searching, and trying applications. Consumers are key (without forgetting business users) to meeting the needs of mobility and touch interactions. To enable developers to create a new experience with Windows for consumer users, Microsoft introduced a new layer in the operating system: *Windows Runtime*, also called *WinRT*.

WinRT is the evolution of the Component Object Model (COM) present in previous versions of Windows, with a completely different type of system (no binary string, no variant, and no RegSvr32) and the deletion of the IDispatch interface and connection points. It solves the main problems of actual applications in the absence of a marketplace in which to find and install applications in a secure mode, without administration permission. WinRT improves the performance and memory cost of necessary wrappers for the interoperability scenarios; it then simplifies the use of native language with the managed language (as with C# and VB.NET) and makes not-blocking the call to the input/output (I/O) device (net, disk, and so on). It also provides standard contracts for the data exchange among applications—and among applications and the operating system.

WinRT integrates the .NET Common Language Runtime (CLR) as a subplatform and doesn't substitute it; it is responsible for many tasks of application memory management through the Garbage Collector, the compilation of the Intermediate Language (IL) code through the just in time (JIT) compiler. Some aspects of the .NET platform influenced many choices of WinRT—for example, the metadata format (ECMA-335), a standard that defines the Common Language Infrastructure (CLI), in which applications written in multiple high-level languages can be executed in different system environments (http://www.ecma-international.org/publications/standards/Ecma-335.htm) and libraries. The type system supports class, methods, properties, delegates, and events such as the .NET languages. The base types are bool, int, float, enum, guid, type, and object. The string, at a binary level, is a value type (not nullable), immutable and compatible with STL (wstring) and .NET (String). The reference types are all types that implement a WinRT interface; the others are value types. There are observable collections and dictionaries, too (Vector and Map). For user interfaces, there is a native implementation of XAML. Windows Presentation Foundation (WPF) and Silverlight don't run in immersive mode, only in desktop mode, but there is a special portable library that allows the creation of DLL libraries shared between Windows Store apps, Desktop, Silverlight, Windows Phone, and Xbox applications!

Figure 2-1 shows the Windows 8 platform. You can see the WinRT layer as a set of object-oriented class libraries shared across programming languages. This is possible because the WinRT metadata are CLI metadata stored in a separate WINMD file (because native code that is processor-specific can't contain metadata) and can be reflected like CLI assemblies.

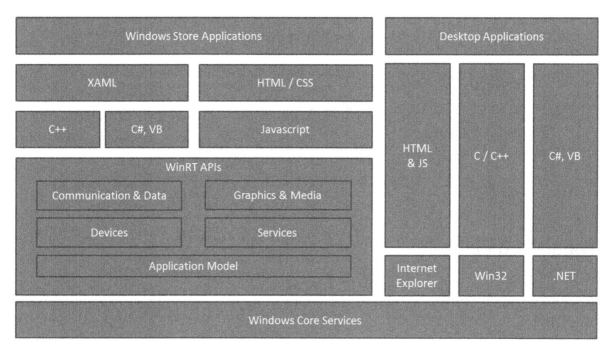

Figure 2-1. *Windows 8 platform*

These WinRT APIs can be grouped into five logical blocks based on their functionalities:

- *Application Model*: Provides all functionalities for application life cycle management

- *Communication and Data*: Provides all functionalities for data storage and communication between the internal and the external world

- *Graphics and Media*: Provides all functionalities for media management

- *Devices*: Provides all functionalities for managing available hardware devices

- *Services*: Provides all functionalities to connect to services such as Skydrive, Bing, Azure Mobile, and Xbox Live

In Figure 2-2, you see these blocks detailed in subcomponents (discussed later in this chapter). Now we make some observations on application life cycle management, the importance of a responsive user interface (UI), and the sandbox in which the applications run. Notice that some items in the picture contain the suffix *(one asterisk) or ** (double asterisks). The meaning of these asterisks is to show what feature has been updated (*) and what features have been added (**) from the first version of the WinRT application programming interface (API) to version 8.1.

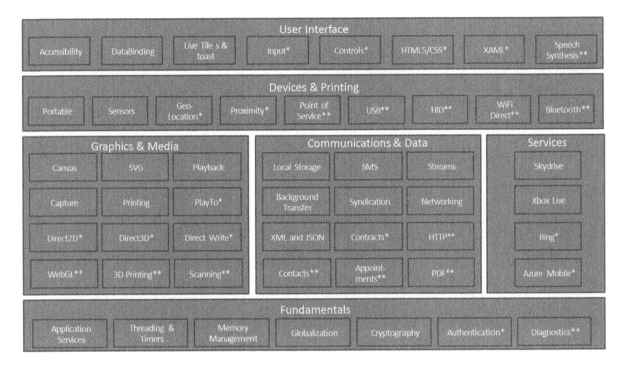

***Figure 2-2.** WinRT functionality blocks*

When an application is activated for the first time, its process is created and running, and the user interface is launched in full screen mode. If another application is activated, the first is hidden and is suspended after 5 seconds, sending a message to the application to save the current state. If it is reactivated, the system sends a resume message to the app for loading the saved state, and the process becomes active. If the available memory is too low, all suspended processes will be closed without notification messages to improve performance. Figure 2-3 shows application life cycle management.

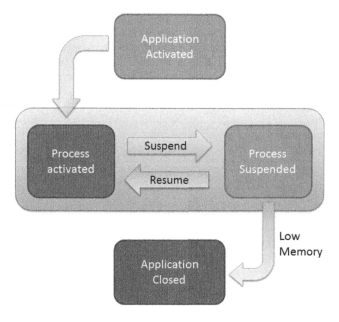

Figure 2-3. *Application life cycle management*

One of the problems of the previous version of Windows was installing and uninstalling applications without administration privilege. WinRT solves this problem in a way that doesn't affect security. All Windows Store applications can be exclusively installed from the Windows 8 Store (the only exception is the installation through Visual Studio for developers' purposes), the Microsoft Marketplace in which all developers can deploy its applications. The installation package, a zip folder with an `.appx` extension, contains an application manifest with the required information for the package installation, the application code files, a section called BlockMap with the hashes of all the application files, and a signature for the package validation.

The application manifest is an `.xml` file named `appxmanifest.xml` that explicitly declares all the capabilities required by the application: file access, device access, network and identity, file type association, and contracts. Don't worry; it isn't necessary to manually edit this file because Visual Studio has a visual editor for this purpose.

When you choose an application from the store for the installation, the system downloads the package, validates it, checks the integrity of all files through the hashes in BlockMap and checks the requirements declared in the manifest file. A component called Security Broker checks this manifest file to ensure that nothing can be used without user authorization (see Figure 2-4).

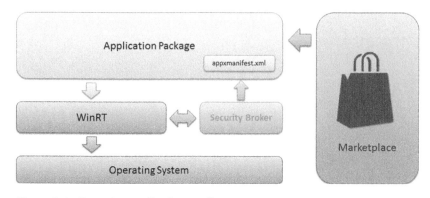

Figure 2-4. *Execution application sandbox*

To allow compatibility among programming languages and WinRT, the projection mechanism was introduced to remap and fit the libraries' metadata. For example, it solves the problem of JavaScript that uses CamelCase notation for properties and methods, PascalCase for types, and lowercase for events; while C++ and .NET use PascalCase notation for all. The projections are specific for every language; Microsoft provides projections for C++, JavaScript, and .NET; but in the future, other companies might provide projections for their languages. See Figure 2-5.

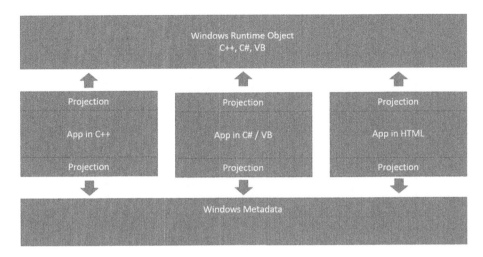

Figure 2-5. *Metadata compatibility through projections*

Application Model

The Application Model component of WinRT APIs refers to fundamental components of the library responsible for application management. It's composed of six main blocks:

- Application Services

- Threading & Timers

- Memory Management

- Authentication

- Cryptography

- Globalization

- Diagnostics

The application services are located in the `Windows.ApplicationModel` namespace and contain the entire API for managing the application life cycle and handling operating system events. For example, the window of an immersive application, its thread, and its state changes are managed through the `Windows.ApplicationModel.Core` classes and interfaces (see Figure 2-6).

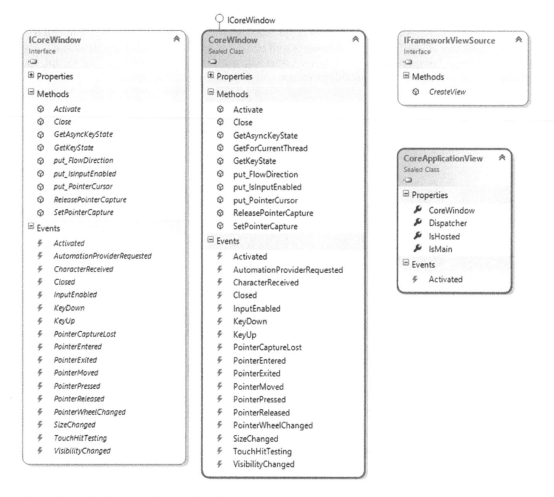

Figure 2-6. *Windows.ApplicationModel.Core classes and interfaces*

Another interesting element is the Windows.ApplicationModel.Background namespace, which provides classes that enable an app to manage background tasks. Although the user interfaces of the immersive mode can appear to be monotasking, Windows is a multitasking operating system, so you can execute different applications at the same time and, with the background tasks, also execute more work items that do not require user interaction. Usually you use these kinds of tasks for call services, reacting to a change of a system condition, showing a notification, and so on. Later, we'll analyze how to use this important feature, but now we are looking for a WinRT API that provides this functionality. Figure 2-7 shows the main classes and interfaces involved in background task management.

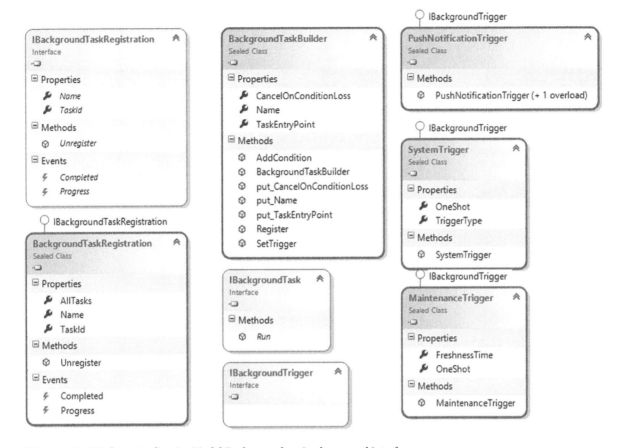

Figure 2-7. Windows.ApplicationModel Background main classes and interfaces

Like the main object-oriented frameworks, you need to implement an interface that establishes the contract between your implementation and the system that executes your code. This interface is IBackgroundTask, which is required to implement the simple Run() method. Without a user interface, there must be another entry point for the execution of the task implemented, so you need to register your code for triggering an event with the SetTrigger() and Register() methods of the BackgroundTaskBuilder class. SetTrigger() accepts any implementation of the IBackgroundTrigger interface; WinRT offers PushNotificationTrigger, SystemTrigger, and MaintenanceTrigger, which allow you to handle the main events of the Windows 8 system. The Register() method returns an instance of the BackgroundTaskRegistration class, which is useful for handling Completed and Progress events.

With the marketplace system, the programmer can check some conditions of application usage, such as the license state for managing an evaluation version of the app. The reference namespace for this purpose is Windows.ApplicationModel.Store, which exposes the classes shown in Figure 2-8.

Figure 2-8. *Windows.ApplicationModel.Store classes*

The most important item is `CurrentApp`, a static class that exposes all information that you need: the application identifier, the license information as an instance of the `LicenseInformation` class, and the link of the Windows Store web catalog. The `LicenseInformation` class provides two Boolean values, `isActive` and `isTrial`, that you can use in your application to enable or disable functionality.

The good news is that you don't need to wait for the publication of your application for testing these values because the namespace provides the `CurrentAppSimulator` class, too. You can use this static class to simulate the `CurrentApp` behavior.

The remaining components of the `Windows.ApplicationModel` namespace are these:

- `Windows.ApplicationModel.Activation`: Defines the items that support event handling for the contracts and extensions supported by Windows

- `Windows.ApplicationModel.Appointments`: Defines the items that support the creation of appointments in a calendar

- `Windows.ApplicationModel.Calls`: Defines the items that support event handling for the lock screen

- `Windows.ApplicationModel.Contacts`: Defines the items that support the use of the Contact Picker to select and acquire information about contacts

- `Windows.ApplicationModel.DataTransfer`: Defines the items used for the data exchange among applications such as the Clipboard

- `Windows.ApplicationModel.Resources`: Defines the items that simplify access to the application resource, such as strings

- `Windows.ApplicationModel.Search`: Defines the items that support the use of the search panel (discussed in the next section)

We will analyze these components in the sample applications, but now we focus on the `Windows.Security` namespace that provides the items for the authentications and protections of the immersive applications.

Windows 8 natively integrates Windows Live Services for user authentication and provides the API for this purpose in the `Windows.Security.Authentication.OnlineId` as well as different authentication services, such as `OAuth` and `OpenID` with the API in the `Windows.Security.Authentication.Web` namespace, providing all the mechanisms for the single sign-on (SSO) feature. Figure 2-9 shows the classes for the use of Windows Live services.

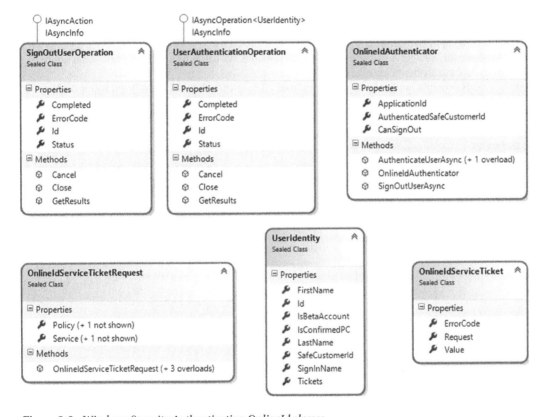

Figure 2-9. *Windows.Security.Authentication.OnlineId classes*

The main operations are shown by the `OnlineIdAuthenticator` class through the `AuthenticateUserAsync()` and `SignOutUserAsync()` methods. Note that they are asynchronous operations; you can retrieve the instance of the `UserIdentity` class, which contains all the information about the user, calling the `GetResult()` method of the `UserAuthenticationOperation` retrieved by `AuthenticateUserAsync()`.

Web services authentication is provided by a single static class called `WebAuthenticationBroker` (see Figure 2-10). The operation is performed by the static asynchronous method `AuthenticateAsync()`, which returns an instance of the `WebAuthenticationResult` class.

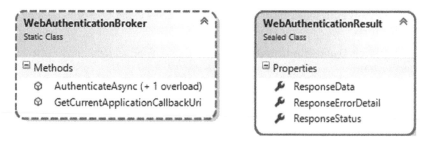

Figure 2-10. *Windows.Security.Authentication.Web classes*

For storing in a shared and secure way, user identification information can be used for the classes of the Windows. Security.Credentials namespace, whereas encrypt and decrypt information can be used for the classes of the Windows.Security.Cryptography namespace.

Starting from Windows 8.1, new ways of authentication are possible. We can now use fingerprint scans, smart cards, and virtual smart cards to authenticate users.

The marketplace adds possible application customers from all countries that Windows Store supports. We can choose our application to be sold in only a particular country, but why should we close the possibilities of the global market? The System.Globalization namespace (see Figure 2-11) can help manage differences between many target cultures. We can use different types of calendars, different languages, a 12-hour clock instead of a 24-hour clock, and so on.

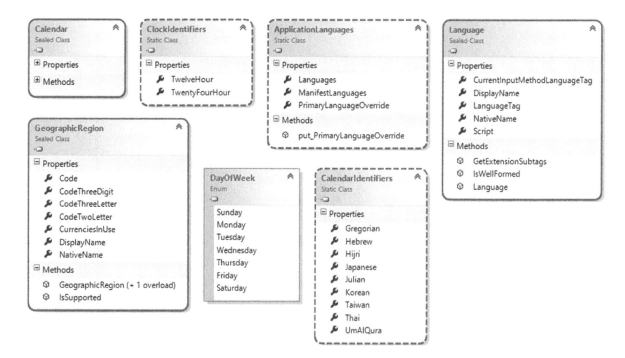

Figure 2-11. *Windows.Globalization classes and enumerations*

To optimize application performance, you should run all tasks in parallel. For this purpose, WinRT provides the `Windows.System.Threading` and `Windows.System.Threading.Core` namespaces (see Figure 2-12), in which the `ThreadPool` static class exposes two overloads of `RunAsync()` methods to run the parallelizable codes in separate threads. A thread pool is more efficient than a single thread because it can schedule work items when threads become available. You cannot control the order in which the threads are executed, but you can use a `ThreadPoolTimer` to delay the execution from the scheduling start and set a `WorkItemPriority` based on your needs.

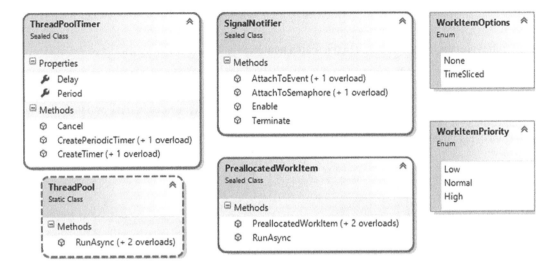

Figure 2-12. *Windows.System.Threading classes and enumerations*

You can preallocate a work item before submitting it to the thread pool with the `PreallocatedWorkItem` class of the `Windows.System.Threading.Core` namespace. This namespace contains another interesting class, `SignalNotifier`, which can be used to create parallel work items to respond to named events or semaphores created by the Win32 COM object.

Communication and Data

The Communication and Data components of WinRT APIs are referred to the components of the library responsible for the communication of the application with the operating system and the external world, and support to the local and cloud storage. There are 12 main blocks:

- Contracts
- Local and Cloud Storage
- Networking
- SMS
- Streams
- XML and JSON
- Background Transfer
- Syndication

- HTTP

- Contacts

- Appointments

- PDF

The contracts establish the communication among applications, and among the applications and the operating system by using a publisher/subscriber relation. There are many contracts in Windows 8; we now take a look at the following:

- *Search*: Integrates the application data in the search panel

- *Share*: Shares documents, video, images, and so on

The goal of the search contract is to reuse the search functionality offered by the operating system, with the result being a centralized and user-friendly feature. Through the contract, the application provides its data, and the user can choose the application in the search criteria, too. The search contract uses the `Windows.ApplicationModel.Search` classes shown in Figure 2-13 to manage the data exchange.

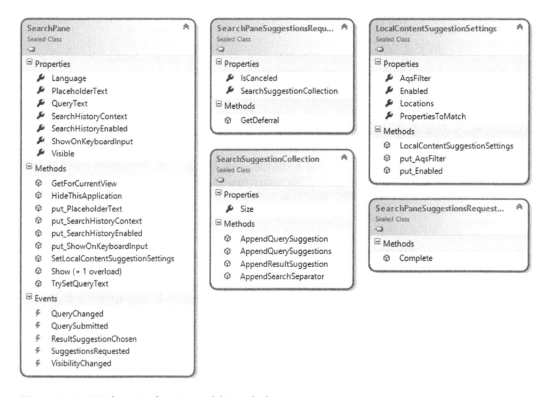

Figure 2-13. *Windows.ApplicationModel.Search classes*

The main class is SearchPane, which provides the GetForCurrentView() method to retrieve a reference to the search pane that can be used in the application. The Show() method shows the search panel and the property. QueryText contains the search text provided by the user. You can subscribe to the events offered by this class for managing the phases of search operations; for example, QueryChanged for when the user changes the search text, or SuggestionRequested and ResultSuggestionChosen for managing the search suggestions provided to users by the application. In the next chapters, we'll show you how to use this interesting feature to improve the user experience of your application.

The share contract enables communication between applications using the Share Panel provided by the operating system. In the share contract, the source and the target application in the contract can be internal or external to the operating system (for example, your application and Facebook or Twitter). The namespace that contains the classes for this functionality is Windows.ApplicationModel.DataTransfer (its most important classes are shown in Figure 2-14). In the DataPackage class, we store the data to share, classified according to following types:

- Plain text

- Uniform Resource Identifier (URI)

- HTML

- Formatted text

- Bitmaps

- Files

- Developer-defined data

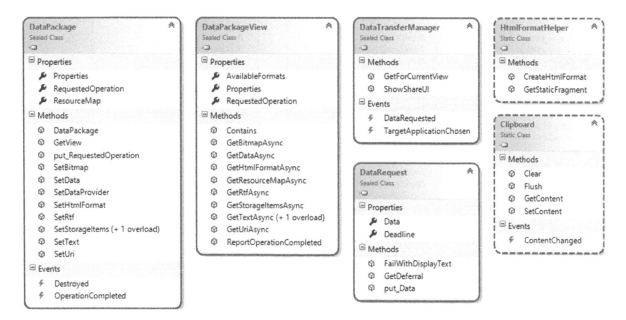

Figure 2-14. *Windows.ApplicationModel.DataTransfer classes*

For sharing the data stored in an instance of DataPackage class, we can use the DataTransferManager instance class associated with the current window that can be retrieved using the method GetForCurrentView(). When a user clicks a Share or Connect charm, the DataRequested event of the DataTransferManager fired; now we can share the data with the application selected by the user.

Our application can also be a target of data sharing; we'll analyze this opportunity in the book sample application. Each application needs to keep the information; in Windows 8, you can use three main solutions:

- External services
- Local storage
- Cloud storage

External services can usually be applied when your Windows Store app is a client of an external application and the connection availability to the services is a strong requirement for the application. *Local storage* is a useful solution for applications that need to work also in disconnected mode, using an application reserved space of the device disk. *Cloud storage*, which includes the use of Skydrive services, is a good solution for saving the application data on the user's cloud space. The WinRT API provides native objects for local storage; cloud storage is provided through an external API such as Windows Live SDK.

The classes for managing the local storage are located in the Windows.Storage namespace, in which you can find the classes shown in Figure 2-15.

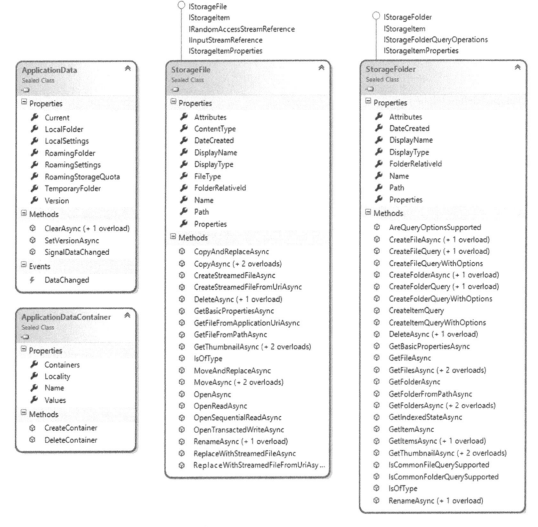

Figure 2-15. *Windows.Storage main classes*

The `ApplicationData` class provides the local storage access point through the `Current` property, with which you can retrieve an `ApplicationDataContainer` class instance using its `LocalSettings` property and an instance of the `StorageFolder` class from its `LocalFolder` property. The `LocalFolder` class provides asynchronous methods for creating files and folders in local storage.

The web services of the WinRT API are available on the `Windows.Web` namespace, in which you can find the main classes shown in Figure 2-16. You can iterate with Syndication web standards for exchanging data in XML format.

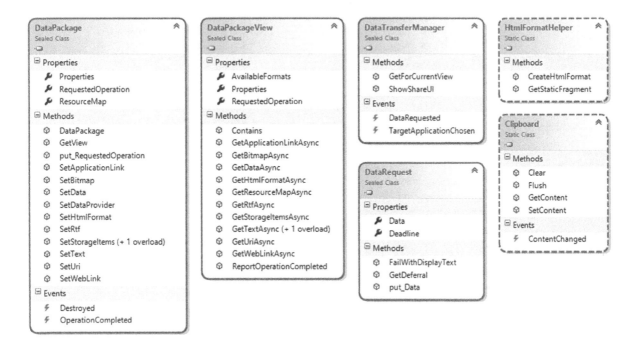

Figure 2-16. *Windows.Web main classes*

Windows 8 implements the concept of notifications, already introduced in Windows Phone 7, which enable the system to send and receive asynchronous notification from cloud services. There are many types of notifications, including these:

- Toast notification

- Raw notification

- Tile notification

- Badge notification

These notifications are available starting from the `Windows.Networking.PushNotifications` namespace that contains the main classes shown in Figure 2-17. The main class is `PushNotificationChannel`, which exposes the `PushNotificationReceived` event that fires when a notification occurs. An instance of this class can be created from the `PushNotificationChannelManager` static class. The enumeration `PushNotificationType` enumerates the possible type of notification. (Details on the notifications' functionalities and workflow will be explained in Chapter 9.)

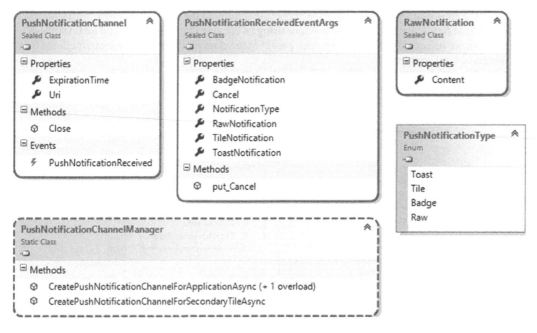

Figure 2-17. *Windows.Networking.PushNotifications main classes*

As notifications, all the network functionalities offered by the Windows Runtime API are located in the namespace Windows.Networking, in which you can find the following:

- Advanced download and upload transfer capabilities (Windows.Networking .BackgroundTransfer)

- Information about connectivity, usage, and data plan information (Windows.Networking .Connectivity)

- Mobile broadband account management (Windows.Networking.NetworkOperators)

- Support connection between devices that are within close range (Windows.Networking .Proximity)

- Access to socket and WebSocket for network communications (Windows.Networking .Sockets)

Windows 8 also provides the Short Message System (SMS) service, but it is in the Windows.Device.Sms namespace because it's strictly connected to the device that Windows 8 runs. The SmsDevice class exposes all necessary objects for SMS operations: call SendMessageAsync() to send a SMS and subscribe to SmsMessageReceived to manage SMS receive events. See Figure 2-18.

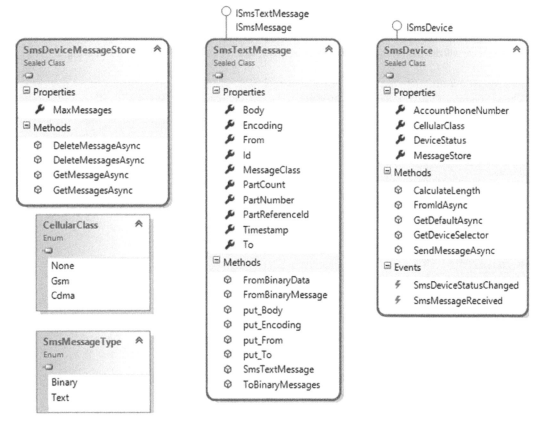

Figure 2-18. *Windows.Device.SMS main classes*

For reading and writing a sequential and random access stream, you can use the `Windows.Storage.Streams` namespace, in which specified stream type reader and writer classes usually support you in operations with data. For example, `FileInputStream` and `FileOutputStream` enable you to read and write file data. Very useful is the `Windows.Data.XML` namespace, which provides all the classes for managing XML data with two child namespaces:

- `Windows.Data.Xml.Dom` explores the XML data tree
- `Windows.Data.Xml.Xsl` transforms XML data in other XML formats through the XSLT transformation process.

Windows 8.1 introduces a new HTTP Client API located in the `Windows.Web.Http` namespace. This namespace provides the following:

- HTTP verbs
- Authentication
- Support for SSL
- Cookies management

The main class is `HttpClient`, which is similar to the ASP.NET version.

Graphics and Media

Graphics and media enable the developer to handle various aspects related to physical display, photos, audio, and video. The first namespace we will discuss is `Windows.Graphics.Display`, which contains the objects shown in Figure 2-19.

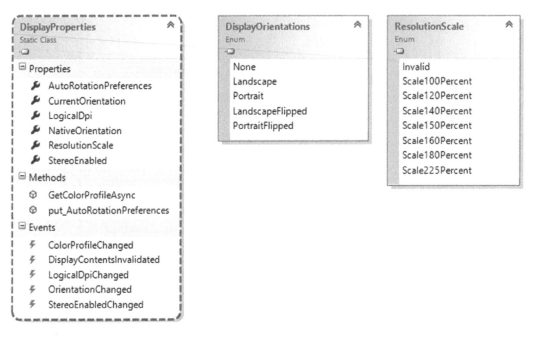

***Figure 2-19.** Windows.Graphics.Display classes and enumerations*

DisplayProperties, which is the main class of the namespace, enables you to get information about the physical display of the device. The most common properties are AutoRotationPreferences, CurrentOrientation, and LogicalDPI, which return the default orientation, the current orientation, and the number of pixels for inches for the current resolution, respectively. Notice that the first one returns an object of the DisplayOrientations enum type. Through public events, we can handle all changes of state for these properties. For example, LogicalDpiChanged is triggered when the LogicalDpi or ResolutionScale properties were modified because of a zoom in/out on the screen or a change to the screen resolution. OrientationChanged is triggered when users change the ways they move devices in their hands (here we are referring to a tablet!).

The Windows.Graphics.Imaging namespace lets you manipulate different image formats (based on system known codecs). Figure 2-20 shows the most useful elements in this namespace.

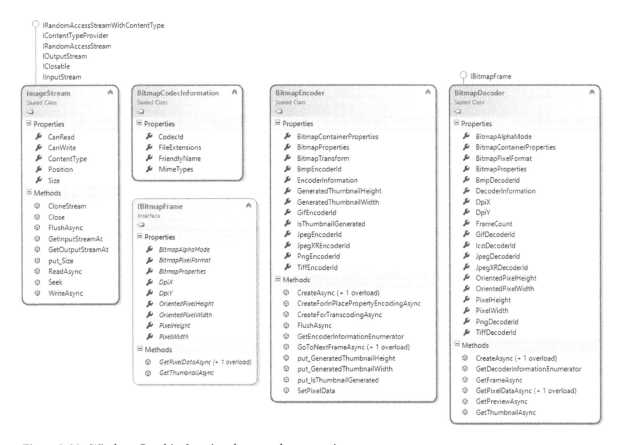

Figure 2-20. *Windows.Graphics.Imaging classes and enumerations*

ImageStream is a class that allows memorization of image data based on a stream format. It is possible to manage the image data using the ReadAsync() and WriteAsync() methods. Other methods, such as Seek(), GetInputStreamAt(), and GetOutputStreamAt(), can be used to position on the stream. An instance of the ImageStream class can also be used as input for the CreateAsync() method inside the BitmapDecoder and BitmapEncoder classes. These classes allow you to read an image or create, manage, and save an image in a file. The CreateAsync() method (overload included) gets an inherited object of IRandomAccessStream. Moreover, both classes contain the GetDecoderInformationEnumerator() method, which returns an object of the System.Collection. Generic.IReadOnlyList<Windows.Graphics.Imaging.BitmapCodecInformation> type. Finally, GetPreviewAsync() and GetThumbnailAsync() are useful whenever we need a preview or a thumbnail, returning a Windows.Graphics. Imaging.ImageStream object.

Inside the Windows.Graphics namespace is the Windows.Graphics.Printing namespace (discussed later). Windows.Media contains the classes shown in Figure 2-21.

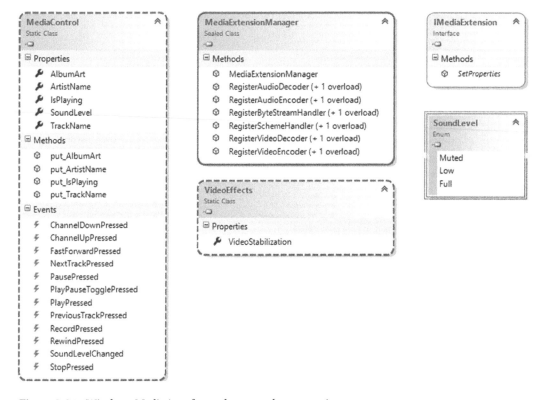

Figure 2-21. *Windows.Media interfaces, classes, and enumerations*

The MediaControl class allows applications to subscribe to notifications by audio and video systems on the device whenever it is triggered. It is possible to handle events that are triggered whenever a user presses a button related to webcam or audio settings on the device. As shown in Figure 2-21, the MediaControl class contains events such as PlayPressed, StopPressed, and RecordPressed. By managing these events, we can specify what instruction is executed when they're triggered (e.g., manipulating the AV stream). Other information about playing media can be retrieved using MediaControl properties such as TrackName, ArtistName, IsPlaying, and SoundLevel (the last one is an enumeration; refer to Figure 1-19).

In the same namespace is the MediaExtensionManager class, which enables registering a codec for a specific audio/video stream. But there are some restrictions:

- Registration is valid only for the lifetime of the MediaExtensionManager instance.

- Registration is valid only for the current application.

- A plug-in can override media formats on the device.

Last but not least is the VideoEffects class, which allows a decrease in video shaking by the VideoStabilization property. This property takes as input the name of the effect to apply to the video.

The Windows.Media.Capture namespace contains all the classes for photos, audio recordings, and videos captured (see Figure 2-22).

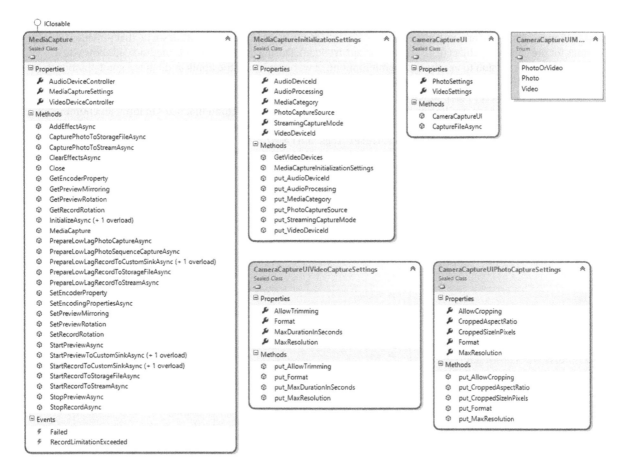

Figure 2-22. *Windows.Media.Capture classes and enumerations*

The MediaCapture class is used to save audio, videos, and photos. These capabilities are supplied by the following methods:

- Photo
  - CapturePhotoToStorageFileAsync
  - CapturePhotoToStreamAsync
- Audio/video
  - StartPreview[...]Async (where ... are the different overloads)
  - StartRecord[...]Async (where ... are the different overloads)
  - StopPreviewAsync()
  - StopRecordAsync()

In one available overload, stream capture needs to be initialized using the InitializeAsync() method, which takes in input a class of Windows.Media.Capture.MediaCaptureInitializationSettings type that provides initial settings for the capturing object (e.g., StreamingCaptureMode). During the first use, this method will show you a pop-up asking permission to use the device microphone or webcam inside the application. It is a good practice to use InitializeAsync() inside the main UI thread of your app.

The CameraCaptureUI class, which shows a full-screen UI to capture a single video or photo, is in the same namespace. Photo or video can be saved using the CaptureFileAsync() method that takes in input an enumeration of CameraCaptureUIMode type that defines the type of input: audio, video, or photo. All the information related to this class is set using CameraCaptureUIPhotoCaptureSettings and CameraCaptureUIVideoCaptureSettings.

The Windows.Media.Devices namespace has classes to help manage audio, video, and communications such as webcams or microphones (integrated or plugged). Figure 2-23 summarizes the most common classes.

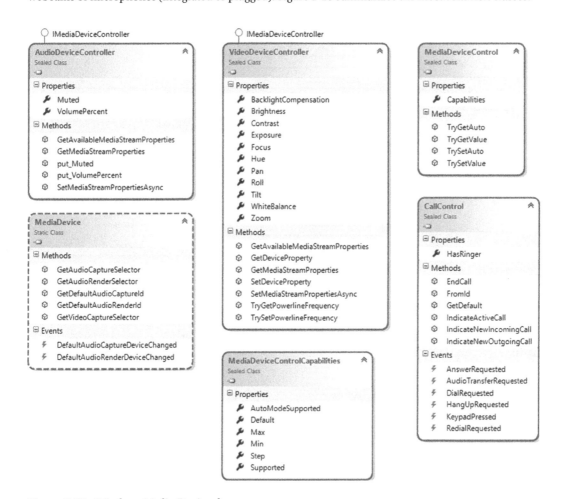

Figure 2-23. *Windows.Media.Device classes*

`MediaDevice` is the most important class in this namespace. It is a static class that contains five methods:

- `GetAudioCaptureSelector()` returns the device ID for capturing audio.

- `GetAudioRenderSelector()` returns the device ID for rendering audio.

- `GetDefaultAudioCaptureId()` returns the default device ID for capturing audio.

- `GetDefaultAudioRenderId()` returns the default device ID for rendering audio.

- `GetVideoCaptureSelector()` returns the device ID for capturing video.

`GetDefaultAudioCaptureId()` and `GetDefaultAudioRenderId()` return the default device ID for capturing or rendering audio in a specific role: default (e.g., media) or communication.

In the same namespace are the following classes:

- `AudioDeviceController` sets properties as `Muted` or `VolumePercent`.

- `VideoDeviceController`, `MediaDeviceControl`, and `MediaDeviceControlCapabilities` retrieve and manage settings related to the camera (e.g., zoom, brightness, focus, and supported encoding properties).

- `CallControl` handles calls on a device that provides phone capabilities.

The `Windows.Media.MediaProperties` namespace (see Figure 2-24) contains classes that allow management of properties related to the media stream. `AudioEncodingProperties`, `ImageEncodingProperties`, and `VideoEncodingProperties` help to set audio, photo, and video properties. The `ContainerEncodingProperties` class enables setting up properties about media containers. A *media container* stores information related to a media stream and contains the following:

- A header with all the properties on a media stream (such as the number and the format type)

- An index to allow random access to the content

- Content metadata (artist, title, and so on)

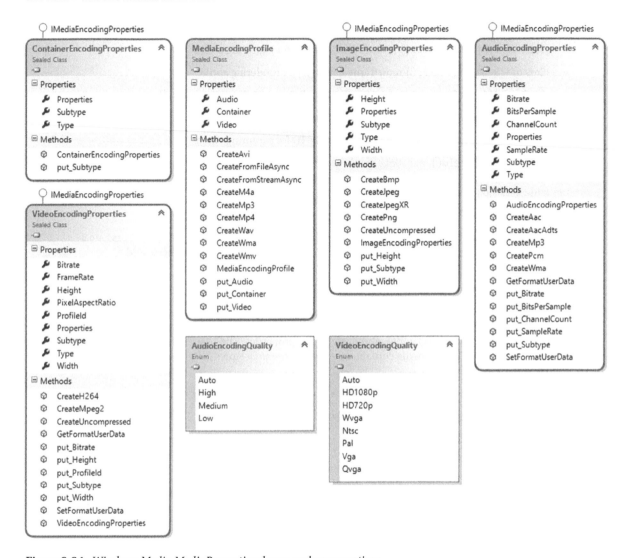

Figure 2-24. *Windows.Media.MediaProperties classes and enumerations*

The word *container* is more often used than *file* because it is common to refer to a container in a live streaming context. You can use a container without having to save it to a file.

Figure 2-25 shows the content of Windows.Media.Playlists. This namespace contains only one class, Playlist, which manages different playlist formats. Thanks to the methods LoadAsync() and SaveAsync() of Playlist, you can read and save playlists in different formats using the PlaylistFormat enumeration.

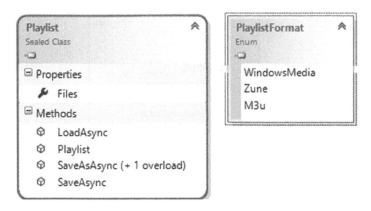

Figure 2-25. *Windows.Media.Playlists classes and enumerations*

The Windows.Media.PlayTo namespace helps to send audio, photo, and video toward remote certified devices. This feature is based on the Digital Living Network Alliance (DLNA) technology that allows streaming media over Wi-Fi (see http://en.wikipedia.org/wiki/Digital_Living_Network_Alliance). An application that needs to use the PlayTo feature has to register with the SourceRequested event inside the PlayToManager class. This event is triggered whenever a user clicks the Device item inside an application on the right. But it is really recommended to use a specific Play To app button inside the application to open up the Play To flyout. This feature can be enabled programmatically by calling the Windows.Media.PlayTo.PlayToManager.ShowPlayToUI() method (supported only in Windows 8.1). The PlayToManager class manages all the settings related to the PlayTo feature.

As a destination for a media stream, you can also choose a specified target using the property DefaultSourceSelection. Using the PlayToReceiver class, you can create a custom software PlayTo receiver that allows you to play (or display), stop, or manage content stored on computers inside the network (see Figure 2-26).

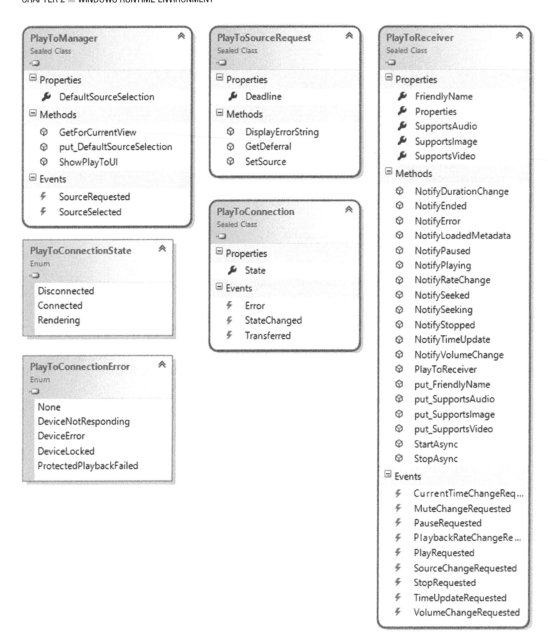

Figure 2-26. *Windows.Media.PlayTo classes and enumerations*

The Windows.Media.Protection namespace provides classes to manage Digital Rights Management (DRM) media contents (see Figure 2-27). The MediaProtectionManager class can be passed as input to the following:

- A media playback API

- The msSetMediaProtectionManager attribute inside the tag's video or audio

Figure 2-27. *Windows.Media.Protection classes*

The last namespace in `Windows.Media` is `Windows.Media.Transcoding` (see Figure 2-28), which transcodes audio and video files. *Transcoding* a media file means converting it from one format to another. But that's not all! You can also add effects or trim pieces from the file.

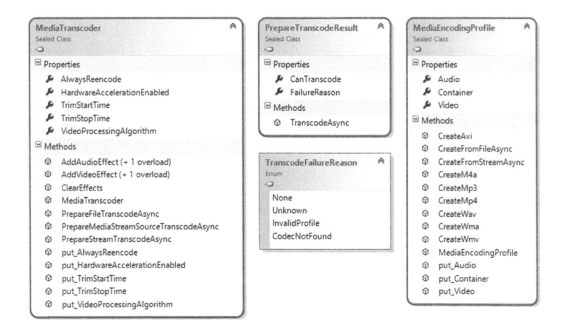

Figure 2-28. *Windows.Media.Transcoding classes and enumerations*

Whereas the `MediaTranscoder` instance stores an object to convert, the `PrepareFileTranscodeAsync` class is used to transcode an audio or video stream to a target format. This class contains a method called `TranscodeAsync()` that takes as input an object of `MediaEncodingProfile` that provides some of the following methods:

- `CreateMp3()`
- `CreateMp4()`
- `CreateWav()`
- `CreateWma()`
- `CreateWmv()`

`PrepareFileTranscodeAsync` returns an instance of `PrepareTranscodeResult` that notifies the operation outcome by `FailureReasonProperty` (this property returns a value of `TranscodeFailureReason` enumeration).

Windows 8 is a user-centric operating system that not only helps developers but also supports hardware designers to provide the best UX. With Windows 8, a hardware vendor can customize components in the printing system to give access to all functionalities of the device. Before the arrival of Windows 8, Windows used the v3 printer driver model that functioned in desktop mode until now. Starting with this version, Windows supports a redesigned printer driver model. It's called the v4 printer driver model and it integrates Windows Store apps to provide a better UX with a customized print UI. The framework of classes that helps device manufacturers create v4 drivers is fully integrated with the `Windows.Graphics.Printing` namespace (shown in Figure 2-29) that you can use in your apps to participate in printing.

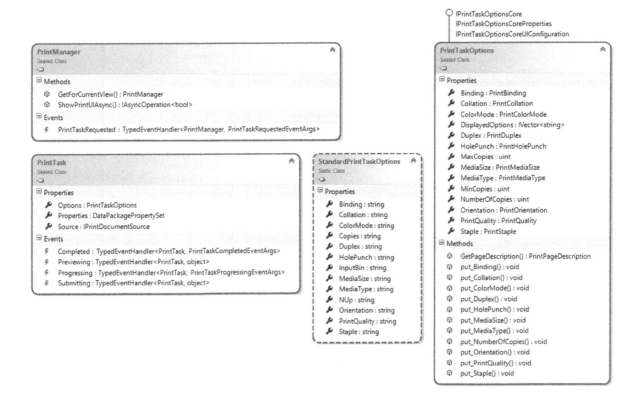

Figure 2-29. *The Windows.Graphics.Printing namespace*

The `Windows.Graphics.Printing` namespace contains two main classes: `PrintManager` and `PrintTask`. `PrintManager`, which is the entry point for printing, allows you to subscribe to the `PrintTaskRequested` event that fires when the user selects the Devices charm. This event uses the `PrintTaskRequestedEventArgs` class as an argument, which enables you to create an instance of `PrintTask` that contains the content to print and options about the process. For example, accessing the `DisplayedOptions` property of the `Options` property contained in `PrintTask` enables you to easily manage options exposed by the default print UI, such as `Copies` or `PrintQuality` (a list of standard print options are exposed by the `StandardPrintTaskOptions` class).

`PrintTask` is the core class on which `Printing` is based. Every `PrintTask` is a printing operation and can transit through four states:

- *Preview* is managed by the `Previewing` event that occurs when the system makes a print preview.

- *Submit* is managed by the `Submitting` event that fires when the user chooses to print the document.

- *Progress* is managed by the `Progressing` event that fires when pages are submitted to the printer, providing information about the remaining pages to print.

- *Complete* is managed by the `Completion` event that occurs when the process is finished, providing information about the way the process is completed (successful, canceled, or failed).

When we talk about printing in Windows 8, we must talk about the `Windows.UI.Xaml.Printing` namespace (see Figure 2-30). If you use XAML, you know that through this technology you can prepare `UIElements` (the base class used by languages based on XAML used as the core for components implementation) to be printed. These functionalities are exposed under the `Windows.UI.Xaml.Printing` namespace from the `PrintDocument` class that automatically interacts with `PrintManager` and allows you to create a page (written with XAML) and prints it as a document.

Figure 2-30. *PrintDocument class*

To conclude, use `Windows.Graphics.Printing` when you need to print your own document format and you require greater control over the printing process; use `Windows.UI.Xaml.Printing` when you need to print `UIElements`.

The Windows 8.1 update brings also supports 3D printing. Two classes are responsible for the communication with a 3D printer: `IXpsDocumentPackageTarget3D` and `IXpsOMPackageWriter3D`. The first is the job containing all the details and a print queue. The second contains the methods to send data into the Windows spooler as an Open Packaging Conventions (OPC) package. (You can find more information here: `http://msdn.microsoft.com/en-us/magazine/cc163372.aspx`). In a few words, this package is based on two containers: *parts* and *contents* (see Figure 2-31).

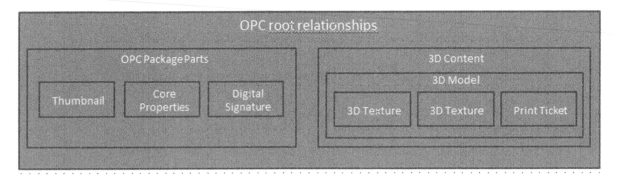

Figure 2-31. *OPC package*

In the content, there is a 3D model component that contains XML markup to define the object to print.

Devices and Printing

Minimum device requirements for Windows 8 are not too restrictive and focus on tablet and hybrid tablet-laptop devices. To install Windows 8 on a tablet, it has to provide the capabilities shown in Table 2-1.

Table 2-1. *Device Capability Requirements*

Category	Type	Description
Storage	Space	At least 100 GB of free space after the installation of the operating system
Firmware	Firmware type	Unified Extensible Firmware Interface (UEFI) firmware required
Networking	WLAN and Bluetooth 4.0	These two components are required
Graphics	GPU	Direct3D10 support
Graphics	Screen resolution	Minimum 1366 x 768
Touch	Five-finger touch	Requires a touch monitor with five points of touch
Camera	Front/user facing camera	Minimum 720p camera
Sensors	Ambient light sensor	Necessary for auto-adjust screen brightness
Sensors	Magnetometer	
Sensors	Accelerometer	
Sensors	Gyroscope	
Device	USB 2.0	At least one USB 2.0 controller with a port exposed
Output	Speaker	A speaker for audio output is required

In addition to these components, others are available that are not required for the producer, such as the optional A-GPS device that is ready to be managed from the system (and your app). When we talk about the Device and Printing components of the WinRT API, it means the part of the library responsible for management of the following:

- Geolocation

- Portable

- Sensors

- NFC devices

Although these components are not required, you can write your app to exploit these components, giving the Windows Store the task of managing the installation on the appropriate device.

`Geolocation` is located under the `Windows.Devices.Geolocation` namespace (see Figure 2-32) that enables your app to retrieve the device's geographic location, provided from multiple devices:

- Wi-Fi triangulation

- IP Geolocation

- GPS devices

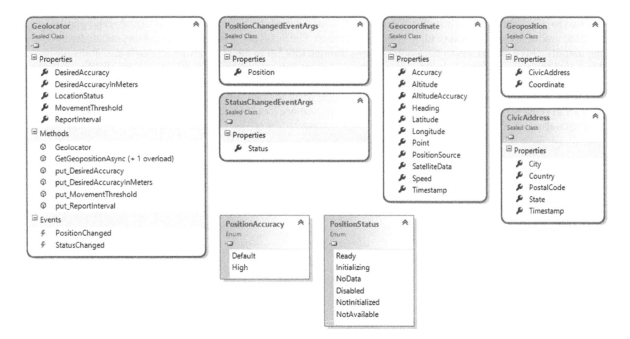

Figure 2-32. *Geolocation namespace diagram*

`Geolocator` is the entry point of `Geolocation` and provides events to track changes of position (identified by the `GeoPosition` class that exposes the `Geocoordinate` and `CivicAddress` linked to the current position) and events to track status changes. (It allows your app to know when the location device is ready to use.)

When you create your app, you'll find APIs to manage Media Transfer Protocol (MTP) device services through Windows Portable Devices (WPDs) inside the `Windows.Devices.Portable` namespace (shown in Figure 2-33). WPD offers an infrastructure able to standardize data transfers between applications and portable devices such as portable media players, digital still cameras, and mobile phones.

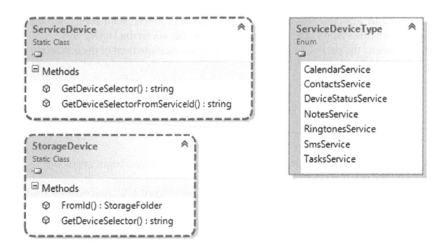

Figure 2-33. *Class diagram of the Windows.Devices.Portable namespace*

MTP is the evolution of the Picture Transfer Protocol (PTP), with which you can transfer images from digital cameras to computers without installing a driver. MTP allows more types of devices, such as digital audio players and portable media, to communicate with the operating system. The ServiceDevice static class allows you to discover and identify a MTP device service for a WPD. Access through this API to the MTP device service is available only to Windows Store apps, giving privileged access by the device manufacturer. The StorageDevice class enables your apps to access a storage device.

When you think about an app for tablets, you certainly assume that the device can be equipped with sensors (e.g., Accelerometer). The Windows.Devices.Sensors namespace (see Figure 2-34) has several classes that manage sensors.

Figure 2-34. *Diagram of a subset of the Windows.Devices.Sensors namespace*

The Accelerometer class manages the sensors that measure the G-force applied along the three axes. If you come from a Windows Phone platform, note that this class exposes an event called Shaken that occurs when the device is shaken. The Compass class gives you information about true north and magnetic north.

■ **Note** The measurement of magnetic north is optional and depends on the capabilities of the sensor; only the true north measurement is required. Remember that the Compass sensor is not required.

The Gyrometer class reports the angular velocity with respect to the three axes and enables your app to manage the rotation velocity of the device. Inclinometer manages the inclination of the device and reports information about pitch, roll, and yaw. These terms are usually used for aeronautical, nautical, and automobile purposes:

- *Pitch* is the leaning back or forth of the muzzle.

- *Roll* is the oscillation around the longitudinal axis.

- *Yaw* is the oscillation around a vertical axis passing through the center of gravity of the item.

Through this sensor, you can evaluate how much a user tilts the device compared with the three axes. LightSensor measures the ambient light using LUX as units. Using this sensor (if it's present), you can personalize the user experience depending on the available light (e.g., you can adaptively change the color of your UI depending on ambient light, with a high-contrast combination if there is too much light, and vice versa).

Finally, you can retrieve information about the orientation of the device using OrientationSensor, which returns a matrix (3 x 3) with rotation values and a Quaternion. You can use this sensor to adjust the in-game prospective of a player, depending on the orientation of the device.

■ **Note** Avoid using OrientationSensor in your Windows Store apps if it's not necessary. Windows Store apps already support different orientations that change layouts relative to device orientation.

The last sensor is the simplified version of OrientationSensor called SimpleOrientationSensor. This simplified version allows you to detect the current orientation of the device and its face-up and face-down status. For example, you can use this sensor in a messenger app that shows the user as unavailable when the device is face down and then notifies other users that it has come back when the device is face up.

Near field communication (NFC) is a standard for communication between devices and covers protocol and data format, whereas communication is based on the existing radio-frequency identification (RFID) that regulates close communication (no more than a few centimeters). The Windows.Devices.Proximity namespace (see Figures 2-35 and 2-36) contains APIs to support this standard. Using these APIs, you can write an app that shares content with another computer near a user device. The entry point to use Proximity in order to know when a device enters and leaves proximity is the ProximityDevice class (see Figure 2-35), which exposes two events:

- DeviceArrived: This event occurs when a compatible device enters the proximate range.

- DeviceDeparted: This event occurs when a connected device leaves the proximate range.

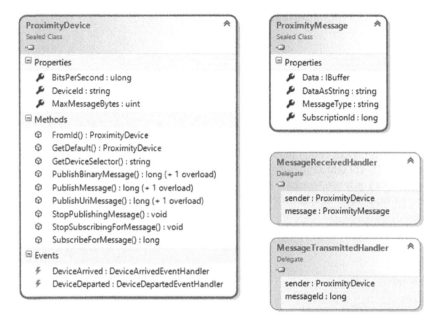

Figure 2-35. *Windows.Devices.Proximity namespace: ProximityDevice involved classes*

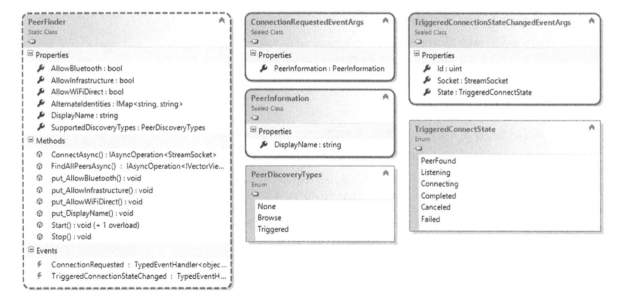

Figure 2-36. *Proximity namespace: PeerFinder involved class diagram*

For example, you can use proximity in a massive multiplayer role playing game (MMRPG), in which a user taps a device to help another user. Or in an app that manages contacts, the user can simply share a business card with a tap. The Windows.Devices.Proximity namespace exposes another interesting class named PeerFinder (see Figure 2-36) that helps you find close devices (using different types of connection technologies, such as Wi-Fi Direct or Bluetooth) that run your application to establish long-term connections.

Windows 8.1 also brings in new APIs to support the following types of device:

- Human Interface Device (HID)

- Point of Service (PoS)

- USB

- Bluetooth

- Wi-Fi Direct

HIDs are supported on different type of transport: USB, Bluetooth, Bluetooth LE, and I²C. (Get more information on HID here: http://msdn.microsoft.com/it-it/library/windows/hardware/jj126202.aspx.) There are few limitations to the HID devices API: first, we can only use Windows 8.1 built-in drivers to access the device through the API (unfortunately, vendor drivers are not supported). It might also block top-level collection that can take advantage of the following usage pages:

- `HID_USAGE_PAGE_UNDEFINED`

- `HID_USAGE_PAGE_GENERIC`

- `HID_USAGE_GENERIC_KEYBOARD`

- `HID_USAGE_GENERIC_KEYPAD`

- `HID_USAGE_GENERIC_SYSTEM_CTL`

- `HID_USAGE_PAGE_KEYBOARD`

- `HID_USAGE_PAGE_CONSUMER`

- `HID_USAGE_PAGE_DIGITIZER`

- `HID_USAGE_PAGE_SENSOR`

- `HID_USAGE_PAGE_BARCODE_SCANNER`

- `HID_USAGE_PAGE_WEIGHING_DEVICE`

- `HID_USAGE_PAGE_MAGNETIC_STRIPE_READER`

- `HID_USAGE_PAGE_TELEPHONY`

The namespace to access HID devices is `Windows.Devices.HumanInterfaceDevice`, in which the main classes to retrieve data from a device are `HidDevice` and `HidInputReport` (see Figure 2-37). `HidDevice` enables connection to a device using the `GetDeviceSelector()` method to create a selector for a HID device and then the `FromIdAsync()` method to open a connection. Instead, to retrieve data, methods such as `GetNumericControl()` and `GetBooleanControl()` in `HidInputReport` can be used.

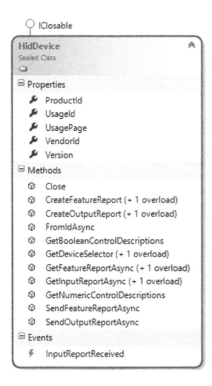

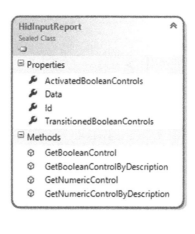

Figure 2-37. HID main classes inside the Windows.Devices.HumanInterfaceDevice namespace

Because Windows 8 is created to run on different kinds of devices, PoS support can be really useful if you want to create an application to handle payments in a shop. This API is contained in the `Windows.Devices.PointOfService` namespace and it supports barcode scanners and magnetic stripe readers. Depending on what device you use, you can instantiate a `BarcodeScanner` class or a `MagneticStripeReader` class (see Figure 2-38).

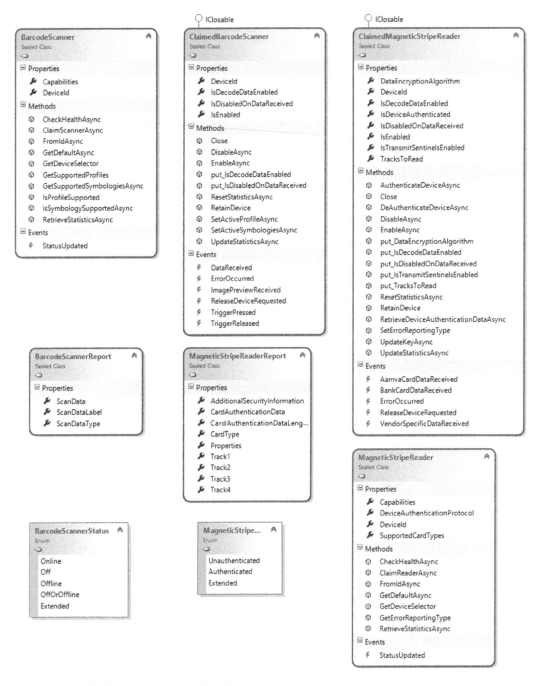

Figure 2-38. *Windows.Devices.PointOfService namespace main classes*

For a barcode scanner, use the `BarcodeScanner.GetDefaultAsync()` method (or `BarcodeScanner.ClaimScannerAsync()` method for exclusive use) to connect to a device. Then subscribe to the `ClaimedBarcodeScanner.DataReceived()` event. Finally, use the `ClaimedBarcodeScanner.EnableAsync()` method to retrieve data.

For a magnetic stripe reader, use the `MagneticStripeReader.GetDefaultAsync()` method (or `MagneticStripeReader.ClaimReaderAsync` method for exclusive use) to connect to a device. Then subscribe to the `ClaimedMagneticStripeReader.BankCardDataReceived` or `ClaimedMagneticStripeReader.AamvaCardDataReceived` event. Finally, use the `ClaimedMagneticStripeReader.EnableAsync()` method to retrieve data.

The USB API allows communication to a USB device for which Windows does not provide any built-in drivers. There are few requirements:

- The USB device has to use the `Winusb.sys` driver.

- Information about the device has to be provided in the app manifest (capability).

- The device has to belong to one of these USB device classes:

    - CDC control class (class code: 0x02; subclass code: any; protocol code: any)

    - Physical class (class code: 0x05; subclass code: any; protocol code: any)

    - PersonalHealthcare class (class code: 0x0f; subclass code: 0x00; protocol code: 0x00)

    - ActiveSync class (class code: 0xef; subclass code: 0x01; protocol code: 0x01)

    - PalmSync class (class code: 0xef; subclass code: 0x01; protocol code: 0x02)

    - DeviceFirmwareUpdate class (class code: 0xfe; subclass code: 0x01; protocol code: 0x01)

    - IrDA class (class code: 0; subclass code: 0x02; protocol code: 0x00)

    - Measurement class (class code: 0xfe; subclass code: 0x03; protocol code: any)

    - Vendor-specific class (class code: 0xff; subclass code: any; protocol code: any)

The `Windows.Devices.Usb` namespace contains all the classes to interact with a USB device. Figure 2-39 shows the main classes.

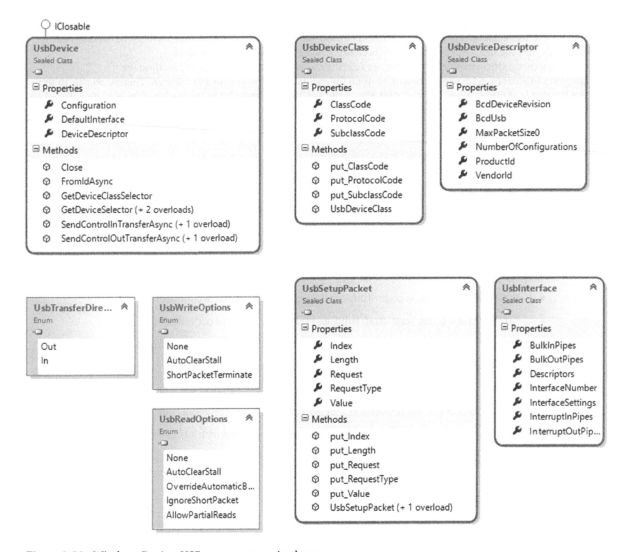

Figure 2-39. *Windows.Devices.USB namespace main classes*

To connect to a USB device, we need to use the UsbDevice.GetDeviceSelector() to retrieve the device information and then use the UsbDevice.FromIdAsync() to pass the device information previously retrieved.

Bluetooth APIs are contained inside the Windows.Devices.Bluetooth.RFCOMM and Windows.Devices. Bluetooth.GenericAttributeProfile namespaces (see Figure 2-40). These APIs take advantage of the RFCOMM Protocol or GATT Profile (used for Bluetooth LE devices) to communicate with devices. Notice that the Bluetooth device needs to be discovered and paired before it can be used through the APIs.

Figure 2-40. *Windows.Devices.Bluetooth.RFCOMM and Windows.Devices.Bluetooth.GenericAttributeProfile namespace main classes*

Finally, Wi-Fi Direct APIs enable us to include the possibility to connect to Wi-Fi Direct–supported devices in the app. The `WiFiDirectDevice` class manages connections through devices using the `GetDeviceSelector()` method and the `FromIdAsync()` method. Figure 2-41 shows the `Windows.Devices.WiFiDirect` namespace classes.

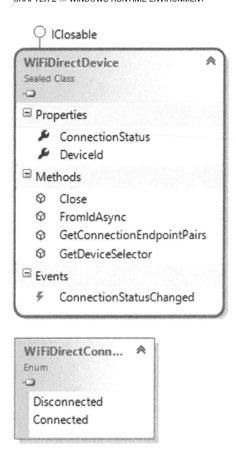

Figure 2-41. *Windows.Devices.WiFiDirect namespace*

Conclusion

Learning about the library that is the basis of the main new features of Windows 8 is essential for understanding how to develop applications that take full advantage of the platform created by Microsoft. This chapter analyzed the main components of Windows Runtime for the development of Windows Store apps, which will be useful in the following chapters, in which you design and implement your first application.

■ ■ ■

CHAPTER 3

Designing the User Experience

This chapter introduces you to controls available for Windows Store apps development and discusses when to use them to provide a better User Experience (UX). But before we start talking about controls, we want to discuss some concepts that you need to keep in mind while you develop your app. We will introduce you to some principles to remember when you develop an app for Touch UX.

Touch Design Principles

Windows Store apps are designed to be "touched" by the user on a tablet, so you should design your app considering postures that users will assume when working with your application. If you look at people using tablets, you'll see that while the tablet is in the landscape position, the hands are near the bottom-left and -right corners; in portrait position, the hands are near the center. You should include controls near the users' hands. For the same reason, you should put content to be read (when possible) farther from their hands.

User Experience (UX) is a mandatory concept in Windows Store apps. If your application is designed to allow interaction using hands, remember that fingers aren't precise like the mouse. When you add a control to the user interface (UI), remember to create it with a dimension that allows easy control for the user. Of course, it's not easy to choose the correct dimensions, but assuming a medium finger with a width about 11 millimeters, consider the following:

- Fundamental actions must be provided by controls with good dimensions, so consider using a 50-by-50 pixel area (minimum) because an incorrect interaction with your app can disappoint users.

- Incorrect touch situations can be resolved using controls with a minimum size of 40 x 40 pixels.

- If you don't have enough space on your UI, you can resolve an incorrect touch situation with only one gesture by using 30 x 30 pixels as the minimum size.

In any case, remember that if two controls that can be touched are close, you must set a minimum of 30 pixels' padding between them to avoid accidental interaction.

Now that you know some basics of touch interaction, we can start talking about controls and why you should choose one control instead of another.

Control Library

This section discusses the rich control library available for Windows 8. We first explore the set of common controls that are part of UI design from early versions of Windows and then we'll discuss the new controls introduced to help you to get the best from Windows 8, providing better UX.

The base class of all Windows Store apps controls is UIElement, which inherits from DependencyObject (which, like every class in the .NET Framework, inherits from the Object class). Figure 3-1 shows a diagram of base classes that are used by the framework to design the UI. All start from the DependencyObject class to create a class that participates in the dependency property system, which means that a control can take part in the binding mechanism. The UIElement class exposes a set of methods and events that help you manage a lot of standard behaviors such as clicking or double-clicking.

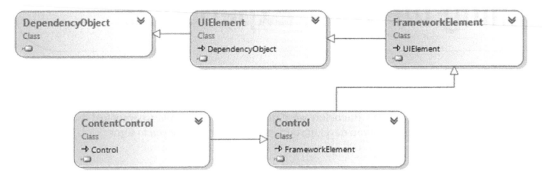

Figure 3-1. *UI base classes inheritance diagram*

The direct descendant of the UIElement class is FrameworkElement, which extends the functionalities of base classes and adds support to the Loaded/Unloaded event and a lot of functionality relative to binding.

Another thing to consider in your application development using XAML is the concept introduced by ContentControl. When a control inherits from this class, it can define (single element) content. For example, Button inherits (indirectly) from this class and can define content such as text, an image, or another control.

This is a summary of base classes that you must know in order to understand how you can customize behaviors, styles, and control templates.

Common Controls

The controls library for Windows Store apps contains a lot of elements that aren't unknown to Silverlight, Windows Presentation Foundation (WPF), or more generally to Windows developers. These elements include Button, ComboBox, CheckBox, RadioButton, TextBox, TextBlock, Image, Hyperlink, HyperlinkButton, PasswordBox, Slider, and shapes.

Button

Button is the core of user interaction. The primary purpose of this control is to reply to a click with an event, starting an elaboration. In Windows Store apps, Button appears as shown in Figure 3-2, and you can define a button that contains simply a text or other framework elements such as an image (see Figure 3-3).

Figure 3-2. *Example of a button*

Figure 3-3. *Button with an image*

In order to be compliant with the Microsoft guidelines about the use of buttons, you must avoid using them for navigation (with the exception of buttons such as Back and Next). Instead, you should use buttons for actions such as form submission (see Figures 3-4 and 3-5) or resetting (see Figure 3-6), and for starting an immediate action such as a save operation.

Figure 3-4. *Standard submit button*

Figure 3-5. *Submit button with specific text*

Figure 3-6. *Reset button*

Figure 3-3 shows a button with an image inside. This button offers information about something in the app, but when you define a custom layout for a button, remember that what you use as the content of your button will be critical for users to understand. You should use a self-explanatory text without too much information, which can be confusing. For the same reason, you shouldn't edit the content of a Submit button if not required for localization in order to provide a consistent UX between various apps.

CheckBox

CheckBox (see Figure 3-7) gives a choice of checking or unchecking itself (some check boxes can be in indeterminate states). CheckBox is useful when you want to give not-mutually-exclusive choices to the end user; when the user must answer a question with a yes or no response (e.g., the Terms of Service agreement shown in Figure 3-8); or for a mixed choice with check boxes grouped under another check box that, if checked, selects all or none of the grouped check boxes.

Figure 3-7. *CheckBox examples*

Figure 3-8. *Yes or no response check box*

Here are some best practices for CheckBox and its use:

- ToggleSwitch is another control with a behavior similar to CheckBox (discussed in the "New Controls" section). But according to the Windows Store apps guidelines, you must use CheckBox if a manipulation represents a change of status; if your selection represents an action, you must use ToggleSwitch. So if the choice will be part of a submitted form, use CheckBox; if the selection causes an immediate submit, use ToggleSwitch.

- If you want to choose the best control for disabling a feature or to switch something on/off in your app, use ToggleSwitch instead of CheckBox.

- If your purpose is to allow users to check more than one option, use CheckBox because a set of check boxes provides the mental scheme for this goal.

TextBox

A lot of applications work on text, and TextBox (shown in Figure 3-9) is a control that allows users to input text in a single or multiline way. Because you'll often use a TextBox in your application, you must remember a lot of rules to use it. One of these rules concerns the format of the text. If you need to have text that requires a particular format (e.g., a product key), you should use TextBox to re-create the specific format and not apply a format to the text inside the text box.

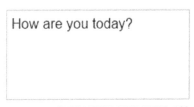

Figure 3-9. *An example of TextBox*

Text input appears to be an easy concept, but you must follow some rules in order to provide a good UX to the user. For example, if the user can input the path of a file directly in a text box, you must provide a button that allows the user to select a correct value. Another interesting example is a complex text format in which the text must be on multiple lines and must be formatted and enriched with styles. In this case, you must use RichEditBox (a Rich text box for HTML) instead.

Another way to use a TextBox is for messaging applications. In this case, you probably will use formatted text. If your application manages short messages with limited length, you must provide a way for users to see how many characters they can still write (see Figure 3-10).

How are you today?

CHARACTERS REMAINING: 100

Figure 3-10. *Example of limited-length TextBox*

TextBox exposes a lot of properties, and some of them must be learned to work better with TextBox (see Table 3-1).

Table 3-1. *Main Properties of TextBox*

Name		Description
XAML text	HTML value	Contains the text written in TextBox
MaxLength	maxLength	Contains the max number of characters that can be written in TextBox
AcceptsReturn	isMultiLine	Indicates whether TextBox allows newline or carriage return characters
SelectedText	use selectionStart and selectionEnd	Contains the text actually selected in TextBox
TextWrapping	use the TextArea control	Indicates whether the text can automatically wrap when reach the maximum TextBox width
IsTextPredictionEnabled	autocomplete	Indicates whether the autocomplete feature is active for TextBox
IsSpellCheckEnabled	spellcheck	Enables the spell check engine to inspect the text inside TextBox

HyperlinkButton

HyperlinkButton helps you create a button with a URI to navigate. Depending on the format of the URI you use, Windows will start the relative software. If you write an URI that starts with http, the default browser will be used; if your URI starts with mailto, Windows will ask users if they want to start Mail software.

HyperlinkButton (shown in Figure 3-11) should be used only for navigation purposes, inside or outside of your application. When you use this control, remember to set a tooltip on the link for users to see, even when they touch the link. You should also put additional information in the tooltip, keeping the text of the link short enough

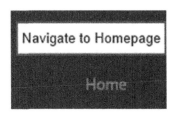

Figure 3-11. *An example of HyperlinkButton with a tooltip*

RadioButton

RadioButton is another control that helps with user choice, but unlike CheckBox, RadioButton options (shown in Figure 3-12) are mutually exclusive and grouped. Its name is due to the way the options work, just like presets on a radio, which can be selected only one at time.

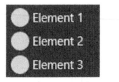

Figure 3-12. *An example of RadioButton*

Because this control has been used since the dawn of the graphical interface, we believe it's appropriate to describe some best practices for its use. Sometimes we have found applications in which RadioButton was used to collect a choice between two elements (for example, I agree/I don't agree, Yes/No, True/False). This kind of choice is better expressed with a single CheckBox. You should use a RadioButton when you want to emphasize selectable options, forcing the user to pay attention to the choice. If you don't need to draw attention to various options, you can use a ComboBox control that helps save space on the UI.

Remember to create a RadioButton that encloses a label inside it, allowing the user to select the element by touching the bullet and by touching the label. When you create two or more RadioButton groups, you should separate them by using a label that indicates their purpose because if you put a group near another group without a logical sense, the user might find it difficult to make the correct choice.

ToggleSwitch

Starting from the first version of Windows Phone, Microsoft has a new control named ToggleSwitch. ToggleSwitch, just like CheckBox, helps you collect user choices; but according to Metro design guidelines, you must use ToggleSwitch when a choice triggers an immediate change. For example, Figure 3-13 shows a ToggleSwitch that allows the user to enable or disable notification from the application. When the user switches between On and Off, the application activates or deactivates the notification system, giving the right feedback to users (they know that when they touch the ToggleSwitch, the relative change becomes effective immediately).

Figure 3-13. *An example of ToggleSwitch*

On and Off are the default labels for this control, but if you need to use a specific label you can customize it (e.g., Show/Hide), giving the user the right information in context. Of course, if there isn't a real need to change these labels, consider leaving standard values. And for situations that require a change to the label, make sure that the text does not exceed four characters or else you will have space problems.

ToggleSwitch inherits a lot of properties from the Control class and extends it with a property (see the descriptions in Table 3-2).

Table 3-2. *Most Important ToggleSwitch Properties*

XAML Property	HTML Data-Win-Options Attribute	Description
Header	title	A single UIElement that acts as a header of the control (in Figure 3-13, it is the word *Notifications*).
HeaderTemplate	N/A	With this template, you can bind a DataTemplate as header.
OnContent	labelOn	With this property, you can define a single UIElement that acts as content when the control is in an on state.
OffContent	labelOff	With this property, you can define a single UIElement that acts as content when the control is in an off state.
OnContentTemplate OffContentTemplate	N/A	With these two templates, you can define how to bind data when the control is in on or off states.

ToggleButton

ToggleButton is a button that can switch between two states (Checked/Unchecked). ToggleButton is the base class of CheckBox and RadioButton (see the class diagram in Figure 3-14). If you need to create a custom control that toggles between checked and unchecked states, use ToggleButton as the base class.

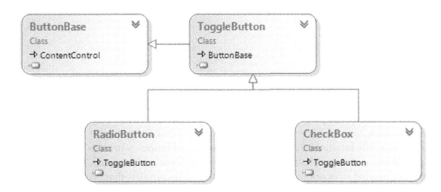

Figure 3-14. *ToggleButton class diagram*

The ToggleButton control (see Figure 3-15) exposes the IsChecked property that stores the information about the state of the control and the IsThreeState property that, if enabled, allows the control to assume the indeterminate state.

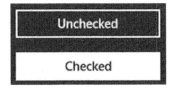

Figure 3-15. *How ToggleButton displays*

■ **Note**   The ToggleButton control is not available for HTML.

ProgressBar and ProgressRing

When developing new Windows Store apps, you can use two controls to show users that your application is doing something:

- *ProgressBar*: It's not a really new control, but it was redesigned from its Windows Phone introduction (see Figure 3-16). This control can be used in two ways:

    - To show progress about an operation (e.g., files to download, tasks to complete, and so on)

    - Simply to show that something is going on in your application but not provide information about progress (indeterminate, as shown in the bottom left of Figure 3-16)

- *ProgressRing*: A new control introduced with Windows 8 that shows a dotted ring when activated (see the top right part of Figure 3-16).

Figure 3-16. *Examples of ProgressBar and ProgressRing*

Following Microsoft best practices about the use of progress controls, you must use these controls for any application operations that need more than 2 seconds to complete. You should not use ProgressBar or ProgressRing to track progress about a task made by a user. To follow the Microsoft guidelines, you should use a "determinate" ProgressBar to track operations with a predictable duration (e.g., file download/upload). The use of an "indeterminate" ProgressBar should be dedicated to operations with an unpredictable duration that don't require a "block" of UI (e.g., connection to a service that can be cancelled).

Of course, some cases require stopping user interactions while an operation with an undefined duration runs. In these cases, you should use ProgressRing (e.g., installing a new feature). Obviously, we reiterate that your application must be user-centric; if an operation blocks users from performing other things for more than 10 seconds, you must provide a way to cancel this operation.

Per the Microsoft guidelines, when you create a ProgressBar, it must be accompanied by two labels. The first must be placed above the ProgressBar to act as a title; the second is placed below the ProgressBar to display the status of the operation (see Figure 3-17).

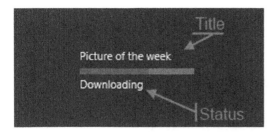

Figure 3-17. *An example of ProgressBar*

Sometimes progress controls are incorrectly used; for example, if your app loads a list of messages from the hard drive while you load the oldest messages, displaying a progress control could be counterproductive because it wastes space on the UI. Background operations that have a little importance for the user (e.g., sending voice messages) don't need progress control, either. In these cases, Microsoft recommends using ellipses instead (e.g., sending voice message . . .).

When you work with a ProgressBar, you might need to switch between determinate and indeterminate modality—for example, when an action starts with an operation with undefined duration and after information about the progress can be provided from the context. For example, your app executes a download of a file and you can't predict how long the connection to the server will take, so you start with an indeterminate state. Later, when you are downloading the file from a server, you can switch to determinate modality because you know how much data you have downloaded and how much is left.

When the interaction with an AppBar (discussed in the next section) produces a task that blocks the UI, show the ProgressBar inside the AppBar. If it is clear what is tracked, you can put the ProgressBar in the top of the AppBar without the status and title.

AppBar

Every application needs a menu with some functions that help users interact with elements on the UI. AppBar is the control that makes it easy. When you design your application, you can place the AppBar in the top or bottom of your page using the TopAppBar and BottomAppBar properties of the Page class. (You can easily remember that TopAppBar refers to the AppBar shown in the *top* of the screen, and BottomAppBar refers to the *bottom* part of the screen.)

When you choose where to put a button, you must remember that these two positions are conceptually different: you should put the TopAppBar that allows the user to navigate in your app in the top of your application; with BottomAppBar, you will put the classic toolbar with commands and tools.

In Figure 3-18, TopAppBar shows four buttons that refer to the navigation of the application.

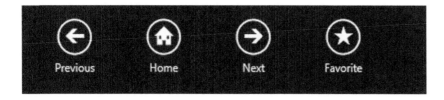

Figure 3-18. *Example of TopAppBar*

In Figure 3-19, the BottomAppBar shows a set of buttons divided by use. On the left side, you can see the buttons that are used to create and modify the set of elements displayed, and on the right side are the controls that interact with items adding additional functionality compared with create, read, update, and delete (CRUD) operations.

Figure 3-19. *Example of BottomAppBar*

Creating menus for an app is both difficult and easy. It's easier from the point of view of the developer because the Windows 8 platform allows us to easily create them, but it could be difficult to design a good menu. First, if your app needs a lot of items in a menu, consider grouping them logically. Avoid using labels such as *Advanced* or *More*: the first because newbie users might be afraid of it, and the second because it might create confusion about the functionalities exposed in this submenu.

When you design an application, always remember that your app can be executed in portrait and landscape mode or snapped view. If you put up to ten commands in the AppBar, it will be automatically redrawn by the system (adjusting padding and hiding labels) to fit the new space. In snapped view, Windows will create two rows of commands, so if you want to avoid this behavior, you must limit your AppBar to five elements.

You can use AppBar to show contextual commands: you will set the dismissal mode of the AppBar to *sticky*, which means that your AppBar will remain open until you close it programmatically. For example, you should set sticky mode when users select items from a list to remove them; when they start to select, the AppBar appears with the Remove command available and enabled. When they end by activating the Remove command, you must hide the AppBar programmatically from your code. Be careful when you use sticky mode in a page that requires scrolling horizontally because you must resize the scrolling area in order to put the scrollbar on top of the AppBar.

Another important rule refers to the Login and Logout commands. They must be moved to the Settings charm of your application; if the login is required for your app, consider putting it on the main page.

When you design your AppBar, remember that out of the box you will have a lot of styles for buttons (shown in Figure 3-20) that you can use to provide the same UX across applications.

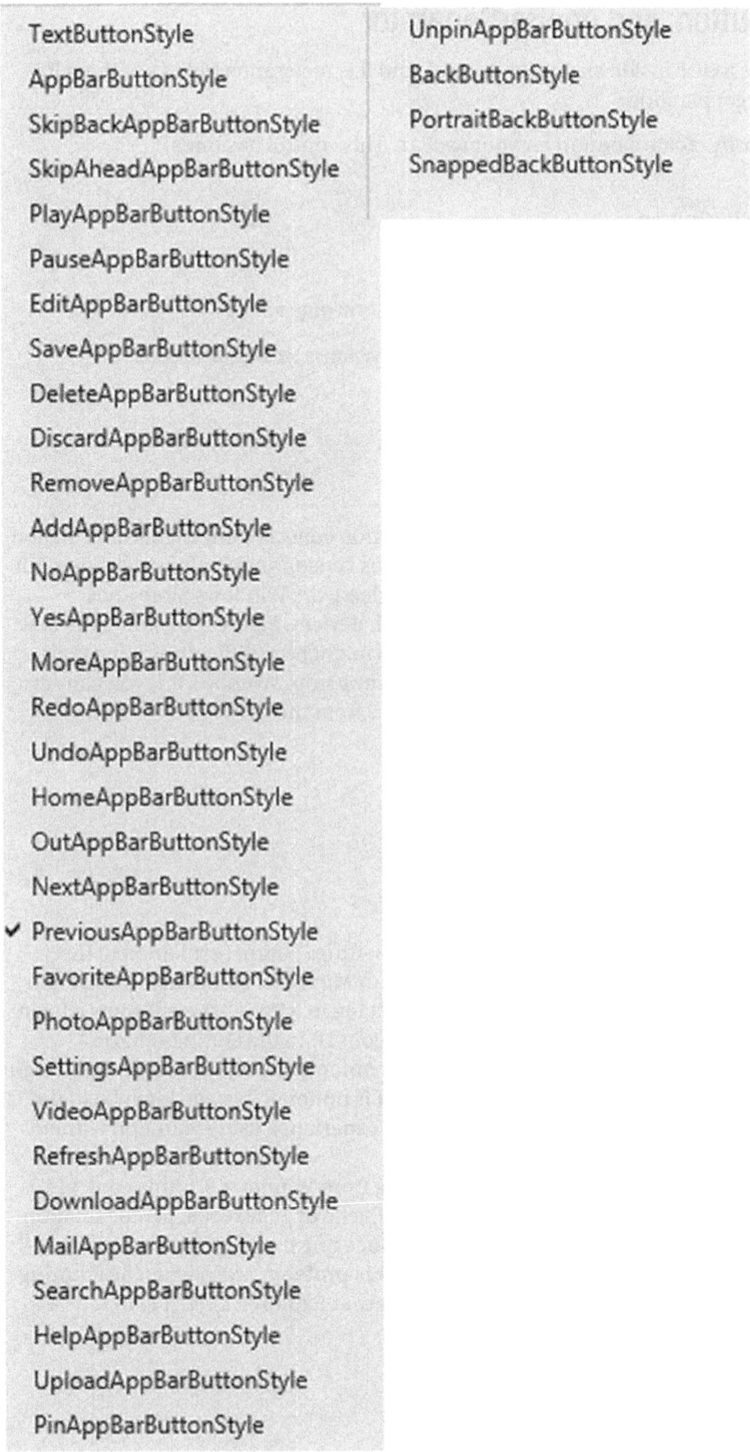

TextButtonStyle
AppBarButtonStyle
SkipBackAppBarButtonStyle
SkipAheadAppBarButtonStyle
PlayAppBarButtonStyle
PauseAppBarButtonStyle
EditAppBarButtonStyle
SaveAppBarButtonStyle
DeleteAppBarButtonStyle
DiscardAppBarButtonStyle
RemoveAppBarButtonStyle
AddAppBarButtonStyle
NoAppBarButtonStyle
YesAppBarButtonStyle
MoreAppBarButtonStyle
RedoAppBarButtonStyle
UndoAppBarButtonStyle
HomeAppBarButtonStyle
OutAppBarButtonStyle
NextAppBarButtonStyle
✓ PreviousAppBarButtonStyle
FavoriteAppBarButtonStyle
PhotoAppBarButtonStyle
SettingsAppBarButtonStyle
VideoAppBarButtonStyle
RefreshAppBarButtonStyle
DownloadAppBarButtonStyle
MailAppBarButtonStyle
SearchAppBarButtonStyle
HelpAppBarButtonStyle
UploadAppBarButtonStyle
PinAppBarButtonStyle

UnpinAppBarButtonStyle
BackButtonStyle
PortraitBackButtonStyle
SnappedBackButtonStyle

Figure 3-20. Visual Studio menu of available button styles

AppBarButton, AppBarToggleButton, and AppBarSeparator

Windows 8.1 introduces three new controls to use inside an AppBar control, and it is recommended to use them if your application has Windows 8.1 as its target platform:

- AppBarButton allows you to easily create a button for your AppBar. This control has three properties:

  - Label sets the content for the button.

  - Icon sets the image for the button.

  - IsCompact sets the view mode for the button (with or without showing Label).

- AppBarToggleButton creates a button that can have two states (i.e., play/pause) inside an AppBar.

- AppBarSeparator logically separates AppBarButton.

PasswordBox

Users' personal information is valuable and should be protected. If your application collects some of this information, the first security block that you can furnish is a password. Everyone from previous versions of Windows development will appreciate our choice to put PasswordBox in the "New Controls" section. Indeed, the Windows Store apps version of PasswordBox has been strongly redesigned, focusing on UX with touch devices. Figure 3-21 shows the new PasswordBox with an eye drawing on the right side. Users with strong passwords might have difficulty writing their passwords onscreen, so they can touch the "eye" to see the written text. And starting from Windows 8.1, you can set a header to the control using the Header property, which does not accept any focus from the UI.

Figure 3-21. *An example of PasswordBox*

If your app needs the user to log in, you should move the logon UI to the Settings charm (explained in the "Contracts and Extensions" section of this chapter) to keep your app in line with Microsoft guidelines about login controls. Of course, if your app *requires* that the user have an account and must log in with it, you will show a login UI in your app when it starts the first time. After the login, you must put the logout UI in the Settings charm.

If your app requires access with an account for some functionality about contents shown, you can put the login UI inside the container that you want to use to show contents. When a login UI is optional, put the login UI in the Settings charm to access other functionalities because the user can get a great experience using your app without an account.

The WebView control allows you to use a smart iframe inside code. Starting from Windows 8.1, this control has some advantages, such as the support for HTML5 (but not all features like AppCache or IndexedDB, geolocalitation and Clipboard access), navigation, and capability to display a web site that does not support frame or iframe visualization. A well-known bug called "airspace problem" has been fixed. This problem arose when attempting to overlap XAML elements. Also, WebView now supports history and uses Internet Explorer 11 (IE11) in document mode.

New Controls in Windows 8.1

Windows 8.1 introduces the following new controls:

- DatePicker (XAML)
- TimePicker (XAML)
- CommandBar
- Flyout (XAML)
- MenuFlyout (XAML)
- SettingsFlyout (XAML)
- SearchBox (XAML & HTML)
- Hub (XAML and HTML)
- BackButton (HTML)
- NavBar (HTML)

DatePicker and TimePicker enable you to use a specific control to let users choose date and time (see Figure 3-22). These controls are really useful because they were really difficult to create previously They can receive input by mouse, keyboard or even touch; and are localizable. You can also use pattern to format the date or time and, thanks to the Header property, there's no need to add a label for them. Now you can use them in your XAML applications.

Figure 3-22. *An example of DatePicker and TimePicker*

CommandBar lets you easily customize a bottom bar in your applications. It allows AppBarButton or AppBarToggleButton to use glymps for button styles. It can also be compact.

Flyout controls let you show a pop-up with text or other controls inside it that can be easily dismissed by clicking outside of it. It is usually attached to a Button by using Attached Properties. MenuFlyout and SettingFlyout are designed to show a menu of items or a menu of settings (similar to the Setting charm). SettingFlyout now enables you to easily create a panel for setting, saving you from a really bad headache. Figure 3-23 shows an example of Flyout and MenuFlyout.

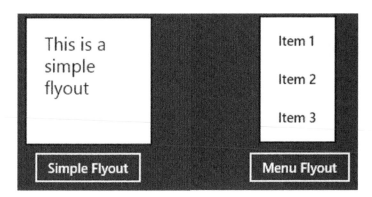

Figure 3-23. *An example of Flyout*

The SearchBox control lets you use a search feature inside your app. It can be now included as a control in the markup and supports full templating, styling, and the Input Method Editor (IME). Figure 3-24 show an example of a SearchBox control.

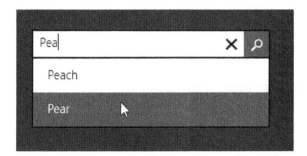

Figure 3-24. *An example of a SearchBox control*

The Hub control is a great addition to the Windows Store app controls. It allows you to show heterogeneous data provided from different sources in a simple and very spectacular way. It is divided into HubSection controls that define areas with their own data source. It is also possible to create a Hub app using the specific template in the project creation step. A great example of a Hub control is the Bing Sports app shown in Figure 3-25.

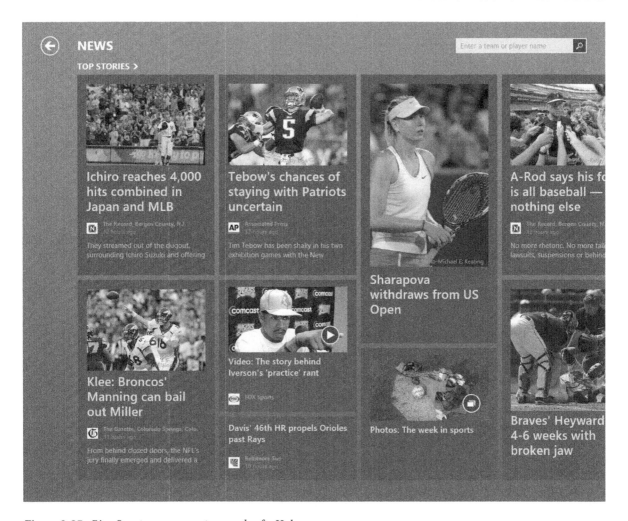

Figure 3-25. *Bing Sports app: a great example of a Hub app*

The BackButton control allows you to easily handle navigation between windows in your app. The BackButton can access the navigation stack to determine whether the user can navigate backward; if not, the button is automatically disabled.

The NavBar control lets you create a top AppBar to provide an easy way to navigate inside your app. The NavBar is built using the NavBarContainer that contains one or more NavBarCommands. This is a very customizable control that also provides paging for NavBarCommand. Figure 3-26 shows an example of NavBar:

Figure 3-26. *NavBar example*

List Management Controls

Regardless of which approach is used to develop Windows Store apps (discussed in detail in Chapter 4), *list controls* show a list of items placed in different ways, depending on the control used. List controls in Metro style are included in a namespace called `Windows.UI.Xaml.Control` (XAML) or `WinJS.UI` (HTML).

ItemsControl

For XAML, `ItemsControl` is the main control to show data collection. Although it's not commonly used to achieve this scope, all controls used to display collections of data inherit from it. Figure 3-27 shows a class diagram that displays the hierarchy among the list controls of `Windows.UI.Xaml.Control`.

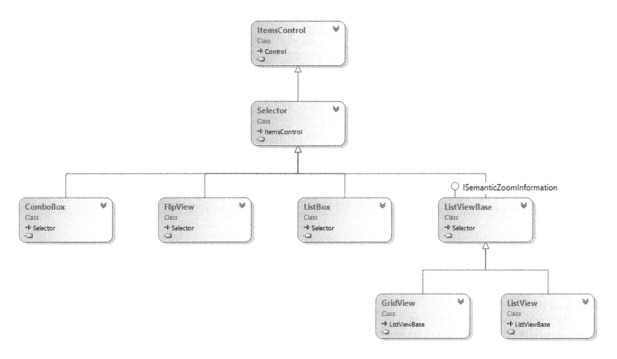

Figure 3-27. *List control class diagram*

All the controls inherit from `ItemsControl`, passing by the `Selector` class. This class gives you the ability to select items. Figure 3-28 shows a simple example of `ItemsControl` usage.

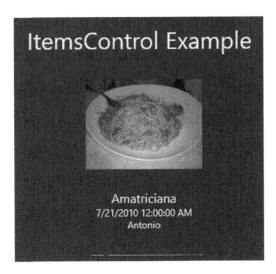

Figure 3-28. *An example of ItemsControl*

This control does not provide an automatic vertical scrollbar for its content; you have to use a `ScrollViewer`.

Public members of `ItemsControl` are frequently used in a derived control to set its layout or features. These members are shown in Figure 3-29 (surrounded by red rectangles).

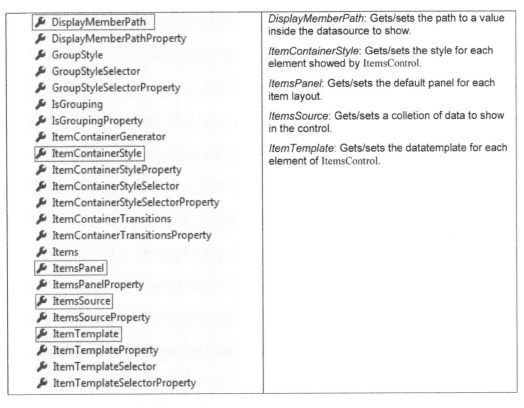

Figure 3-29. *ItemsControl public members*

HTML and JavaScript (JS) don't have an ItemsControl class, but they contain all the following controls (the namespace is Win.JS.ControlName). Starting from the left, the first control is the ComboBox control, which displays a read-only text box that, once selected, shows a drop-down list and allows users to select an item inside the list. It is also possible, starting from Windows 8.1, to set an header to the control by using the Header property, which does not accept any focus from the UI.

Figures 3-30, 3-31, and 3-32 show selection examples for a ComboBox control.

Figure 3-30. *A ComboBox example*

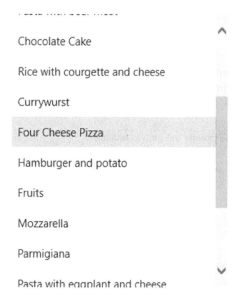

Figure 3-31. *Open ComboBox*

Figure 3-32. *Selected item in ComboBox*

The FlipView control allows users to "flip" among data collections. This control is ideal when you need to display pictures (see Figure 3-33).

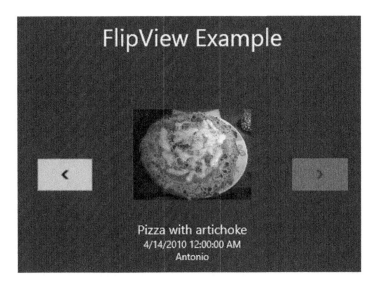

Figure 3-33. *FlipView example*

The declaration is similar to the other controls because `FlipView` inherits from the `ItemsControl` class. So you can use a layout control such as `StackPanel` inside the `DataTemplate`, filled by other controls. Figure 3-33 shows an output sample of `FlipView`. The arrows help navigate between the items.

One annoying problem related to `FlipView` is the difference of the transition between items. If you use touch, there is a smooth transition; but if you use the mouse and the arrow, or switch among items programmatically, there is no transition. Fortunately, this problem has been solved in the Windows 8.1 version with the `UseTouchAnimationsForAllNavigation` property.

The `ListBox` control is represented as a list of selectable items. Figure 3-34 shows a simple example.

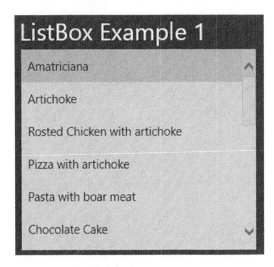

Figure 3-34. *ListBox example*

You can create a complex structure inside the ListBox with any kind of controls within (see Figure 3-35).

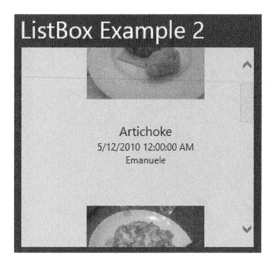

Figure 3-35. *A complex structure inside a ListBox*

As shown in Figure 3-36, GridView and ListView inherit from ListViewBase. This class contains common features used in both controls and implements ISemanticZoomInterface.

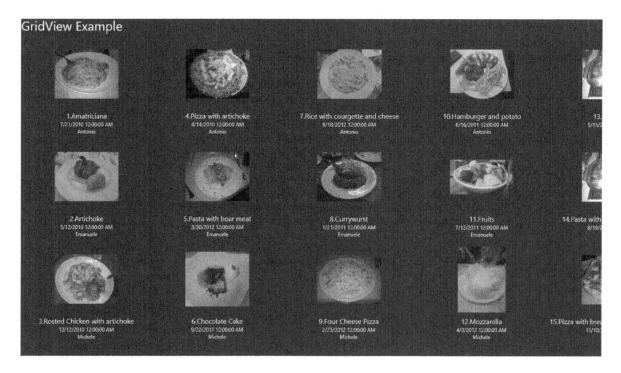

Figure 3-36. *Items order inside a GridView*

GridView is a data control that shows items in a grid. It provides a definition for columns and rows, and data can be associated using the ItemsSource property. GridView has an high level of customization and also allows grouping and sorting of items. Figure 3-36 shows an example of its usage.

It's interesting the way GridView lays the object in the output: the number in the title of a picture shows that the placing will be by columns.

ListView, which is the most complete list control, has great flexibility and enables you to represent a complex data layout.

Figure 3-37 shows the result. Although ListView looks very similar to the ListBox control, it is flagged as obsolete, so using ListView is highly recommended. Also, ListView is a *touch-and-animation-ready* control that provides a touch-spaced layout.

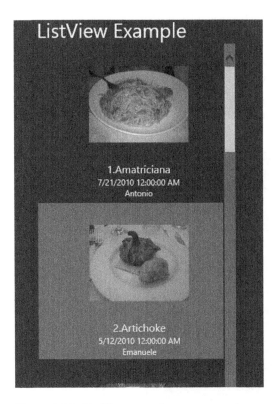

Figure 3-37. *ListView example*

Orientation and Layout

When you create an application, one of the main problems is how to locate objects inside the application. With Windows 8, you have to consider different aspects, mostly regarding different targeting devices in which this operating system (OS) will run.

Different Screen, Same Windows Version

One of the first goals of Windows 8 is its support for different devices and screen resolutions. Regardless of the device, a UI will always remain the same, thanks to screen-resolution scaling capabilities. So whenever you use a tablet or a multimonitor setup, your UI will be able to adapt its aspect based on the device's resolution. Windows 8 does the following:

- Provides the same interface on all devices

- Helps developers build their apps that look the same on all devices

Screen devices can be classified in three different ways:

- *Screen size*: The size of the screen, usually measured in inches (e.g., 13.3" or 15.6").

- *Screen resolution*: The number of pixels on a screen (e.g. 1366 x 768).

- *Pixel density*: The number of pixels within a physical area of the screen, which is usually measured in *dots per inch (DPI)*. The larger the screen resolution, the higher the pixel density.

Regardless of this classification, screen devices can have different ratios. For example, Figures 3-38, 3-39, and 3-40 show how object layouts adapt with different screen sizes and resolutions.

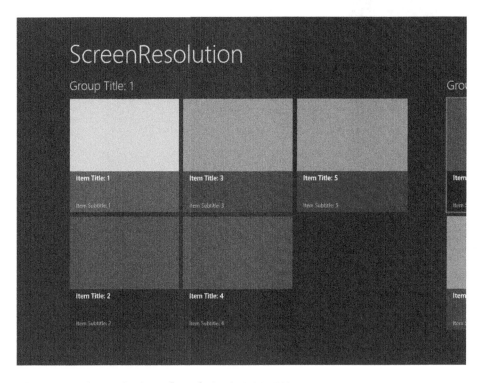

Figure 3-38. *Screen size is 10.6"; resolution is 1024 x 768*

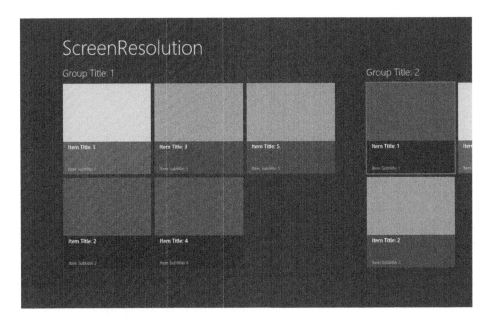

Figure 3-39. *Screen size is 12"; resolution is 1280 x 800*

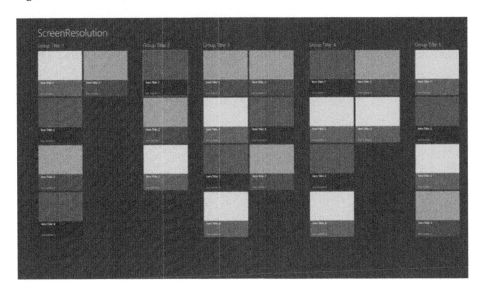

Figure 3-40. *Screen size is 27"; resolution is 2560 x 1440*

Here's a list of Windows 8–supported screen sizes, default resolutions, and DPI densities:

- **10.6"**
    - 2560 x 1440 (291 DPI)
    - 1920 x 1080 (218 DPI)
    - 1366 x 768 (155 DPI)

- **11.6"**
    - 2560 x 1440 (253 DPI)
    - 1920 x 1080 (190 DPI)
    - 1366 x 768 (135 DPI)

- **12"**
    - 1280 x 800 (125 DPI)
- **14"**
    - 1920 x 1080 (157 DPI)
    - 1366 x 768 (112 DPI)

- **15.6"**
    - 1920 x 1080 (141 DPI)
- **17"**
    - 1920 x 1080 (130 DPI)
- **23"**
    - 1920 x 1080 (96 DPI)
- **27"**
    - 2560 x 1440 (109 DPI)

All these screen resolutions have one thing in common: a minimum resolution of 1024 x 768 (see Figure 3-41).

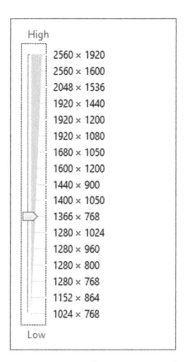

Figure 3-41. *Different screen resolutions with a minimum of 1024 x 768*

A minimum resolution is chosen to help developers tailor their applications without regard to the way content fits in resolutions lower than 1024 x 768 and to avoid targeting their applications for a specific resolution.

Choosing a minimum resolution is based on the following:

- It's the resolution in which Metro UI and its content fits the best.

- Web sites are generally designed for a resolution of 1024 x 768.

- The majority of Windows 7 users don't use a lower resolution than 1024 x 768 (http://blogs.msdn.com/b/b8/archive/2012/03/21/scaling-to-different-screens.aspx).

- The default or suggested resolution for Windows 8 is 1366 x 768.

Whenever we use a larger screen or a higher resolution, more objects will be filled on the screen (refer to Figures 3-38, 3-39, and 3-40).

In particular, there are two different techniques for settling objects in the UI:

- *Adaptive*: The higher the screen resolution, the higher number of objects in the UI.

- *Scale*: The higher the screen resolution, the larger the objects in the UI (games have benefits using this technique).

Pixel density might be a problem, too! Different screen resolutions have different DPIs, so a developer can use three percentages to scale images and ensure that they won't be blurry:

- 100 percent when no scaling is applied

- 140 percent for HD tablets

- 180 percent for quad-XGA tablets

To help developers create layouts for their applications, Windows 8 developing tools include a set of built-in features such as XAML attributes or CSS3 Flexible Box. And you haven't heard the last of this!

Visual Studio 2013 provides a simulator with a setting option for the device resolution (see Figure 3-42). Blend for Visual Studio 2013 provides a menu to select both the resolution and DPI of the destination platform (see Figure 3-43). These tools help developers simplify their work.

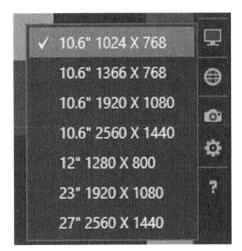

Figure 3-42. *Screen resolution setting in Visual Studio 2013 Simulator*

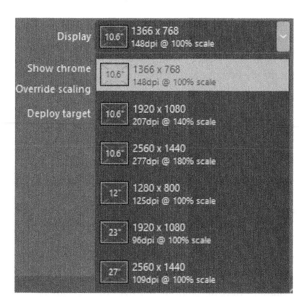

Figure 3-43. *Screen resolution setting in Blend 5*

Windows 8 also introduces improvements for multimonitor support. A multimonitor setup helps you to be more productive by parallellizing work on different screens. According to recent research, people usually use a first (main) monitor for work; a second monitor for e-mail or web browsing; and a third monitor for news, social networks, and chat. Microsoft has listened to people who have commented on the Windows Feedback Program, designing the best way to support multimonitor setups.

Major features are the following:

- *Taskbar on all monitors*: This option is fully customizable; you can set ways to show the taskbar on secondary screens.

- *Universal access*: Now you can use the Start button or charms on every monitor.

- *Side-by-side Windows Store apps*: You can have multiple Windows Store apps on different monitors.

- *Desktop backgrounds*: You can set multiple background images or span one image on different monitors.

Layout

In Windows 8 (but not the later version starting from version 8.1), there are three different view states for Windows Store apps:

- Full screen view (see Figure 3-44)

Figure 3-44. *An example of full screen view*

- Snapped view (see Figure 3-45)

Figure 3-45. *An example of snapped and fill views*

- Fill view (see Figure 3-46)

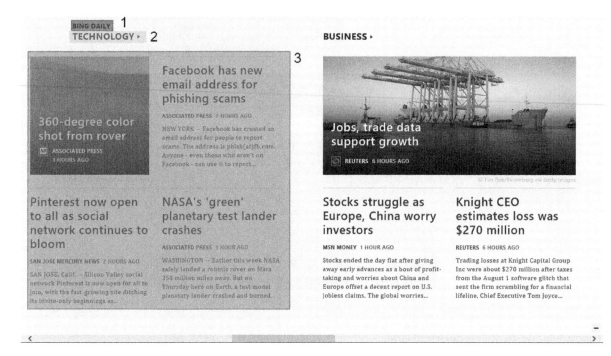

Figure 3-46. *A screenshot from the Windows Store News app (full screen view)*

Full screen view uses the whole screen to show an application. Snapped and fill views are enabled only if the horizontal resolution is 1366 pixels or greater.

In this view state, 320 pixels are used for the snapped portion (the left side of Figure 3-45); 1046 pixels are dedicated to the fill view (the right side of Figure 3-45). The remaining 22 pixels are used for the splitter.

To make a great app, consider the different view states and follow these rules:

- Don't change the context; maintain the user state and just resize the app.

- Don't use controls to modify the view state (this is the splitter's job!).

- Use the application's API to understand view state changing.

- Adjust the content in a stack shape (see Figures 3-46 and 3-47).

Figure 3-47. *A screenshot from the Windows Store News app (snapped view)*

In Figure 3-46, the highlighted section (referring to 1, 2, and 3) is set in a stack layout visible in Figure 3-47. This way, users always have the information needed to maintain the previous state shown in full screen view.

Things have changed in Windows 8.1, however. The snapped and fill views are gone. Every app can be resizable with a default minimum width of 500 pixels that can be reduced to 320 pixels. It is possible to have two Windows Store apps open on the same screen and to resize each one, and an app can open in one or more new windows at the same time. Also, as many as three apps can be on the same full HD (1080-pixel) screen. For this reason, Microsoft guidelines strongly recommend creating apps that work at any available size (especially the low ones).

To improve navigation, it is also recommended to adapt controls such as AppBar, NavBar, SearchBox, or Flyout to lower resolution. There are also few changes in the ApplicationView class: some methods, such as the TryUnsnap or Value properties, no longer work if the target platform is Windows 8.1.

Figure 3-48 shows a screenshot with the new windowing modes:

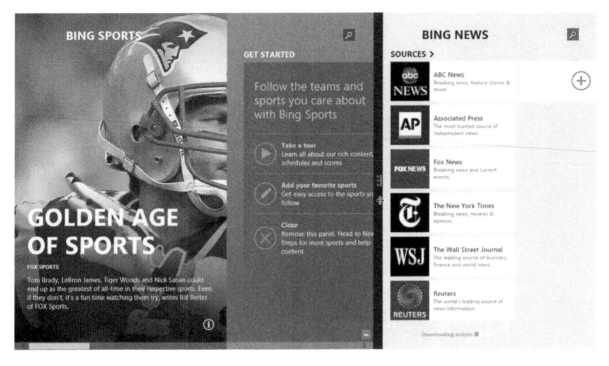

Figure 3-48. *New windowing modes in Windows 8.1*

Now that you have a good knowledge of screen settings, you can learn how to set controls in your UI.

Creating a layout means choosing the right container for controls. The choice depends on the type of application that you want to develop. The main layout controls in the control library are as follows:

- XAML
    - Canvas
    - Grid
    - Stack Panel
    - Virtualizing Stack Panel
- HTML/CSS
    - Combination of HTML5 elements and CSS3 styles

A *canvas* is a drawing area, and all controls inside a canvas are positioned by absolute value (these values correspond to the distance from the top/left corner). Because of absolute positioning, it cannot be used in applications that need a scalable interface. Figure 3-49 shows an example of positioning a button inside a canvas.

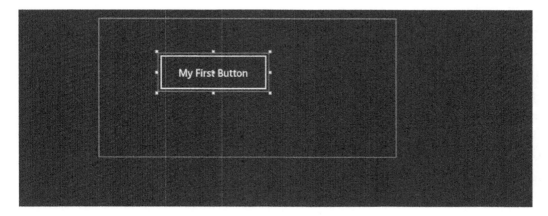

Figure 3-49. *A button inside a canvas*

The Grid control helps create a grid structure. It can have rows and columns, and a cell can contain any other control. Before you use it, the number of the rows and columns needs to be defined, and there are several ways to set the size of the columns/rows. With the asterisk (*) you can autosize the cells, depending on the space available inside the screen. Figure 3-50 shows an example of a grid declaration.

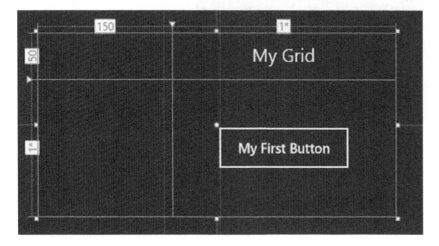

Figure 3-50. *A grid with a text block and one button*

StackPanel enables you to position controls consecutively and set directions, such as horizontal or vertical. Figures 3-51 and 3-52 show examples of the StackPanel control.

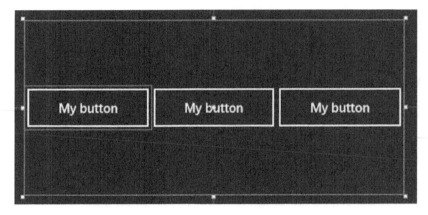

Figure 3-51. *StackPanel with horizontal orientation*

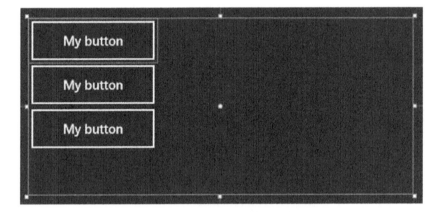

Figure 3-52. *StackPanel with vertical orientation*

Orientation

Tablet devices usually provide a gyroscope or an accelerometer to detect screen orientation changes. There are two types of orientation: *landscape* (see Figure 3-53) and *portrait* (see Figure 3-54).

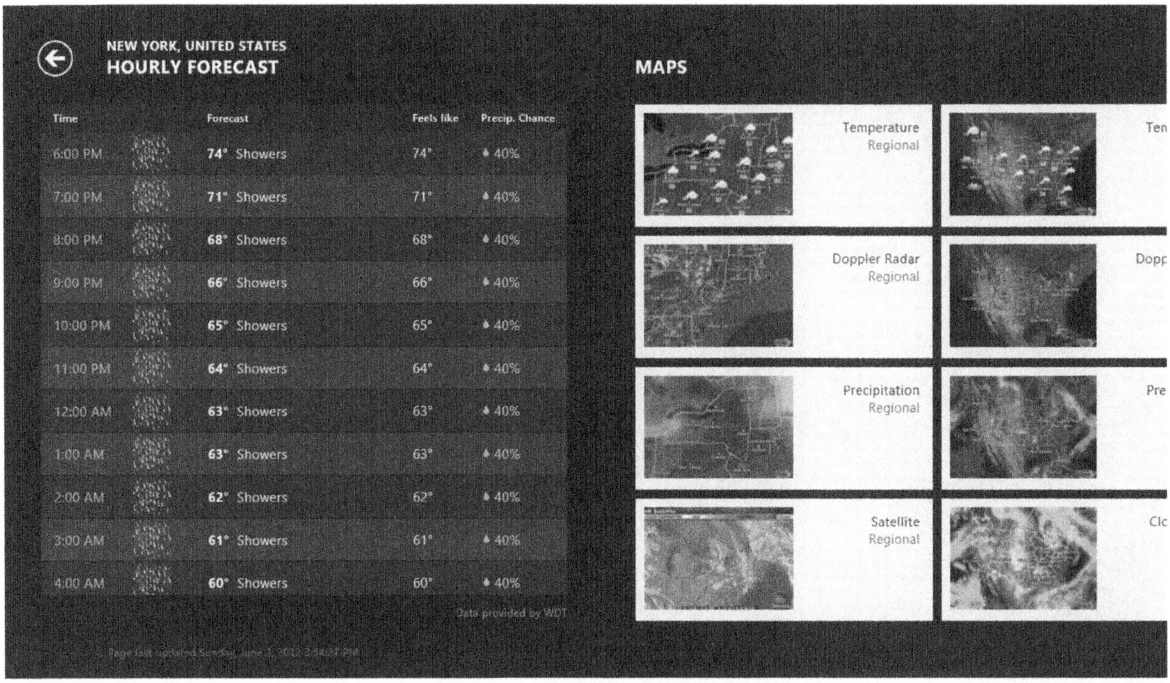

Figure 3-53. Landscape orientation

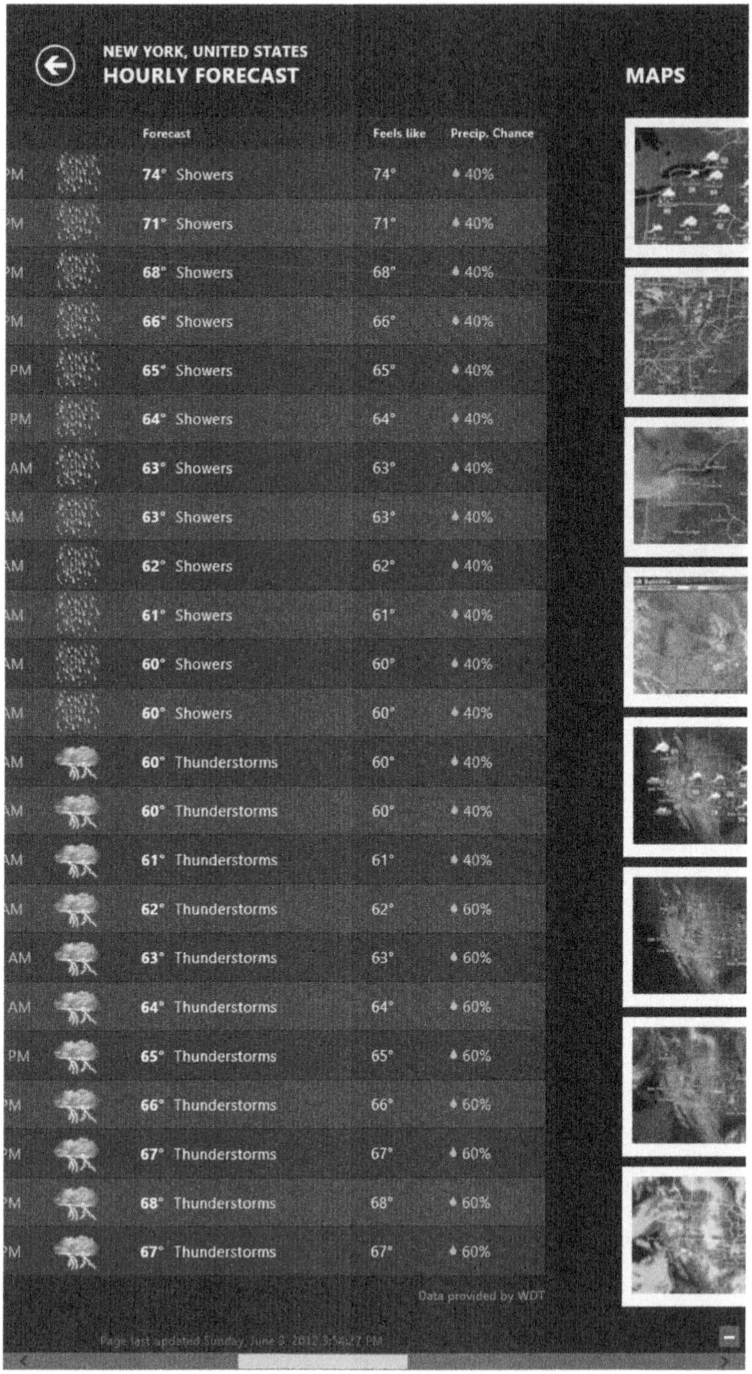

Figure 3-54. *Portrait orientation*

Developers have to identify orientation changes in their applications, which can be done using media queries in CSS or using managed code catching the OrientationChanged event in the code-behind.

Developers can test orientation while developing the application using Visual Studio 2013 Simulator or Blend for Visual Studio 2013 (see Figure 3-55).

Figure 3-55. *Blend view support*

Semantic Zoom

Semantic zoom is a new way to use zoom features to display contents. It is a touch-based technique that allows navigation, display, and management of a large set of related data. It uses the pinch and stretch gesture to show more or less information, and to navigate with the help of panning and scrolling gestures.

Two modes (or zoom levels) display the content:

- *Zoomed-in*: Contents are displayed in details, showing additional information such as photos or item-related data

- *Zoomed-out*: Contents are summarized into semantic-based groups, allowing the user to quickly navigate them

Figures 3-56 and 3-57 illustrate the difference between the modes.

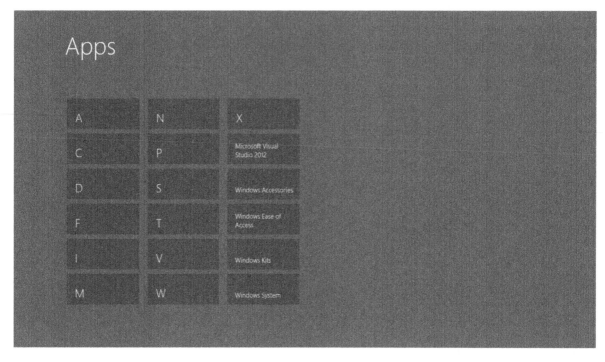

Figure 3-56. *An example of zoom-out on apps*

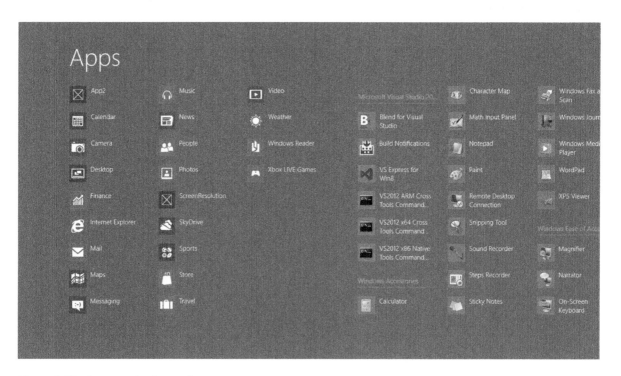

Figure 3-57. *An example of zoom-in on apps*

In addition to the pinch gesture, you can reach semantic zoom using the mouse or keyboard. With the mouse, you can hold down the Ctrl key while scrolling with the scroll wheel. With the keyboard, you can hold down the Ctrl and Shift keys and press the + or – keys.

Panning and scrolling gestures can help navigation by localizing the content and then zooming in on it.

At first sight, semantic zoom might be confused with optical zoom. Actually, they are different, even though they share the same interactions and behaviors. *Optical zoom* increases the level of details in a content area; *semantic zoom* changes the level of details in which they're shown, giving the data a different perspective.

Here are some recommendations for developers using semantic zoom. First, always define two levels of zoom. It's important to balance what contents are shown in the different levels to avoid having to repeat information and to simplify the navigation. They must leave enough space among the elements to let the user zoom in or zoom out. Also, the space for the element has to be big enough to use a finger (more information can be found in the touch targeting size section of this chapter).

Developers should organize the content in sorted groups and take advantage of the pages (but being careful not to overdo!). Finally, borders should be used only for semantic zoom control.

Contracts and Extensions

Contracts and extensions are the core of the interaction of an app with other apps or the OS. In this era of social networks, people need to communicate, so when you write an app, don't consider it stand-alone. Your app must be ready to satisfy users' needs: they want to *tweet* what they're doing now or share what great news they read in your app. You can do this and much more with contracts and extensions. Windows 8 allows you to create applications that define an agreement with the OS or with other apps. When the agreement is made with Windows, it's called an *extension*; when the agreement is made with another application, it's called a *contract*.

The following sections describe each one and explain what you need to know in order to follow Microsoft guidelines. You'll learn how to use them while we develop the case study.

Contracts

A *contract* defines the interaction between apps (source and target) mediated by a broker (the contract) that defines what is required by your app to participate.

Types of contracts include the following:

- Share contracts
- Search contracts
- Settings contracts
- Play To contracts
- App to App Picker contracts
- Cached File Updated contracts

Share Contract

One of the most important features for a user-centric system is the chance to share contents with other apps and services. Users love to share information, and with Windows 8 the Share charm is always near their fingers.

You can set your application to be a target of the *Share contract* by adding a Share target contract file to your project. This file allows you to declare the data formats and file types your applications supports. When your application has this contract as a target, remember that when Windows activates your application, it will open in the snapped view state. It is a good practice to specify which page of your application to show.

When you write your app to participate as a target, keep in mind some best practices that help provide a better UX:

- Avoid providing a way to leave the sharing context in your app; if users open your app for sharing, you must hide everything that is not relevant for this function.

- Don't provide a back button; when activated to share, your app adds a back button that navigates to the share target selection. Avoid using multiple pages when your app acts as a target.

- Put the button that shares the contents in an easily accessible location (normally the bottom-right corner) and provide the simplest UX to the user for sharing contents rapidly.

Of course, if an app acts as a target, other apps can act as a source. In this case, in your application you must declare the type of content shares and how many format types your application supports so it will be more interesting. Source apps should also follow some best practices:

- If your application shares contents available on the Web, share a link to the online content rather than the content itself.

- When you prepare the package to share, respect user selections. For example, if the user wants to share a portion of text, you must share only the selected text, not the entire page or document.

- Provide some additional information (e.g., title, description, link, thumbnail, and so on), which allows the target apps to improve their UX, providing the best look and feel to their users.

- To always provide the same UX, don't create your own share button in your application.

When users want to share something from your app, they press the Share button in the Charm Bar (shown in Figure 3-58). If your application is a source for sharing, the system will show something similar to the screen shown in Figure 3-59. (Of course, the displayed items may vary, depending on which contents your app shares because only applications that can manage them will be displayed.)

Figure 3-58. *Share button in the Charm Bar*

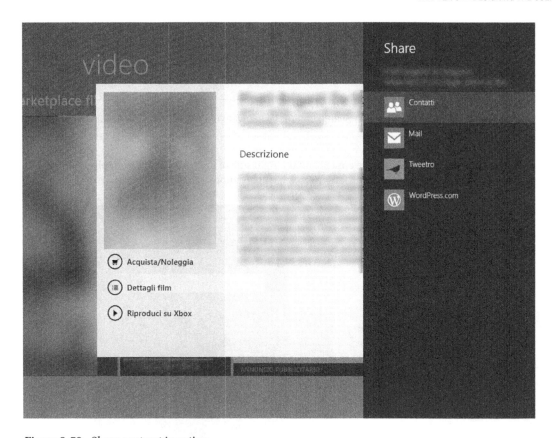

Figure 3-59. *Share contract in action*

Search Contract

Suppose that your app manages contents and you want these contents to be searchable everywhere in the system. This is what a *Search contract* offers: users can access data located in your app everywhere in the system or on the Web, and you gain a lot of points in the UX. Windows provides a search pane opened by the Search charm that sorts applications by frequency of use (see Figure 3-60).

Figure 3-60. *Search button*

When you develop an application that participates in a Search contract, you can be sure that the user will find your functionality easy to use and friendly because it is well integrated with the OS and offers a good UX. If you need another good reason to integrate a Search contract in your applications, consider that your app will be more visible to users for more use.

■ **Note**   You can write an app that participates in a Search contract wherever your app stores data (locally or remotely).

If you use Windows 8 (not 8.1 or later), a pane appears on the right side of the screen when you select the Search charm (see Figure 3-61). If your application is in the foreground, it will be automatically highlighted.

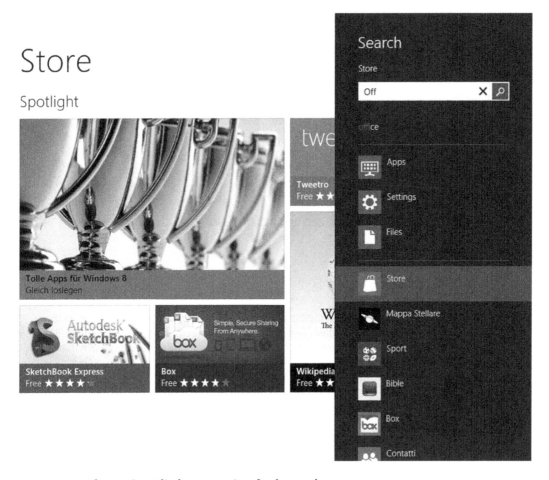

Figure 3-61. *The App Store displays suggestions for the search query*

Things are different in Windows 8.1: the Search charm has been redesigned. Now when you search something through the Search charm, you can choose where to find it (see Figure 3-62). After you press Enter, another window powered by Bing displays all results from different sources (see Figure 3-63).

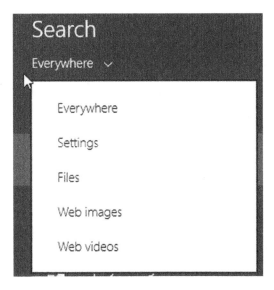

Figure 3-62. *The App Store displays suggestions for the search query (Windows 8.1)*

Figure 3-63. *The App Store displays suggestions for the search query (Windows 8.1)*

Because the Search contract is part of the UX core provided by Windows 8, you must follow some guidelines when you participate in this contract.

If you are using Windows 8.1, try to integrate the SearchBox control over the Search charm; otherwise, avoid in-app UI elements that provide the same functionalities of the Search charm because your app may become difficult to use. Provide search functionalities directly in your UI only for the Find in Page feature when users expect to remain on the same page (this doesn't happen when they use the search pane that opens a new UI). The Find in Page feature is particularly useful if your application manages documents. UI controls for Find in Page functionalities normally are located in the AppBar, which must stay open (in sticky mode) while the user uses this functionality.

When the Search contract is the main application on the screen, it will be asked for suggestions, depending on the search query. You should always provide a list of suggestions (refer to Figure 3-61).

Your application can provide two types of suggestions:

- *Query suggestions*: Suggestions for query text that the user inputs

- *Result suggestions*: Results that match the query actually written by the user

You should always provide search suggestions to speed up query input, providing the same result that a search shows if the user inputs the truncated text. For example, if your app manages messages, and the user searches for "Holidays," you should provide all messages that contain this word (refer to your relevance algorithm).

Participating in this contract enables your app to provide suggestions about the search query, allowing users to navigate directly to the details of the selected item. It speeds up the navigation, which helps the UX. You should provide no more than five suggestions; if your app provides query suggestions and result suggestions, you must limit the result to one item.

Some best practices to follow when your app participates in this contract include these:

- You should provide a way to see what the user is looking for in the search page.

- Combine the ListView control and the Search contract to provide the same UX of Windows 8 (see Figure 3-64).

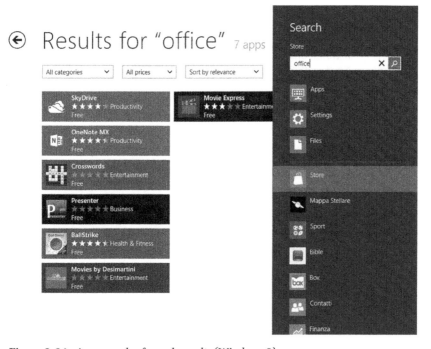

Figure 3-64. *An example of search results (Windows 8)*

- If something is important to show, move it to the left side of the screen because the Search charm appears on the right side over your application, hiding information on the search results page.

- Provide a way to see why an item inside your application matches the search query. If the user looks for "Holidays," you should show the word *Holidays* inside the description or the title of the image in your application.

- Provide a way to refine the search in your application. For example, if your application contains images and text, you should provide a set of filters to limit the result to images or text in the search page results.

- When you contact a service to collect suggestions, use the SearchPaneSuggestionsRequestDeferral class, which allows you to signal when your app finishes collecting suggestions.

Settings Contract

The user touches the Settings charm (shown in Figure 3-65), and if your app participates in the *Settings contract*, you can define a Settings page (see Figure 3-66). The Settings contract gives users access to your app's settings from the Settings charm. The purpose of the Settings contract is to give uniform access to app settings so users feel that the apps are all integrated within the system.

Figure 3-65. *Settings button in app charms*

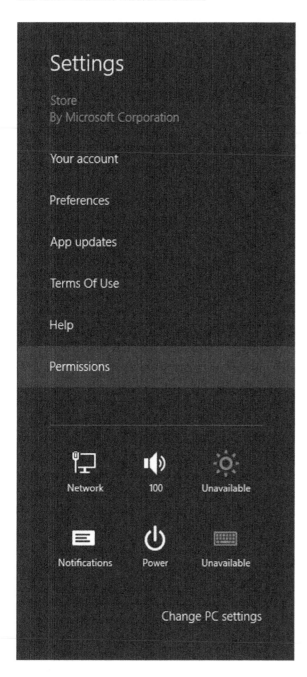

Figure 3-66. *Example of the Settings pane*

To participate in this contract, your application will use the SettingsCommand class that creates a setting entry that you can add to the ApplicationCommands list (you'll see how to use this class when the application's setting console in Chapter 7 is discussed). By default, if your application was downloaded from the Windows Store, Windows provides two entries: one for permissions relative to your application; the other to rate and review your application (not available for side-loaded enterprise apps).

We never tire of repeating that UX is the core concept of Windows 8, and to enable the user to obtain the best experience from your application, you must follow some simple rules:

- Choose well when determining the settings to include in the Settings pane, which includes settings that influence the app's behaviors.

- Use the Settings charm to provide information not accessed very often, such as help or copyright info.

- Group similar settings to reduce entry points. For example, group uncommon settings under one entry point to allow more common settings under their own entry point (e.g., group any About policy support information under the About entry). Remember to limit entry points to four.

- Avoid the use of app settings to change the application workflow; instead, use AppBar for this purpose. Don't navigate in your application when users press the Settings charm because they must be in the same place where they started when the setting windows close.

- Limit the settings hierarchies to two levels in order to provide an easy-to-use menu.

Play To Contract

Imagine that your app shows videos, and your potential users are watching the video on their tablets while riding the subway. They get home and decide to finish seeing the film on their new Digital Living Network Alliance (DLNA)–compatible televisions. If your application participates in the Play To contract, your users can stream the video by simply pressing the Play To charm. It's easy to accomplish this: you handle only the SourceRequested event of the PlayToManager class, which fires when the user selects the Devices charm, and then pass the media element to the PlayToSourceRequestedEventArgs class.

As with other contracts, you should follow some best practices:

- If your application manages videos, provide a way to stream them.

- Register as the source of this contract only if you have contents to share.

- If you share content with this contract, you must allow the user to continue navigating, providing a way to keep the media element available.

App to App Picker Contract and Cached File Updated Contract

Modern OSs on tablets all have the same core concept: apps. The user needs to have an immersive application, but these apps don't integrate because every app is stand-alone. To solve this problem in Windows 8, you can participate in the *App to App Picker contract*, which enables apps to access files inside other apps.

Although the App to App Picker contract provides opening and saving file capabilities, the *Cached File Updated contract* allows you to update files.

The Cached File Updated contract allows your app to track file changes in order to update these files in a central repository. For example, the SkyDrive application in Windows 8 allows you to share contents with other apps and keep files updated with the SkyDrive service.

Extensions

Although contracts enable interaction with other apps, *extensions* enable you to integrate with the OS. Extensions available in Windows 8 include these:

- Account Picture Provider

- AutoPlay

- Background Tasks

- Contact Picker

- File Activation

- Print Task Settings

- Protocol Activation

Account Picture Provider

This extension allows users to open an app if they want to change their profile picture. Suppose that your application edits images with some effects. Users of your app would use images edited within your software as profile pictures just by clicking a button.

If your application allows users to change profile pictures, you can use three types of media:

- Small format image

- Large format image

- Video

These three types can be set by your application in the same call, but remember that when you set a large image or a video, you must always associate a small image as a thumbnail.

AutoPlay

With this extension, your application can open a device when it is added to the system. For example, if your application edits images, it will be an option when a user connects a new device such as a camera, USB drive, or Secure Digital (SD) card; or when the user starts a share using proximity.

Background Tasks

As discussed earlier, in Windows 8 only one application at a time is executed, reserving available resources for the foreground app. You need some gears to keep the app's information up to date. One of these gears is the Background Tasks extension that you can use if you want to do work when your app is not active. Although background tasks are very helpful in most scenarios (e.g., downloading e-mail), avoid using background tasks for Search for Extraterrestrial Intelligence (SETI) workloads, for example, because it will drain the battery.

Starting a background task requires an event that triggers and launches the task. The triggers that raise various trigger events are described in Table 3-3.

Table 3-3. *Trigger Types*

Trigger Type	Event	Occurrence
SystemEventTrigger	InternetAvailable	When an Internet connection is available
SystemEventTrigger	ControlChannelReset	When a network channel is reset
SystemEventTrigger	NetworkStateChange	When a network state changes, such as when passing from a free to a paid connection
SystemEventTrigger	OnlineIdConnectedStateChange	When the online ID associated with the account changes (refers to the online ID used by Windows Live)
SystemEventTrigger	ServicingComplete	When the system ends to update the application
SystemEventTrigger	SmsReceived	When a new Short Message System (SMS) is received by an installed mobile broadband device
SystemEventTrigger	TimeZoneChange	When the time zone changes on the device (e.g., when the system adjusts the clock for Daylight Saving Time [DST] or when the user moves around the world)
SystemEventTrigger	UserAway	When the user is absent
SystemEventTrigger	UserPresent	When the user is present
ControlChannelTrigger	ControlChannelTrigger	On incoming messages on the control channel
MaintenanceTrigger	MaintenanceTrigger	When it is time for maintenance background tasks
PushNotificationTrigger	PushNotificationTrigger	When raw notifications arrive on the WNS channel
TimeTrigger	TimeTrigger	When a time event occurs

When you subscribe to a trigger in your task, you can set zero or more conditions to be satisfied in order to start the task. For example, if your app manages e-mail, you can set a condition that an Internet connection must be available. Task conditions are described in Table 3-4.

Table 3-4. *Task Conditions*

Condition	Description
InternetAvailable	An Internet connection must be available
InternetNotAvailable	An Internet connection must be unavailable
SessionConnected	The session must be connected
SessionDisconnected	The session must be disconnected
UserNotPresent	The user state must be set to away
UserPresent	The user state must be set to present

When one of the triggers described here fires, the BackgroundTask infrastructure looks for apps registered for it and launches the background task.

With Background Tasks, you can provide information about updating tiles in your app, and if your app is authorized to publish on a locked screen, you can provide information about the state of your app. For example, if your app manages messages, you can show the number of unread messages. You'll see how to implement background tasks in Chapter 7, when we talk about how to implement them in an app.

Contact Picker

Your app can register to provide contact data so that when an app requires contact information, your application appears as a source. Imagine that you are writing a messaging app with a specific contact list. Other apps on the system can use the list of contacts your app provides, even outside of your own app. This extension is another important part of UX because it provides cross-app integration.

File Activation

Immersive apps are cool, but when users come from previous versions of Windows, they look for an application that opens certain file types. For this reason, Windows 8 introduced the File Activation extension. When you declare in your app that you can open certain files, the OS lists your app as a possible file destination. When your app has been activated, you can handle the ActivationKind relative to the open file. Of course, because Windows 8 is a user-centric OS, you can't set the default app to use for a file type within your app, but Windows will ask users to choose the app that they want as the default.

Printer Task Settings

When you think of a personal computer, you associate it with a printer; and when you think of a printer, you think of the software products that manage them. Every printer manufacturer produces its own software to manage the printer, and some of them also tell users about cartridge status.

Windows 8 offers some benefits to manufacturers. The app relative to a device is automatically downloaded from the Windows Store when the user connects the device. Immersive apps for printers can be useful; for example, your application can show the status of the printer in the tile and the cartridge status. Because your app will be distributed through the Windows Store if you produce an update, it will be shown to all users. This is a great leap for the UX because when users connect to a device, they will be immediately ready to work with its software.

Protocol Activation

With Protocol Activation, you can manage particular protocols. For example, consider an application that supports Voice over Internet Protocol (VoIP). With this extension, the app can manage every hyperlink that uses the callto:\\ protocol. This extensions works like the File Activation extension: it is activated by the system when the user selects your application to manage a protocol that you should specify in the App.Manifest. You will manage the ActivationKind named protocol while your app handles the activated event.

Conclusion

This chapter helped you create an application with better UX, showed you how to choose the right control from the rich control library to provide a consistent UX between apps, and how to further integrate your app with other apps (and the system).

Chapter 4 introduces you to ways of developing applications for the Windows 8 platform and discusses reasons for choosing one over another.

CHAPTER 4

■ ■ ■

Choose Your Way

Although this book is about the C# and Visual Basic (VB) languages, it also introduces all the possibilities offered by the Windows Runtime (WinRT) platform. If you are interested in a language other than the ones presented in this book, you can find an appropriate book in the Apress catalogue. This chapter analyzes the tools and the differences between them, focusing attention on XAML and C# or VB for developing the Windows Store App.

Choosing Your Way

Why are very different languages used to develop Windows Store App applications? As you saw in Chapter 2, WinRT allows the use of more languages to invoke the application programming interface (API) through the projections. Out of the box, Microsoft enables the possibility of using C#, VB, JavaScript (JS), and C++ as programming languages, and HTML5 (with CSS3) and XAML for the user interface (UI) definition.

Choose the language you know and are comfortable using. Of course, there are differences with namespaces, objects, and ways to write code, but by understanding the application model and the features offered by WinRT, you can use the language that is most productive for you. If you are a web developer, you probably will choose HTML 5, CSS 3, and JS. If you are a Silverlight, Windows Presentation Foundation (WPF), or Windows Phone developer, you will choose XAML and C# or VB. If you are a C++ developer, you need to learn only about XAML and use your experience in C++ language to develop a Windows Store App.

If you are a Windows Phone developer, you can be happy: most of your knowledge about Windows Phone can be ported on Windows Store Apps without effort, but remember that the user experience (UX) is different. For example, panorama and pivot controls are not present, and the target devices are bigger than smartphones. Many controls are equal, and Microsoft design language guidelines are similar, but the user and the use can be very different.

The key is to think about your potential users and to concentrate on satisfying user requirements. The language you use is only a tool: choose the one that is most familiar.

Using XAML and the .NET Languages

XAML is a markup language introduced by Microsoft with the WPF technology, with the big objective of creating for desktop applications the separation between contents and presentation already existing in the web application with HTML and CSS. The eXtensible Application Markup Language (XML) uses a XML declarative syntax to instantiate .NET UI components and initializes their properties.

XAML Views and Binding

Chapter 3 introduced many controls to use inside a Windows Store App view. Let's see how to use them in XAML markup. First, a view is a subclass of the Page class, which means that the root element of an XAML view is a Page element that can contain a layout controls with UI elements:

```
<Page
    x:Class="BlankApplication.MainPage"
    xmlns="http://schemas.microsoft.com/winfx/2006/xaml/presentation"
    xmlns:x="http://schemas.microsoft.com/winfx/2006/xaml"
    xmlns:local="using: BlankApplication">
    <Page.Resources>

    </Page.Resources>
    <Grid>

    </Grid>
</Page>
```

A Page (or the application in general) can contain more elements, and many of them might have the same property values. In this case, you can group common properties in a resource style to be reused in many contexts. For example, with this markup you can set the font size to 48 pixels and the background to red for all buttons in a Page:

```
<Page.Resources>
    <Style TargetType="Button">
        <Setter Property="FontSize" Value="48" />
        <Setter Property="Background" Value="Red" />
    </Style>
</Page.Resources>
```

The Page.Resources section defines all resources of the current page. Through its Setter properties, the Style element defines all the property values applied with the style. The required TargetType property selects the possible UI elements target of the style in the example Button elements. If you don't specify the optional x:Name property, the style will be applied to all elements that match the TargetType property, which is very useful for a homogenous application look and feel. If you want to create a style for specified elements that match the style's TargetType, you can set the property x:Name and use the XAML binding syntax to bind it to the elements. The previous example then becomes the following:

```
<Page.Resources>
    <Style x:Name="MyButtonStyle" TargetType="Button">
        <Setter Property="FontSize" Value="48" />
        <Setter Property="Background" Value="Red" />
    </Style>
</Page.Resources>
```

And the Button target of the style can be declared as follows:

```
<Button Content="Click Me" Style="{StaticResource MyButtonStyle}" />
```

One of the most important features introduced by the XAML syntax is declarative binding. By using starting and ending braces, you can indicate to the compiler that the content is not simply a string; it is an expression to evaluate during the parsing process. In the previous example, the Style property is binding to the MyButtonStyle resource.

But the power of the binding expression can be appreciated when is used to bind UI controls with application model class properties or other UI control properties. For example, to show a Slider current value in a TextBlock, you can use the following XAML:

```
<Slider Name="MySlider" Minimum="0" Maximum="100" Width="500" />
<TextBlock Text="{Binding ElementName=MySlider, Path=Value}" />
```

The binding is bidirectional by default, but you can specify a property called Mode that can have one of these three values:

- OneTime: The binding is applied only once

- OneWay: For unidirectional binding

- TwoWay: For bidirectional binding (default)

When you bind a UI control with a data class property, the ElementName is not used because the Source instance of the class will be set typically through the DataContext property of the UI element or its parent, or the Source property of the binding. Look at this code:

C#
```
public class User
{
    public string Name { get; set; }
    public string Surname { get; set; }
}
```

VB
```
Public Class User
    Public Property Name As String
    Public Property Surname As String
End Class
```

If you have a domain class that represents a generic user of the application, you can set an instance of this class to the DataContext page, which will make it available to the page controls for the binding. You can create an instance of this class from the XAML, but the instance is usually created by a method of a business class. If you want to have a UserManager business class, you can write the following code:

C#
```
User myUser = userManager.GetUser();
this.DataContext = myUser;
```

VB
```
Dim myUser as User = userManager.GetUser()
Me.DataContext = myUser
```

The XAML binding expression of a form that permits user field management can be written as follow:

```
<TextBlock Text="Name: " />
<TextBox Text="{Binding Path=Name}" />
<TextBlock Text="Surname: " />
<TextBox Text="{Binding Path=Surname}" />
```

If the only binding property to set is Path, you can omit it; in the example, you can write {Binding Name} and {Binding Surname}.

XAML has many other features, and the binding expressions have many other options (we will explain them when they are used).

VB and C# Windows Store App Template

Now look at the project template for XAML and C# (on the left) and VB (on the right) in Figure 4-1.

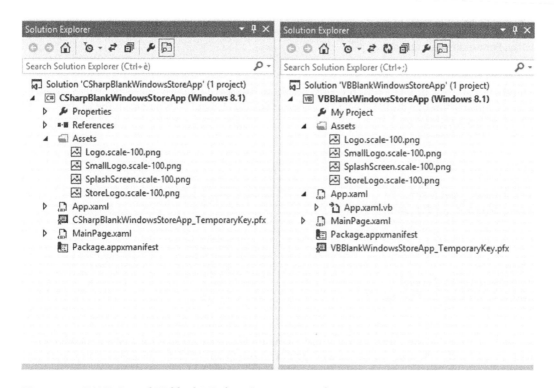

Figure 4-1. *XAML C# and VB blank Windows Store App template*

A Windows Store App page has one XAML file and a correspondent code file with a .cs or .vb extension. Figure 4-1 shows MainPage.xaml and the corresponding MainPage.xaml.cs and MainPage.xaml.vb files. A special file is App.xaml (with the .cs and .vb files), which is used to manage the application life cycle. In the Windows 8.1 version, there is no need to keep the StandardStyle file because default styles are now part of the framework.

The Asset folder contains the required images used for the application: Logo.png, SmallLogo.png, SplashScreen.png, and StoreLogo.png.

A Quick Introduction to JavaScript and C++
HTML 5 and JavaScript

If you are a web developer, the good news is that you can reuse your skills for developing Windows Store Apps. After the great success of HTML 5 and CSS 3, Microsoft looks at the future: supporting the current draft of this standard (the final release is attending for 2014) in its browser, Internet Explorer (IE) and in its platform to meet the needs of the web developers with the many options offered by the new specifics.

Hypertext Markup Language (HTML) is a language that was born in the 1980s to supporting hypertext, the electronic text composed of linked pages available through the World Wide Web. Since the 1980s, the language has evolved and been standardized by the W3C (World Wide Web Consortium). It has two main objectives: a correct syntax for a correct semantic interpretation by the main browser and new features to adapt an old language to the new web requirements.

Windows Store Apps for JS support HTML 5. This means that you can use new tags in the markup code and implement some JS code for features in your apps.

Another very useful feature introduced with HTML 5 (and most used with Windows Store Apps), are the data-* attributes. You can use these attributes to store custom data in the page; for example, to store a validation message. Many JS frameworks, such as jQuery mobile and unobtrusive validation jQuery plugins, use this attribute. In the Windows Store, apps8 data-* are used to indicate the control used in the page and its parameter values. These values are used from the Windows Store App JS framework: WinJS.

C++

C++ programmers can develop Windows Store Apps without learning another language by using the knowledge garnered by years of experience. Unfortunately, Windows 8.1 architecture imposes some limitations on the classical C++ application development.

Here are some things you can do with C++:

- Write components for HTML5 and the JS UI

- Write the code-behind of the XAML UI

- Write the game engine for the DirectX UI

Games are very popular for users, and C++ with DirectX allows you to create high-performance 2D and 3D games, accessing the powerful hardware available on the PC and tablet as the Tegra processors. If you are interested in high-performance applications, C++ can be your best choice. The internal modules of Window 8.1 are also written in C++ and expose an external surface for the WinRT calls and for native calls.

What Language Should You Choose?

As we said at the beginning of this chapter, it makes sense to choose one language you already know or prefer to use to develop your application. This choice helps you write code easily and decreases development time. Even though all the languages available to develop the Windows Store App share the same API subsystem, there are some variations due to language design that can make the difference in term of learning curve and performance. The main reasons to choose one language over any other are the *requirements*, which are all the features you want to introduce in your app. Based on these requirements`, you can choose the language that gives the best performance with less development effort. Let's see what the differences are, starting with the creation of a UI.

XAML vs. HTML and CSS

Once again, based on the kind of application you are developing and what requirements you have, one language will be the best fit for you. Take, for example, the creation of a Windows Store App for a graphic-intensive game: of course, it is possible to use JS, but there might be a bit of performance degradation. As a matter of fact, controls such as Canvas or using Scalable Vector Graphics (SVG) don't have the same performance as other technologies. For example, Canvas controls rebuild all pixels of the shapes to create motion, asking for resource to the runtime subsystem (remember that Windows Store Apps written in JS run by a process called *wwahost*, which provides a subset of IE features).

In this case, XAML for the UI and C++ plus the DirectX API have the best performance (DirectX is a set of APIs for game development). In this case, shapes rendering is more efficient.

C#, VB, C++, and JavaScript

A wise choice is to use a language you already know so you can reuse our skills during development. But sometimes you need to choose another way.

Indeed, considering what functional requirements are, it is possible to choose one language among the others. Let's go back for a moment to the game application: if it is a 3D graphic-intensive game, C++ is the best choice because C++ is a low-level language that has low memory consumption). Native code differs from managed code because it lacks a Garbage Collector (GC) that is a component for handling memory inside programs (creating and freeing memory allocation). Besides, native code is directly compiled into machine code, whereas managed code is compiled into Microsoft Intermediate Language (MSIL). Of course, you can use C# to create a game application; just be aware of a minimal degradation of performance during execution.

A different case is porting. In this case, it is recommended to reuse the same technology or language and what is already created, and then adapt it to WinRT. If it is a WPF, Silverlight, or Windows Phone application, migration is simple. On the other hand, if it is a Windows Forms application, it might take more effort and time. If it is an ASP.NET application instead, it is recommended to use C# or VB; that's why rewriting the whole back end in JS is not so simple. In the end, if it is a mobile application in HTML 5 and JS (or jQuery), it is better to use these technologies.

Another requirement might be the use of a programming pattern inside the code. C# and VB are object-oriented languages, and it is easier to also create a complex architecture using patterns such as Domain Driven Design or Test Driven Development. In this case, a database is often used to host data. As you will learn in Chapter 8, there are some differences that can help you decide on the best language or technology to use.

Few observations are linked to code obfuscation and the destination platform. Remember the following:

- JS is written in plain text.

- C#/VB is compiled in managed code (MSIL) and can be decompiled with tools such as .NET Reflector or ILspy.

- C++ is unmanaged code that generates machine code, and it is not easy to decompile (you will need a disassembler and few sleepless nights).

The destination platform could also be a decision point. .NET languages support "Any CPU" compilation, which means that the output assembly could run on x86 or x64 platforms (remember that the output assembly is in MSIL and needs a Common Language Runtime [CLR] to execute). It's different for C++, in which the destination platform must be specified. Table 4-1 summarizes the key point differences.

Table 4-1. *Supported options by language*

	C#/ VB	C++	JS
Level	Middle	Low	High
Type system	Static & Dynamic	Static	Dynamic
Garbage Collector	Yes	No (just ref-counted pointers)	Yes
Output	Assembly (MSIL)	Machine Code	Plain Text

Now you know that there are many reasons why one language is chosen over the others. What helps to make the decision is always the context (i.e., requirements, porting, game applications, and so on).

Conclusion

This chapter discussed the C# and VB languages that are used in this book to develop Windows Store Apps. You learned that there are other languages available in the platform, and you can choose one by considering your requirements. Of course, the simple way is to always choose what you already know; this way, you can maintain a lower development effort in less time.

CHAPTER 5

■ ■ ■

Managing the Application Life Cycle

To make the most of Windows Store apps development, you must understand a lot of core concepts in order to have control over the behavior of your application. One of these is the application life cycle, which is a basic concept for writing a good application that resumes its state correctly when the user reopens an application after a suspension.

Dissecting the Application Life Cycle

The first step of the application life cycle, just after the user downloads it from the Windows Store, is the NotRunning state, which is also the starting state when your app is crashed or closed. In the NotRunning state, your app can assume the Running state, which happens in only two cases:

- When the user opens your application by touching the tile or a notification

- When your app is chosen by the user to interact with another application using "Contracts and Extensions" (refer to Chapter 3 for an in-depth discussion)

Figure 5-1 shows different application execution states:

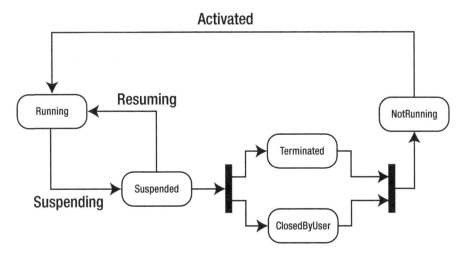

Figure 5-1. *Windows Store app life cycle*

An application is activated when passing from a NotRunning to a Running state. You can initialize all resources required for application execution by overriding the OnLaunched event.

There is a best practice that you must keep in mind: this transition is related to the time that the splash screen is visible on the user's screen device. For this reason, every background task needs to be as fast as possible to give control over your application to the user. If you need to load a large amount of data or connect to a service, you should not do it in the OnLaunched event; you should use an *extended splash screen* to avoid forcing the user having to wait for completion.

Suppose that the user leaves your application and returns to the Start screen or switches to another application: your app is still running. If you use the closing gesture, swiping the app from the top of the bottom of the screen, the app is still running, but it saves resources. This behavior is introduced with Windows 8.1.

If you want to permanently close your app, you have to use the close gesture. Hold the app thumbnail for about 2 seconds on the bottom of the screen, until it flips over. Then the runtime will maintain the app running for about 10 seconds until it will be suspended and then closed. When the user switches from or to the app, the VisibilityChanged event is called. This event can be used to manage an interaction (for example, stopping a timer if your app is a game).

The app will remain in a Suspended state until it is terminated by the operating system (OS) for memory reasons or from a closing gesture. The transition to the Suspended state raises the Suspending event, which you should handle to save the application state and release resources that your application requires.

Windows can manage many applications in a Suspended state to ensure that users can switch quickly between them. Of course, applications should not remain in a Suspended state, so they are terminated to recover resources. You need to remember that your application does not receive notifications about terminating, so you have only one opportunity to save the state of your application: the Suspending event.

By the way, although you cannot manage any terminating event, you can know how the application was terminated by evaluating the PreviousExecutionState of Activated event arguments. This property returns one of the following values from the ApplicationExecutionState enumeration:

- Terminated (or closed by the OS)

- ClosedByUser

- NotRunning

There is a lot of information to know about application termination. Unlike desktop applications, when you develop an immersive application you must keep in mind that your app can't offer a functionality to close itself, except in rare cases such as security issues. In that event, Windows will consider your application to be crashed, which could be a problem for users because when your app crashes (raises an exception or stops responding), the user is asked for consent to send a report to Microsoft with a subset of the error information (as discussed in Chapter 4). If you programmatically close your application with a button, you could receive a problem report every time a user closes your application. If the application crashes when it starts, there is no notification of the crash (unless you have your own internal code that tracks this issue) and the ApplicationExecutionState value will be NotRunning.

As you can see in Figure 5-1, from the Suspended state your app can reach the Running state by passing the Resuming event that fires when the user switches to it. When resumed, your app will start from the same point it was before being suspended, and you can handle the Resuming event to refresh contents of your application or require some resources from the system.

This is a quick overview of the application life cycle, but theory is nothing without practice. The following sections contain some code examples of how to manage the various events raised during the life cycle. Because this book is based on the C# and VB.NET languages, we will show you code for these languages supported by Windows Store apps, and you can be inspired by the language that meets your requirements and knowledge.

Activated Event

You start managing the `Activated` event in order to follow a logical flow. In this chapter, you will use a simple app; in Chapter 6, you will learn about Windows Store app creation in detail. For now, just create a project inside Visual Studio 2013. Inside of the section of your favorite programming language, choose the Blank App template to create a new Windows Store app, as shown in Figure 5-2. The figure shows the C# section, but the steps are the same for the other languages. Let's see how to handle an `Activated` event in different languages.

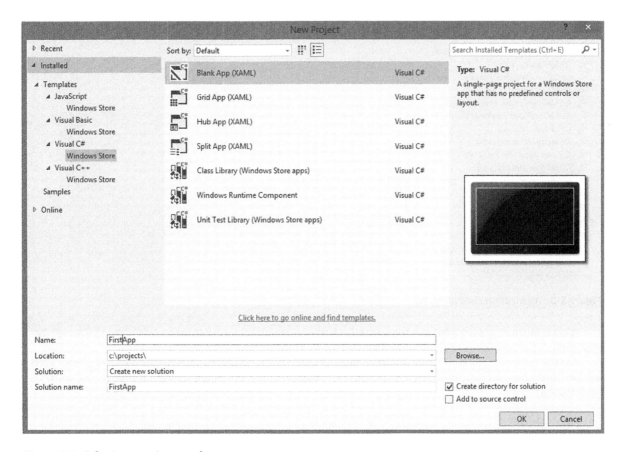

Figure 5-2. *Selecting a project template*

After your project is created, you will see a default implementation of the `OnLaunched` method inside the `App.xaml.cs` file. This file represents the main class of the application and inherits from the `Application` class (shown in Figure 5-3). This class exposes methods, events, and properties that represent the behavior of the application inside the OS.

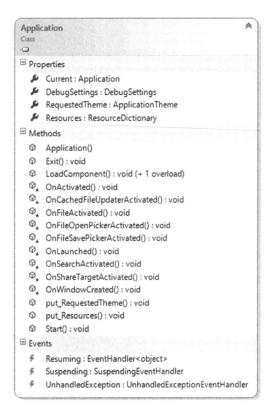

Figure 5-3. *Application class diagram*

What is interesting are the OnLaunched and OnActivated methods that you will override in order to manage the application's Launching and Activation events.

The OnLaunched method will be called when the user executes the application explicitly; conversely, OnActivated will be called whenever your application is launched for other situations (for example, when it answers to Contract subscription).

C#

In C#, the OnLaunched method looks like this (App.xaml.cs):

```csharp
        protected override async void OnLaunched(LaunchActivatedEventArgs e)
        {

#if DEBUG
            // Show graphics profiling information while debugging.
            if (System.Diagnostics.Debugger.IsAttached)
            {
                // Display the current frame rate counters
                this.DebugSettings.EnableFrameRateCounter = true;
            }
#endif
```

```
        Frame rootFrame = Window.Current.Content as Frame;

        // Do not repeat app initialization when the Window already has content,
        // just ensure that the window is active

        if (rootFrame == null)
        {
            // Create a Frame to act as the navigation context and navigate to the first page
            rootFrame = new Frame();
            //Associate the frame with a SuspensionManager key
            SuspensionManager.RegisterFrame(rootFrame, "AppFrame");
            // Set the default language
            rootFrame.Language = Windows.Globalization.ApplicationLanguages.Languages[0];

            if (e.PreviousExecutionState == ApplicationExecutionState.Terminated)
            {
                // Restore the saved session state only when appropriate
                try
                {
                    await SuspensionManager.RestoreAsync();
                }
                catch (SuspensionManagerException)
                {
                    //Something went wrong restoring state.
                    //Assume there is no state and continue
                }
            }

            // Place the frame in the current Window
            Window.Current.Content = rootFrame;
        }
        if (rootFrame.Content == null)
        {
            // When the navigation stack isn't restored navigate to the first page,
            // configuring the new page by passing required information as a navigation
            // parameter
            if (!rootFrame.Navigate(typeof(GroupedItemsPage)))
            {
                throw new Exception("Failed to create initial page");
            }
        }
        // Ensure the current window is active
        Window.Current.Activate();
    }
```

The default implementation evaluates the PreviousExecutionState property of LaunchActivatedEventArgs to see whether its value is equal to the Terminate value of the ApplicationExecutionState enumeration that you can see in the class diagram shown in Figure 5-4. Remember this diagram because you will refer to it when you evaluate other values of ApplicationExecutionState for other transitions. By checking the PreviousExecutionState, you can restore a saved state. The #if DEBUG statement enables the framerate counter on the top of the screen (starting in Windows 8.1).

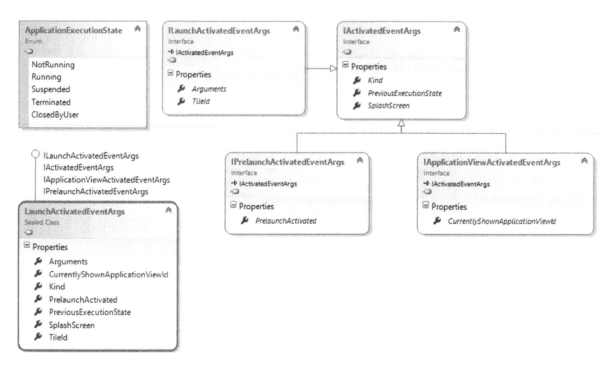

Figure 5-4. *Application activation class and enumeration*

The remaining code allows the application to start using a root content of your application as an instance of the MainPage application page.

To manage the application activation completely, you must handle the OnActivated event this way:

```
protected override void OnActivated(IActivatedEventArgs args)
{
    switch (args.Kind)
    {
        case ActivationKind.CachedFileUpdater:
            //Do something here
            break;
        case ActivationKind.CameraSettings:
            //Do something here
            break;
        case ActivationKind.ContactPicker:
            //Do something here
            break;
        case ActivationKind.Device:
            //Do something here
            break;
        case ActivationKind.File:
            //Do something here
            break;
```

```
        case ActivationKind.FileOpenPicker:
            //Do something here
            break;
        case ActivationKind.FileSavePicker:
            //Do something here
            break;
        case ActivationKind.PrintTaskSettings:
            //Do something here
            break;
        case ActivationKind.Protocol:
            //Do something here
            break;
        case ActivationKind.Search:
            //Do something here
            break;
        case ActivationKind.ShareTarget:
            //Do something here
            break;
    }
}
```

In this code, you are preparing your application to manage various types of activation, evaluating the Kind property of the IActivatedEventArgs interface (see Figure 5-5). You may be wondering why you use an interface. You do so because you'll have a different implementation of IActivatedEventArgs depending on ActivationKind. (It will be clarified when we talk about contracts and extensions).

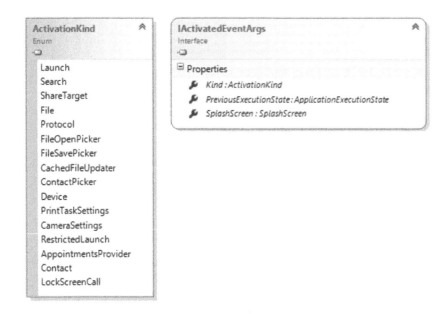

Figure 5-5. *Activation arguments class diagram*

VB

As soon as you create your project, a file named App.xaml.vb is created. In this file is a standard implementation of the OnLaunched method that looks like this:

```vb
    Protected Overrides Sub OnLaunched(e As
Windows.ApplicationModel.Activation.LaunchActivatedEventArgs)
#If DEBUG Then
        ' Show graphics profiling information while debugging.
        If System.Diagnostics.Debugger.IsAttached Then
            ' Display the current frame rate counters
            Me.DebugSettings.EnableFrameRateCounter = True
        End If
#End If

        Dim rootFrame As Frame = TryCast(Window.Current.Content, Frame)

        ' Do not repeat app initialization when the Window already has content,
        ' just ensure that the window is active

        If rootFrame Is Nothing Then
            ' Create a Frame to act as the navigation context and navigate to the first page
            rootFrame = New Frame()
            If e.PreviousExecutionState = ApplicationExecutionState.Terminated Then
                ' TODO: Load state from previously suspended application
            End If
            ' Place the frame in the current Window
            Window.Current.Content = rootFrame
        End If
        If rootFrame.Content Is Nothing Then
            ' When the navigation stack isn't restored navigate to the first page,
            ' configuring the new page by passing required information as a navigation
            ' parameter
            If Not rootFrame.Navigate(GetType(MainPage), e.Arguments) Then
                Throw New Exception("Failed to create initial page")
            End If
        End If

        ' Ensure the current window is active
        Window.Current.Activate()
    End Sub
```

If you compare this code with C# code, you'll notice that there's no difference between the implementations except for a slight difference in syntax. And this consideration is valid also for the OnActivated override, which looks like this:

```vb
Protected Overrides Sub OnActivated(args As IActivatedEventArgs)
    Select Case args.Kind
        Case ActivationKind.CachedFileUpdater
            'Do something here
        Case ActivationKind.CameraSettings
            'Do something here
```

```
            Case ActivationKind.ContactPicker
                'Do something here
            Case ActivationKind.Device
                'Do something here
            Case ActivationKind.File
                'Do something here
            Case ActivationKind.FileOpenPicker
                'Do something here
            Case ActivationKind.FileSavePicker
                'Do something here
            Case ActivationKind.PrintTaskSettings
                'Do something here
            Case ActivationKind.Protocol
                'Do something here
            Case ActivationKind.Search
                'Do something here
            Case ActivationKind.ShareTarget
                'Do something here
        End Select
    End Sub
```

That's all you have to do to manage the activation of your application. Now you learn how to manage the VisibilityChanged event.

Visibility Changed Event

When the visibility of the application changes, the VisibilityChanged event fires, allowing you to manage this change. All you need to do is to manage the VisibilityChanged event of CoreWindow class. In Figure 5-6, you can see a class diagram that shows the classes used to manage this event.

Figure 5-6. *CoreWindow and VisibilityChangedEventArgs class diagrams*

To simulate a real situation in your C# and VB.NET code, you will stop a `DispatcherTimer` that measures time elapsed in a game.

■ **Note** `DispatcherTimer`, which is a class available only in a Windows Store app, provides a `Timer` that is integrated in a `Dispatcher` queue. If you use this class, you can refer from your code to a UI object; if you use a simple `Timer` and do something on a UI thread, you will get a `CrossThreadException`.

First, declare the `DispatcherTimer` and a `CoreWindow` reference to subscribe to the `VisibilityChanged` event. You start the timer when visibility is `true`; you'll stop it when it is `false`. Let's play!

C#

As mentioned, you declare a private member of the DispatcherTimer type in the App class (App.xaml.cs) and you initialize it inside the constructor, using 1 second as the TimeSpan to set the value of the Interval property of DispatcherTimer.

```
private DispatcherTimer _timer;
```

...

```
public App()
{
    this.InitializeComponent();
    this.Suspending += OnSuspending;
    timer = new DispatcherTimer
    {
        Interval = TimeSpan.FromSeconds(1)
    };
}
```

Another thing that you need is a private member of the CoreWindow type, which you'll initialize in the OnLaunched method, getting an instance from the static method GetForCurrentThread of the CoreWindow class:

```
private CoreWindow coreWindow;
```

...

```
coreWindow = CoreWindow.GetForCurrentThread();

coreWindow.VisibilityChanged +=
    (s, e) =>
    {
        if (e.Visible)
            timer.Start();
        else
            timer.Stop();
    };
```

■ **Note**   You can get the same instance of CoreWindow by navigating the Current static property of the Window static class and looking for the CoreWindow property.

In this way, when the app loses visibility, the timer stops running and starts again when the app becomes visible. Of course, this is only an example of how to manage the VisibilityChanged event, and the code inside the event handler will change based on your own application.

VB

As in C#, the first thing that you need is an instance of DispatcherTimer created in this way:

```
Dim _timer = New DispatcherTimer() With {.Interval = TimeSpan.FromSeconds(1)}
```

Then you need to add an event handler for the VisibilityChanged event, which is like this in VB:

```
Private Sub VisibilityChanged(sender As Windows.UI.Core.CoreWindow,
args As Windows.UI.Core.VisibilityChangedEventArgs)
        If args.Visible Then
            _timer.Start()
        Else
            _timer.Stop()
        End If
End Sub
```

Now that you have an event handler, you will get an instance of CoreWindow. Because VB is a managed language like C#, you create an instance of CoreWindow inside the App class and then you can get the CoreWindow instance inside the OnLaunched event in two ways:

```
Dim _coreWindow As Windows.UI.Core.CoreWindow
...
_coreWindow = coreWindow.GetForCurrentThread()
Or
_coreWindow = Window.Current.coreWindow;
```

There is no difference between these two methods because you will always get the same instance. The last thing to do is to subscribe the event handler to the event, and you will do it inside the OnLaunched method in this way:

```
AddHandler coreWindow.VisibilityChanged, AddressOf VisibilityChanged
```

That's it.

Suspending Event

As mentioned before, an app in the running state can reach only the Suspended state, which happens raising the Suspending event. Here you'll learn how to handle this event. Again, be careful about the Windows Store app's execution model; there is no assurance that the VisibilityChanged and Suspending events raise one after the other in a short time.

When the OS fires the suspending event, it saves the actual state of your application in order to resume from the same point later. In this way, the user gets the impression that the app is running in the background. The Suspending event is where you'll save app data and release resources such as devices because the OS doesn't notify your app while terminating.

Figure 5-7 shows a diagram of classes used during the Suspending event. The starting point is the SuspendingEventArgs class that contains a property of the SuspendingOperation class. SuspendingOperation contains a GetDeferral method that you can use during your process of saving in order to ask for "extra time" before the suspension ends. This method returns an object of the SuspendingDeferral class, in which you'll call the Complete method to notify that your operation ended.

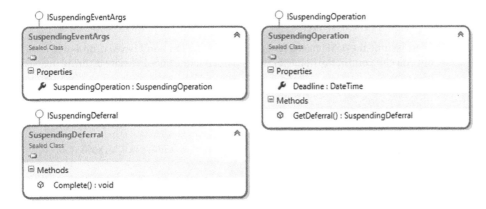

Figure 5-7. *Classes used in a Suspending event*

C#

Managing the Suspending event in C# is really simple. The first thing that you need is an event handler in App.xaml.cs:

```
private async void OnSuspending(object sender, SuspendingEventArgs e)
{
    var deferral = e.SuspendingOperation.GetDeferral();
    await SuspensionManager.SaveAsync();
    deferral.Complete();
}
```

In the first line of code, you get an object of the SuspendingDeferral class in order to notify the OS that your operations ended in the last line of code. Now that you have an event handler, you can attach your handler to the event:

```
this.Suspending += OnSuspending;
```

app is an instance of your application that you can refer to by using the this keyword if you are working in App.xaml.cs or using the Current static property of the Application object:

```
Application.Current.Suspending += OnSuspending;
```

VB

The code to manage the Suspending event in VB is also really simple:

```
AddHandler Application.Current.Suspending, AddressOf OnSuspending
Private Async Sub OnSuspending(sender As Object, e As SuspendingEventArgs) Handles Me.Suspending
    Dim deferral As SuspendingDeferral = e.SuspendingOperation.GetDeferral()
    Await Common.SuspensionManager.SaveAsync()
    deferral.Complete()
End Sub
```

Resuming Event

From the Suspended state, your app can assume the NotRunning and Running states. You don't have control over the transition to the NotRunning state, but you can control the behavior when passed to the Running state by firing the Resuming event.

C#

Managing the Resuming event is really easy. The event handler can be implemented as follows in App.xaml.cs:

```
void OnResuming(object sender, object e)
{
    //Place your code here
}
```

Attach the event handler to the Resuming event in the App() constructor:

```
this.Resuming += OnResuming;
```

VB.NET

In the App.xaml.vb file, use this code:

```
AddHandler Application.Current.Resuming, AddressOf App_Resuming

Private Sub App_Resuming(sender As Object, e As Object)
        ' TODO: Refresh network data
End Sub
```

Conclusion

In this chapter, you have seen different ways to handle application life cycle event inside your application. It is important to understand that data is not loaded or saved automatically when your app is terminated. You need to save it on the available storage as the local storage or the cloud storage to recover it when app is loaded again or refresh it if necessary. Understanding the life cycle of a Windows Store app is necessary to avoid unexpected behavior during runtime.

CHAPTER 6

■ ■ ■

Start Up Your App

The main objective of this book is to teach you how to create a Windows 8.1 application with the tools and languages (C# and VB) offered by Microsoft. After the previous five chapters where we explained the required basic concepts to entry in the platform, using the Microsoft Design Language guidelines with the Windows 8.1 Runtime and the languages available within the Microsoft tools, we are ready now to illustrate how to prototype your app.

Design the User Interface

In the design process, the best way to show customers and programmers the product you want create to make a mockup of the views that compose the application user interface. There are many solutions for this purpose, some free and some for a fee, some for creating static mockups and others for creating functional mockups. If you want to stay on the Microsoft stack, you can use Microsoft SketchFlow to create a mockup application that permits the actors in the project to try the application flow and give you feedback. This tool is released with the enterprise version of Microsoft Expression Blend and allows you to create a WPF or Silverlight application that shows a functional mockup and captures user feedbacks.

For static mockups, there are two Microsoft products, Visio and PowerPoint Storyboard template. Visio allows you to create many types of diagrams, with various components and also typical UI components. The PowerPoint Storyboard template is a new tool, introduced with Team Foundation Server 2012; it's a free template that allows you to create static mockups, adding user interface components (you can also include Windows 8.x and Windows Phone elements) on PowerPoint slides. At the end of your work, you have a PowerPoint presentation to show to your collaborators and customers. Otherwise, if you want to use a non-Microsoft product such as Balsamiq Mockups, you can download the stencils for Windows Store apps directly at http://msdn.microsoft.com/en-us/library/windows/apps/dn144786.aspx.

For this book's purposes, we will use the PowerPoint Storyboard template, choosing from the assets the Windows 8.1 Application components available through the last version of the template. In the following images, we will show you how to create a mockup for an application that saves a user's favorite places.

Figure 6-1 shows the Start screen of the app with mouse pointer about to click the app tile. Figure 6-2 shows what happens after the user clicks the app title: the main view of the app appears, showing the grid visualization of the places.

Start

User Name

Figure 6-1. *Mockup of the Start screen*

MyApp

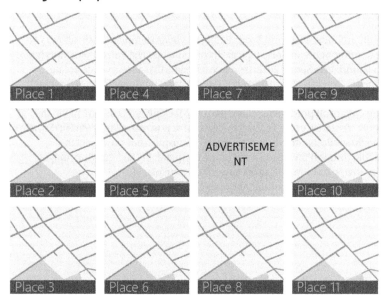

Figure 6-2. *Main page of the app*

Note that Figure 6-1 does not provide a real value to your mockup, but it will help you involve the observer in order to mimic the user experience.

The view in Figure 6-2 is based on the standard Windows Store Grid template available starting with Visual Studio 2013, but in the tile, you will visualize the title of the item and a map snapshot. You can also show an example of what happens when you select one or more elements by clicking or tapping: a special border will indicate that the user's selection was a success (as shown in Figure 6-3). By PowerPoint storyboarding, you can also show the application bar (Figure 6-4) where you can see the available operations.

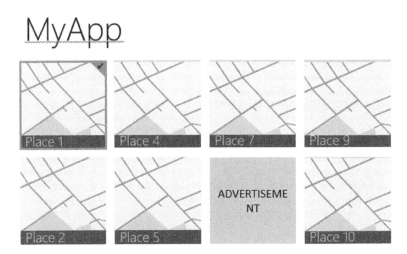

Figure 6-3. *Item selection*

Figure 6-4. *Application bar*

Finally, Figure 6-5 shows an example of how to create a mockup for an item detail page.

Figure 6-5. *Item detail page*

Using this kind of tool can help to simplify the design of your application and avoid misunderstanding with the stakeholders. Use it as much as possible!

Choose the Right Tool

When your mockup is complete, it's time to start coding your app. Even if the Visual Studio editor is equal to Blend, this latter is still the best choice for designers. For this reason we'll introduce you to Blend in this section and identify core functionalities that you can use in this application.

Starting with VS2012, Blend is integrated with VS, so you can find in the contextual menu of Blend-compatible projects an item labeled Edit in Blend (shown in Figure 6-6). This menu will open the solution in Blend and, if you select a file, open it in the editor.

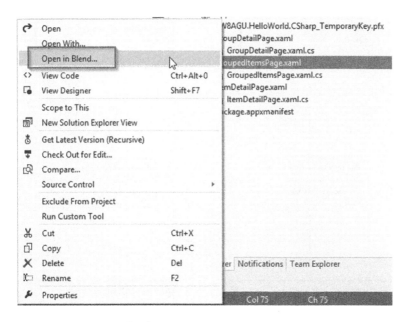

Figure 6-6. *Open in Blend menu*

When you need to work with layout and styles, Blend should be your first choice because it's made for this. Blend ships with two workspaces, Design and Animation. Every workspace has its own widget disposition. As you can imagine, the first one is dedicated to designing the UI, while the second one facilitates your work on animations. This is the main difference between the UI design approach in VS or Blend: both are good for design, but Blend is better for animation.

There are three types of animations:

- *Transition Animations*: Good for transition effects

- *Theme Animations*: Good for animation with a theme

- *Custom Animations*: For every case not covered by the previous two

Transition animations are used to render a control and are visible in the class diagram show in Figure 6-7. If you want to apply one of these transitions, you can simply add one them to the `TransitionCollection` of a control in the following way:

```
<Button>
  <Button.Transitions>
      <TransitionCollection>
       <EntranceThemeTransition FromHorizontalOffset="-229"/>
     </TransitionCollection>
  </Button.Transitions>
</Button>
```

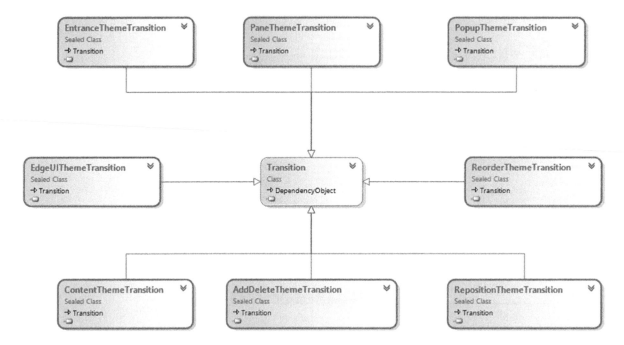

Figure 6-7. *Transition class diagram*

In this example, we create an instance of EntranceThemeTransition with an initial offset of -229 pixels to the Button, so when rendered it will appear with the effect of an entrance from the left.

Theme animations are built-in animations that are used in standard Windows Store app controls. This type of animation is based on TimeLine class and must be triggered explicitly, because you must use them in conjunction with a storyboard.

■ **Note** A storyboard is the class used to define changes of value in a control's dependency properties in a period. A storyboard can only be started by using the StoryboardName.Begin() method, because you cannot use triggers to modify the aspect of a control, only the VisualStateManager.

When you use a ThemeAnimation, you add it as a child of Storyboard in this way:

```
<Storyboard x:Name="MyStory">
   <FadeOutThemeAnimation TargetName="MyControl"  />
</Storyboard>
```

And in your code-behind you must write MyStory.Begin() both for C# and VB.

The last category of animations is custom animations. Under this category are classified the classical storyboards written in XAML. This type of animation has two categories:

- Dependent
- Independent

Dependent animation is an animation that needs information from the UI thread; for this reason by default it's not executed, so requires an opt-in from the app developer to enable it (`PointAnimation.EnableDependentAnimation = true`). When enabled, this animation type runs smoothly on the UI thread, but when the system starts doing something, the storyboard can stutter. For this reason, you should avoid dependent animations.

To create an independent animation your storyboard must respect these requirements:

- Duration of the animation set to 0 (zero)
- Animation can target
  - `UIElement.Opacity`
  - `Canvas.Left` or `Canvas.Top`
  - `Brush` (using `SolidColorBrush`)
  - `RenderTransorm, Projection, Clip`
  - `ObjectAnimationUsingKeyFrames`

Conclusion

In this chapter, you took the first step in the creation of a Windows Store app. You also took a quick tour in Blend for Visual Studio. Starting in the next chapter, you will go deep inside the Windows RT features. So let the fun begin!

CHAPTER 7

■ ■ ■

Take Advantage of the Environment

In this chapter, you will learn how to integrate your apps with the operating system, adding the ability to activate functionality directly from the Charm Bar. The first section explores geolocation and sensors integration. You will start sharing media content through the Digital Living Network Alliance (DLNA) protocol participating in the Play To contract.

In the third section, you'll see how to integrate your apps with the system, activating a Background Task that will wait for an available Internet connection (but you will often see other types of activations) to perform tasks that will keep your app useful even when closed, such as contacting your remote web service.

Finally, and importantly, you will take advantage of the environment with charms to implement contracts. The first contract that you will implement is the Settings contract because usually your app requires a place to manage settings to customize the user experience (UX). Then you will learn about the Share charm, with which you can integrate through the Share contract.

Sensors

In this section, you will see how to enrich the UX in an app with the use of various sensors. First, you will see how to use the Geolocation namespace (Windows.Devices.Geolocation) that will help us to retrieve the position of the device using GeoCoordinate (Latitude, Longitude, and Altitude). Later you will learn how Windows 8.1 supports a wide range of sensors and how you can access them through the classes contained in Windows.Device.Sensors namespace. This namespace offers the following classes to support the relative sensor:

- Accelerometer
- Compass
- Gyrometer
- Inclinometer
- LightSensor
- OrientationSensor
- SimpleOrientationSensor

SimpleOrientationSensor doesn't refer to a real class of sensor; it's a simplified version of the orientation sensor that helps you to easily access information about the current orientation of the device without the need to interpret the SensorQuaternion that you can retrieve by using of OrientationSensor.

Geolocation

The core class to manage is the Geolocator class available in the Windows.Devices.Geolocation namespace (shown in Figure 7-1). Classes contained in this namespace are responsible to manage Geolocation (as the namespace suggest). The Geolocator class is the entry point for these functionalities, through PositionChanged and StatusChanged, events which respectively rise when the position of the device changes and when position data availability changes states (every state will be expressed through a PositionStatus value). Otherwise, if you need a single position check, you can use the available GetLocationAsync method.

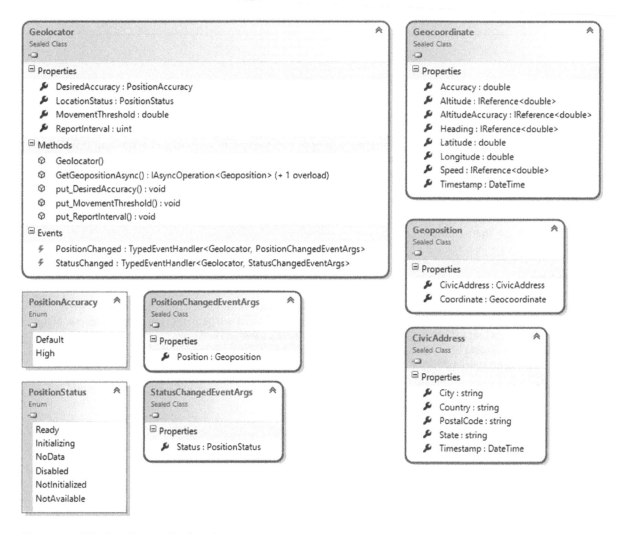

Figure 7-1. *Windows.Devices.Geolocation namespace*

The Geolocator class has other interesting members such as the DesiredAccuracy property, which you can use to express the accuracy needed by your app, and the MovementThreshold property, which you can set to specify the threshold before the PositionChanged event fires.

When the PositionChanged event fires, you can get the actual position of the device by accessing the Position property of the PositionChangedEventArgs instance passed as an argument of the event handler.

The type of `Position` property is `Geoposition`, which provides information such as `CivicAddress` and `Geocoordinate`. `CivicAddress` provides information about the `Country`, `State`, `City`, and `PostalCode` of the current position.

`Geocoordinate` provides low-level information about the following:

- `Latitude`: The angular distance north or south of the earth's equator, measured in degrees along a meridian, as on a map or globe

- `Longitude`: The distance in degrees east or west of the prime meridian at 0 degrees, measured by the angle between the plane of the prime meridian and that of the meridian through the point in question, or by the corresponding time difference

- `Altitude`: The height of something above a reference level, especially above sea level or above the earth's surface

- `Speed`: The actual speed of the device expressed as meters per seconds

- `Heading`: The actual direction of the device expressed in degrees relative to true north

- `Accuracy`: The accuracy of a location in meters

■ **Note** *True north*, also known as *geodetic north*, is the direction from any point toward the North Pole.

Remember that only `Latitude`, `Longitude`, and `Accuracy` are always provided; whereas `Altitude`, `Accuracy`, `Heading`, and `Speed` are provided only if available. You should keep this in mind to avoid possible `NullReferenceExceptions`.

Prepare the UI

To show a map in XAML, you can use the Bing Maps SDK for Windows 8.1 Store apps (because this SDK adds a control for XAML), which is available here:
`http://visualstudiogallery.msdn.microsoft.com/224eb93a-ebc4-46ba-9be7-90ee777ad9e1`

Before you can use `Map` control in your app, you need a Bing Maps key that you can get in this way:

1. Connect to `http://www.bingmapsportal.com/`.

2. Log on with a Windows Live account.

3. Create a new Bing Maps key. Don't worry about the application name; you can use a key on every app.

4. Inside the `App.xaml` file, create a resource identified by the `BingCredentials` key in this way: `<x:String x:Key="BingMapKey">`*your key*`</x:String>`, where "your key" is the Bing Maps key created before. This is a good practice if your app uses this control in other pages, and it is a good way to keep only information about how to draw the view inside the XAML.

XAML

■ **Note**   For this version of the library, you must change Target CPU to a specific platform instead of Any CPU.

After the installation, add a reference to Bing Maps, as shown in Figure 7-2, so you can import the Bing.Maps namespace into your code.

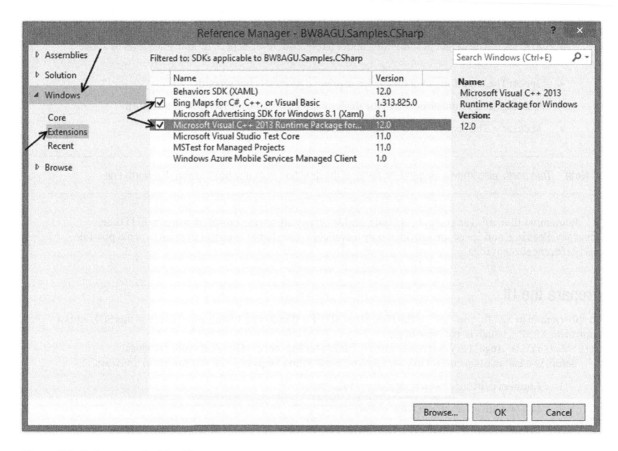

Figure 7-2. *Referencing the Bing.Maps namespace*

If your solution is configured to build for Any CPU, your project won't compile and will notify you that something has gone wrong (as you can see Figure 7-3).

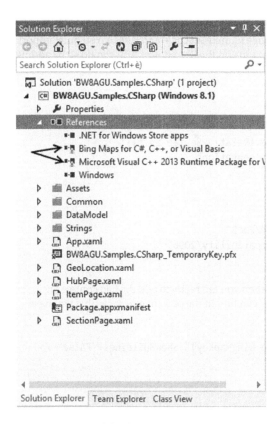

Figure 7-3. *Invalid reference*

To solve this problem, open the Configuration Manager from the Build menu of Visual Studio. From the Configuration Manager, you can select the target platform for projects inside your solution, changing the selected value of the Active Solution Platform combo box (see Figure 7-4).

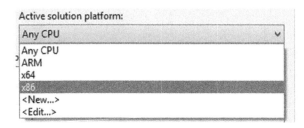

Figure 7-4. *Active solution platform drop-down list*

Now you are ready to include Map control inside your application and you will do it in a project dedicated to this chapter named BW8AGU.Samples.CSharp/BW8AGU.Samples.VB in a page named GeoLocationSample. You must import the Bing.Maps namespace inside the page of your app where you want to add the Map control. You can do so by adding the bold XAML as an attribute of the Page element in XAML:

```
<Page
    x:Name="pageRoot"
    x:Class="BW8AGU.Samples.CSharp.GeoLocationSample"
    DataContext="{Binding DefaultViewModel, RelativeSource={RelativeSource Self}}"
    xmlns="http://schemas.microsoft.com/winfx/2006/xaml/presentation"
    xmlns:x="http://schemas.microsoft.com/winfx/2006/xaml"
    xmlns:local="using:BW8AGU.Samples.CSharp"
    xmlns:common="using:BW8AGU.Samples.CSharp.Common"
    xmlns:maps="using:Bing.Maps"
    xmlns:d="http://schemas.microsoft.com/expression/blend/2008"
    xmlns:mc="http://schemas.openxmlformats.org/markup-compatibility/2006"
    mc:Ignorable="d">
```

In this way, you have imported the Bing.Maps namespace, and then you are ready to add the Map control on your user interface (UI). You will do it using the map element that you can find in the maps namespace (that you have imported):

```
<maps:Map x:Name="MapControl" Credentials="{StaticResource BingMapKey}" ShowBuildings="False" />
```

Find Me Everywhere

The control is ready to show the position that you'll retrieve using a GeoLocator instance. You just have to do two steps:

1. Declare in the app manifest that your application will use Location capability.

2. Use Location capability in your code.

To declare that your application will use Location capability, you must open the app manifest and, in Capabilities tab, check Location (see Figure 7-5).

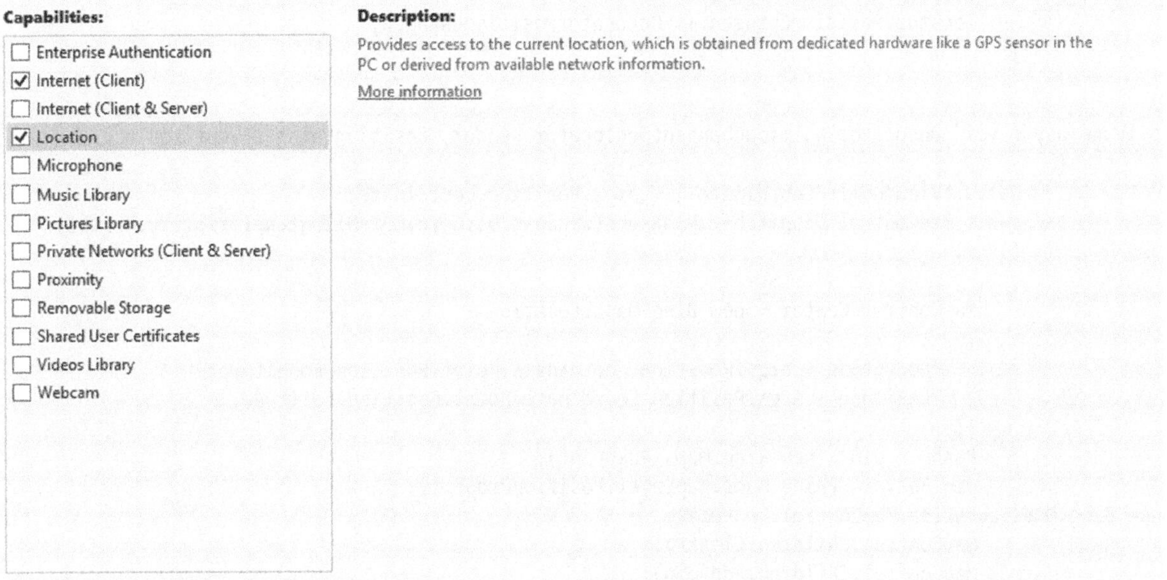

Capabilities:

- ☐ Enterprise Authentication
- ☑ Internet (Client)
- ☐ Internet (Client & Server)
- ☑ Location
- ☐ Microphone
- ☐ Music Library
- ☐ Pictures Library
- ☐ Private Networks (Client & Server)
- ☐ Proximity
- ☐ Removable Storage
- ☐ Shared User Certificates
- ☐ Videos Library
- ☐ Webcam

Description:

Provides access to the current location, which is obtained from dedicated hardware like a GPS sensor in the PC or derived from available network information.

More information

Figure 7-5. *Using the Location capability*

To use location capability in your code, at the class level you can declare a Geolocator type variable and you can create a method to initialize it. If you need to track the position of the user in your app (e.g., the Navigation app), you can subscribe to the PositionChanged event, and if your code retrieves the position without the use of an async pattern, you can subscribe to the StatusChanged event in order to detect the state of Geolocator. Now choose the language that is appropriate for you and follow your directives.

In the code-behind of your XAML file, you must include the Windows.Devices.Geolocation and Bing.Maps namespaces so you need an instance that you declare inside the page class as a class private field. After the declaration, you will write a method that initializes the instance with an accuracy of 2 meters and a threshold of 1 meter. Finally, you must subscribe to the PositionChanged event with an event handler that will report information on the UI, updating the map center and updating the viewmodel used by the UI with information about longitude, latitude, and other data provided by location services. You can do it with the following code:

C#

```
using Bing.Maps;
using Windows.Devices.Geolocation;

public sealed partial class GeoLocationSample : Page
 {
        private Geolocator locator = null;

     private void InitializeGeolocator()
       {
           if (locator == null)
           {
               locator = new Geolocator();
               locator.DesiredAccuracyInMeters = 2;
```

```csharp
                locator.MovementThreshold = 1;
                locator.PositionChanged += OnLocatorPositionChanged;
            }
        }

private async void OnLocatorPositionChanged(Geolocator sender, PositionChangedEventArgs args)
        {
            DefaultViewModel["Coordinate"] = args.Position.Coordinate;
            await MapControl.Dispatcher.RunAsync(Windows.UI.Core.CoreDispatcherPriority.Normal,
            () =>
            {
                MapControl.Center = new Bing.Maps.Location
                {
                    Longitude = args.Position.Coordinate.Point.Position.Longitude,
                    Latitude = args.Position.Coordinate.Point.Position.Latitude,
                };
                Pushpin pin = new Bing.Maps.Pushpin();
                pin.SetValue(Bing.Maps.MapLayer.PositionProperty,
new Bing.Maps.Location(MapControl.Center));
                MapControl.Children.Clear();
                MapControl.Children.Add(pin);

                MapControl.SetZoomLevel(10,TimeSpan.FromSeconds(1));
            });
        }
    ...
    }
```

VB

```vbnet
Imports Bing.Maps
Imports Windows.Devices.Geolocation

public sealed partial class GeoLocationSample : Page
 {
        Private locator As Geolocator

Private Async Sub InitializeGeolocator()
        If locator Is Nothing Then
            locator = New Geolocator()
            locator.DesiredAccuracyInMeters = 2
            locator.MovementThreshold = 1
            AddHandler locator.PositionChanged, AddressOf OnLocatorPositionChanged
            Dim actualPosition = Await locator.GetGeopositionAsync()
            AddHandler locator.StatusChanged, AddressOf OnStatusChanged
        End If
    End Sub

Private Async Sub OnLocatorPositionChanged(sender As Geolocator, args As PositionChangedEventArgs)
        DefaultViewModel("Coordinate") = args.Position.Coordinate
        Await MapControl.Dispatcher.RunAsync(Windows.UI.Core.CoreDispatcherPriority.Normal, Sub()
```

```
        MapControl.Center = New Bing.Maps.Location() With {
            .Longitude = args.Position.Coordinate.Point.Position.Longitude,
            .Latitude = args.Position.Coordinate.Point.Position.Latitude
        }
        Dim pin As Pushpin = New Bing.Maps.Pushpin()
        pin.SetValue(Bing.Maps.MapLayer.PositionProperty, New Bing.Maps.Location(MapControl.Center))
                                        MapControl.Children.Clear()
                                        MapControl.Children.Add(pin)

        MapControl.SetZoomLevel(10, TimeSpan.FromSeconds(1))

        End Sub)
    End Sub
    ...
```

This code uses the Geolocator class to track the user position continuously. However, nothing until now has called the InitializeGeolocator method; for this scope, you have a button on the UI to start tracking the user position, and all you have to write is the following:

C#

```
private void OnGetPositionButtonClick(object sender, RoutedEventArgs e)
        {
            InitializeGeolocator();
        }
```

VB

```
Private Sub OnGetPositionButtonClick(sender As Object, e As RoutedEventArgs) Handles
GetPositionButton.Click
        InitializeGeolocator()
    End Sub
```

Windows.Device.Sensors

Windows.Device.Sensors is the namespace that contains all classes that you can use to access to sensors. In this namespace, shown in Figure 7-6, you can find classes to manage:

- Accelerometer
- Compass
- Gyrometer
- Inclinometer
- LightSensor
- OrientationSensor

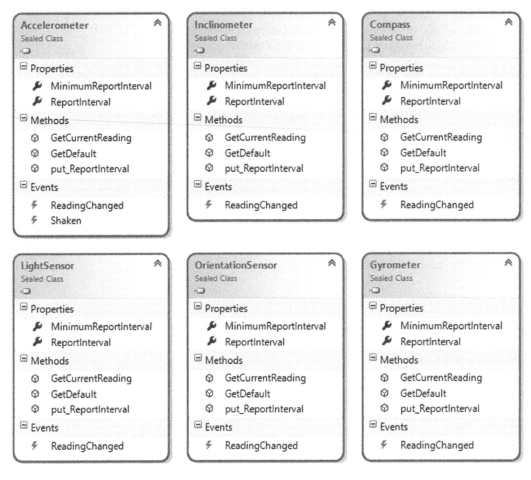

Figure 7-6. *Windows.Devices.Sensors namespace*

All these classes offer the same methods and events (with the exception of the Shake event in the Accelerometer class). Every class can be activated in the same way:

1. Create an instance.

2. Subscribe to the ReadingChanged event.

3. Manage the reading changed event argument.

About the third step: you need to see it through because every class uses its own event argument implementation.

Moreover, as you can deduce from Figure 7-6, every sensor can be used following the same programming model. For this reason, we will show you how to use a Compass sensor so that you learn how to also use other sensors. Of course, every sensor will provide different kind of data, as shown in Figure 7-7.

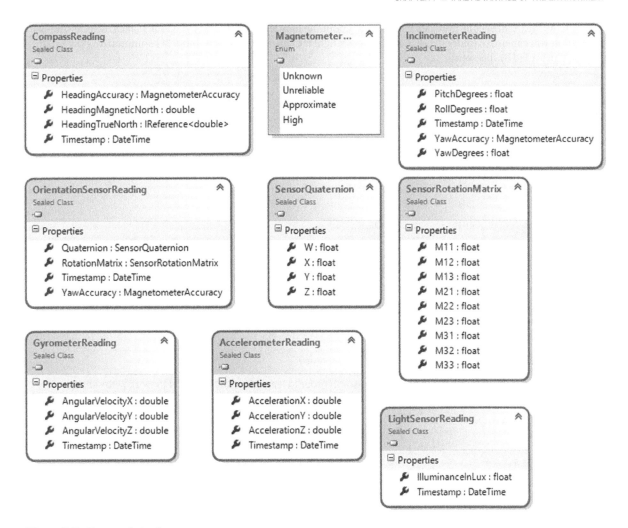

Figure 7-7. *Sensors data classes*

For the Compass sensor, the CompassReading class contains Heading data (Accuracy, Magnetic North, True North) and the timestamp of the measurement. Just like the Inclinometer reading the *accuracy* is expressed by an enumeration that shows how accurate the reading is.

Inclinometer provides information about Pitch, Roll, and Yaw through the InclinometerReading class. Using data provided by this sensor, we could retrieve the position of the device against the horizon.

OrientationSensorReading is the class used by OrientationSensor to understand how the device is oriented, against spherical coordinates. The Quaternion property is the SensorQuaternion type that contains values of versors in a mathematical notation.

Gyrometer provides data through the GyrometerReading class that exposes four properties. Three properties are dedicated to the angular velocity of the device against three axes, and the last one is the TimeStamp of the measurement.

The behavior of Accelerometer is similar to Gyrometer, but it provides information about the acceleration of the device on three axes.

Finally, the LightSensor provides information about the light that hits the device. IlluminanceInLux assumes values that you can use to understand at which type of light is exposed the device. Table 7-1 summarizes how to use the value provided by this sensor.

Table 7-1. *Illuminance Values*

Lighting Condition	From (lux)	To (lux)
Pitch Black	0	10
Very Dark	11	50
Dark Indoors	51	200
Dim Indoors	201	400
Normal Indoors	401	1000
Bright Indoors	1001	5000
Dim Outdoors	5001	10,000
Cloudy Outdoors	10,001	30,000
Direct Sunlight	30,001	100,000

Compass Example

In this section, you see how to use the Compass sensor in order to learn the code required to work with sensors. Your UI will be simple and will show information retrieved by the sensor in text form.

XAML

```
<Grid Grid.Row="1">
        <Grid.RowDefinitions>
            <RowDefinition Height="36"/>
            <RowDefinition Height="36"/>
            <RowDefinition Height="36"/>
            <RowDefinition Height="36"/>
        </Grid.RowDefinitions>
        <Grid.ColumnDefinitions>
            <ColumnDefinition Width="118"/>
            <ColumnDefinition Width="Auto"/>
            <ColumnDefinition/>
        </Grid.ColumnDefinitions>
        <TextBlock Grid.Row="0" Text="Magnetic North" />
        <TextBlock Grid.Row="1" Text="True North" />
        <TextBlock Grid.Row="2" Text="Heading Accuracy" />
        <TextBlock Grid.Row="0" Grid.Column="1" Text="{Binding CompassData.MagneticNorth}" />
        <TextBlock Grid.Row="1" Grid.Column="1" Text="{Binding CompassData.TrueNorth}" />
        <TextBlock Grid.Row="2" Grid.Column="1" Text="{Binding CompassData.Accuracy}" />
        <Button Grid.Row="3" Content="Get Data" Click="OnGetDataButtonClick" />
    </Grid>
```

C#

```csharp
using Windows.Devices.Sensors;

private void OnGetDataButtonClick(object sender, RoutedEventArgs e)
        {
            var compass = Compass.GetDefault();
            if (compass == null)
            {
                this.DefaultViewModel["CompassData"] =
                    new
                    {
                        MagneticNorth = "Compass not found",
                        TrueNorth= "Compass not found",
                        Accuracy = "Compass not found"
                    };
            }
            else
            {
                var reading = compass.GetCurrentReading();
                compass.ReadingChanged += OnCompassReadingChanged;
                SetCompassReading(reading);
            }
        }

private void SetCompassReading(CompassReading reading)
        {
            this.DefaultViewModel["CompassData"] =
                new
                {
                    MagneticNorth = reading.HeadingMagneticNorth,
                    TrueNorth = reading.HeadingTrueNorth,
                    Accuracy = reading.HeadingAccuracy
                };
        }

        private void OnCompassReadingChanged(Compass sender, CompassReadingChangedEventArgs args)
        {
            SetCompassReading(args.Reading);
        }
```

VB

```vbnet
private void OnGetDataButtonClick(object sender, RoutedEventArgs e)
        {
            var compass = Compass.GetDefault();
            if (compass == null)
            {
                this.DefaultViewModel["CompassData"] =
                    new
```

```
                {
                    MagneticNorth = "Compass not found",
                    TrueNorth= "Compass not found",
                    Accuracy = "Compass not found"
                };
            }
            else
            {
                var reading = compass.GetCurrentReading();
                compass.ReadingChanged += OnCompassReadingChanged;
                SetCompassReading(reading);
            }
        }

        private void SetCompassReading(CompassReading reading)
        {
            this.DefaultViewModel["CompassData"] =
                new
                {
                    MagneticNorth = reading.HeadingMagneticNorth,
                    TrueNorth = reading.HeadingTrueNorth,
                    Accuracy = reading.HeadingAccuracy
                };
        }

        private void OnCompassReadingChanged(Compass sender, CompassReadingChangedEventArgs args)
        {
            SetCompassReading(args.Reading);
        }
```

Media

Windows 8.1 offers various ways to manage Media elements, even a good update to the MediaElement control (that was limited in Windows 8), which offers a standardized way to present media onscreen.

Stream Media Element

This section discusses using the Play To contract to stream Media elements contained in your application to DLNA devices. The capability to stream media is provided by classes (shown in Figure 7-8) that you can find in the Windows.Media.PlayTo namespace. Inside this namespace, you can find other classes that can act as DLNA clients.

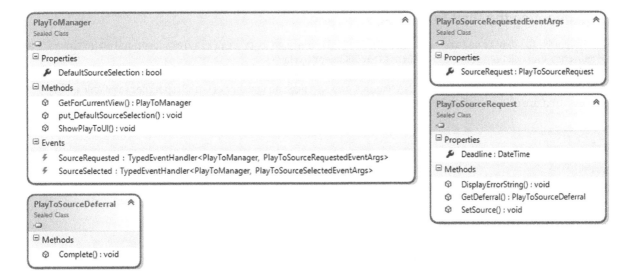

Figure 7-8. *PlayToSource fundamental classes*

The entry point for the Play To contract is `PlayToManager`, which returns an instance of itself through the `GetForCurrentView` method and allows you to subscribe to two events: `SourceRequested` and `SourceSelected`.

`SourceRequested` fires when the user interacts with the `Device` charm. The `EventArg` for this event is `PlayToSourceSelectedEventArgs`, which contains the body of the request contained in the `PlayToSourceRequest` class. This type allows you to set a source for the stream (that you can get from a `MediaElement` or `Image` control). That is all you have to know to start streaming your contents.

In your app, you'll simulate a video application that will allow the user to stream a video during its reproduction to a DLNA-ready client (such as Xbox 360).

■ **Note**   If you want to test code in this section, you must have a DLNA–compliant client device. If you don't have one, you can use Window Media Player to receive the stream. To enable this feature, start Windows Media Player, open the Stream menu, and select Allow Remote Control Of My Player to enable this feature.

Prepare the UI

Before you start using the `PlayToManager` class, you need to add a `MediaElement` control to your page:

XAML

Inside the XAML file, you need one thing:

```
<MediaElement Source="{Binding Path='Path'}" AutoPlay="False" x:Name="mediaElement" />
```

Implementing the Play To Contract

To implement the Play To contract, you must declare and retrieve an instance of `PlayToManager` and an instance of `Dispatcher` that will help you avoid the `CrossThreadException` later.

To start using the Play To contract, you need an instance of `PlayToManager` (contained in the `Windows.Media.PlayTo` namespace) that is the entry point for DLNA features. You also need an instance of `CoreDispatcher` (available in the `Windows.UI.Core` namespace) in order to stream contents asynchronously.

C#

```
...
using Windows.Media.PlayTo;
using Windows.UI.Core;
...
public sealed partial class PlayToSample : Page
    {
        private PlayToManager playtoManager = null;
        private CoreDispatcher dispatcher;
    ...
}
```

VB

```
...
Import Windows.Media.PlayTo
Import Windows.UI.Core
...
public sealed partial class PlayToSample : Page
    {
        private PlayToManager playtoManager = null;
        private CoreDispatcher dispatcher;
    ...
}
```

Of course, you must initialize it before use. For this reason, you will write the `InitPlayToManager` method that initializes both the `PlayToManager` and `Dispatcher` objects.

C#

```
private void InitPlayToManager()
{
    dispatcher = Window.Current.CoreWindow.Dispatcher;
    if (playtoManager == null)
    {
      playtoManager = PlayToManager.GetForCurrentView();
      playtoManager.SourceRequested += OnPlayToSourceRequested;
      playtoManager.SourceSelected += OnPlayToSourceSelected;
    }
}
```

VB

```vb
Private Sub InitPlayToManager()
        dispatcher = Window.Current.CoreWindow.Dispatcher
        If playtoManager Is Nothing Then
                playtoManager = PlayToManager.GetForCurrentView()
                AddHandler playtoManager.SourceRequested, AddressOf OnPlayToSourceRequested
                AddHandler playtoManager.SourceSelected, AddressOf OnPlayToSourceSelected
        End If
End Sub
```

This method will be called inside the LoadState method that was previously written in order to be sure that these objects are initialized when the page is loaded.

C#

```csharp
protected override void LoadState(Object navigationParameter, Dictionary<String, Object> pageState)
{
...
   InitPlayToManager();
...
}
```

VB

```vb
Protected Overrides Sub LoadState(navigationParameter As [Object], pageState As Dictionary(Of
[String], [Object]))
    ...
        InitPlayToManager()
    ...
End Sub
```

As you have seen, in the InitPlayToManager method, you subscribe to the SourceRequested and SourceSelected events with the OnPlayToSourceSelected and OnPlayToSourceRequested event handlers. The first fires after the user selects the device from the device pane; this event might be useful to retrieve information about the specific device that the user selects. The second one fires when the user selects the Device charm and must be used to provide content to the stream.

C#

```csharp
private void OnPlayToSourceSelected(PlayToManager sender, PlayToSourceSelectedEventArgs args)
{
   //Report the name of the client
}

private async void OnPlayToSourceRequested(PlayToManager sender, PlayToSourceRequestedEventArgs e)
        {
                await dispatcher.RunAsync(Windows.UI.Core.CoreDispatcherPriority.Normal,
                    () =>
```

```
        {
            PlayToSourceDeferral deferral = e.SourceRequest.GetDeferral();
        PlayToSourceRequest sr = e.SourceRequest;
            sr.SetSource(videoMediaElement.PlayToSource);
            deferral.Complete();
        });
    }
```

VB

```
Private Sub OnPlayToSourceSelected(sender As PlayToManager, args As PlayToSourceSelectedEventArgs)
        'Report the name of the client
End Sub

Private Async Sub OnPlayToSourceRequested(sender As PlayToManager, e As
PlayToSourceRequestedEventArgs)
    Await coreDispatcherInstance.RunAsync(Windows.UI.Core.CoreDispatcherPriority.Normal,
        Async Sub()
        Dim deferral As PlayToSourceDeferral = e.SourceRequest.GetDeferral()
        Dim sr As PlayToSourceRequest = e.SourceRequest
        'Set the media element as source for incoming SourceRequest
        sr.SetSource(videoMediaElement.PlayToSource)
        deferral.Complete()
    End Sub)
End Sub

private async void OnPlayToSourceRequested(PlayToManager sender, PlayToSourceRequestedEventArgs e)
        {
            await dispatcher.RunAsync(Windows.UI.Core.CoreDispatcherPriority.Normal,
                () =>
                {
                    PlayToSourceDeferral deferral = e.SourceRequest.GetDeferral();
                    PlayToSourceRequest sr = e.SourceRequest;
                    sr.SetSource(videoMediaElement.PlayToSource);
                    deferral.Complete();
                });
        }
```

Background Task

With version 8, Windows introduced a new concept of application behavior. Every app works only while it is in the foreground, but the environment offers various ways to "simulate" that your app is still working:

- *Background Task*: "Queues" a task in order to update data inside the application

- *Push Notification*: Notifies from the outside that something is ready for the application

- *Background Transfer API*: Starts a transfer that requires a long time and must continue while the application is suspended

- *Playback Manager*: Provides content to play to the playback infrastructure

- *File Share contract*: Shares contents between applications

This section discusses Background Tasks in Windows 8.1, which are enriched in this edition of the OS. This feature enables your app to run code in the background, allowing you to write real-time applications such as a chat or a Voice over Internet Protocol (VOIP) app. As you read before, a Background Task works even if your app is suspended or not running. While you build one, you can specify a set of conditions that must be verified to run the task and one trigger that launches the task. Figure 7-9 shows how the Background Task system works.

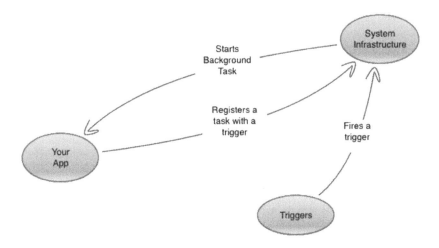

Figure 7-9. *BackgroundTask process*

First, register a task that will start with a specific trigger (see Table 7-2) with optional conditions (see Table 7-3). When a trigger fires, the system infrastructure looks for Background Tasks registered for it. If conditions (optionally) associated with the task are fulfilled, the task starts independently from the application status. In the case of unsatisfied conditions, the infrastructure waits until all conditions are satisfied and then executes the task. This mechanism is called *latching* because the infrastructure latches the trigger to a fired state.

Table 7-2. *Background Task Triggers*

Trigger Type	Event	When it Fires
ControlChannelTrigger	ControlChannelTrigger	When the control channel receives a message
MaintenanceTrigger	MaintenanceTrigger	When the device is plugged in
PushNotificationTrigger	PushNotificationTrigger	When a raw notification arrives
SystemEventTrigger	InternetAvailable	When the Internet becomes available
SystemEventTrigger	LockScreenApplicationAdded	When an app tile is added to the lock screen
SystemEventTrigger	LockScreenApplicationRemoved	When an app tile is removed from the lock screen
SystemEventTrigger	ControlChannelReset	When a network channel is reset
SystemEventTrigger	NetworkStateChange	When a change on network connectivity occurs
SystemEventTrigger	OnlineIdConnectedStateChange	When the online ID associated with the account changes
SystemEventTrigger	ServicingComplete	When the app is updated

(continued)

Table 7-2. (*continued*)

Trigger Type	Event	When it Fires
SystemEventTrigger	SessionConnected	When the session is connected
SystemEventTrigger	SessionDisconnected	When the session is disconnected
SystemEventTrigger	SmsReceived	When a new Short Message System (SMS) message is received (if the device supports it)
SystemEventTrigger	TimeZoneChange	When the time zone changes (e.g., for automatic clock regulation for Daylight Saving Time [DST])
SystemEventTrigger	UserAway	When the user is absent
SystemEventTrigger	UserPresent	When user is present
TimeTrigger	TimeTrigger	After a time period elapses
LocationTrigger	LocationTrigger	When user is inside a Geofencing

Table 7-3. *Background Task Conditions*

Condition	Meaning
InternetAvailable	The Internet must be available.
InternetNotAvailable	The Internet must be unavailable.
SessionConnected	The session must be connected (logged in).
SessionDisconnected	The session must be disconnected (logged out).
UserNotPresent	The user must have the status set to away.
UserPresent	The user must have the status set to present.

Every trigger type described in Table 7-2 reflects a class of framework (see Figure 7-10) that even shows the SystemTriggerType enumeration, which reflects events that are classified as SystemEvent.

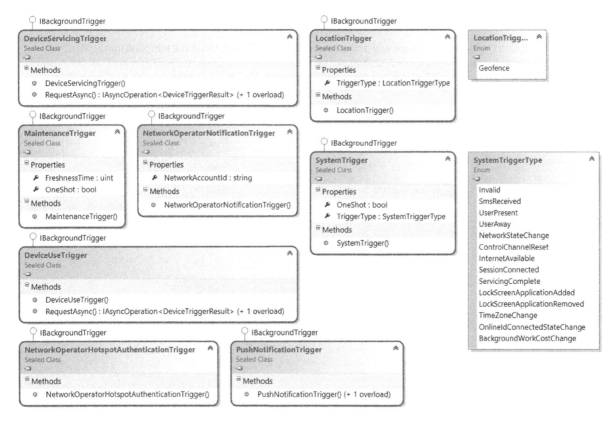

Figure 7-10. *Trigger classes*

In this example, you'll implement the infrastructure for an app that downloads messages from a server. Because you don't know that the user will be always connected, you can create a Background Task that will synchronize with the server when the Internet becomes available. Figure 7-11 shows how to add a Background Task.

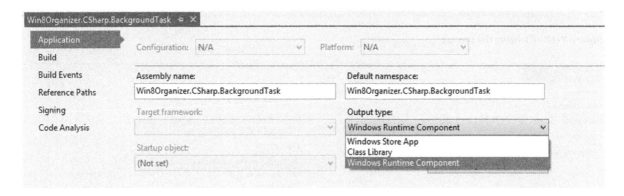

Figure 7-11. *Adding a Background Task*

Implementing the Background Task

When you work with C# and VB, you must add a new project to your solution using the template for the Windows Runtime Component, as shown in Figure 7-12. You do this because when you create a Background Task, the output type of the project must be set to Windows Runtime Component (see Figure 7-13), allowing the Background Task infrastructure to manage it.

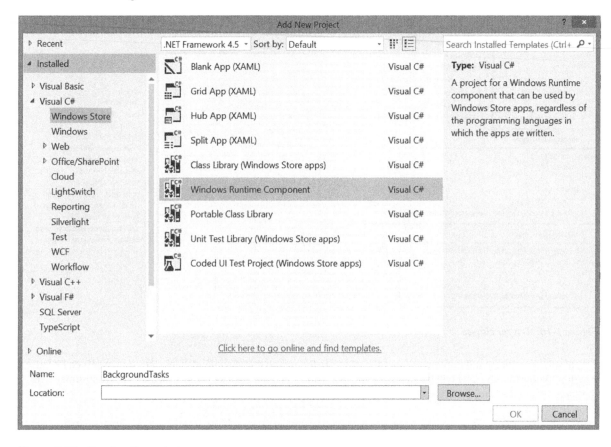

Figure 7-12. *Creating the project*

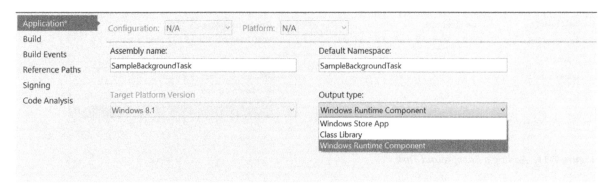

Figure 7-13. *Project output type*

When the project is created, delete the autogenerated class and create a new class named DownloadMessagesBackgroundTask. This class must be declared as sealed if you work with C# and as NotInheritable if you use VB. In the declaration of the class, you must always implement the IBackgroundTask interface containing only one method named Run (see Figure 7-14). Remember that when the Background Task works for a long time, you should use the BackgroundTaskDeferral to tell the infrastructure of Windows 8.1 that your async process has finished.

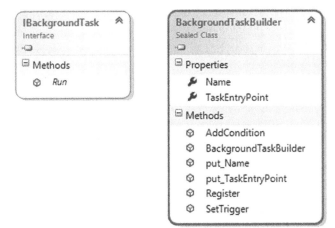

Figure 7-14. *Background Task essential class and interface for C#, C++, and VB*

Then your code will look like this, where MessagesDownloader is your class that exposes an operation that simulates the download of 20 messages:

C#

```
using Windows.ApplicationModel.Background;

namespace SampleBackgroundTask
{
    public sealed class DownloadMessagesBackgroundTask : IBackgroundTask
    {
        public async void Run(IBackgroundTaskInstance taskInstance)
        {
            BackgroundTaskDeferral deferral = taskInstance.GetDeferral();
            await MessagesDownloader.GetMessagesAsync();
            deferral.Complete();
        }
    }
}
```

VB

```vb
Imports Windows.ApplicationModel.Background

Namespace SampleBackgroundTask
    Public NotInheritable Class DownloadMessagesBackgroundTask
        Implements IBackgroundTask
        Public Async Sub Run(taskInstance As IBackgroundTaskInstance) Implements IBackgroundTask.Run
            Dim deferral As BackgroundTaskDeferral = taskInstance.GetDeferral()
            Await MessagesDownloader.GetMessagesAsync()
            deferral.Complete()
        End Sub
    End Class
End Namespace
```

Registering the Background Task

After the implementation of the Background Task, the most interesting part of the code to write is the registration of the Background Task. In Figure 7-14, you can see the essential class and interface involved in Background Task creation. IBackgroundTask is the previous interface that we developed in the introduction to the Background Task. BackgroundTaskBuilder is the class to use to register the Background Task in the system.

To register a Background Task you will create a private method named RegisterBackgroundTask that you can call wherever you prefer in your code. This method will do these next steps:

1.   Retrieves all tasks registered for the current application

2.   Looks for a task with a name equal to the string in the SaveTaskName constant

3.   If it is the first time that you are registering the Background Task, it creates an instance of BackgroundTaskBuilder:

   a.   Sets as the name the content of the SaveTaskName constant

   b.   Sets as the TaskEntryPoint the full name of the SaveBackgroundTask type

   c.   Registers a trigger with the Internet available

   d.   Registers the Background Task and subscribes to the Progress (reporting) event and the Completed event.

4.   If it is not the first registration, it:

   a.   Gets the task from the collection of registered tasks

   b.   Subscribes to the Progress (reporting) event, and the Completed event.

As you can read in the step-by-step method description, two events, Progress and Completed, are subscribed to, exposed by the BackgroundTaskRegistration class. By handling the Completed event, you can notify users that the Background Task has finished or simply use it to unregister the BackgroundTaskRegistration. The Progress event fires when you set the Progress property of the IBackgroundTaskInstance argument inside the Run method.

C#

```csharp
public sealed partial class BackgroundTaskSample : Page
{
private const string GetMessagesTaskName = "GetMessagesTask";
        private void RegisterBackgroundTask()
        {
            var registeredTasks = BackgroundTaskRegistration.AllTasks;
            bool alreadyRegistered = registeredTasks.Any(t =>
t.Value.Name.Equals(GetMessagesTaskName));
            if (!alreadyRegistered)
            {
                BackgroundTaskBuilder backgroundTaskBuilder = new BackgroundTaskBuilder();
                backgroundTaskBuilder.Name = GetMessagesTaskName;
                backgroundTaskBuilder.TaskEntryPoint =
typeof(SampleBackgroundTask.DownloadMessagesBackgroundTask).FullName;
                backgroundTaskBuilder.SetTrigger(
                    new SystemTrigger(SystemTriggerType.InternetAvailable, true));

                var registration = backgroundTaskBuilder.Register();
                registration.Progress += OnSaveBackgroundTaskProgressReported;
                registration.Completed += OnSaveBackgroundTaskCompleted;

            }
            else
            {
                //Use the task already registered
                var task = registeredTasks.First(t => t.Value.Name.Equals(GetMessagesTaskName));
                task.Value.Progress += OnSaveBackgroundTaskProgressReported;
                task.Value.Completed += OnSaveBackgroundTaskCompleted;
            }
        }

        private void OnSaveBackgroundTaskCompleted(BackgroundTaskRegistration sender,
BackgroundTaskCompletedEventArgs args)
        {
            //Put here the code to manage the end of a task
            //Notify the user about the end of the execution
        }

        private void OnSaveBackgroundTaskProgressReported(BackgroundTaskRegistration sender,
BackgroundTaskProgressEventArgs args)
        {
            //Put here the code to manage progress of a task
            //Notify task progress
        }
}
```

VB

```vb
Public NotInheritable Class BackgroundTaskSample
    Inherits Page
...
Private Const GetMessagesTaskName As String = "GetMessagesTask"
    Private Sub RegisterBackgroundTask()
        Dim registeredTasks = BackgroundTaskRegistration.AllTasks
        Dim alreadyRegistered As Boolean = registeredTasks.Any(Function(t)
t.Value.Name.Equals(GetMessagesTaskName))
        If Not alreadyRegistered Then
            Dim backgroundTaskBuilder As New BackgroundTaskBuilder()
            backgroundTaskBuilder.Name = GetMessagesTaskName
            backgroundTaskBuilder.TaskEntryPoint = GetType(DownloadMessagesBackgroundTask).FullName
            backgroundTaskBuilder.SetTrigger(New SystemTrigger(SystemTriggerType.InternetAvailable, True))

            Dim registration = backgroundTaskBuilder.Register()
            AddHandler registration.Progress, AddressOf OnSaveBackgroundTaskProgressReported

            AddHandler registration.Completed, AddressOf OnSaveBackgroundTaskCompleted
        End If

    End Sub

    Private Sub OnSaveBackgroundTaskCompleted(sender As BackgroundTaskRegistration, args As
BackgroundTaskCompletedEventArgs)
        'Put here the code to manage the end of a task
        'Notify the user about the end of the execution
    End Sub

    Private Sub OnSaveBackgroundTaskProgressReported(sender As BackgroundTaskRegistration, args As
BackgroundTaskProgressEventArgs)
        Throw New NotImplementedException()
    End Sub
End Class
```

Declaring the Background Task

You've now created your Background Task and written code to register it in the system. But to make everything work, you must declare in the application manifest that you intend to benefit from the Background Task infrastructure. To do so, open the application manifest and click the Declarations tab; then open the Available Declarations combo box (see Figure 7-15). From the list, select Background Task and click the Add button.

Available Declarations:

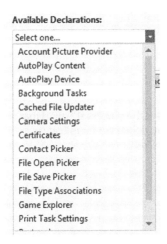

Figure 7-15. *Declaring Background Tasks*

This operation will open a panel like the one in Figure 7-16, in which you can set the entry point and task types. There is a clarification that you must keep in mind about the configuration of task types: remember that `TimeTrigger`, `PushNotificationTrigger`, `ControlChannelTrigger` and some `SystemTriggerTypes` (`SessionConnected`, `ControlChannelReset`, `UserPresent`, and `UserAway`) require that your app is in lock screen to work. To complete this operation, call the `RequestAccessAsync` method of the `BackgroundExecutionManager` class, which will ask the users whether they want to add the application to the lock screen.

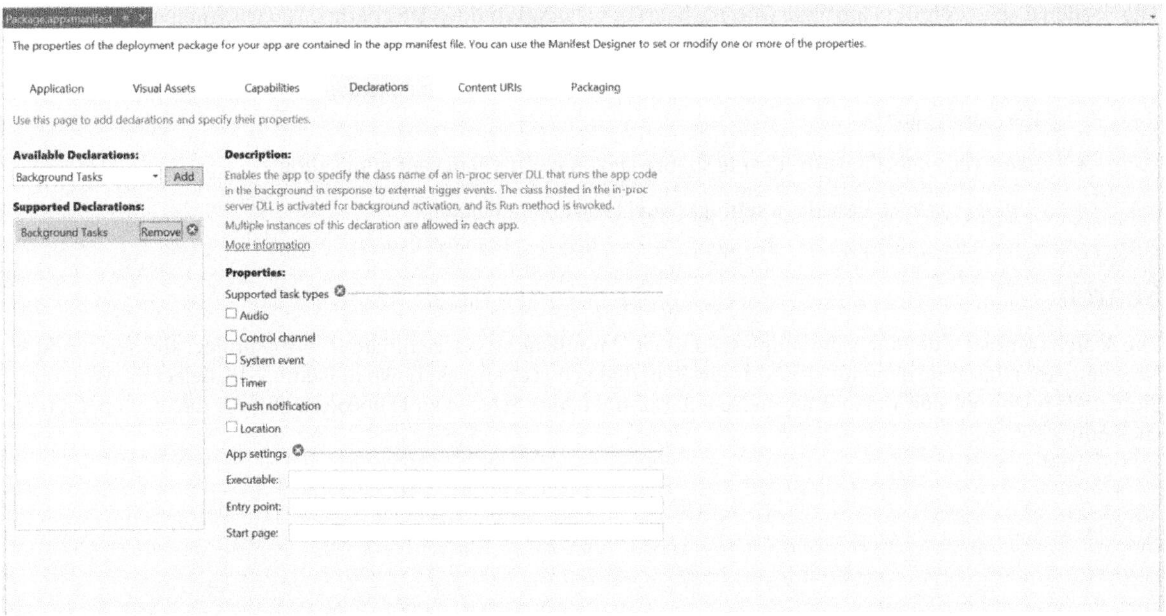

Figure 7-16. *Configuring Background Tasks*

For C# and VB projects, you must declare the entry point of the Background Task that is the full name of the class that implements `IBackgroundTask`. In this case, it is set to `SampleBackgroundTask.DownloadMessagesBackgroundTask`.

Debugging Background Tasks

Soon after the registration of the Background Task in the Debug Location bar, you can see the process ID (PID) that Windows gives to your app and a combo button that allows you to fire events to help you debug your application. Inside the combo box, you can see the name that you have given to your task (see Figure 7-17).

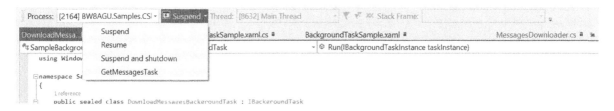

Figure 7-17. *Background Task debugging*

If you click your Background Task, it will run, enabling you to debug your code.

Charms

This section discusses how to integrate with the heart of the new Windows UI: charms. You will implement the following:

- *Search contract*: Provides suggestions based on a list of names and results after a query from the search pane

- *Share contract*: Allows the user to share as text the content of your application

- *Settings contract*: Provides a settings panel for your application

Search

The Search contract is definitely the simplest contract to implement; just right-click the app project and select Add ➤ New Item from the context menu. The Add New Item dialog box opens, as shown in Figure 7-18. Select the Windows Store node on the left side and look for the Search Contract item. Select it and choose a name for the result page; then click Add.

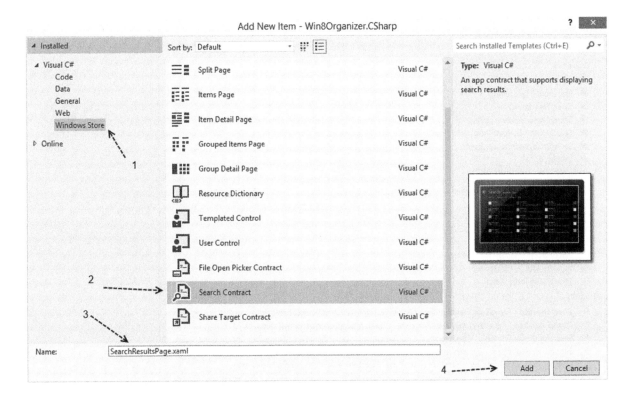

Figure 7-18. *Adding a Search contract*

When you add a Search contract to your project, Visual Studio automatically adds a new class named `BooleanNegationConverter`. Now you must declare that your app is a search provider in the application manifest. Open the app manifest; under Declaration, add the Search entry.

In version 8.1, Microsoft introduced the `SearchBox` control because the use of the Charm Bar is not as intuitive as hoped because not all users read the OS user manual. For this reason, you can add search functionality on your own app using the `SearchBox` control. This control is not properly related to the use of Search charm, but you should to see how to provide search results in your app using both ways, so you can choose which one meets your needs.

Search Contract

The core class that the Search contract is based on is `SearchPane` (shown in Figure 7-19). The most important method of `SearchPane` is `GetForCurrentView`, which returns an instance of `SearchPane` that you can use as an entry point for search functionality. Another interesting member is the `ShowOnKeyboardInput` property that, if set to `true`, automatically shows the search panel if the user writes something. `SearchPane` also exposes several events that you can handle if you want to collect information about the usage of this functionality.

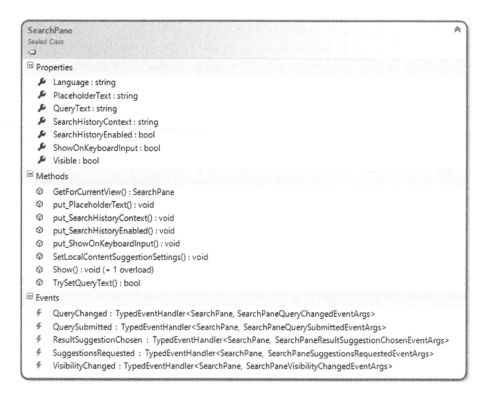

Figure 7-19. *SearchPane class*

Adding a Search contract is not the only way to provide search functionality in your app. You can subscribe to the QuerySubmitted event that delegates to your handler all the work to do. For example, you can use it in a game to provide hints based on the query submitted.

When the user starts searching, your app can provide suggestions to autocomplete the word. To do it, you must handle the SuggestionsRequested event that fires when the user changes the text in the search panel.

Another interesting event is ResultSuggestionChosen, which fires when the user hits a suggestion. This event should be handled to collect suggestions usage information in order to see the most frequently used suggestions and increase their points in your relevance algorithm.

For Win8Organizer, you start from the provided suggestions; in AppointmentManager, two new methods were added to support search functionality. The first is GetSearchSuggestions, which accepts a string as input and returns a list (a maximum of five elements) of the string that will populate the suggestions list. The second method, GetAppointmentsFiltered, accepts the string to query, looks for it inside the description or subject of the appointments, and returns a collection of appointments; we suggest limiting the number of items in the result page if they're too many to be charged.

Providing Suggestions

To provide suggestions inside your app, you subscribe to the SuggestionsRequested event with the OnSearchSuggestionRequested handler, declaring a SearchPane object at the class level of the AppointmentsGrouped page; the code will look like the examples in the next two sections.

■ **Note**   You must declare a SearchPane in order to initialize it inside the OnLaunched method, subscribing the SuggestionsRequested event in order to provide suggestions while the user writes a query.

C#

```csharp
sealed partial class App : Application
{

protected override async void OnLaunched(LaunchActivatedEventArgs e)
    {
        SearchPane.GetForCurrentView().SuggestionsRequested += OnSearchSuggestionRequested;
    }

}

private async void OnSearchSuggestionRequested(SearchPane sender,
SearchPaneSuggestionsRequestedEventArgs args)
        {
            var deferral = args.Request.GetDeferral();
            var suggestions = await SuggestionProvider.GetSuggestionsAsync(args.QueryText);
            args.Request.SearchSuggestionCollection.AppendQuerySuggestions(suggestions);
            deferral.Complete();
        }
```

VB

```vb
NotInheritable Class App
    Inherits Application

    Protected Overrides Async Sub OnLaunched(e As LaunchActivatedEventArgs)
...
        AddHandler SearchPane.GetForCurrentView().SuggestionsRequested, AddressOf
OnSearchSuggestionRequested
    End Sub

    Private Async Sub OnSearchSuggestionRequested(sender As SearchPane, args As
SearchPaneSuggestionsRequestedEventArgs)
        Dim deferral = args.Request.GetDeferral()
        Dim suggestions = Await SuggestionProvider.GetSuggestionsAsync(args.QueryText)
        args.Request.SearchSuggestionCollection.AppendQuerySuggestions(suggestions)
        deferral.Complete()
    End Sub
```

Providing Results

We have added the SearchResultsPage before, which in standard implementation comes ready to manage a query and provide filters in results. Because it is up to you to decide how to show search results in your app, we will concentrate on what you need to do in order to complete the implementation of the Search contract.

You must override the OnSearchActivated Method, which fires even when the application was closed but activated as a Search provider. In this method, you will do the same work as with the Launched method, changing the destination page.

C#

```
protected async override void OnSearchActivated(Windows.ApplicationModel.Activation.
SearchActivatedEventArgs args)
        {
            var previousContent = Window.Current.Content;
            var frame = previousContent as Frame;

            // If the app does not contain a top-level frame, it is possible that this
            // is the initial launch of the app. Typically this method and OnLaunched
            // in App.xaml.cs can call a common method.
            if (frame == null)
            {
                // Create a Frame to act as the navigation context and associate it with
                // a SuspensionManager key
                frame = new Frame();
                SuspensionManager.RegisterFrame(frame, "AppFrame");

                if (args.PreviousExecutionState == ApplicationExecutionState.Terminated)
                {
                    // Restore the saved session state only when appropriate
                    try
                    {
                        await SuspensionManager.RestoreAsync();
                    }
                    catch (SuspensionManagerException)
                    {
                        //Something went wrong restoring state.
                        //Assume there is no state and continue
                    }
                }
            }

            frame.Navigate(typeof(SearchResultsPage), args.QueryText);
            Window.Current.Content = frame;

            // Ensure the current window is active
            Window.Current.Activate();
        }
```

VB

```
Protected Overrides Async Sub OnSearchActivated(args
As Windows.ApplicationModel.Activation.SearchActivatedEventArgs)
        Dim previousContent = Window.Current.Content
        Dim frame = TryCast(previousContent, Frame)

        ' If the app does not contain a top-level frame, it is possible that this
        ' is the initial launch of the app. Typically this method and OnLaunched
        ' in App.xaml.cs can call a common method.
        If frame Is Nothing Then
            ' Create a Frame to act as the navigation context and associate it with
            ' a SuspensionManager key
            frame = New Frame()
            SuspensionManager.RegisterFrame(frame, "AppFrame")

            If args.PreviousExecutionState = ApplicationExecutionState.Terminated Then
                ' Restore the saved session state only when appropriate
                Try
                    Await SuspensionManager.RestoreAsync()
                    'Something went wrong restoring state.
                    'Assume there is no state and continue
                Catch generatedExceptionName As SuspensionManagerException
                End Try
            End If
        End If

        frame.Navigate(GetType(SearchResultsPage), args.QueryText)
        Window.Current.Content = frame

        ' Ensure the current window is active
        Window.Current.Activate()
    End Sub
```

SearchBox

SearchBox is a new control that allows your app to implement an in-app search behavior. It is important to remember that you must choose which strategy you want in your app. If you want the SearchBox, forget using the SearchPane because it requires the activation of the contract (including the contract in the app) that will make the SearchBox unable to work.

In the XAML file, the code needed to include the control looks like this:

```
<SearchBox Height="40" Width="200" />
```

Using this control, you can provide (in your app) the same UX that Windows provides in the SettingsPane, but we suggest putting the control in a position in which the user can easily find it.

Providing Suggestions

In this example, we provide suggestions to the control, using the list of files accessible to the app.

C#

```csharp
private void navigationHelper_LoadState(object sender, LoadStateEventArgs e)
        {
            var settings = new Windows.ApplicationModel.Search.LocalContentSuggestionSettings
            {
                Enabled = true
            };
            settings.Locations.Add(Windows.Storage.KnownFolders.MusicLibrary);
            settings.Locations.Add(Windows.Storage.KnownFolders.PicturesLibrary);
            musicSearchBox.SetLocalContentSuggestionSettings(settings);
        }
```

VB

```vb
Private Sub navigationHelper_LoadState(sender As Object, e As LoadStateEventArgs)
    Dim settings = New Windows.ApplicationModel.Search.LocalContentSuggestionSettings() With {
        .Enabled = True
    }
    settings.Locations.Add(Windows.Storage.KnownFolders.MusicLibrary)
    settings.Locations.Add(Windows.Storage.KnownFolders.PicturesLibrary)
    mediaSearchBox.SetLocalContentSuggestionSettings(settings)
End Sub
```

With this approach, suggestions about the files container are shown in the Music and Pictures Library, so you can apply this code in a music application.

Sharing

In recent years, the Internet has changed the way people live. They are always connected and every day they share work with others using software. So you should allow your users to share contents from your app because if your application favors user activity, they use it more readily.

The entry point for share source functionality is the DataTransferManager class (shown in Figure 7-20) that allows you to manage the Search charm activation through the DataRequested event. When this event fires, you can populate a DataPackage with data taken from the content you intend to distribute. You can put different types of data inside the DataPackage:

- SetText adds a text as the body of your share

- SetBitmap adds an image as part of the data

- SetStorageItems adds files or folders stored

- SetUri adds an URI to the DataPackage

- SetRtf adds contents in Rich Text Format

- SetHtmlFormat adds HTML as body of the DataPackage

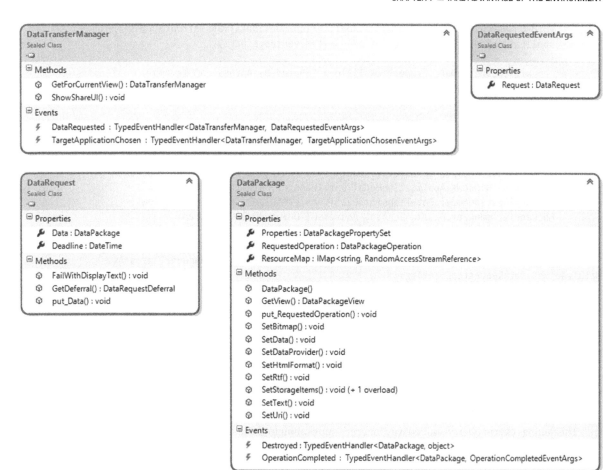

Figure 7-20. *Share source core classes*

Preparing Data to Share

To prepare your app to share content, you must modify the code-behind of your page, getting an instance of
DataTransferManager and subscribing the DataRequested event. Inside, the event handler will fill the DataPackage
with contents about the appointment:

C#

```
private void navigationHelper_LoadState(object sender, LoadStateEventArgs e)
        {
            Windows.ApplicationModel.DataTransfer.DataTransferManager manager =
Windows.ApplicationModel.DataTransfer.DataTransferManager.GetForCurrentView();
            manager.DataRequested += OnShareDataRequested;
        }
```

```
private void OnShareDataRequested(Windows.ApplicationModel.DataTransfer.DataTransferManager sender,
Windows.ApplicationModel.DataTransfer.DataRequestedEventArgs args)
        {
            args.Request.Data.Properties.Title = "Shared by Apress Sample App";
            args.Request.Data.SetText(shareableTextBox.Text);
        }
```

VB

```
Private Sub NavigationHelper_LoadState(sender As Object, e As Common.LoadStateEventArgs)
    Dim manager As Windows.ApplicationModel.DataTransfer.DataTransferManager =
    Windows.ApplicationModel.DataTransfer.DataTransferManager.GetForCurrentView()
        AddHandler manager.DataRequested, AddressOf OnShareDataRequested
    End Sub

Private Sub OnShareDataRequested(sender As DataTransfer.DataTransferManager, args As
DataTransfer.DataRequestedEventArgs)
        args.Request.Data.Properties.Title = "Shared by Apress Sample App"
        args.Request.Data.SetText(shareableTextBox.Text)
    End Sub
```

Settings

Most of the applications require a settings panel, a part of the UI dedicated to app configuration, in which users can decide whether they want another color for text or how often the application can try to connect to the server. For this reason, Microsoft UI engineers introduced the Settings charm.

The Settings charm offers a unified way for every application to show a menu of settings. It was discussed theoretically in Chapter 3, and in this section you get your hand dirty with the code required to participate in this contract. Every Windows Store app has two default entries inside the Settings pane:

- *Rate*: Used to rate the application in the Windows Store

- *Permissions*: Helps the user to choose app-specific permissions about capabilities

To help you become familiar with some concepts, we'll create a settings pane that will be applied when user navigates starts the application. For accuracy, remember that you can apply a new layout to your settings pane page by page, in order to offer a specific settings pane between pages. This is in contrast with what you see implemented in a lot of applications because a settings pane is intended to be global across the application; however, this example is intended to explain the extreme freedom that you have.

Add a folder to your project and name it SettingsPanels. Inside this folder, add a UserControl named ApplicationSettingsPanel.

As with other contracts, there is a class that acts as the entry point for the ApplicationSettings namespace (shown in Figure 7-21). This class exposes the GetForCurrentView method, already seen in other contracts, that returns an instance of SettingsPane specific for the current view you are using. The other method is Show, which opens the Settings panel.

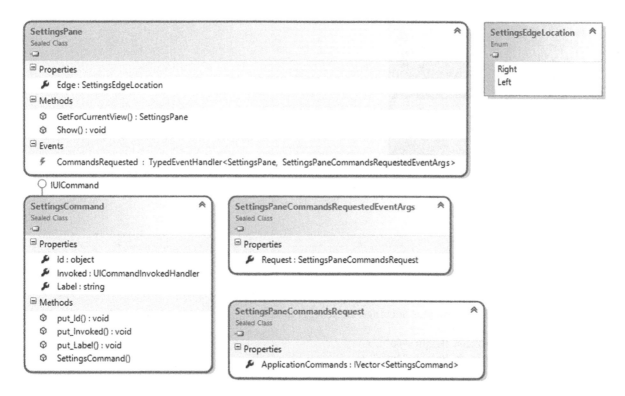

Figure 7-21. *ApplicationSettings namespace*

What you haven't yet seen is the Edge property that indicates whether the Settings pane will appear on the left or right side of the screen. This property helps you (if you evaluate it) to define in which side of the screen your settings view must appear.

Last but not least is the CommandsRequested event that fires when the user interacts with the Settings charm. This event accepts as an EventArg a SettingsPaneCommandRequestedEventArgs that contains the Request property, which in turn contains a collection of SettingsCommand.

SettingsCommand is what is called an "entry point" for settings in Chapter 3. Every instance of this class is an entry for a submenu that will be designed as a UserControl.

Application Settings

The Application Settings panel (shown in Figure 7-22) enables you to choose the language that your application must use and whether it must use push notification.

Figure 7-22. *Application Settings panel*

XAML

To create this panel, we'll skip a lot of uninteresting XAML that defines the template and visual state for the back button so it's really easy to read, and you can navigate from the code attached to this book. Here is the XAML required to create the panel shown in Figure 7-22:

```
<Grid Background="{StaticResource SettingsPanelBackgroundBrush}" >
      <Grid.RowDefinitions>
          <RowDefinition Height="80" />
          <RowDefinition Height="Auto" />

      </Grid.RowDefinitions>

      <Grid Grid.Row="0" >
          <Grid.ColumnDefinitions>
              <ColumnDefinition Width="*" />
          </Grid.ColumnDefinitions>

          <StackPanel Margin="40,20,10,0" Orientation="Horizontal" Grid.Column="0"
VerticalAlignment="Center" HorizontalAlignment="Left">
              <Button Click="OnApplicationSettingsBackButtonClick"  Style="{StaticResource
BackButtonStyle}"/>
                  <TextBlock FontSize="25" Text="Application Settings" />
          </StackPanel>
      </Grid>
      <Grid Grid.Row="1" >

          <StackPanel Margin="40,20,10,0" >
              <TextBlock Text="Choose your language" />
              <ComboBox x:Name="languageCombobox" ItemTemplate="{StaticResource
CultureInfoDataTemplate}" />
          </StackPanel>
      </Grid>
  </Grid>
```

CultureInfoDataTemplate is a data template created this way:

```xml
<DataTemplate x:Key="CultureInfoDataTemplate">
    <TextBlock Text="{Binding EnglishName}" />
</DataTemplate>
```

C#

```csharp
public ApplicationSettings()
{
    this.InitializeComponent();
    Loaded += OnLoaded;
}

private void OnLoaded(object sender, RoutedEventArgs e)
{
    languageCombobox.ItemsSource = ApplicationSettingsHelper.Instance.AvailableLanguages;
    languageCombobox.SelectedItem = ApplicationSettingsHelper.Instance.CurrentCulture;
    languageCombobox.SelectionChanged += OnLanguageSelectionChanged;
}

private void OnLanguageSelectionChanged(object sender, SelectionChangedEventArgs e)
{
    //Set the language immediately (from Settings Charm guidelines)
    ApplicationSettingsHelper.Instance.CurrentCulture = e.AddedItems.First() as CultureInfo;
}

private void OnApplicationSettingsBackButtonClick(object sender, RoutedEventArgs e)
{
    Popup parent = this.Parent as Popup;
    if (parent != null)
    {
        parent.IsOpen = false;
        SettingsPane.Show();
    }
}
```

A Helper class was used previously. This time, you use ApplicationSettingsHelper, which is a singleton application that helps you populate the Settings panel and has the following implementation:

```csharp
public class ApplicationSettingsHelper
    {
        private static ApplicationSettingsHelper instance = new ApplicationSettingsHelper();

        private ApplicationSettingsHelper()
        {
            AvailableLanguages =
                new ObservableCollection<CultureInfo>
                {
```

```
                new CultureInfo("en-US"),
                new CultureInfo("it-IT"),
            };
    }

    public static ApplicationSettingsHelper Instance
    {
        get
        {
            return instance;
        }
    }

    public ObservableCollection<CultureInfo> AvailableLanguages { get; set; }

    public CultureInfo CurrentCulture
    {
        //Read Settings in Get
        get;
        //Save Settings in Set
        set;
    }
}
```

VB

```
Public Sub New()
        Me.InitializeComponent()
        AddHandler Me.Loaded, AddressOf OnLoaded
End Sub

Private Sub OnLoaded(sender As Object, e As RoutedEventArgs) Handles Me.Loaded
        languageCombobox.ItemsSource = ApplicationSettingsHelper.Instance.AvailableLanguages
        languageCombobox.SelectedItem = ApplicationSettingsHelper.Instance.CurrentCulture
AddHandler languageCombobox.SelectionChanged, AddressOf OnLanguageSelectionChanged
End Sub

Private Sub OnLanguageSelectionChanged(sender As Object, e As SelectionChangedEventArgs)
        'Set the language immediatly (from Settings Charm guidelines)
        ApplicationSettingsHelper.Instance.CurrentCulture = TryCast(e.AddedItems.First(),
CultureInfo)
End Sub

Private Sub OnApplicationSettingsBackButtonClick(sender As Object, e As RoutedEventArgs)
        Dim parent As Popup = TryCast(Me.Parent, Popup)
        If parent IsNot Nothing Then
                parent.IsOpen = False
                SettingsPane.Show()
        End If
End Sub
```

A Helper class was used previously. This time, you use ApplicationSettingsHelper, which is a singleton application that helps you populate the Settings panel and has the following implementation:

```
Public Class ApplicationSettingsHelper
    Private Shared m_instance As New ApplicationSettingsHelper()

    Private Sub New()
        AvailableLanguages = New ObservableCollection(Of CultureInfo)()
        AvailableLanguages.Add(New CultureInfo("en-US"))
        AvailableLanguages.Add(New CultureInfo("it-IT"))
        }
    End Sub

    Public Shared ReadOnly Property Instance() As ApplicationSettingsHelper
        Get
            Return m_instance
        End Get
    End Property

    Public Property AvailableLanguages() As ObservableCollection(Of CultureInfo)
        Get
            Return m_AvailableLanguages
        End Get
        Set(value As ObservableCollection(Of CultureInfo))
            m_AvailableLanguages = value
        End Set
    End Property
    Private m_AvailableLanguages As ObservableCollection(Of CultureInfo)

    Public Property CurrentCulture() As CultureInfo
        'Read Settings in Get
        Get
            Return m_CurrentCulture
        End Get
        'Save Settings in Set
        Set(value As CultureInfo)
            m_CurrentCulture = value
        End Set
    End Property
    Private m_CurrentCulture As CultureInfo
End Class
```

Activating the Settings Charm on Master

You can now start creating an InitSettingsPane method inside the App.xaml.cs file that gets an instance of SettingsPane and subscribes to the CommandsRequest event with the OnSettingsPaneCommandsRequested handler. This handler clears the application commands collection (that populates the Settings entry in the Search panel).

When you create a `SettingsCommand`, you must provide three things:

- An identifier
- A label to show on the panel
- A method that accepts an `IUICommand` object

This method is triggered when the user chooses an item from the panel. To simplify your life, we'll create a class named `SettingsPanelHelper` to create a pop-up that will have an instance of a `CustomControl` as a Child. Your code will look like this:

C#

```csharp
#region Settings Contract

        private SettingsPane settingsPane = null;

        private void InitSettingsPane()
        {
            settingsPane = Windows.UI.ApplicationSettings.SettingsPane.GetForCurrentView();
            settingsPane.CommandsRequested += OnSettingsPaneCommandsRequested;
        }

        private void OnSettingsPaneCommandsRequested(SettingsPane sender,
SettingsPaneCommandsRequestedEventArgs args)
        {
            args.Request.ApplicationCommands.Clear();
            args.Request.ApplicationCommands.Add(
                new SettingsCommand(
                    "applicationCommand",
                    "Application",
                    ApplicationCommandInvokedHandler));

            args.Request.ApplicationCommands.Add(
                new SettingsCommand(
                    "tileCommand",
                    "Tile and Notifications",
                    TileCommandInvokedHandler));
        }

        private void ApplicationCommandInvokedHandler(IUICommand command)
        {
            ApplicationSettings content =
                new ApplicationSettings
                {
                    Width = 346,
                    Height = Window.Current.Bounds.Height
                };
            Popup settingsPopup = SettingsPanelHelper.CreateSettingsPanel(content, Window.Current.Bounds);
            settingsPopup.IsOpen = true;
        }

        #endregion
```

VB

```vb
Private Sub InitSettingsPane()
    settingsPane = Windows.UI.ApplicationSettings.SettingsPane.GetForCurrentView()
    AddHandler settingsPane.CommandsRequested, AddressOf OnSettingsPaneCommandsRequested
End Sub

Private Sub OnSettingsPaneCommandsRequested(sender As SettingsPane, args As
SettingsPaneCommandsRequestedEventArgs)
    args.Request.ApplicationCommands.Clear()
    args.Request.ApplicationCommands.Add(New SettingsCommand("applicationCommand", "Application",
ApplicationCommandInvokedHandler))
End Sub

Private Sub ApplicationCommandInvokedHandler(command As IUICommand)
    Dim content As New ApplicationSettings() With { _
        .Width = 346, _
        .Height = Window.Current.Bounds.Height _
    }
    Dim settingsPopup As Popup = SettingsPanelHelper.CreateSettingsPanel(content, Window.Current.
Bounds)
    settingsPopup.IsOpen = True
End Sub
```

Again, you use a `Helper` to improve the readability of the code. The `CreateSettingsPanel` of this class helps you create a pop-up that will contain the `UserControl` that is the `SettingsPane`. The implementations of this class are discussed in the following section.

A Look Inside SettingsPanelHelper

`SettingsPanelHelper` is a class that we wrote to support you with your development of Windows Store apps. It enables you to avoid always writing the same code to show a Settings pane. The code is really simple: you accept a `UserControl` that will be the content of the pop-up that the `CreateSettingsPanel` method returns. You also accept a `Rect` instance that will be used to pass the actual resolution reserved to your application and a double with a default value of 346 that specifies the size of the pop-up. This method evaluates whether the Search panel appears on the left or right side of the screen and creates a pop-up that will be positioned in the right side.

C#

```csharp
public class SettingsPanelHelper
{
    public static Popup CreateSettingsPanel(UserControl content, Rect bounds, double settingsSize = 346)
    {
    Popup p = new Popup
    {
        IsLightDismissEnabled = true,
        Width = settingsSize,
        Height = bounds.Height
    };
```

```
  p.ChildTransitions = new TransitionCollection
  {
     new PaneThemeTransition
     {
        Edge = SettingsPane.Edge == SettingsEdgeLocation.Right
           ? EdgeTransitionLocation.Right
           : EdgeTransitionLocation.Left
     }
  };
  p.SetValue(Canvas.LeftProperty,
     SettingsPane.Edge == SettingsEdgeLocation.Right ? (bounds.Width - settingsSize) : 0);

  p.SetValue(Canvas.TopProperty, 0);
  p.Child = content;
  return p;
  }
}
```

VB

```
Imports Windows.UI.ApplicationSettings
Imports Windows.UI.Xaml.Controls.Primitives
Imports Windows.UI.Xaml.Media.Animation

Public Class SettingsPanelHelper
    Public Shared Function CreateSettingsPanel(content As UserControl, bounds As Rect, Optional
settingsSize As Double = 346) As Popup
        Dim p As New Popup() With { _
            .IsLightDismissEnabled = True, _
            .Width = settingsSize, _
            .Height = bounds.Height _
        }
        p.ChildTransitions = New TransitionCollection()
        Dim transition As New PaneThemeTransition()
        transition.Edge = If(SettingsPane.Edge = SettingsEdgeLocation.Right,
EdgeTransitionLocation.Right, EdgeTransitionLocation.Left)
        p.ChildTransitions.Add(transition)

        p.SetValue(Canvas.LeftProperty, If(SettingsPane.Edge = SettingsEdgeLocation.Right,
(bounds.Width - settingsSize), 0))
        p.SetValue(Canvas.TopProperty, 0)

        p.Child = content
        Return p
    End Function
End Class
```

Conclusion

With Windows 8.1, it is really simple to integrate your app with others. The use of contracts follows the same flow for all of them, which translates into a brief learning curve when you have to use a new contract. In the next chapter, you'll see how to persist the data of your application so you can save information about settings.

CHAPTER 8

■ ■ ■

Data Management

This chapter explains how an app can manage data through the new API available in WinRT. We will take a look at data access and manipulation in different types of storage and how to handle user settings. Step by step, we will show these features using examples.

Handling Data in a Windows Store App

The **Windows Storage APIs** are a simple way to access and manipulate data and files whether they are on the local machine or elsewhere (such as the cloud). The APIs are located in the Windows.Storage namespace. All the languages available for developing Windows Store apps allow the use of Windows Storage APIs but unfortunately there are slight differences (as we explain later in this chapter). But first of all, we have to point out that there are two different kinds of data that you can access or use inside your app:

- *App Data*: The data created, used, and dismissed by the application to maintain runtime state, user preferences, and general settings.

- *User Data*: The data created by a user that uses the application, like documents or media files.

Both kinds of data can be stored on the local machine and, depending on what folder is used, permissions must be set. Indeed, Windows Store app has restrictions regarding folder access: in order to read the content of a specific folder, you have to set the relative *app capability* in your app using the **package manifest**. This can be opened inside Visual Studio 2013 by double-clicking in Solution Explorer the Package.appmanifest item, and opening the Package Designer, as shown in Figure 8-1.

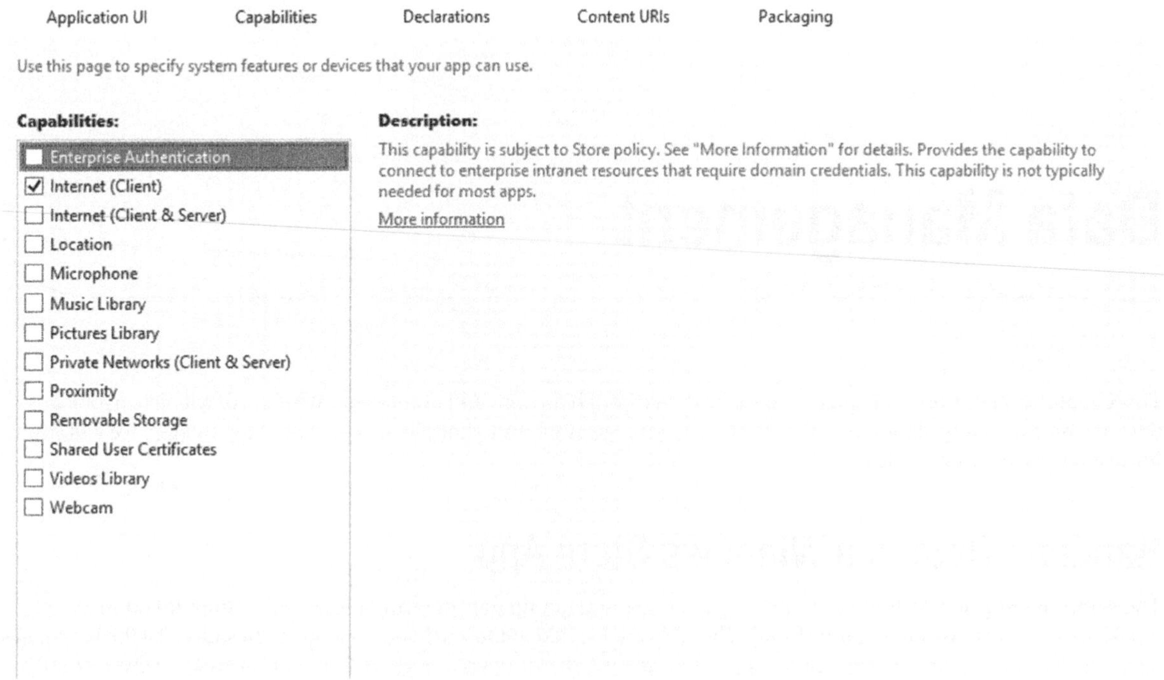

| Application UI | Capabilities | Declarations | Content URIs | Packaging |

Use this page to specify system features or devices that your app can use.

Capabilities:

- ■ Enterprise Authentication
- ☑ Internet (Client)
- ☐ Internet (Client & Server)
- ☐ Location
- ☐ Microphone
- ☐ Music Library
- ☐ Pictures Library
- ☐ Private Networks (Client & Server)
- ☐ Proximity
- ☐ Removable Storage
- ☐ Shared User Certificates
- ☐ Videos Library
- ☐ Webcam

Description:

This capability is subject to Store policy. See "More Information" for details. Provides the capability to connect to enterprise intranet resources that require domain credentials. This capability is not typically needed for most apps.

More information

Figure 8-1. *The Package Designer*

In the Capabilities section, you can select what folder an app can access.

■ **Note**   The DocumentsLibrary capability is dropped starting with Windows 8.1. However, it can be enabled manually by editing the Package.appmanifest and compiling the app, but we advise you to avoid this technique. And note that you should use the DocumentsLibrary capability just for specific situations (like embedded content), not to store data! For more information, go to blogs.msdn.com/b/wsdevsol/archive/2013/05/09/dealing-with-documents-how-not-to-use-the-documentslibrary-capability-in-windows-store-apps.aspx.

Table 8-1 shows the available capabilities with their relative location.

Table 8-1. *Location and Capability*

Location	Capability
Documents Library (until Windows v.8)	DocumentsLibrary (file extension in app manifest)
Music Library	MusicLibrary
Pictures Library	PicturesLibrary
Videos Library	VideosLibrary
Homegroup Libraries	One of the following: MusicLibrary PicturesLibrary VideosLibrary
Removable devices	RemovableDevices
Media Server Devices (DLNA)	One of the following: MusicLibrary PicturesLibrary VideosLibrary
Universal Naming Convention (UNC)	PrivateNetworkClientServer + InternetClient or InternetClientServer + EnterpriseAuthentication (if needed) + File extension in app manifest

Whenever an app tries to access to a folder without the proper capability, a System.UnauthorizedAccessException is raised, as shown in Figure 8-2.

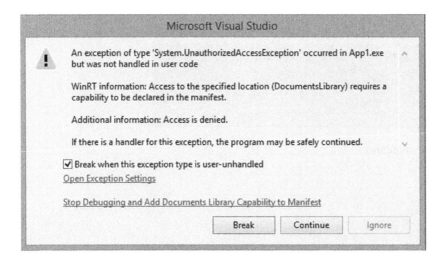

Figure 8-2. *A pop-up in Visual Studio 2013 shows the System.UnauthorizedAccessException*

App Capabilities help developers take full control of what information apps can access or use. Besides, when a Windows Store app is submitted to the Windows Store, the description is checked to see if it matches all enabled capabilities. As a result, a customer always knows what data is used before he buys the app. Figure 8-3 shows a description sample from the Contacts app.

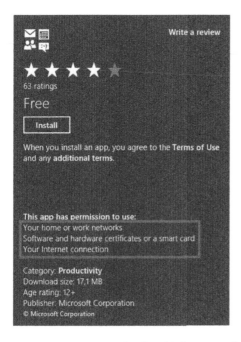

Figure 8-3. *An example of enabled app capabilities from Windows Store*

A good practice is to show on the first use of the app what capability is going to be enabled (Figure 8-4). And of course you can always check what app capabilities are allowed inside the app by using the permission section in the settings charm (Figure 8-5).

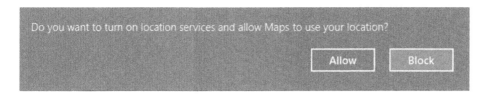

Figure 8-4. *A pop-up asking to use a capability*

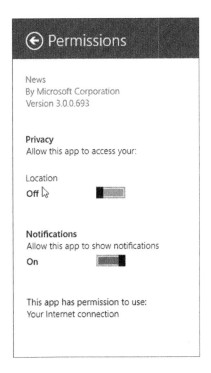

Figure 8-5. *Permission section in settings charm*

Once you have enabled app capabilities for your app, you must choose the way to access data: thanks to Storage APIs, you have a simple way to do that!

Managing App Data

In a desktop app, all app data is stored inside the system registry, installation folder, or user profile folder (like AppData); guidelines suggest to always use one of these locations! Otherwise, when you develop a Windows Store app, you can't access data directly where is stored, but you can use something called **data stores**: these are similar to data containers and are created per-user once a Windows 8 Store app is installed.

There are three different types of data stores (Figure 8-6):

- *Local Data*: Data stored on the local machine.

- *Roaming Data*: Data stored on the cloud.

- *Temporary Data*: Data stored on the local machine in a temporary folder.

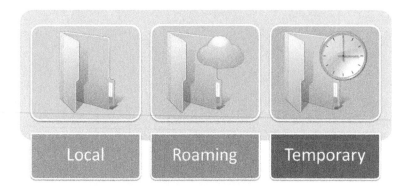

Figure 8-6. *The three data stores*

Of course, you know that local data stores keep your app data somewhere on the local machine, but only the Storage APIs take care of accessing and manipulating it.

So why are data stores helpful? Using data stores offers some advantages. The first is isolation, which helps to avoid data being shared in other apps or in other user instances. Next is the lifetime of the data, which is closely related to the app lifetime: when you install an app, data is maintained in data stores and will remain so until the app is uninstalled (except for roaming data, as you will see later).

Moreover, when you install updates, data is updated too, allowing for the possibility of versioning: with this feature you can prevent a bad headache caused by incompatibility between data application versions. The way to do this is simple: just check the version. If it is less than the installed app version, it needs to be updated.

Choosing one data store or the other depends on what the data contains and how long it needs to be kept. Let's see in detail how data stores work.

Local Data

Local data can be used to maintain information about the configuration of the app and to store large dataset without any storage limit. This kind of storage is ideal if there is no need to share this data with other app instances on other devices. Figure 8-7 shows the Storage APIs main classes.

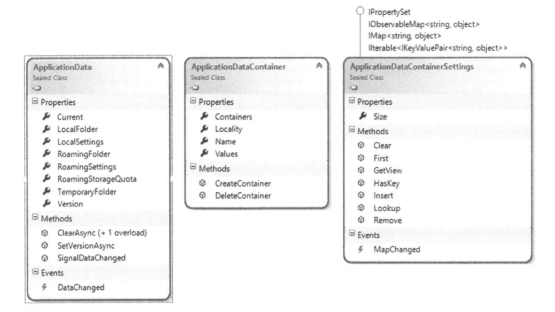

Figure 8-7. Windows Storage API main classes

These APIs allow storing of both data and files. Data is stored inside **containers**, which are created whenever they are needed, and help to hide (and simplify) the access to the system registry. Containers can be nested up to 32 levels. In the following code, a LocalSettings object is user to retrieve or store local information:

C#

```csharp
public CultureInfo CurrentCulture
{
    get
    {
        var localSettings = Windows.Storage.ApplicationData.Current.LocalSettings;

        if (localSettings.Containers.ContainsKey("localization"))
        {
            var cultureName = localSettings.Containers["localization"].Values["language"] as String;
            return (cultureName != null) ? new CultureInfo(cultureName) : CultureInfo.CurrentCulture;
        }

        return new CultureInfo("en-US");
    }
    set
    {
        var localSettings = Windows.Storage.ApplicationData.Current.LocalSettings;
```

```
        if (!localSettings.Containers.ContainsKey("localization"))
        {
            //Create a new container
            localSettings.CreateContainer("localization",
Windows.Storage.ApplicationDataCreateDisposition.Always);
        }

        localSettings.Containers["localization"].Values["language"] = value.Name;
    }
}
```

VB

```
Public Property CurrentCulture() As CultureInfo
    Get
        Dim localSettings = Windows.Storage.ApplicationData.Current.LocalSettings
        Dim culture As CultureInfo

        If localSettings.Containers.ContainsKey("localization") Then
            Dim cultureName = TryCast(localSettings.Containers("localization").Values("language"),
[String])
            culture = New CultureInfo(cultureName)
        Else
            culture = CultureInfo.CurrentCulture
        End If

        Return culture
    End Get
    Set(value As CultureInfo)
        Dim localSettings = Windows.Storage.ApplicationData.Current.LocalSettings

        If Not localSettings.Containers.ContainsKey("localization") Then
            'Create a new container
            localSettings.CreateContainer("localization",
Windows.Storage.ApplicationDataCreateDisposition.Always)
        End If

        localSettings.Containers("localization").Values("language") = value.Name
    End Set
End Property
```

Sometimes you need to store more values that are logically related. Storage APIs provide a specific ApplicationDataCompositeValue (Figure 8-8). This type helps keep different values together, solving the problems associated with data concurrency, consistency, and integrity.

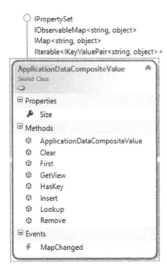

Figure 8-8. ApplicationDataCompositeValue class

The code below shows how to create a composite value.

C#

```csharp
public CultureInfo CurrentCultureDetailed
{
    get
    {
        var localSettings = Windows.Storage.ApplicationData.Current.LocalSettings;

        if (localSettings.Containers.ContainsKey("localization"))
        {
            ApplicationDataCompositeValue composite =
(ApplicationDataCompositeValue)localSettings.Containers["localization"].Values["language"];

            return (composite != null) ? new CultureInfo(composite["selectedLanguage"].ToString())
                : CultureInfo.CurrentCulture;
        }

        return new CultureInfo("en-US");
    }
    set
    {
        var localSettings = Windows.Storage.ApplicationData.Current.LocalSettings;

        if (!localSettings.Containers.ContainsKey("localization"))
        {
            //Create a container
            localSettings.CreateContainer("localization",
                Windows.Storage.ApplicationDataCreateDisposition.Always);
        }
```

```
            ApplicationDataCompositeValue composite = new ApplicationDataCompositeValue();
            composite["selectedLanguage"] = value.Name;
            composite["lastChangeTime"] = DateTime.Now.ToString();

            localSettings.Containers["localization"].Values["language"] = composite;
    }
}
```

VB

```
Public Property CurrentCultureDetailed() As CultureInfo
    Get
        Dim localSettings = Windows.Storage.ApplicationData.Current.LocalSettings

        If localSettings.Containers.ContainsKey("detailedLocalization") Then
            Dim composite As ApplicationDataCompositeValue =
                DirectCast(localSettings.Containers("detailedLocalization").Values("language"),
                    ApplicationDataCompositeValue)

            Return If((composite IsNot Nothing), New
CultureInfo(composite("selectedLanguage").ToString()),
                        CultureInfo.CurrentCulture)
        Else
            Return New CultureInfo("en-US")
        End If
    End Get
    Set(value As CultureInfo)
        Dim localSettings = Windows.Storage.ApplicationData.Current.LocalSettings

        If Not localSettings.Containers.ContainsKey("detailedLocalization") Then
            'Create a container
            localSettings.CreateContainer("detailedLocalization",
                                        Windows.Storage.ApplicationDataCreateDisposition.Always)
        End If

        Dim composite As New ApplicationDataCompositeValue()
        composite("selectedLanguage") = value.DisplayName
        composite("lastChangeTime") = DateTime.Now.ToString()

        localSettings.Containers("detailedLocalization").Values("language") = composite
    End Set
End Property
```

Besides settings, the Storage APIs also store files using CreateFileAsync() and GetFileAsync() methods from the LocalFolder object. Files are accessed both in read and write mode. Because of the lack of a binary type inside WinRT, sometimes files can be used as substitute. Some good examples are the SaveAsync() and RestoreAsync() methods inside the SuspensionManager class, shown next.

C#

```csharp
public static async Task SaveAsync()
{
    try
    {
    // Save the navigation state for all registered frames
    foreach (var weakFrameReference in _registeredFrames)
    {
        Frame frame;
        if (weakFrameReference.TryGetTarget(out frame))
        {
            SaveFrameNavigationState(frame);
        }
    }

        // Serialize the session state synchronously to avoid asynchronous access to shared
        // state
        MemoryStream sessionData = new MemoryStream();
        DataContractSerializer serializer =
            new DataContractSerializer(typeof(Dictionary<string, object>), _knownTypes);
        serializer.WriteObject(sessionData, _sessionState);

        // Get an output stream for the SessionState file and write the state asynchronously
        StorageFile file = await
            ApplicationData.Current.LocalFolder.CreateFileAsync(sessionStateFilename,
            CreationCollisionOption.ReplaceExisting);
        using (Stream fileStream = await file.OpenStreamForWriteAsync())
        {
            sessionData.Seek(0, SeekOrigin.Begin);
            await sessionData.CopyToAsync(fileStream);
            await fileStream.FlushAsync();
        }
    }
    catch (Exception e)
    {
        throw new SuspensionManagerException(e);
    }
}

public static async Task RestoreAsync()
{
    _sessionState = new Dictionary<String, Object>();

    try
    {
        // Get the input stream for the SessionState file
        StorageFile file =
            await ApplicationData.Current.LocalFolder.GetFileAsync(sessionStateFilename);
```

```csharp
        using (IInputStream inStream = await file.OpenSequentialReadAsync())
        {
            // Deserialize the Session State
            DataContractSerializer serializer =
                new DataContractSerializer(typeof(Dictionary<string, object>), _knownTypes);
            _sessionState = (Dictionary<string, object>)serializer.ReadObject(inStream.AsStreamForRead());
        }

        // Restore any registered frames to their saved state
        foreach (var weakFrameReference in _registeredFrames)
        {
            Frame frame;
            if (weakFrameReference.TryGetTarget(out frame))
            {
                frame.ClearValue(FrameSessionStateProperty);
                RestoreFrameNavigationState(frame);
            }
        }
    }
    catch (Exception e)
    {
        throw new SuspensionManagerException(e);
    }
}
```

VB

```vbnet
Public Shared Async Function SaveAsync() As Task
    Try

        ' Save the navigation state for all registered frames
        For Each weakFrameReference As WeakReference(Of Frame) In _registeredFrames
            Dim frame As Frame = Nothing
            If weakFrameReference.TryGetTarget(frame) Then
                SaveFrameNavigationState(frame)
            End If
        Next

        ' Serialize the session state synchronously to avoid asynchronous access to shared
        ' state
        Dim sessionData As New MemoryStream()
        Dim serializer As New Runtime.Serialization.DataContractSerializer(
            GetType(Dictionary(Of String, Object)), _knownTypes)
        serializer.WriteObject(sessionData, _sessionState)

        ' Get an output stream for the SessionState file and write the state asynchronously
        Dim file As Windows.Storage.StorageFile =
            Await Windows.Storage.ApplicationData.Current.LocalFolder.CreateFileAsync(
            sessionStateFilename, Windows.Storage.CreationCollisionOption.ReplaceExisting)
```

```vbnet
        Using fileStream As Stream = Await file.OpenStreamForWriteAsync()
            sessionData.Seek(0, SeekOrigin.Begin)
            Await sessionData.CopyToAsync(fileStream)
            Await fileStream.FlushAsync()
        End Using
    Catch ex As Exception
        Throw New SuspensionManagerException(ex)
    End Try
End Function

Public Shared Async Function RestoreAsync() As Task
    _sessionState = New Dictionary(Of String, Object)()

    Try

        ' Get the input stream for the SessionState file
        Dim file As Windows.Storage.StorageFile =
            Await Windows.Storage.ApplicationData.Current.LocalFolder.GetFileAsync(sessionStateFilename)
        If file Is Nothing Then Return

        Using inStream As Windows.Storage.Streams.IInputStream =
Await file.OpenSequentialReadAsync()

            ' Deserialize the Session State
            Dim serializer As New Runtime.Serialization.DataContractSerializer(
                GetType(Dictionary(Of String, Object)), _knownTypes)
            _sessionState = DirectCast(serializer.ReadObject(inStream.AsStreamForRead()),
                Dictionary(Of String, Object))
        End Using

        ' Restore any registered frames to their saved state
        For Each weakFrameReference As WeakReference(Of Frame) In _registeredFrames
            Dim frame As Frame = Nothing
            If weakFrameReference.TryGetTarget(frame) Then
                frame.ClearValue(FrameSessionStateProperty)
                RestoreFrameNavigationState(frame)
            End If
        Next
    Catch ex As Exception
        Throw New SuspensionManagerException(ex)
    End Try
End Function
```

To access a file programmatically, you can use the StorageFile object (Figure 8-9). Remember that it is a really good practice to use this Local Store just for data that is not needed on other devices or just for a large set of data.

Figure 8-9. *StorageFile and StorageFolder classes*

Through this object you can also use the IsEqual property to check if two files are equal. Also, StorageFolder includes a few methods to get files or folders async:

- GetFileAsync, to get a file asynchronously
- GetFilesAsync, to get a collection of files asynchronously

- GetFoldersAsync, to get a folder asynchronously

- GetItemAsync, to get a file or a sub-folder asynchronously

It is also possible to use the method TryGetItemAsync to retrieve a file without worrying about an exception when a file is not found. In this case, the method returns null.

Roaming Data

Roaming data stores are an innovative way to simplify data management inside Windows Store apps. The use of this feature allows users to have the same user experience on different devices, thereby avoiding multiple configurations. In addition, users are able to resume their activities when switching from one device from another (such as from a home PC to a tablet).

Once a user has installed an app, he usually sets an initial configuration. This step can take some time, and repeating the entire procedure on different devices is frustrating. Roaming data provides really good assistance for this: after the first configuration, all user preferences are set to be roaming. Afterwards, when user installs the Windows Store app on other devices, the user preferences are already available. Of course, the developer should check the existence of settings and retrieve them from the cloud. The most interesting aspect is that the application just needs to retrieve the settings using the Storage APIs object without any further configuration (e.g., services, login)! In this way you can guarantee a full user experience.

All roaming data is synched to the cloud, using the user's Microsoft account. The synch process is not immediate and there is also a limit on the storage size that can be checked using the ApplicationData.Current. RoamingStorageQuota property.

C#

```
var quota = ApplicationData.Current.RoamingStorageQuota; //Usually 100KB
```

VB

```
Dim quota = ApplicationData.Current.RoamingStorageQuota
```

If this limit is exceeded, data won't be synched until the roaming data is less than the limit again. Because of this, you should use roaming data only for small information like user preferences or small data files. It is also a good practice to avoid sending the content of web pages and instead send links directly. Typically you should choose at design time what data will roam, thereby avoiding serious headaches later. Here is how to take advantage of Roaming Data using the RoamingSettings object.

C#

```
get
{
    var roamingSettings = Windows.Storage.ApplicationData.Current.RoamingSettings;

    if (roamingSettings.Containers.ContainsKey("localization"))
    {
        var cultureName = roamingSettings.Containers["localization"].Values["language"] as String;
        return (cultureName != null) ? new CultureInfo(cultureName) : CultureInfo.CurrentCulture;
    }

    return new CultureInfo("en-US");
}
```

```
set
{
    var roamingSettings = Windows.Storage.ApplicationData.Current.RoamingSettings;

    if (!roamingSettings.Containers.ContainsKey("localization"))
    {
        //Create a container
        roamingSettings.CreateContainer("localization",
Windows.Storage.ApplicationDataCreateDisposition.Always);
    }

    roamingSettings.Containers["localization"].Values["language"] = value.Name;
}
```

VB

```
Get
        Dim roamingSettings = Windows.Storage.ApplicationData.Current.RoamingSettings

        If roamingSettings.Containers.ContainsKey("localization") Then
            Dim cultureName =
                TryCast(roamingSettings.Containers("localization").Values("language"), [String])
            Return If((cultureName IsNot Nothing),
                    New CultureInfo(cultureName), CultureInfo.CurrentCulture)
        End If

        Return New CultureInfo("en-US")
End Get
Set(value As CultureInfo)
        Dim roamingSettings = Windows.Storage.ApplicationData.Current.RoamingSettings

        If Not roamingSettings.Containers.ContainsKey("localization") Then
            'Create a container
            roamingSettings.CreateContainer("localization",
                                    Windows.Storage.ApplicationDataCreateDisposition.Always)
        End If

        roamingSettings.Containers("localization").Values("language") = value.Name
    End Set
```

It is possible to roam a group of settings together using the ApplicationDataCompositeValue object, increasing data consistency:

C#

```
get
{
    var roamingSettings = Windows.Storage.ApplicationData.Current.RoamingSettings;

    if (roamingSettings.Containers.ContainsKey("localization"))
    {
        ApplicationDataCompositeValue composite =
            (ApplicationDataCompositeValue)roamingSettings.Containers["localization"].Values["language"];
```

```
        return (composite != null) ? new CultureInfo(composite["selectedLanguage"].ToString())
            : CultureInfo.CurrentCulture;
    }

    return new CultureInfo("en-US");
}
set
{
    var roamingSettings = Windows.Storage.ApplicationData.Current.RoamingSettings;

    if (!roamingSettings.Containers.ContainsKey("localization"))
    {
        //Create a container
        roamingSettings.CreateContainer("localization",
            Windows.Storage.ApplicationDataCreateDisposition.Always);
    }

    ApplicationDataCompositeValue composite = new ApplicationDataCompositeValue();
    composite["selectedLanguage"] = value.Name;
    composite["lastChangeTime"] = DateTime.Now.ToString();

    roamingSettings.Containers["detailedLocalization "].Values["language"] = composite;
}
```

VB

```
Get
    Dim roamingSettings = Windows.Storage.ApplicationData.Current.RoamingSettings

    If roamingSettings.Containers.ContainsKey("detailedLocalization") Then
        Dim composite As ApplicationDataCompositeValue =
            DirectCast(roamingSettings.Containers("detailedLocalization").Values("language"),
                ApplicationDataCompositeValue)

        Return If((composite IsNot Nothing),
                    New CultureInfo(composite("selectedLanguage").ToString()),
CultureInfo.CurrentCulture)
    Else
        Return New CultureInfo("en-US")
    End If
End Get
Set(value As CultureInfo)
    Dim roamingSettings = Windows.Storage.ApplicationData.Current.RoamingSettings

    If Not roamingSettings.Containers.ContainsKey("detailedLocalization") Then
        'Create a container
        roamingSettings.CreateContainer("detailedLocalization",
                                        Windows.Storage.ApplicationDataCreateDisposition.Always)
    End If
```

```
    Dim composite As New ApplicationDataCompositeValue()
    composite("selectedLanguage") = value.DisplayName
    composite("lastChangeTime") = DateTime.Now.ToString()

    roamingSettings.Containers("detailedLocalization").Values("language") = composite
End Set
```

In order to better the user experience, you can use a special setting to override the order of the data synch process, the HighPriority setting. Like the previous examples, is sufficient to create a container named HighPriority.

The roaming engine will automatically prioritize this container among the others. It is not suggested to use the HighPriority option to store settings related to user preferences; instead it's better to memorize the last action or state before an app is suspended (e.g., save the number of the actual page of an opened book). Then, when the app is resumed, either on the same machine or another device, the values stored inside the HighPriority container will be read. The HighPriority container can also store composite values, but be aware that there is a limit of 8kb. If the container size hits this limit, the container will be roamed just like the others with no priority. In the default template for a Windows Store app, if you suspend an app, an event called SaveAsync() saves the state for you. You can use the same method to roam information on app suspension with HighPriority:

C#

SuspensionManager.cs:
```
// Save last suspending time
var storageSettings = ApplicationData.Current.RoamingSettings;
storageSettings.Values["HighPriority"] = DateTime.Now.ToString();
```

App.xaml.cs:
```
//Get the last suspending time
var roamingSettings = Windows.Storage.ApplicationData.Current.RoamingSettings;
if (roamingSettings.Values.Count > 0 && roamingSettings.Values["HighPriority"] != null)
{
    DateTime lastSuspensionTime =
Convert.ToDateTime(roamingSettings.Values["HighPriority"].ToString());
}
```

VB

SuspensionManager.vb:
```
' Save last suspending time
Dim storageSettings = ApplicationData.Current.RoamingSettings
storageSettings.Values("HighPriority") = DateTime.Now.ToString()
```

App.xaml.vb:
```
Dim roamingSettings = Windows.Storage.ApplicationData.Current.RoamingSettings
If roamingSettings.Values.Count > 0 And Not roamingSettings.Values("HighPriority") Is Nothing Then
    Dim lastSuspensionTime As DateTime =
        Convert.ToDateTime(roamingSettings.Values("HighPriority").ToString())
End If
```

A Windows Store application automatically checks for new roaming data. Inside the app, it is enough to register to handle the DataChanged() event. Of course, the synchronization between devices is not immediate and it is not recommended to use this technique to exchange data among PCs. Here is a usage example of forcing the trigger of the DataChanged() event by calling SignalDataChanged() event.

C#

RoamingData.xaml.cs:
```csharp
public RoamingData ()
{
    this.InitializeComponent();
    this.initComboBoxes();

    Windows.Storage.ApplicationData.Current.DataChanged +=
        new TypedEventHandler<Windows.Storage.ApplicationData, object>(DataChangedHandler);

    var roamingSettings = Windows.Storage.ApplicationData.Current.RoamingSettings;
    roamingSettings.Values["lastRoamingSettingDate"] = DateTime.Now.ToString();
    Windows.Storage.ApplicationData.Current.SignalDataChanged();
}

async void DataChangedHandler(Windows.Storage.ApplicationData sender, object args)
{
    // DataChangeHandler may be invoked on a background thread,
    // so use the Dispatcher to invoke the UI-related code on the UI thread.
    await this.Dispatcher.RunAsync(CoreDispatcherPriority.Normal, () =>
    {
        var roamingSettings = Windows.Storage.ApplicationData.Current.RoamingSettings;
        if (roamingSettings.Values.Count > 0)
        {
            DateTime lastSuspensionTime = Convert.ToDateTime(
                    roamingSettings.Values["lastRoamingSettingDate"].ToString());
        }
    });
}
```

VB

RoamingData.xaml.vb:
```vbnet
Public Sub New()
    InitializeComponent()
    Me._navigationHelper = New Common.NavigationHelper(Me)
    AddHandler Me._navigationHelper.LoadState,
        AddressOf NavigationHelper_LoadState

    'Get quota
    Dim quota = ApplicationData.Current.RoamingStorageQuota
    'Usually 100KB
    RoamingDataQuota.Text = [String].Format("{0} KB", quota.ToString())
```

```vbnet
    'Roaming data - Single value
    RoamingSettingsSingleValue.Text = CurrentCulture.DisplayName

    'Roaming data - Composite data
    CurrentCultureDetailed = New CultureInfo("en-US")
    GetCompositeData()

    'Roaming Data - DataChanged Event Handler
    AddHandler Windows.Storage.ApplicationData.Current.DataChanged, AddressOf DataChangeHandler

    Dim roamingSettings = Windows.Storage.ApplicationData.Current.RoamingSettings
    roamingSettings.Values("lastRoamingSettingDate") = DateTime.Now.ToString()
    Windows.Storage.ApplicationData.Current.SignalDataChanged()
End Sub

Private Async Sub DataChangeHandler(ByVal appData As Windows.Storage.ApplicationData, ByVal o As
Object)
    ' DataChangeHandler may be invoked on a background thread,
    ' so use the Dispatcher to invoke the UI-related code on the UI thread.

    Await Me.Dispatcher.RunAsync(CoreDispatcherPriority.Normal,Sub()
    Dim roamingSettings = Windows.Storage.ApplicationData.Current.RoamingSettings
    Dim lastSuspensionTime As DateTime =
            Convert.ToDateTime(roamingSettings.Values("lastRoamingSettingDate").ToString())

    DataChangedInvoked.Text = "Yes"
    End Sub)
End Sub
```

Roaming data also provides application data versioning to avoid incompatibility between app versions. When the data settings inside a Windows Store app are upgraded or the format is modified, there is no automatic mechanism to upgrade data to the new version. It is up to the developer to check if the app data has the same version. Note that data is roamed only if the version between apps matches. The Windows Storage APIs simplify version checking by providing the Application.Version property to verify the version number and the ApplicationData.SetVersionAsync() to set the version number:

C#

RoamingData.xaml.cs
```csharp
...//Roaming Data - Check data version
        VersionHelper.CheckVersion();
...
```

VersionHelper.cs
```csharp
public static class VersionHelper
{
    public static void CheckVersion()
    {
        uint version = ApplicationData.Current.Version;
```

```csharp
    switch (version)
    {
        case 0:
            //Need to upgrade data from v0 to v1
            Upgrade_Version0_to_Version1();
            break;
        case 1:
            //Right version, do nothing...
            break;
        default:
            throw new Exception("Unexpected ApplicationData Version: " + version);
    }
}

static async void Upgrade_Version0_to_Version1()
{
    await ApplicationData.Current.SetVersionAsync(1,
        new ApplicationDataSetVersionHandler(SetVersion1Handler));
}

private static void SetVersion1Handler(SetVersionRequest setVersionRequest)
{
    SetVersionDeferral deferral = setVersionRequest.GetDeferral();

    //Change the data format for all needed settings
    ApplicationData.Current.LocalSettings.Values["LocalData"] = "this-is-a-new-data-format";

    deferral.Complete();
}
}
```

VB

RoamingData.xaml.vb
```vbnet
'Roaming Data - Check data version
VersionHelper.CheckVersion()
...
```

VersionHelper.vb
```vbnet
Public NotInheritable Class VersionHelper
    Private Sub New()
    End Sub
    Public Shared Sub CheckVersion()
        Dim version As UInteger = ApplicationData.Current.Version

        Select Case version
            Case 0
                'Need to upgrade data from v0 to v1
                Upgrade_Version0_to_Version1()
                Exit Select
```

```vb
            Case 1
                'Right version, do nothing...
                Exit Select
            Case Else
                Throw New Exception("Unexpected ApplicationData Version: " + version)
        End Select
    End Sub

    Private Shared Async Sub Upgrade_Version0_to_Version1()
        Await ApplicationData.Current.SetVersionAsync(1,
                            New ApplicationDataSetVersionHandler(AddressOf SetVersion1Handler))
    End Sub

    Private Shared Sub SetVersion1Handler(setVersionRequest As SetVersionRequest)
        Dim deferral As SetVersionDeferral = setVersionRequest.GetDeferral()

        'Change the data format for all needed settings
        ApplicationData.Current.LocalSettings.Values("LocalData") = "this-is-a-new-data-format"

        deferral.Complete()
    End Sub

    Public Shared ReadOnly Property AppVersion() As UInteger
        Get
            Return ApplicationData.Current.Version
        End Get
    End Property
End Class
```

In addition to settings, an app can also roam files. For this scope, the ApplicationData namespace contains the RoamingFolder object. It is important to open and close any handles to the files before the roaming process starts. Here is an extended version of the previous SaveAsync() and RestoreAsync() examples inside the SuspensionManager class.

C#

```csharp
public static async Task SaveAsync()
{
    try
    {
        // Save the navigation state for all registered frames
        foreach (var weakFrameReference in _registeredFrames)
        {
            Frame frame;
            if (weakFrameReference.TryGetTarget(out frame))
            {
                SaveFrameNavigationState(frame);
            }
        }
```

```
            // Serialize the session state synchronously to avoid asynchronous access to shared
            // state
            MemoryStream sessionData = new MemoryStream();
            DataContractSerializer serializer =
                new DataContractSerializer(typeof(Dictionary<string, object>), _knownTypes);
            serializer.WriteObject(sessionData, _sessionState);

            // Get an output stream for the SessionState file and write the state asynchronously
            StorageFile file = await
                ApplicationData.Current.RoamingFolder.CreateFileAsync(sessionStateFilename,
                CreationCollisionOption.ReplaceExisting);
            using (Stream fileStream = await file.OpenStreamForWriteAsync())
            {
                sessionData.Seek(0, SeekOrigin.Begin);
                await sessionData.CopyToAsync(fileStream);
                await fileStream.FlushAsync();
            }
        }
        catch (Exception e)
        {
            throw new SuspensionManagerException(e);
        }
    }

    public static async Task RestoreAsync()
    {
        _sessionState = new Dictionary<String, Object>();

        try
        {
            // Get the input stream for the SessionState file
            StorageFile file =
                await ApplicationData.Current.RoamingFolder.GetFileAsync(sessionStateFilename);
            using (IInputStream inStream = await file.OpenSequentialReadAsync())
            {
                // Deserialize the Session State
                DataContractSerializer serializer =
                    new DataContractSerializer(typeof(Dictionary<string, object>), _knownTypes);
                _sessionState = (Dictionary<string, object>)serializer.ReadObject(inStream.AsStreamForRead());
            }

            // Restore any registered frames to their saved state
            foreach (var weakFrameReference in _registeredFrames)
            {
                Frame frame;
                if (weakFrameReference.TryGetTarget(out frame))
                {
                    frame.ClearValue(FrameSessionStateProperty);
                    RestoreFrameNavigationState(frame);
                }
            }
        }
```

```
    catch (Exception e)
    {
        throw new SuspensionManagerException(e);
    }
}
```

VB

```vb
Public Shared Async Function SaveAsync() As Task
    Try

        ' Save the navigation state for all registered frames
        For Each weakFrameReference As WeakReference(Of Frame) In _registeredFrames
            Dim frame As Frame = Nothing
            If weakFrameReference.TryGetTarget(frame) Then
                SaveFrameNavigationState(frame)
            End If
        Next
        ' Serialize the session state synchronously to avoid asynchronous access to shared
        ' state
        Dim sessionData As New MemoryStream()
        Dim serializer As New Runtime.Serialization.DataContractSerializer(
            GetType(Dictionary(Of String, Object)), _knownTypes)
        serializer.WriteObject(sessionData, _sessionState)

        ' Get an output stream for the SessionState file and write the state asynchronously
        Dim file As Windows.Storage.StorageFile =
            Await Windows.Storage.ApplicationData.Current.RoamingFolder.CreateFileAsync(
            sessionStateFilename, Windows.Storage.CreationCollisionOption.ReplaceExisting)
        Using fileStream As Stream = Await file.OpenStreamForWriteAsync()
            sessionData.Seek(0, SeekOrigin.Begin)
            Await sessionData.CopyToAsync(fileStream)
            Await fileStream.FlushAsync()
        End Using
    Catch ex As Exception
        Throw New SuspensionManagerException(ex)
    End Try
End Function

''' <summary>
''' Restores previously saved <see cref="SessionState"/>.  Any <see cref="Frame"/> instances
''' registered with <see cref="RegisterFrame"/> will also restore their prior navigation
''' state, which in turn gives their active <see cref="Page"/> an opportunity restore its
''' state.
''' </summary>
''' <returns>An asynchronous task that reflects when session state has been read.  The
''' content of <see cref="SessionState"/> should not be relied upon until this task
''' completes.</returns>
Public Shared Async Function RestoreAsync() As Task
    _sessionState = New Dictionary(Of String, Object)()
```

```
    Try

            ' Get the input stream for the SessionState file
            Dim file As Windows.Storage.StorageFile =
                Await Windows.Storage.ApplicationData.Current.RoamingFolder.GetFileAsync
(sessionStateFilename)
            If file Is Nothing Then Return

            Using inStream As Windows.Storage.Streams.IInputStream = Await file.OpenSequentialReadAsync()

                ' Deserialize the Session State
                Dim serializer As New Runtime.Serialization.DataContractSerializer(
                    GetType(Dictionary(Of String, Object)), _knownTypes)
                _sessionState = DirectCast(serializer.ReadObject(inStream.AsStreamForRead()),
                    Dictionary(Of String, Object))
            End Using

            ' Restore any registered frames to their saved state
            For Each weakFrameReference As WeakReference(Of Frame) In _registeredFrames
                Dim frame As Frame = Nothing
                If weakFrameReference.TryGetTarget(frame) Then
                    frame.ClearValue(FrameSessionStateProperty)
                    RestoreFrameNavigationState(frame)
                End If
            Next
    Catch ex As Exception
            Throw New SuspensionManagerException(ex)
    End Try
End Function
```

Make sure to check if roaming a file exceeds the roaming storage quota!

Temporary Data

Temporary data stores can be used as a temporary area to store information. It is important to understand that files in this location can be deleted at any time by the operating system internal tasks (for example, the Disk Cleanup utility). For this reason, it is not guaranteed that these files are always available during app execution. Here is how to manage this type of data using the TemporaryFolder object:

C#

TempDataHelper.cs
```csharp
public async static void SaveTempData(string data)
{
    ;
    StorageFile tempFile =
        await ApplicationData.Current.TemporaryFolder.CreateFileAsync("temporary.txt",
        CreationCollisionOption.ReplaceExisting);
    await FileIO.WriteTextAsync(calFile, data);
}
```

```csharp
public async static Task<String> GetTempData()
{
    try
    {
        StorageFile tempFile = await
ApplicationData.Current.TemporaryFolder.GetFileAsync("temporary.txt");
        String content = await FileIO.ReadTextAsync(tempFile);
        return content;
    }
    catch
    {
        throw new Exception("Data not found!");
    }
}
```

TempData.xaml.cs
```csharp
private void SaveTempDataButton_Click(object sender, RoutedEventArgs e)
{
    TempDataHelper.SaveTempData(UserTempDataTextBox.Text);
}

private async void GetTempDataButton_Click(object sender, RoutedEventArgs e)
{
    StoredTempData.Text = await TempDataHelper.GetTempData();
}
```

VB

TempDataHelper.vb
```vb
Public NotInheritable Class TempDataHelper
    Private Sub New()
    End Sub
    Public Shared Async Sub SaveTempData(data As String)
        Dim tempFile As StorageFile =
            Await ApplicationData.Current.TemporaryFolder.CreateFileAsync(
                "temporary.txt", CreationCollisionOption.ReplaceExisting)
        Await FileIO.WriteTextAsync(tempFile, data)
    End Sub

    Public Shared Async Function GetTempData() As Task(Of [String])
        Try
            Dim tempFile As StorageFile =
                Await ApplicationData.Current.TemporaryFolder.GetFileAsync("temporary.txt")
            Dim content As [String] = Await FileIO.ReadTextAsync(tempFile)
            Return content
        Catch
            Throw New Exception("Data not found!")
        End Try
    End Function
End Class
```

TempData.xaml.vb
```vb
Private Sub SaveTempDataButton_Click(sender As Object, e As RoutedEventArgs)
    TempDataHelper.SaveTempData(UserTempDataTextBox.Text)
End Sub

Private Async Sub GetTempDataButton_Click(sender As Object, e As RoutedEventArgs)
    StoredTempData.Text = Await TempDataHelper.GetTempData()
End Sub
```

User Data

Until now you have seen the different ways to handle AppData inside your Windows Store app.

For user data, you need to use other classes to read or write data and files. First, this type of data can be stored in one of the user libraries, installation folders, or accessible folders (based on the available capabilities). Storage APIs offer a simple way to access to these locations using `Windows.Storage.KnownFolders`. Figure 8-10 shows the static properties available in `KnownFolders` static class.

Figure 8-10. *KnownFolders Properties*

You can access PicturesLibrary after the related capability is enabled in `Package.appxmanifest`:

C#

UserData.xaml.cs
```csharp
        private async void SaveDataButton_Click(object sender, RoutedEventArgs e)
        {
            StorageFile userFile = await KnownFolders.PicturesLibrary.CreateFileAsync("userdata.txt",
CreationCollisionOption.ReplaceExisting);
            await FileIO.WriteTextAsync(userFile, UserDataTextBox.Text);
        }
```

```csharp
    private async void GetDataButton_Click(object sender, RoutedEventArgs e)
    {
        try
        {
            StorageFile userFile = await KnownFolders.PicturesLibrary.GetFileAsync("userdata.txt");
            StoredData.Text = await FileIO.ReadTextAsync(userFile);
        }
        catch
        {
            throw new Exception("Data not found!");
        }
    }
```

VB

UserData.xaml.vb

```vbnet
Private Async Sub SaveDataButton_Click(sender As Object, e As RoutedEventArgs)
    Dim userFile As StorageFile =
        Await KnownFolders.PicturesLibrary.CreateFileAsync("userdata.txt",
                                                CreationCollisionOption.ReplaceExisting)
    Await FileIO.WriteTextAsync(userFile, UserDataTextBox.Text)
End Sub

Private Async Sub GetDataButton_Click(sender As Object, e As RoutedEventArgs)
    Try
        Dim userFile As StorageFile = Await KnownFolders.PicturesLibrary.GetFileAsync("userdata.txt")
        StoredData.Text = Await FileIO.ReadTextAsync(userFile)
    Catch
        Throw New Exception("Data not found!")
    End Try
End Sub
```

Starting in Windows 8.1 it is also possible to use another class to retrieve all libraries folders: StorageLibrary. With this object you can easily handle your libraries thanks to integration with the FilePicker object.

FilePicker and FolderPicker

In the previous section you saw how to access user libraries. The problem is that KnownFolders is the only available location inside the app (if the relative app capability is enabled). If you want to store files in another location, you can take advantage of the FilePicker class.

The FilePicker is a user-driven control that allows a user to choose the location for a file. This helps to minimize the number of enables capabilities in the app and simplify the submission process to the Windows Store.

The following images show an example of FilePicker: you can see the current location (Figure 8-11), a scrollable menu to navigate in the local folders (Figure 8-12), and the list of selected items (Figure 8-13).

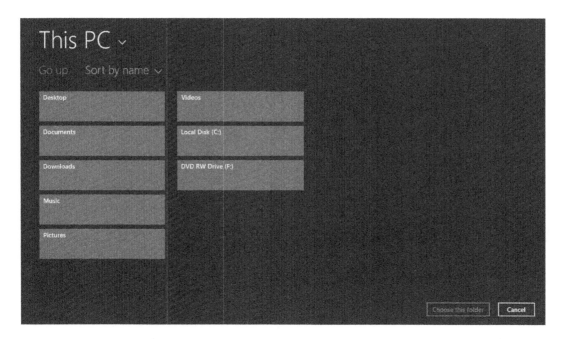

Figure 8-11. *An example of FilePicker*

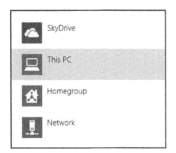

Figure 8-12. *FilePicker available folders*

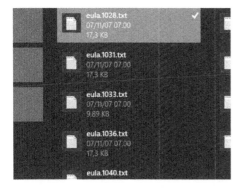

Figure 8-13. *Selected file inside FilePicker*

Once a file is picked using the FilePicker, an instance of the StorageFile class is returned.

In addition to FilePicker, the Storage APIs also provide a FolderPicker object that lets the user choose a folder. Once a folder is picked using the FolderPicker, an instance of StorageFolder is returned.

In order to use the FilePicker or the FolderPicker object, it is necessary to follow these steps:

1. Create and customize a FilePicker/FolderPicker object, setting different properties before the control. Some of these properties are listed in Table 8-2.

Table 8-2. *FilePicker/FolderPicker Properties*

Property	Description	Possible Values
ViewMode	Item Visualization	List, Thumbnail
SuggestedStartLocation	Default folder	A file system location
fileTypeFilter	A list of different extension to filter showed items	List of extensions

2. Show the FilePicker/FolderPicker using

    a. pickSingleFileAsync() (just one file)

    b. pickMultipleFileAsync() (multiple files, returning a list of storage files)

    c. pickSingleFolderAsync() (just one folder)

Also remember that file picker can be opened both in split-screen and a full-screen display.

Let's add the code inside your Organizer app:

C#

UserData.xaml.cs
```
public async void GetFile()
{
    FileOpenPicker openPicker = new FileOpenPicker();
    openPicker.ViewMode = PickerViewMode.List;
    openPicker.SuggestedStartLocation = PickerLocationId.Desktop;
    openPicker.FileTypeFilter.Add(".txt");
    StorageFile file = await openPicker.PickSingleFileAsync();

    if (file != null)
    {
        //do something
    }
}
```

UserData.xaml.cs
```
public async void GetFolder()
{
    FolderPicker openPicker = new FolderPicker();
    openPicker.ViewMode = PickerViewMode.List;
    openPicker.SuggestedStartLocation = PickerLocationId.Desktop;
    openPicker.FileTypeFilter.Add(".txt");
    StorageFolder folder = await openPicker.PickSingleFolderAsync();
```

```
    if (folder != null)
    {
        //do something
    }
}
```

VB

UserData.xaml.vb
```
Public Async Sub GetFile()
    Dim openPicker As New FileOpenPicker()
    openPicker.ViewMode = PickerViewMode.List
    openPicker.SuggestedStartLocation = PickerLocationId.Desktop
    openPicker.FileTypeFilter.Add(".txt")
    Dim file As StorageFile = Await openPicker.PickSingleFileAsync()

    If file IsNot Nothing Then
        'do something
    End If
End Sub
```

UserData.xaml.vb
```
Public Async Sub GetFolder()
    Dim openPicker As New FolderPicker()
    openPicker.ViewMode = PickerViewMode.List
    openPicker.SuggestedStartLocation = PickerLocationId.Desktop
    openPicker.FileTypeFilter.Add(".txt")
    Dim folder As StorageFolder = Await openPicker.PickSingleFolderAsync()

    If folder IsNot Nothing Then
        'do something
    End If
End Sub
```

If you need to save a file to a location, you need to use the FileSavePicker. Once the window is opened by calling the PickSaveFileAsync() method, the user can type a name or leave the default file name set using the SuggestedFileName property. It is also possible to set the following:

- The default folder using the SuggestedStartLocation property

- The default extension using the DefaultFileExtension property

Then the user confirms the saving of the file and PickSaveFileAsync() returns a StorageFile object that is the saved file. Remember that it is possible to share your files in other applications by integrating the file picker contracts.

Using SQLite for Windows Store Apps

Sometimes you need to store more structured data than single values or a data file. Often the appropriate choice in this situation is a database. Unfortunately, in a Windows Store app you can't directly access SQL Server or SQL Server CE (the only way is to access to them using services). The available solution is SQLite.

For those who don't know, SQLite is an open source transactional database (more often defined as a library). It is multi-platform and consists of a single file containing all the data (other details at en.wikipedia.org/wiki/SQLite). In order to use SQLite in your application, you need to download it from www.sqlite.org/download.html (Figure 8-14) and install it (Figure 8-15).

| sqlite-wp80-winrt-
3080000.vsix
(2.80 MiB) | A complete VSIX package with an extension SDK and all other components needed t
Visual Studio 2012 targeting Windows Phone 8.0.
(sha1: aa33fd4e3582a315689344e2317e6c8e1e22fb9c) |

Precompiled Binaries for Windows Runtime

| sqlite-winrt80-
3080002.vsix
(4.23 MiB) | A complete VSIX package with an extension SDK and all other components needed t
development with Visual Studio 2012.
(sha1: 0bb0fbf8743402dd6abcc335df9953c4a12e7cd9) |
| sqlite-winrt81-
3080002.vsix
(4.21 MiB) | A complete VSIX package with an extension SDK and all other components needed t
development with Visual Studio 2013.
(sha1: 81fbbca307552a38ed577def2d365ac1b8fcecfc) |

Precompiled Binaries for .NET

System.Data.SQLite   Visit the System.Data.SQLite.org website and especially the download page for sourc

Legacy Source Code Distribution Formats (Not Recommended)

Figure 8-14. *SQLite download page*

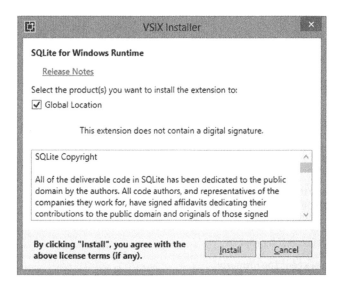

Figure 8-15. *SQLite VSIX Installer window*

Once installed (Figure 8-16), you need to add a reference to your Windows Store app project: right-click the project name in the Solution Explorer, select the References item, and then Add New Reference.

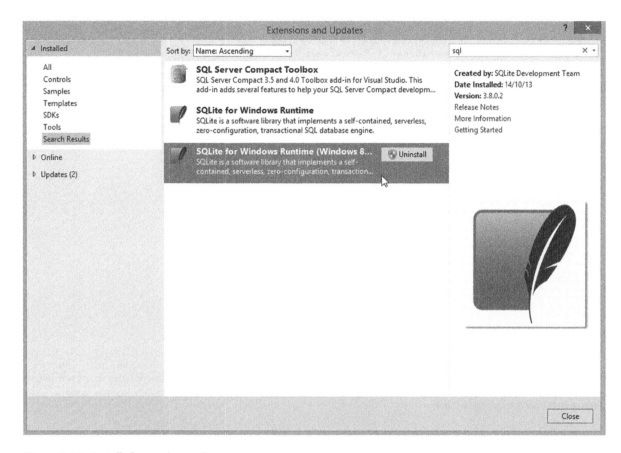

Figure 8-16. *Installed extension section*

Inside the windows that shows up (Figure 8-17), check the SQLite for Windows Runtime item.

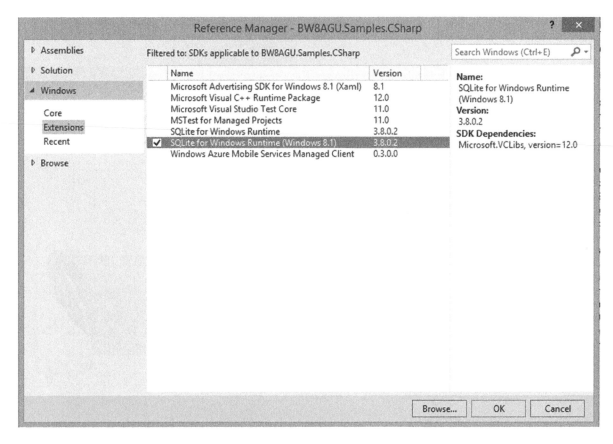

Figure 8-17. *Add reference window*

Now you can add through NuGet a wrapper to connect and use SQLite via the following command:

```
Install-Package sqlite-net
```

You are now ready to learn how to create a table for a SimpleAppointment entity and how to access to it:

C#

```
SQLiteHelper.cs
public async static void CreateDatabase()
{
    var storagePath = Windows.Storage.ApplicationData.Current.LocalFolder;
    var file = await storagePath.TryGetItemAsync("db.sqlite");

    if (file == null)
    {
        var dbPath = System.IO.Path.Combine(
            Windows.Storage.ApplicationData.Current.LocalFolder.Path, "db.sqlite");
```

```csharp
        try
        {
            using (var db = new SQLiteConnection(dbPath))
            {
                db.CreateTable<SimpleAppointment>();
            }
        }
        catch (Exception ex)
        {
            throw ex;
        }
    }
}

public static void AddAppointment(SimpleAppointment appointment)
{
    var dbPath = System.IO.Path.Combine(
        Windows.Storage.ApplicationData.Current.LocalFolder.Path, "db.sqlite");

    try
    {
        using (var db = new SQLiteConnection(dbPath))
        {
            db.RunInTransaction(() =>
                {
                    db.Insert(new SimpleAppointment()
                    {
                        Id = appointment.Id,
                        Subject = appointment.Subject,
                        Location = appointment.Location,
                        StartDate = appointment.StartDate,
                        EndDate = appointment.EndDate
                    });
                }
            );
        }
    }
    catch (Exception ex)
    {
        throw ex;
    }
}

public static SimpleAppointment GetAppointment(int id)
{
    var dbPath = System.IO.Path.Combine(
        Windows.Storage.ApplicationData.Current.LocalFolder.Path, "db.sqlite");
```

```
    try
    {
        using (var db = new SQLiteConnection(dbPath))
        {
            return db.Find<SimpleAppointment>(id);
        }
    }
    catch (Exception ex)
    {
        throw ex;
    }
}
```

SQLiteAccess.xaml.cs
```
private void SaveButton_Click(object sender, RoutedEventArgs e)
{
    SQLiteHelper.AddAppointment(new SimpleAppointment
                                {
                                    Subject = SubjectTextBox.Text,
                                    Location = LocationTextBox.Text,
                                    StartDate = StartDatePicker.Date.Date,
                                    EndDate = EndDatePicker.Date.Date
                                });

    ResultTextBlock.Text = "Appointment saved!";

}

private void ClearButton_Click(object sender, RoutedEventArgs e)
{
    SubjectTextBox.Text = String.Empty;
    LocationTextBox.Text = String.Empty;
    StartDatePicker.Date = DateTime.Now;
    EndDatePicker.Date = DateTime.Now;
}

private void LoadButton_Click(object sender, RoutedEventArgs e)
{
    SimpleAppointment appointment = SQLiteHelper.GetAppointment(1);

    SubjectTextBox.Text = appointment.Subject;
    LocationTextBox.Text = appointment.Location;
    StartDatePicker.Date = appointment.StartDate;
    EndDatePicker.Date = appointment.EndDate;
}

public SQLiteAccess()
{
    this.InitializeComponent();
    this.navigationHelper = new NavigationHelper(this);
```

```
    //Create a SQLite database if not exists
    SQLiteHelper.CreateDatabase();
}

SimpleAppointment.cs
public class SimpleAppointment
{
    [SQLite.PrimaryKey]
    [SQLite.AutoIncrement]
    public int Id { get; set; }
    public string Subject { get; set; }
    public string Location { get; set; }
    public DateTime StartDate { get; set; }
    public DateTime EndDate { get; set; }
}
```

After adding a reference to SQLite in your project, a file named SQLite.cs is added. This file is a wrapper that helps you use SQLite. Unfortunately, there's no official wrapper for SQLite to use with languages other than C#. But there are unofficial wrappers like Visual Basic Sqlite WinRT Wrapper (code.msdn.microsoft.com/windowsapps/Visual-Basic-Sqlite-WinRT-bf6fe131).

There is another good way to use the official library inside your project via a language other than C#. You just need to create a DLL (or WinRT component) and then add it to your project. A good explanation from Tim Heuer is at timheuer.com/blog/archive/2012/08/07/updated-how-to-using-sqlite-from-windows-store-apps.aspx.

Finally, to explore SQLite data inside your db, you can use a tool like SQLite Browser: sourceforge.net/projects/sqlitebrowser.

Retrieving Remote Data

Until now you've faced the management of user data that resides on the same machine where the app is running. More often, however, you need data that is reachable through the Internet using web services.

Happily, Windows Store apps can retrieve remote data through the Internet from different sources, such as Active Server Methods (ASMX), Windows Communication Services, and the new Windows Azure Mobile Services. In this section, we will go to into details on how to retrieve remote data from these sources.

Retrieving Data from Windows Communication Foundation

Windows Store apps support a subset of features of Windows Communication Foundation (WCF for short). Table 8-3 summarizes them.

Table 8-3. *WCF Features for Windows Store Apps*

Binding	`BasicHttpBinding`
	`NetTcpBinding`
	`NetHttpBinding`
	`CustomBinding`

Binding Elements	`BinaryMessageEncodingBindingElement`
	`TextMessageEncodingBindingElement`
	`ConnectionOrientedTransportBindingElement`
	`SslStreamSecurityBindingElement`
	`WindowsStreamSecurityBindingElement`
	`TcpTransportBindingElement`
	`HttpTransportBindingElement`
	`HttpsTransportBindingElement`
	`TransportSecurityBindingElement`

Enconding	`Text` `Binary`

Security Modes	`None`
	`Transport`
	`TransportWithMessageCredential`
	`TransportCredentialOnly (for BasicHttpBinding)`

ClientCredentialType	`None`
	`Basic`
	`Digest`
	`Negotiate`
	`Ntlm`
	`Windows`
	`Username (Message Security)`
	`Windows (Transport Security)`

Transfer Mode	`Buffered`
	`Streamed`
	`StreamedRequest`
	`StreamedResponse`

Serializer	`DataContractSerializer`
	`DataContractJsonSerializer`
	`XmlSerializer`

Misc	`ChannelFactory`
	`DuplexChannelFactory`
	`CallbackBehaviorAttribute`

If you need to add a WCF service to your project, nothing changes from the past. The steps are the following: right-click the Service Reference inside the project in Solution Explorer, choose Add Service Reference, type or paste the URL into the Address box, press the Go button, and once the service shows up, click the Ok button. Visual Studio 2013 takes care to create all related files for the connection. But good news always has bad news behind it: there's no Windows Communication Foundation XML configuration! In Visual Studio 2013, in a project different from a Windows Store app, you can change WCF bindings and behavior using the XML configuration. Instead, in a Windows Store app, you must edit any configuration in the Reference.cs related to the referenced service. To open this file (Figure 8-18), you need to enable the "All files" viewing option (1) and then open and edit Reference.cs file (2).

Figure 8-18. Reference.cs location

Once open, note that all operations are generated using the Task-based asynchronous pattern and the Configure() method is declared as partial class. But why? Unfortunately, every time you update the service reference, all changes to the Configure() method are overwritten. So, if you want to keep your changes stored, you need to implement a partial class for the client (pay attention to namespaces):

C#

FakeServiceClient.cs
```csharp
namespace Win8Organizer.CSharp.Model.FakeServiceReference
{
    public partial class FakeServiceClient :
        System.ServiceModel.ClientBase<Win8Organizer.Csharp.Model.FakeServiceReference.IfakeService>,
            Win8Organizer.Csharp.Model.FakeServiceReference.IfakeService
    {
        static partial void ConfigureEndpoint(System.ServiceModel.Description.ServiceEndpoint
serviceEndpoint,
            System.ServiceModel.Description.ClientCredentials clientCredentials)
        {
            if (serviceEndpoint.Name ==
                FakeServiceReference.FakeServiceClient
                    .EndpointConfiguration.BasicHttpBinding_IfakeService.ToString())
            {
                serviceEndpoint.Binding.SendTimeout = new System.TimeSpan(0, 1, 0);
            }
        }
    }
}
```

VB

```vbnet
Partial Public Class FakeServiceClient
    Inherits System.ServiceModel.ClientBase(Of FakeServiceReference.IFakeService)
    Implements FakeServiceReference.IFakeService
```

```
    Partial Private Shared Sub ConfigureEndpoint(ByVal serviceEndpoint As
System.ServiceModel.Description.ServiceEndpoint,
                                        ByVal clientCredentials As
System.ServiceModel.Description.ClientCredentials)
        ' Implementation is moved after the FakeServiceClient instantiation
        ' because partial method must have empty body
    End Sub

    Public Function GetSimpleAppointmentAsync() As Task(Of FakeServiceReference.SimpleAppointment)
                            Implements FakeServiceReference.IFakeService.
GetSimpleAppointmentAsync
        Return MyBase.Channel.GetSimpleAppointmentAsync
    End Function
End Class
```

Now that you've configured the service reference, you are ready to create a proxy class and retrieve data inside your application. Let's see how to add your app to a WCF Service to get appointments information.

■ **Note**   You need a copy of *Visual Studio Express 2013 for Web* to create a WCF Service.

First, take a look at the FakeService.svc:

C#

IFakeService.cs

```csharp
    [ServiceContract]
    public interface IFakeService
    {

        [OperationContract]
        SimpleAppointment GetSimpleAppointment();
    }

    // Use a data contract as illustrated in the sample below to add composite types to service operations.
    [DataContract]
    public class SimpleAppointment
    {
        [DataMember]
        public int Id { get; set; }

        [DataMember]
        public string Subject { get; set; }

        [DataMember]
        public string Location { get; set; }

        [DataMember]
        public DateTime StartDate { get; set; }
```

```
        [DataMember]
        public DateTime EndDate { get; set; }
    }
```

FakeService.svc.cs
```
public class FakeService : IFakeService
{
    SimpleAppointment IFakeService.GetSimpleAppointment()
    {
        return new SimpleAppointment()
        {
            Id = 1,
            Subject = "New Appointment",
            Location = "12, Kennedy Street, Washington",
            StartDate = DateTime.Now,
            EndDate = DateTime.Now.AddDays(1)
        };
    }
}
```

■ **Note**   You will reuse the same service for VB language.

In Figure 8-18 you saw how to add reference to the FakeService. Now let's see how to call the web service. Remember: web service calls must be asynchronous!

C#

WCFClient.xaml.cs
```
private async void LoadButton_Click(object sender, RoutedEventArgs e)
{
    try
    {
        FakeServiceReference.FakeServiceClient svc = new FakeServiceReference.FakeServiceClient();

        FakeServiceReference.SimpleAppointment appointment = await svc.GetSimpleAppointmentAsync();

        SubjectTextBox.Text = appointment.Subject;
        LocationTextBox.Text = appointment.Location;
        StartDatePicker.Date = appointment.StartDate;
        EndDatePicker.Date = appointment.EndDate;
    }
    catch
    {
        ResultTextBlock.Text = "Oops! Something went wrong!";
    }
}
```

VB

```vb
Private Async Sub LoadButton_Click(sender As Object, e As RoutedEventArgs)
    Try
        Dim svc As New FakeServiceReference.FakeServiceClient

        If svc.Endpoint.Name = FakeServiceReference.FakeServiceClient.EndpointConfiguration.
BasicHttpBinding_IFakeService.ToString() Then
            svc.Endpoint.Binding.SendTimeout = New System.TimeSpan(0, 1, 0)
        End If

        Dim appointment As FakeServiceReference.SimpleAppointment = Await
svc.GetSimpleAppointmentAsync()

        SubjectTextBox.Text = appointment.Subject
        LocationTextBox.Text = appointment.Location
        StartDatePicker.[Date] = appointment.StartDate
        EndDatePicker.[Date] = appointment.EndDate
    Catch
        ResultTextBlock.Text = "Oops! Something went wrong!"
    End Try
End Sub
```

WinRT provides also the SyndicationApi. It is a set of classes that helps retrieve feeds from the Web. The usage is very simple: the class SyndicationClient performs the whole process, starting a connection, reading the feed, and returning a list of SyndicationItem:

C#

RssHelper.cs
```csharp
public async static Task<string> GetFeedTitleAsync()
{
    string response = String.Empty;
    SyndicationFeed feed = new SyndicationFeed();
    SyndicationClient client = new SyndicationClient();

    try
    {
        feed = await client.RetrieveFeedAsync(
            new Uri("http://www.apress.com/index.php/dailydeals/index/rss"));

        response = feed.GetXmlDocument(SyndicationFormat.Rss20).GetXml();
    }
    catch (Exception ex)
    {
        SyndicationErrorStatus status = SyndicationError.GetStatus(ex.HResult);
        if (status == SyndicationErrorStatus.InvalidXml)
        {
            response += "Invalid XML!";
        }
```

```
        if (status == SyndicationErrorStatus.Unknown)
        {
            response = ex.Message;
        }
    }

    return response;
}
```

VB

RSSHelper.vb
```
Public NotInheritable Class RssHelper
    Private Sub New()
    End Sub
    Public Shared Async Function GetFeedTitleAsync() As Task(Of String)
        Dim response As String = [String].Empty
        Dim feed As New SyndicationFeed()
        Dim client As New SyndicationClient()

        Try
            feed = Await client.RetrieveFeedAsync(New
Uri("http://www.apress.com/index.php/dailydeals/index/rss"))

            response = feed.GetXmlDocument(SyndicationFormat.Rss20).GetXml()
        Catch ex As Exception
            Dim status As SyndicationErrorStatus = SyndicationError.GetStatus(ex.HResult)
            If status = SyndicationErrorStatus.InvalidXml Then
                response += "Invalid XML!"
            End If

            If status = SyndicationErrorStatus.Unknown Then
                response = ex.Message
            End If
        End Try

        Return response
    End Function
End Class
```

Starting with Windows 8.1 there is new namespace to handle HTTP web requests and REST web services: Windows.Web.Http. Inside this namespace you can find several helpful objects to achieve simple or complex tasks related to the Web. The features include the following:

- Handling HTTP common verbs (DELETE, GET, PUT and POST)

- Support for common authentication settings and patterns

- Support for SSL

- Customized filters

- Full support for cookies

- Asynchronous operations

The main class is HTTPClient and it allows you to send and receive requests over the HTTP protocol. Using the filtering mechanism, it is possible to customize the request based on the scenario:

C#

HTTPClient.xaml.cs
```
private async void navigationHelper_LoadState(object sender, LoadStateEventArgs e)
{
    // TODO: Create an appropriate data model for your problem domain to replace the sample data
    var item = await SampleDataSource.GetItemAsync((String)e.NavigationParameter);
    //this.DefaultViewModel["Item"] = item;

    ResultTextBlock.Text = await
        new HttpClient().GetStringAsync(
            new Uri("http://www.apress.com/index.php/dailydeals/index/rss"
            )
        );
}
```

VB

HTTPClient.xaml.vb
```
Private Async Sub NavigationHelper_LoadState(sender As Object, e As Common.LoadStateEventArgs)
    ' TODO: Create an appropriate data model for your problem domain to replace the sample data
    Dim item As Data.SampleDataItem = Await
Data.SampleDataSource.GetItemAsync(DirectCast(e.NavigationParameter, String))
    Me.DefaultViewModel("Item") = item

    ResultTextBlock.Text = Await New HttpClient().
        GetStringAsync(New Uri("http://www.apress.com/index.php/dailydeals/index/rss"))
End Sub
```

Retrieving Data from Windows Azure Mobile Services

Some of the big news these days about Windows Store apps is the full support for Windows Azure Mobile Service, which allows you to store structured data on the cloud and provide authentication, push notification, and scalability. All of these features can be configured using a very intuitive portal (which is the same for Microsoft Windows Azure). Let's start from beginning!

First, you need an active Microsoft Account. It can be created at https://signup.live.com/. After creating the account, you must connect to Windows Azure Portal using the Microsoft Account at https://windows.azure.com/ and activate the trial period for Windows Azure (it will last 90 days) and participate in the preview program. Then, in the Windows Azure menu (Figure 8-19) click the New button. Then select Compute and choose Create from the Mobile Service items (Figure 8-20). At this point, you have created a mobile service. You need to provide a URL, like buildingwindows8appsfromthegroundupmobileservice (it is the name of the mobile service and it will appear in the final URL like this: https://buildingwindows8appsfromthegroundupmobileservice.azure-mobile.net/), choose to create or re-use a database, and select the region (Figure 8-21). Click the Next button and type all the information about the new database, such as name, server, login, and password, and then press the Complete button (Figure 8-22).

Figure 8-19. *Windows Azure menu*

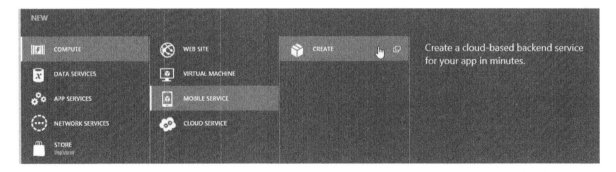

Figure 8-20. *Mobile Service menu*

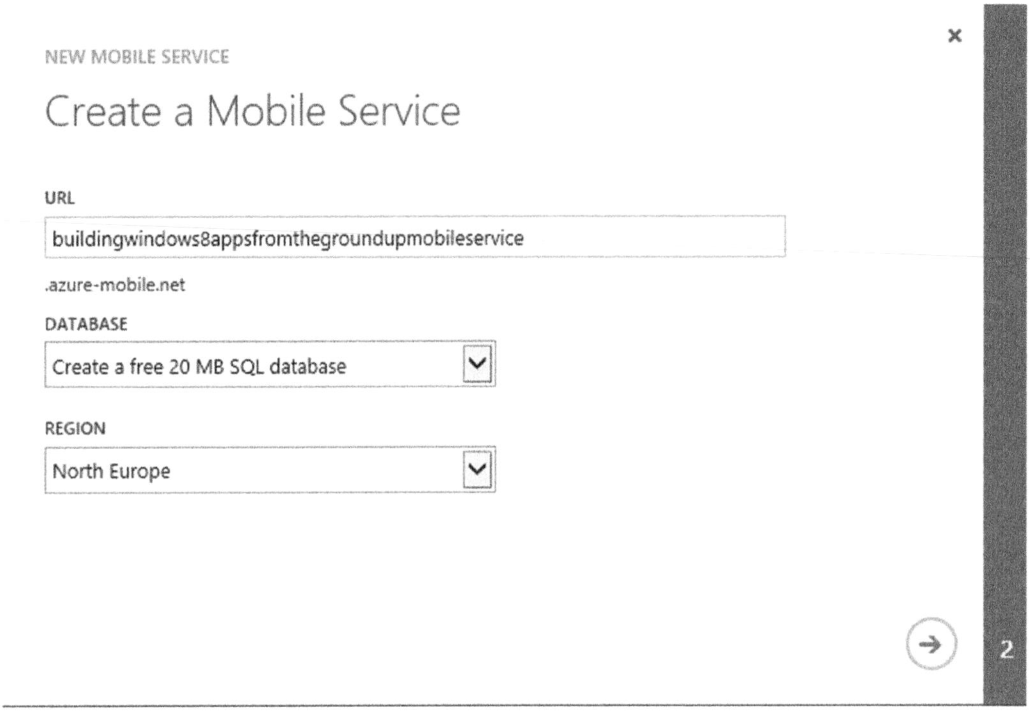

NEW MOBILE SERVICE

Create a Mobile Service

URL

buildingwindows8appsfromthegroundupmobileservice

.azure-mobile.net

DATABASE

Create a free 20 MB SQL database ▾

REGION

North Europe ▾

→   2

Figure 8-21. *Mobile service creation (1)*

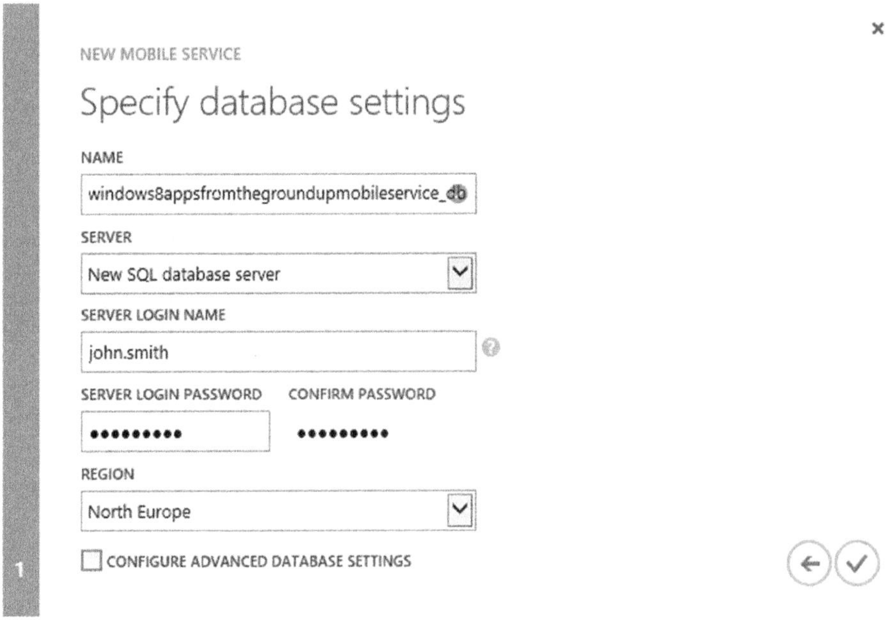

NEW MOBILE SERVICE

Specify database settings

NAME

windows8appsfromthegroundupmobileservice_db

SERVER

New SQL database server ▾

SERVER LOGIN NAME

john.smith   ⊚

SERVER LOGIN PASSWORD   CONFIRM PASSWORD

•••••••••   •••••••••

REGION

North Europe ▾

☐ CONFIGURE ADVANCED DATABASE SETTINGS

← ✓

Figure 8-22. *Mobile service creation (2)*

Through these steps, you have created your first mobile service and you can check out its state using the Windows Azure Portal in the main page by selecting the Mobile Services item on the menu: you can see your buildingwindows8appsfromthegroundupmobileservice in Figure 8-23.

Figure 8-23. *Mobile services summary in Windows Azure Portal*

Clicking the mobile service name brings you to its dashboard (Figure 8-24).

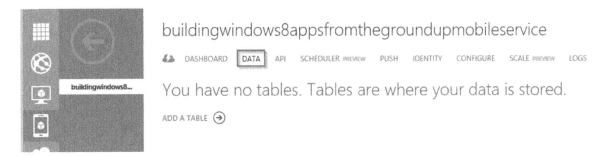

Figure 8-24. *Mobile service dashboard*

In it, select DATA and create a new table named SimpleAppointment by using the "Add a table" button (Figure 8-25).

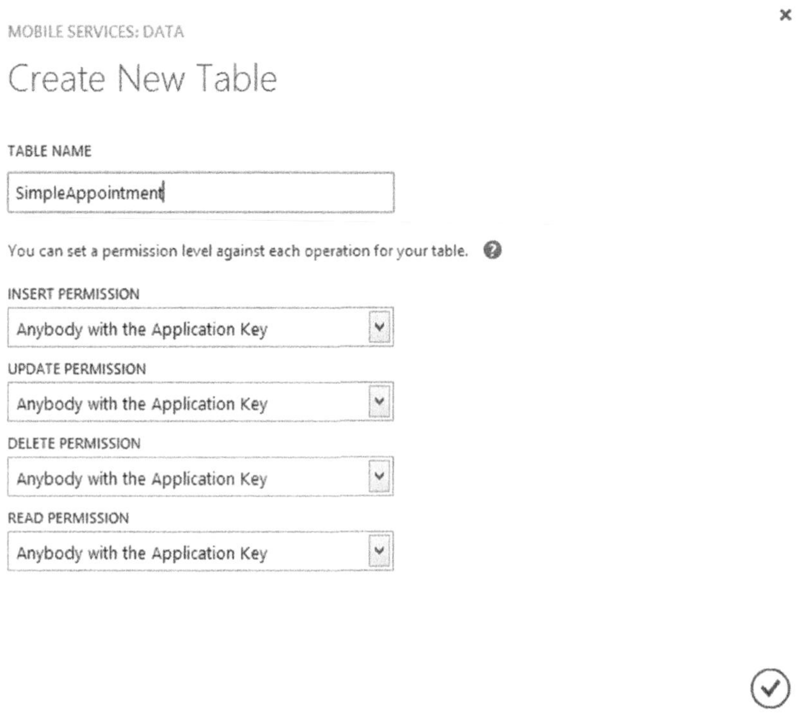

MOBILE SERVICES: DATA

Create New Table

TABLE NAME

SimpleAppointment

You can set a permission level against each operation for your table. ❓

INSERT PERMISSION

Anybody with the Application Key

UPDATE PERMISSION

Anybody with the Application Key

DELETE PERMISSION

Anybody with the Application Key

READ PERMISSION

Anybody with the Application Key

Figure 8-25. *New table creation wizard*

Finally, you have your table (Figure 8-26) and it has just one column (Figure 8-27) to handle all your data.

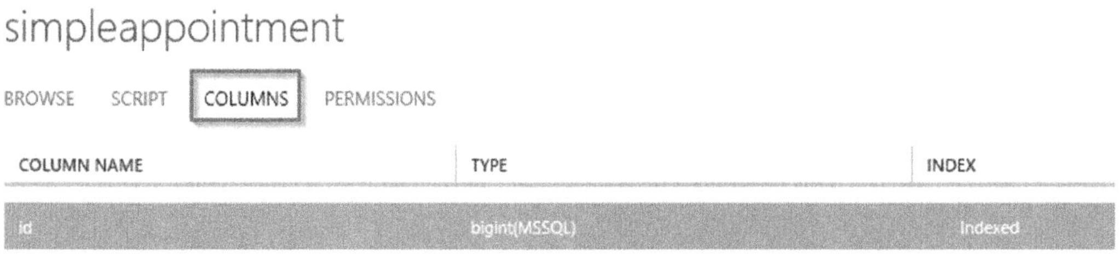

simpleappointment

BROWSE   SCRIPT   COLUMNS   PERMISSIONS

COLUMN NAME	TYPE	INDEX
id	bigint(MSSQL)	Indexed

Figure 8-26. *SimpleAppointment dashboard*

BROWSE   SCRIPT   COLUMNS   PERMISSIONS

COLUMN NAME	TYPE	INDEX
id	bigint(MSSQL)	Indexed

Figure 8-27. *SimpleAppointment columns*

Other items in the Table menu are the following:

- **Browse**: To list all data

- **Script**: To apply some logic to CRUD operations in JavaScript code without the need of an external application (Figure 8-28)

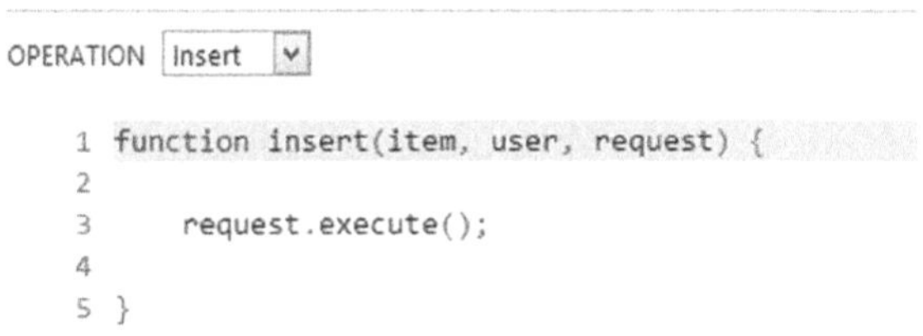

```
OPERATION  Insert  ⌄

1 function insert(item, user, request) {
2
3     request.execute();
4
5 }
```

Figure 8-28. *Script section in Table dashboard*

- **Permission**: To set user permissions to CRUD operations (Figure 8-29)

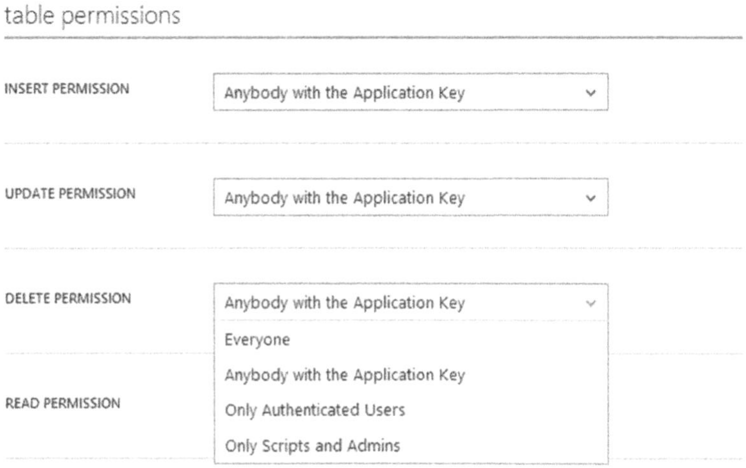

table permissions

| INSERT PERMISSION | Anybody with the Application Key ⌄ |

| UPDATE PERMISSION | Anybody with the Application Key ⌄ |

DELETE PERMISSION	Anybody with the Application Key ⌄
	Everyone
	Anybody with the Application Key
READ PERMISSION	Only Authenticated Users
	Only Scripts and Admins

Figure 8-29. *Permissions section in Table dashboard*

Let's see how to call this service from your Organizer. First, you need to install the Mobile Services SDK (download it at www.windowsazure.com/en-us/develop/mobile/developer-tools/). You can also use a quick and simple NuGet command instead of the previous steps:

```
Install-Package WindowsAzure.MobileServices
```

Then, from your project inside Visual Studio 2013 right-click the project name, select Add, and then select Connected Services (Figure 8-30). Now, in the Service Manager window, select Mobile Services and Import Subscription to open a pop-up to load the subscription file for your Azure Account. If you don't have the subscription file (*.publishsettings), you can simply click Download Subscription File to connect to your account and download it. Once the file is imported, you need to refresh the Services Manager window and your Mobile Service will appear. Just click it and press OK (Figure 8-31).

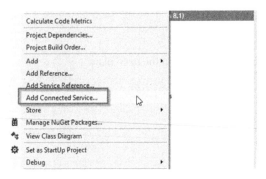

Figure 8-30. *Add a Windows Azure Mobile Service to your project*

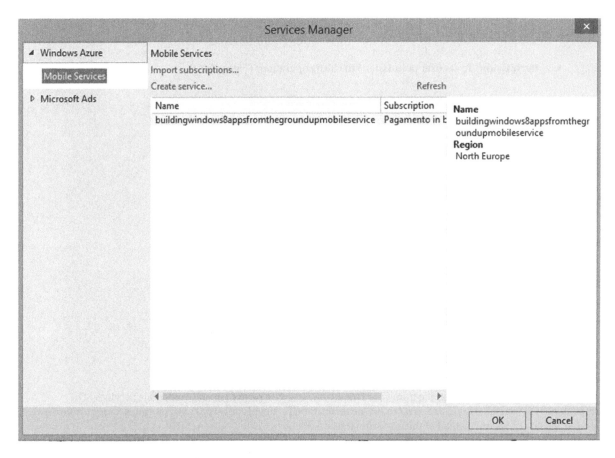

Figure 8-31. *Services Manager window*

To connect your app to the Windows Azure Mobile Service, you need an API key that is automatically added in the previous step inside the `App.xaml.cs` or `App.xaml.vb` and is used to initialize the `MobileServiceClient` class:

C#

```
public static Microsoft.WindowsAzure.MobileServices.MobileServiceClient
    buildingwindows8appsfromthegroundupmobileserviceClient =
    new Microsoft.WindowsAzure.MobileServices.MobileServiceClient(
"https://buildingwindows8appsfromthegroundupmobileservice.azure-mobile.net/",
"YOUR_APP_KEY");
```

VB

```
Public Shared bw8agu_mobileserviceClient As New Microsoft.WindowsAzure.MobileServices.MobileServiceClient(
"https://buildingwindows8appsfromthegroundupmobileservice.azure-mobile.net/",
"YOUR_APP_KEY")
```

This key can be retrieved in the Windows Azure Mobile Services dashboard via the "Connect an existing Windows Store app" item (Figure 8-32).

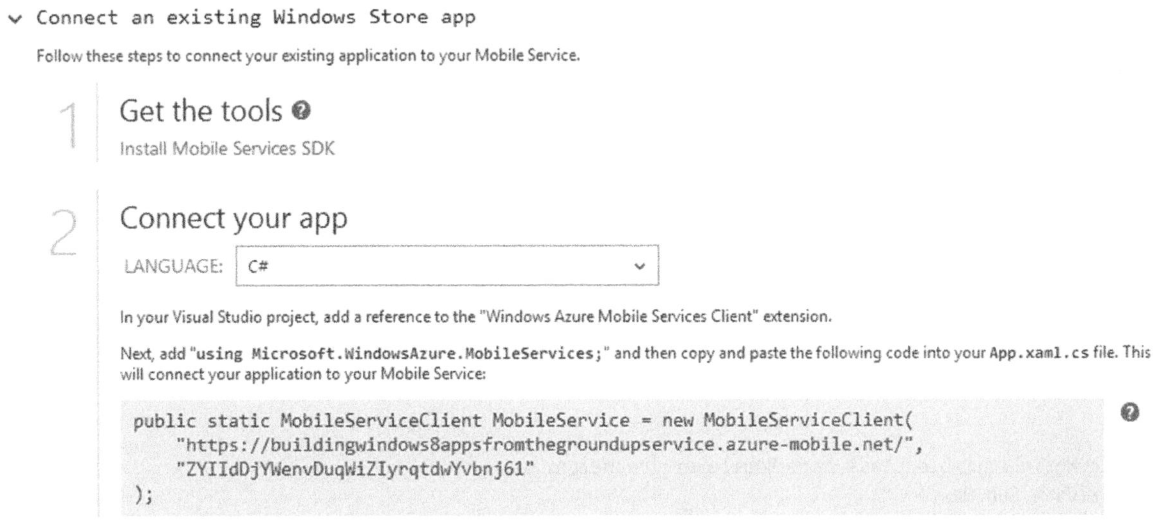

Figure 8-32. *Mobile Service key and address*

Here is how to execute some basic operations on the table behind the Windows Azure Mobile Service just created:

C#

```
public static class AzureMobileServicesHelper
{
    public async static void InsertDataFromAzureMobileSvc(SimpleAppointment item)
    {
        await App.bw8agu_mobileserviceClient.GetTable<SimpleAppointment>()
            .InsertAsync(item);
    }
}
```

```
    public async static Task<MobileServiceCollection<SimpleAppointment, SimpleAppointment>>
GetDataFromAzureMobileSvc()
    {
        try
        {
            IMobileServiceTable<SimpleAppointment> table =
                App.bw8agu_mobileserviceClient
                .GetTable<SimpleAppointment>();

            return await table.ToCollectionAsync<SimpleAppointment>();
        }
        catch (Exception ex)
        { throw ex; }
    }

    public static void UpdateDataFromAzureMobileSvc(SimpleAppointment item)
    {
        try
        {
            IMobileServiceTable<SimpleAppointment> table =
App.bw8agu_mobileserviceClient.GetTable<SimpleAppointment>();

            table.UpdateAsync(item);
        }
        catch (Exception ex)
        {
            throw ex;
        }
    }
}
```

VB

```
Public NotInheritable Class AzureMobileServicesHelper
    Private Sub New()
    End Sub
    Public Shared Async Sub InsertDataFromAzureMobileSvc(item As SimpleAppointment)
        Await App.bw8agu_mobileserviceClient.GetTable(Of SimpleAppointment)().InsertAsync(item)
    End Sub

    Public Shared Async Function GetDataFromAzureMobileSvc() As Task
                As Task(Of MobileServiceCollection(Of SimpleAppointment, SimpleAppointment))
        Try
            Dim table As IMobileServiceTable(Of SimpleAppointment) =
                App.bw8agu_mobileserviceClient.GetTable(Of SimpleAppointment)()

            Return Await table.ToCollectionAsync()
        Catch ex As Exception
            Throw ex
        End Try
    End Function
```

```vbnet
    Public Shared Async Sub UpdateDataFromAzureMobileSvc(item As SimpleAppointment)
        Try
            Dim table As IMobileServiceTable(Of SimpleAppointment) =
                App.bw8agu_mobileserviceClient.GetTable(Of SimpleAppointment)()

            Await table.UpdateAsync(item)
        Catch ex As Exception
            Throw ex
        End Try
    End Sub
End Class
```

The following code can be used to call one of these operations.

C#

AzureMobileServices.xaml.cs

```csharp
private void SaveButton_Click(object sender, RoutedEventArgs e)
{
    try
    {
        AzureMobileServicesHelper.InsertDataFromAzureMobileSvc(new SimpleAppointment
                                        {
                                            Subject = SubjectTextBox.Text,
                                            Location = LocationTextBox.Text,
                                            StartDate = StartDatePicker.Date.Date,
                                            EndDate = EndDatePicker.Date.Date
                                        });

        ResultTextBlock.Text = "Appointment saved!";
    }
    catch (Exception ex)
    {
        ResultTextBlock.Text = ex.Message;
    }

}

private void ClearButton_Click(object sender, RoutedEventArgs e)
{
    SubjectTextBox.Text = String.Empty;
    LocationTextBox.Text = String.Empty;
    StartDatePicker.Date = DateTime.Now;
    EndDatePicker.Date = DateTime.Now;
}
```

```csharp
private async void LoadButton_Click(object sender, RoutedEventArgs e)
{
    SimpleAppointment appointment = (await
AzureMobileServicesHelper.GetDataFromAzureMobileSvc()).FirstOrDefault();

    SubjectTextBox.Text = appointment.Subject;
    LocationTextBox.Text = appointment.Location;
    StartDatePicker.Date = appointment.StartDate;
    EndDatePicker.Date = appointment.EndDate;
}
```

VB

AzureMobileServices.xaml.vb
```vb
Private Sub SaveButton_Click(sender As Object, e As RoutedEventArgs)
    Try
        AzureMobileServicesHelper.InsertDataFromAzureMobileSvc(New SimpleAppointment() With { _
            .Subject = SubjectTextBox.Text, _
            .Location = LocationTextBox.Text, _
            .StartDate = StartDatePicker.[Date].[Date], _
            .EndDate = EndDatePicker.[Date].[Date] _
        })

        ResultTextBlock.Text = "Appointment saved!"
    Catch ex As Exception
        ResultTextBlock.Text = ex.Message
    End Try
End Sub

Private Sub ClearButton_Click(sender As Object, e As RoutedEventArgs)
    SubjectTextBox.Text = [String].Empty
    LocationTextBox.Text = [String].Empty
    StartDatePicker.[Date] = DateTime.Now
    EndDatePicker.[Date] = DateTime.Now
End Sub

Private Async Sub LoadButton_Click(sender As Object, e As RoutedEventArgs)
    Dim appointment As SimpleAppointment = (
        Await AzureMobileServicesHelper.GetDataFromAzureMobileSvc()).FirstOrDefault()
    SubjectTextBox.Text = appointment.Subject
    LocationTextBox.Text = appointment.Location
    StartDatePicker.[Date] = appointment.StartDate
    EndDatePicker.[Date] = appointment.EndDate
End Sub
```

Data just inserted can be showed in the Mobile Services panel on the portal in the used table inside the Data section (Figure 8-33).

simpleappointment

BROWSE   SCRIPT   COLUMNS   PERMISSIONS

id	Subject	Location	StartDate	EndDate
1	First Appointment	10, Wall Street, NY	2013-10-19T22:00:00+00:00	2013-10-19T22:00:00+00:00

Figure 8-33. *SimpleAppointment records*

Last but not least, the Windows Azure Mobile Services portal is a simple and useful environment to check the state and the usage of your services. Indeed, the dashboard shows a chart containing all the API calls, CPU times, and data out info (Figure 8-34). You can also manage notification, scalability, and authentication.

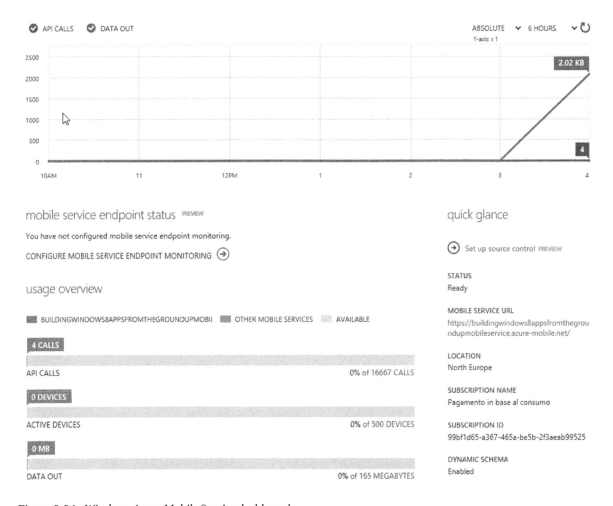

Figure 8-34. *Windows Azure Mobile Service dashboard*

Managing User Info

In this section you'll get a quick look at user info management for issues such as roaming credentials, single sign-on using a web authentication broker, and how to manage user contact. Be aware that some of these features require a valid Microsoft Account and a Windows Store developer account (further information can be found in Chapter 11).

Credential Roaming

With these features, apps can store passwords inside the password vault using the `Windows.Security.Credentials` namespace. The password vault, also called as Credential Locker, is a safe place that allows the credential to roam to other trusted devices. The entire mechanism is based on the following steps.

1. Sign in on Windows 8 using your own credentials. This will mark the machine as a trusted device.

2. Let the user choose to save or not save their password.

Through these steps, credentials will be roamed to the cloud and are available to the other devices (of course if they are trusted devices too!). Figure 8-35 shows the `Windows.Security.Credentials` classes.

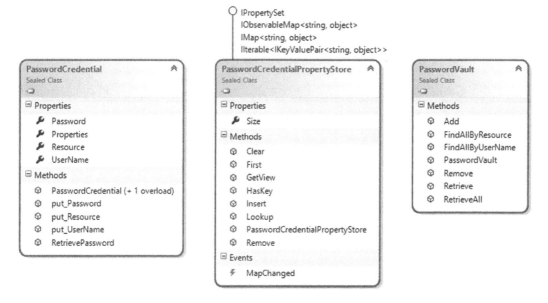

Figure 8-35. *Windows.Security.Credentials classes*

Now, let's see how to memorize and retrieve passwords using the PasswordVault class inside the Login Settings panel (Figure 8-36).

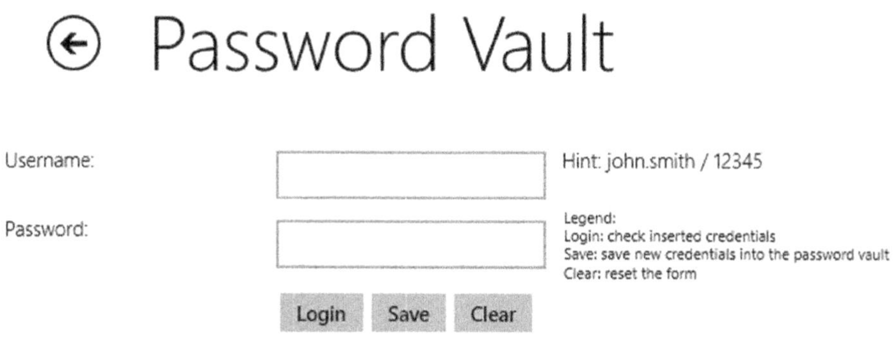

⊕ Password Vault

Username: [   ]   Hint: john.smith / 12345

Password: [   ]   Legend:
Login: check inserted credentials
Save: save new credentials into the password vault
Clear: reset the form

[Login]   [Save]   [Clear]

Figure 8-36. *Login Settings panel*

C#

PasswordVault.xaml.cs

```
private void LoginButton_Click(object sender, RoutedEventArgs e)
{
    if (PasswordVaultHelper.CheckPassword(UsernameTextBox.Text, PasswordTextBox.Password))
    {
        ResultTextBlock.Text = "Login succeeded!";
    }
    else
    {
        ResultTextBlock.Text = "Login failed!";
    }
    ClearTextboxes();
}

private void SaveButton_Click(object sender, RoutedEventArgs e)
{
    PasswordVaultHelper.SavePasswordToVault(UsernameTextBox.Text, PasswordTextBox.Password);

    ResultTextBlock.Text = "Credentials saved!";
    ClearTextboxes();
}

private void ClearButton_Click(object sender, RoutedEventArgs e)
{
    ClearTextboxes();
    ResultTextBlock.Text = String.Empty;
}
```

```csharp
private void ClearTextboxes()
{
    UsernameTextBox.Text = String.Empty;
    PasswordTextBox.Password = String.Empty;
}
```

PasswordVaultHelper.cs
```csharp
public class PasswordVaultHelper
{
    private static PasswordVault vault =
        new Windows.Security.Credentials.PasswordVault();

    public static IList<PasswordCredential> LoadPasswordVault()
    {
        //Load all credentials
        IReadOnlyList<PasswordCredential> creds = vault.RetrieveAll();

        return creds.ToList<PasswordCredential>();
    }

    public static bool CheckPassword(string username, string password)
    {
        bool res = false;

        try
        {
            IReadOnlyList<PasswordCredential> creds = vault.FindAllByUserName(username);

            foreach (PasswordCredential cred in creds)
            {
                cred.RetrievePassword();
                res = cred.Password == password;
            }
        }
        catch
        {
            //do nothing
        }

        return res;
    }

    public static void SavePasswordToVault(string username, string password)
    {
        LoadPasswordVault();

        PasswordCredential cred = new PasswordCredential("BW8AGU", username, password);

        vault.Add(cred);
    }
}
```

VB

PasswordVault.xaml.vb

```vb
Private Sub LoginButton_Click(sender As Object, e As RoutedEventArgs)
    If PasswordVaultHelper.CheckPassword(UsernameTextBox.Text, PasswordTextBox.Password) Then
        ResultTextBlock.Text = "Login succeeded!"
    Else
        ResultTextBlock.Text = "Login failed!"
    End If
    ClearTextboxes()
End Sub

Private Sub SaveButton_Click(sender As Object, e As RoutedEventArgs)
    PasswordVaultHelper.SavePasswordToVault(UsernameTextBox.Text, PasswordTextBox.Password)

    ResultTextBlock.Text = "Credentials saved!"
    ClearTextboxes()
End Sub

Private Sub ClearButton_Click(sender As Object, e As RoutedEventArgs)
    ClearTextboxes()
    ResultTextBlock.Text = [String].Empty
End Sub

Private Sub ClearTextboxes()
    UsernameTextBox.Text = [String].Empty
    PasswordTextBox.Password = [String].Empty
End Sub
```

PasswordVaultHelper.vb

```vb
Public Class PasswordVaultHelper
    Private Shared vault As PasswordVault = New Windows.Security.Credentials.PasswordVault()

    Public Shared Function LoadPasswordVault() As IList(Of PasswordCredential)
        'Load all credentials
        Dim creds As IReadOnlyList(Of PasswordCredential) = vault.RetrieveAll()

        Return creds.ToList()
    End Function

    Public Shared Function CheckPassword(username As String, password As String) As Boolean
        Dim res As Boolean = False

        Try
            Dim creds As IReadOnlyList(Of PasswordCredential) = vault.FindAllByUserName(username)

            For Each cred As PasswordCredential In creds
                cred.RetrievePassword()
                res = cred.Password = password
            Next
            'do nothing
```

```
        Catch
        End Try

        Return res
    End Function

    Public Shared Sub SavePasswordToVault(username As String, password As String)
        LoadPasswordVault()

        Dim cred As New PasswordCredential("BW8AGU", username, password)

        vault.Add(cred)
    End Sub
End Class
```

The Credential Locker also allows you to store multiple credentials, and it's possible to set a default one using the Default property in the PasswordCredential.Properties collection. Besides, you can share credentials across apps using the ApplicationSuiteId property.

Working with Single Sign-On

Many social networks or picture-sharing web sites provide OAuth or Open ID protocols. Using these protocols with single sign-on (SSO), you can avoid re-typing passwords each time you switch between devices. In a Windows Store app, the WebAuthenticationBroker class handles this mechanism without any further interaction by users. Table 8-4 shows the steps to set SSO for a Windows Store app on both the developer and online provider sides.

Table 8-4. *SSO Configuration Steps*

SSO for Developers	1. Use the WebAuthenticationBroker.AuthenticateAsync(WebAuthenticationOptions options, Uri requestUri) method to automatically generate a *callbackUri* checking and merging the value of the app's package *security identifier* **SID** with ms-app://.
	2. Retrieve your app's SID using the WebAuthenticationBroker. GetCurrentApplicationCallbackUri method.
	3. Use the ms-app://<app's-sid> to register your app with your online provider(*).
	4. Use the WebAuthenticationOptions.SilentMode flag to prevent the visualization of any login dialog box from the online provider.
SSO for Online Providers	1. Permit apps to register the ms-app:// scheme as its redirect URI.
	2. Allow the app to use only registered redirect URIs.
	3. Use the protocol flows that don't require implicit grants (e.g., OAuth 2.0).

(*): The ms-app URI can be found on the Developer Portal under the "Manage your cloud services" setting and then "Application Authentication" under Advanced Features.

Let's have a quick look at the WebAuthenticationBroker class. In the following code, you access Facebook and send a post. Remember that you must register the app in the Facebook Developer page using this simple tutorial: https://developers.facebook.com/docs/appcenter/.

C#

```csharp
public static class FacebookHelper
{
    private const string _appID = "<your_app_id>";   //retrieved from Facebook app page
    private const string _url = "https://www.facebook.com/connect/login_success.html";
    private const string _wallUrl = "https://graph.facebook.com/<your_facebook_username>/feed";
    private static string _accessToken = String.Empty;
    private static string _urlAccessToken = String.Empty;

    public static async Task<bool> Authenticate()
    {
        bool res = false;

        try
        {
            String FacebookURL = "https://www.facebook.com/dialog/oauth?client_id=" +
                Uri.EscapeDataString(_appID) +
                "&redirect_uri=" + Uri.EscapeDataString(_url) +
                "&scope=read_stream,user_about_me,read_stream," +
                "publish_stream&display=popup&response_type=token";

            System.Uri requestUri = new Uri(FacebookURL);
            System.Uri callbackUri = new Uri(_url);

            WebAuthenticationResult WebAuthenticationResult =
                await WebAuthenticationBroker.AuthenticateAsync(
                                    WebAuthenticationOptions.None,
                                    requestUri,
                                    callbackUri);

            if (WebAuthenticationResult.ResponseStatus ==
                WebAuthenticationStatus.Success)
            {
                _urlAccessToken = WebAuthenticationResult.ResponseData.ToString();
                _accessToken = _urlAccessToken.Substring(_urlAccessToken.IndexOf('=') + 1);
            }
            else if (WebAuthenticationResult.ResponseStatus ==
                WebAuthenticationStatus.ErrorHttp)
            {
                throw new Exception("HTTP Error: " +
                    WebAuthenticationResult.ResponseErrorDetail.ToString());
            }
            else
            {
                throw new Exception("Error: " +
                    WebAuthenticationResult.ResponseStatus.ToString());
            }

            res = true;
        }
```

```
        catch (Exception Error)
        {
            //log the error somewhere
        }

        return res;
    }

    public static async Task<string> PostOnFacebook(string text)
    {
        string res = String.Empty;

        try
        {
            var client = new HttpClient();

            // Create the HttpContent for the form to be posted.
            var requestContent = new FormUrlEncodedContent(new[] {
                    new KeyValuePair<string, string>("message", text)
                });

            // Get the response.
            HttpResponseMessage response = await client.PostAsync(
                "https://graph.facebook.com/<your_facebook_username>/feed?access_token=" + _accessToken,
                requestContent);

            // Get the response content.
            HttpContent responseContent = response.Content;

            // Get the stream of the content.
            using (var reader = new StreamReader(await responseContent.ReadAsStreamAsync()))
            {
                // Write the output.
                res = reader.ReadToEnd();
            }
        }
        catch (Exception ex)
        {
            //log the error somewhere
            res = ex.Message;
        }

        return res;
    }
}

FacebookAuth.xaml.cs
private async void Authenticate()
{
    bool res = await FacebookHelper.Authenticate();
```

```csharp
        if (!res)
        {
            ResultTextBlock.Text = "Something went wrong!";
        }
    }
}

private void PostButton_Click(object sender, RoutedEventArgs e)
{
    Authenticate();

    PostIt();
}

private async void PostIt()
{
    ResultTextBlock.Text = await FacebookHelper.PostOnFacebook(MessageTextBox.Text);
}
```

VB

FacebookHelper.vb

```vb
Public NotInheritable Class FacebookHelper
    Private Sub New()
    End Sub
    Private Const _appID As String = "<your_app_id>"
    'retrieved from Facebook app page
    Private Const _url As String = "https://www.facebook.com/connect/login_success.html"
    Private Const _wallUrl As String = "https://graph.facebook.com/<your_facebook_username>/feed"
    Private Shared _accessToken As String = [String].Empty
    Private Shared _urlAccessToken As String = [String].Empty

    Public Shared Async Function Authenticate() As Task(Of Boolean)
        Dim res As Boolean = False

        Try
            Dim FacebookURL As [String] = "https://www.facebook.com/dialog/oauth?client_id=" +
                Uri.EscapeDataString(_appID) + "&redirect_uri=" + Uri.EscapeDataString(_url) +
                "&scope=read_stream,user_about_me,read_stream," +
                "publish_stream&display=popup&response_type=token"

            Dim requestUri As System.Uri = New Uri(FacebookURL)
            Dim callbackUri As System.Uri = New Uri(_url)

            Dim WebAuthenticationResult As WebAuthenticationResult =
                Await WebAuthenticationBroker.AuthenticateAsync(WebAuthenticationOptions.None,
requestUri, callbackUri)

            If WebAuthenticationResult.ResponseStatus = WebAuthenticationStatus.Success Then
                _urlAccessToken = WebAuthenticationResult.ResponseData.ToString()
                _accessToken = _urlAccessToken.Substring(_urlAccessToken.IndexOf("="c) + 1)
```

```vb
        ElseIf WebAuthenticationResult.ResponseStatus = WebAuthenticationStatus.ErrorHttp Then
            Throw New Exception("HTTP Error: " + WebAuthenticationResult.ResponseErrorDetail.
ToString())
        Else
            Throw New Exception("Error: " + WebAuthenticationResult.ResponseStatus.ToString())
        End If

        res = True
        'log the error somewhere
    Catch [Error] As Exception
    End Try

    Return res
End Function

Public Shared Async Function PostOnFacebook(text As String) As Task(Of String)
    Dim res As String = [String].Empty

    Try
        Dim client = New HttpClient()

        ' Create the HttpContent for the form to be posted.
        Dim requestContent = New FormUrlEncodedContent(New () {
                                New KeyValuePair(Of String, String)("message", text)})

        ' Get the response.
        Dim response As HttpResponseMessage = Await client.PostAsync(
Convert.ToString("https://graph.facebook.com/<your_facebook_username>/feed?access_token=") & _
accessToken, requestContent)

        ' Get the response content.
        Dim responseContent As HttpContent = response.Content

        ' Get the stream of the content.
        Using reader = New StreamReader(Await responseContent.ReadAsStreamAsync())
            ' Write the output.
            res = reader.ReadToEnd()
        End Using
    Catch ex As Exception
        'log the error somewhere
        res = ex.Message
    End Try

    Return res
End Function
End Class
```

FacebookAuth.xaml.vb

```vb
Private Async Sub Authenticate()
    Dim res As Boolean = Await FacebookHelper.Authenticate()
```

```
    If Not res Then
        ResultTextBlock.Text = "Something went wrong!"
    End If
End Sub

Private Sub PostButton_Click(sender As Object, e As RoutedEventArgs)
    Authenticate()

    PostIt()
End Sub

Private Async Sub PostIt()
    ResultTextBlock.Text = Await FacebookHelper.PostOnFacebook(MessageTextBox.Text)
End Sub
```

Calling the method Authenticate() will open up Facebook login form (Figure 8-37).

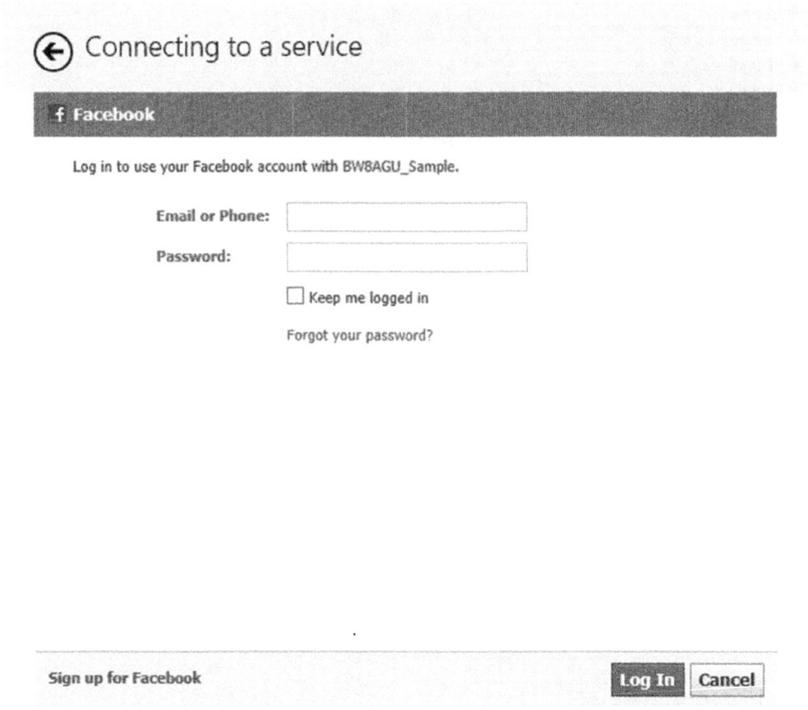

Figure 8-37. *Facebook login pop-up*

Managing User Contacts

The Windows Store API provides an entire namespace to manage contacts: the Windows.ApplicationModel.Contacts namespace. With it you can easily select one or more contacts from your contacts and retrieve information that you need. Figure 8-38 shows the main classes inside the namespace.

Figure 8-38. *Windows.ApplicationModel.Contacts main classes*

The main class is `ContactPicker`. It has the same functionality of the `FilePicker` classes; the only difference that instead of files, you can select contacts.

Before launch, use the `PickSingleContactAsync()` or `PickMultipleContactsAsync()` method to show the picker. It's suggested to set a few properties, such as the following:

- `CommitButtonText`, to help the user to confirm selection

- `SelectionMode`, to set what kind of information you need to retrieve. It allows `ContactSelectionMode` enumeration values.

- Contacts, to select the entire contact

- Fields, to select just certain fields

- DesiredFields, to set what fields you want to use

- The Add() class method accepts as an input a KnownContactField. It allows multiple field declarations, filtering the contact search. For example, if you set just one field, all contacts with that field filled are considered. If you set more than one field, all contacts with any of these filled are considered.

Here is how to use the ContactPicker class.

C#

```
ContactPicker.xaml.cs
private void ContactPickerButton_Click(object sender, RoutedEventArgs e)
{
    GetContact();
}

private async void GetContact()
{
    //Create a new instance of ContactPicker class
    var contactPicker = new Windows.ApplicationModel.Contacts.ContactPicker();
    contactPicker.CommitButtonText = "Select";

    //Set the selection mode
    contactPicker.SelectionMode = ContactSelectionMode.Fields;

    //Set desired fields
    contactPicker.DesiredFieldsWithContactFieldType.Add(ContactFieldType.Email);

    //Open the ContactPicker
    Contact contact = await contactPicker.PickContactAsync();

    if (contact != null)
    {
        ResultTextBlock.Text = contact.FirstName;
    }
}
```

VB

```
Private Sub ContactPickerButton_Click(sender As Object, e As RoutedEventArgs)
    GetContact()
End Sub

Private Async Sub GetContact()
    'Create a new instance of ContactPicker class
    Dim contactPicker = New Windows.ApplicationModel.Contacts.ContactPicker()
    contactPicker.CommitButtonText = "Select"
```

```
'Set the selection mode
contactPicker.SelectionMode = ContactSelectionMode.Fields

'Set desired fields
contactPicker.DesiredFieldsWithContactFieldType.Add(ContactFieldType.Email)

'Open the ContactPicker
Dim contact As Contact = Await contactPicker.PickContactAsync()

If contact IsNot Nothing Then
    ResultTextBlock.Text = contact.FirstName
End If
End Sub
```

Figure 8-39 shows an example of ContactPicker (for privacy, most parts of the image are blanked).

Figure 8-39. *ContactPicker window*

Conclusion

In this chapter, you took a deep look into data management for your Windows Store app. Probably most of the apps you will develop are data-centric, so you must have a good understanding of these concepts to create a functional application with a great user experience.

CHAPTER 9

Listening to the World

The first thing that a user sees after the installation of your app is the tile. This is a static representation of your app on the Start screen and it allows the user to start it; this is true until you do not evolve a static tile in a live tile. At this point of the book you know that Windows 8 keeps only one app active at a time; therefore you should use live tiles to give real-time feedback to the user about the state of the app. You can update app tiles in one of two ways:

- From your app code
- Using push notifications

In this chapter, we will talk about different types of notifications. Most of them are configured with an XML template that we will introduce in specific sections. The scope of this chapter is to explain how to choose the best template.

Notifications Overview

There are several ways to notify the user when the application is not in the foreground.

- *Live Tiles*: Useful to provide information when the user puts your app tile on the Start screen.
- *Badge Notification*: Provides a way to notify users about the status of your application.
- *Lock Screen Notification*: Useful to show textual information on the lock screen.
- *Toast Notification*: Pops up a message that shows information about something that happened in your application (generated from local code or from a remote event).

If the user pins your app on the Start screen, you can provide information through live tiles.

Live Tiles

A live tile is a showcase for your app, and just like a shop, the showcase should persuade people to come in and buy something. For this reason, a live tile must be well designed, providing a good set of helpful information for the user. When we say "helpful information," we mean content that the user will find valuable.

The *more interesting* and *fresh* the *content* shown in your live tile is, the *more the user will want to touch or click it.* This must be a rule when you design your live tile. This rule can be explained in the following way:

- *More interesting:* You must show information related to the user's interests, which can be expanded upon in your app.
- *Fresh*: All the information that you put in your live tile must be current. For example, a weather app should update the live tile to show the forecast for the next day. If the user sees the forecast for three days ago, he/she will reconsider the use of your app.

- *Content:* Choosing what to put inside your live tile is probably the hardest part of its design. The content must be clean, quick to understand, and well positioned. Happily, you can find many templates ready to use for all tile sizes in the framework.

- *More the user will want to touch or click it:* This is not difficult to understand. If your live tile follows the guidelines discussed here, there is a greater possibility that the user will like your app, thereby promoting its tile to a prominent place on their Start screen and using your app frequently.

We mentioned the *square* and *wide* tile sizes. If you look at Figure 9-1 you can see four tile formats.

- The weather app, which shows information about forecast and temperature, is in a **large** tile.

- The desktop uses a **medium** tile.

- The travel app is in a **wide** tile.

- Skype, IE, VS, and Blend are in **small** tiles.

Figure 9-1. *Example of tile sizes*

When choosing which tile size you want to support for your app, note that a wide format is useful for a high level of information, while a square tile is good for a small amount of data. If your app does not support live tiles, you could choose to support at most the square tile in order to avoid wasting space on the Start screen. Wide and large tiles are best suited to be a live tile because they offer a lot of space for information.

You can declare which size of tile your app will support by modifying the app manifest. As you can see in Figure 9-2, you can configure multiple tile sizes; for every size you can provide an image (used as default tile content), and for each image you provide you enable the associated size. An exception is made for the small logo; if you don't provide an image, Windows will scale the medium image. Because Windows runs on multiple types of devices, and every device has its own display resolution, in some scenarios Windows must scale your icon; for this reason you can supply images to be used in that situation.

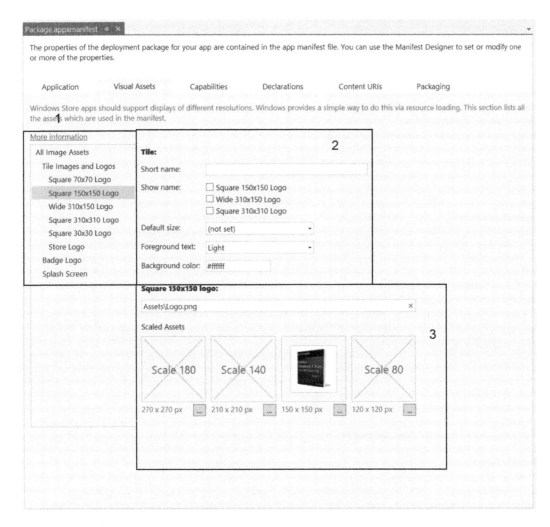

Figure 9-2. Default tile configuration

In Figure 9-2, you can see that we highlighted three areas. In area 1, you can choose which asset you want to configure. In area 2, you can choose the text used as the short name on the tile of your application. Area 3 is contextual to the item that you selected in area 1, and here you can configure the image to be used as a logo.

Every tile size has options for formatting: text only, images only, and peek. Peek templates are dynamic; this means that when you use it, the tile will cycle between two frames—one with primary content and one with additional information. An appropriate scenario for a peek template could be an e-mail app that shows the sender and subject in a primary frame and part of the body in a secondary frame.

Every template is defined via an XML template, and is identified by a value in the **TileTemplateType** enumeration. You can find details about these templates in Appendix A, where you can see examples of them. When you work with live tiles you use mainly two classes, `TileUpdateManager` and `TileNotification`, both of which are shown in Figure 9-3.

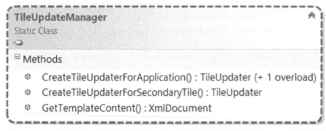

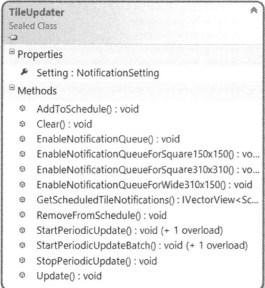

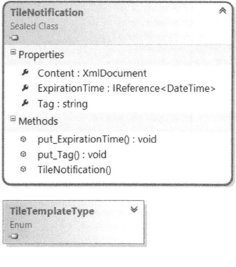

Figure 9-3. *Live tile classes*

TileUpdater is the entry point for live tiles capability. To get an instance of TileUpdater you must invoke TileUpdateManger's methods CreateTileUpdaterForApplication or CreateTileUpdaterForSecondaryTile. With TileUpdater you have complete control of your app tiles (primary and secondary). We will give particular attention to the Update method that accepts a TileNotification instance as a parameter. This method updates the actual layout of your live tiles. If you enable the notification queue, your update will be queued; otherwise your update will overwrite every other update that you've made.

In your example, you'll use the TileSquare150x150PeekImageAndText02 template to update your app tile. The XML content for this template is as follows:

```
<tile>
  <visual version="2">
    <binding template="TileSquare150x150PeekImageAndText02" fallback="TileSquarePeekImageAndText02">
      <image id="1" src="" />
      <text id="1"></text>
      <text id="2"></text>
    </binding>
  </visual>
</tile>
```

Inside your code, you will retrieve the XmlDocument associated with the template, then you will update information about text and image, and then you will update the tile of your app.

C#

```csharp
private void ShowTestNotification(object sender, RoutedEventArgs e)
        {
            var selectedTemplate = TileTemplateType. TileSquare150x150PeekImageAndText02;
            var template = TileUpdateManager.GetTemplateContent(selectedTemplate);

                var textItems = template.GetElementsByTagName("text");
                textItems[0].AppendChild(template.CreateTextNode("Title"));
                textItems[1].AppendChild(template.CreateTextNode("SubTitle"));
                var imgItems = template.GetElementsByTagName("image");
                ((XmlElement)imgItems[0]).SetAttribute("src", "ms-appx:///assets/picture.png");

            var updater = TileUpdateManager.CreateTileUpdaterForApplication();
            updater.Update(new TileNotification(template));
        }
```

VB

```vb
Private Sub ShowTestNotification(sender As Object, e As RoutedEventArgs)
        Dim selectedTemplate = TileTemplateType.TileSquare150x150PeekImageAndText02
        Dim template = TileUpdateManager.GetTemplateContent(selectedTemplate)

        Dim textItems = template.GetElementsByTagName("text")
        textItems(0).AppendChild(template.CreateTextNode("Title"))
        textItems(1).AppendChild(template.CreateTextNode("SubTitle"))
        Dim imgItems = template.GetElementsByTagName("image")
        DirectCast(imgItems(0), XmlElement).SetAttribute("src", "ms-appx:///assets/picture.png")

        Dim updater = TileUpdateManager.CreateTileUpdaterForApplication()
        updater.Update(New TileNotification(template))
End Sub
```

Badge Notification

A badge notification is a little summary shown on your app tile in the bottom right corner. This summary can be numeric, with values from 1 to 99 (every number over 99 appears as 99+), or graphic, using a list of predefined glyphs (shown in Table 9-1). This type of information, for example, would be useful for a messaging application that needs to show how many new messages the user has received, or to alert the user that something has happened.

Table 9-1. *Glyph Values*

Value	Icon
Activity	
Alert	
Available	
Away	
Busy	
NewMessage	
Paused	
Playing	
Unavailable	
Error	
Attention	

■ **Note** Glyph notification is based on a string value (and not an enumeration) to recognize which icon must be applied; for this reason, pay attention when you specify which value should be used.

Badge notification, just like other notification types, is based on an XML template that contains only one element badge with one attribute named value, whose value depends on what type of badge you are going to use. For example, <badge value="25"/> prepares a numeric badge notification, as shown in Figure 9-4. You can change the value to one in Table 9-1 to show an associated image.

Figure 9-4. *Badge notification sample*

To update your app tile the core class is BadgeUpdater and it can call the methods CreateBadgeUpdaterForApplication and CreateBadgeUpdaterForSecondaryTile of BadgeUpdateManager. This class exposes the method GetTemplateContent that can be used to retrieve the XmlDocument to be used for the update.

C#

```
var template = BadgeUpdateManager.GetTemplateContent(BadgeTemplateType.BadgeNumber);
(template.GetElementsByTagName("badge")[0] as XmlElement).SetAttribute("value", 10);
BadgeUpdater updater = BadgeUpdateManager.CreateBadgeUpdaterForApplication();
updater.Update(new BadgeNotification(template));
```

VB

```
Dim template = BadgeUpdateManager.GetTemplateContent(BadgeTemplateType.BadgeNumber)
TryCast(template.GetElementsByTagName("badge")(0), XmlElement).SetAttribute("value", 10)
Dim updater As BadgeUpdater = BadgeUpdateManager.CreateBadgeUpdaterForApplication()
updater.Update(New BadgeNotification(template))
```

Lock Screen Notification

The presence of a lock screen is a privilege that the user gives to your app. He does it because the data in your app is very important to him and he/she wants to be notified in real time about every update.

Lock screen notification is closely linked to badge notification and background tasks; an app that uses badge updates and is chosen by the user to stay in lock screen automatically shows the same notification inside the tile and in lock screen.

For an app to stay in lock screen requires that background task are allowed, because there is no reason that your apps updates its badge directly within the app. For this reason you should use one of the following types of background tasks:

- Control Channel
- Push Notification
- Timer

To use lock screen notification, you must declare it in the Application tab of your application manifest, as shown in Figure 9-5.

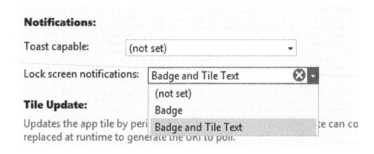

Figure 9-5. *Lock screen notification capability*

To do it correctly you must do at least two things:

- Declare a background task of one of the types listed above.

- Provide a badge logo in the Visual Assets tab, as show in Figure 9-6.

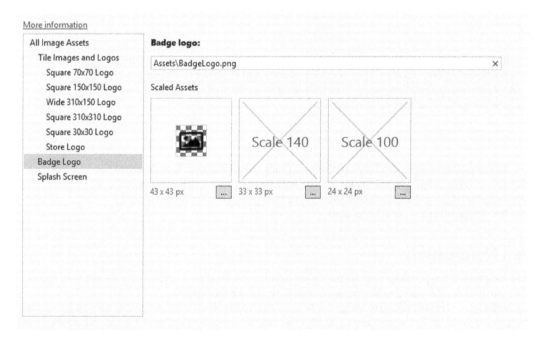

Figure 9-6. *Badge logo configuration*

These settings will allow the code shown for badge notification to update the badge on the Start screen when the user sets your app as lock screen badge.

Toast Notifications

A toast notification is an app-specific pop-up shown regardless of what app is in foreground and can be accompanied by a system sound. This type of notification provides quick access to content in an app. When you use a toast notification, you must keep in mind that is an invasive notification; for this reason you should avoid annoying the user with unwanted messages.

There are two types of toast notifications:

- *Standard Toast*: This type of notification appears for seven seconds in the top-right corner of the screen (top-left for right-to-left languages). This type of notification is useful for IM applications or an organizer app for an incoming invitation.

- *Long-Duration Toast*: This type of notification is really bothersome because it appears for 25 seconds, looping the sound associated with it. This type of notification should be used only in cases where it is necessary to force the user to pay attention to what is happening (such as an invitation to accept an incoming call in a VOIP app).

A toast notification is just like other notifications: it uses an XML template that can be selected from a catalog where every template is identified by a value in `ToastTemplateType` enumeration. In **Table A-2** of Appendix A you can see all the templates available for toast notifications along with the relative code to be used.

Sending Notifications

There are two ways to update a tile: using the `Windows.UI.Notifications` namespace or using push notifications. In previous sections, you've seen how to use `Windows.UI.Notifications` namespace. In this section, you'll see how to use push notifications.

Using a Push Notification

Using a push notification is slightly more complicated than the other notification methods. The core part of the operating system responsible for push notifications is named the **Notification Platform** (composed by three DLLs: `wpnapps.dll` for Windows Push Notification Apps, `wpncore.dll` for Windows Push Notification Core, and `wpnprv.dll` for Windows Push Notification Platform Connection Provider). The notification platform inside the system is responsible for interacting with an app to provide a push notification channel, and to notify your app that something has been received on it. A push notification channel is nothing more than an URI exposed by Windows Push Notification Service (WNS), which is the cloud part (managed by Microsoft) of the notification platform, and is responsible for collecting incoming messages sent to a specific channel and pushing them to the device.

Figure 9-7 is a simple diagram that shows the sequence of steps that are required to send a push notification.

1. Your app requests a push notification channel from the Notification Platform.

2. The Notification Platform asks WNS for a new channel (if the older one has been dropped).

3. The Notification Platform answers your app and provides an URI that identifies the channel.

4. Your app interacts with your service in the cloud that is responsible for storing the information that identifies the device and associates it with the data related to the user.

5. When something must be notified, your device authenticates itself on WNS and sends the message.

6. WNS looks for the device if connected.

    a. If not, it manages a queue of five tile notifications and one badge notification, if the queue is enabled.

    b. If yes, it sends the notification to your app through the Notification Platform.

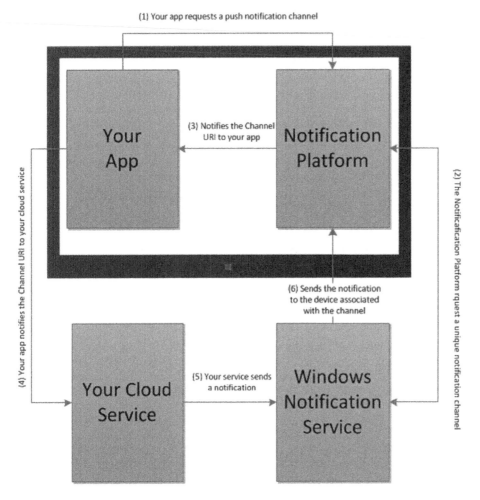

Figure 9-7. *Push notification working schema*

In the class diagram in Figure 9-8, you can see all classes involved in the Push Notification feature. PushNotificationChannelManager is the static class that must be used to create a new push notification channel.

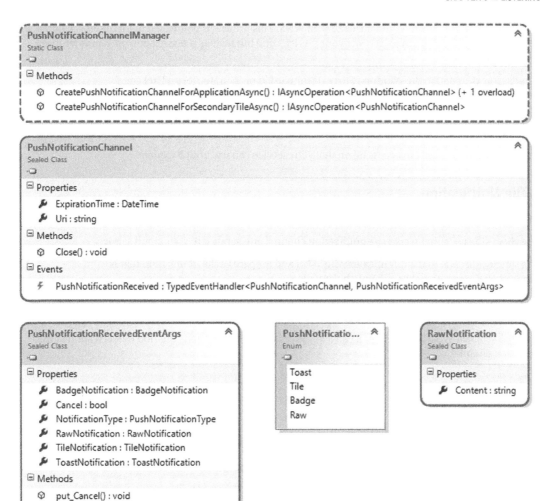

Figure 9-8. *PushNotification namespace*

■ **Note** Every channel expires after 30 days; for this reason you must keep track of the channel in order to update your service data if something changes.

When your app contacts your service to store a channel, remember to use a secure connection to avoid security issues. Every notification channel URI uses the domain notify.windows.com, and if your app receives a different domain, you must avoid sending data to it or you may compromise user privacy.

As discussed, your service must authenticate itself with WNS. This process is composed of three steps, where the first is passive because it doesn't depend on WNS or your service code but instead a registration on Window Store Dashboard.

1. You register your app in the Windows Store Dashboard in order to retrieve a Package security identifier (SID) and a secret key that you will use to authenticate on the server.

2. Your cloud service sends its credentials (Package SID, and key) to WNS using HTTPS protocol according to OAuth 2.0 protocol (you'll see how later).

3. The service answers with an access token that your service can use until it expires.

Sending a Tile Notification

In this section, we'll translate the concept introduced above into code. The code will be separated in two parts:

- The client side code that registers a notification channel and sends it to your cloud service.

- The server side code that authenticates with WNS and prepares a tile notification that is received by the app, thereby updating the app tile.

Client Side

In your App class OnLaunched event handler you'll call a RegisterPushNotifications method that is responsible for creating a notification channel.

C#

```
private async void RegisterPushNotifications()
{
    var channel = await PushNotificationChannelManager
        .CreatePushNotificationChannelForApplicationAsync();
    channel.PushNotificationReceived += OnPushNotificationReceived;
    NotificationHelper.StoreNotificationChannel(channel.Uri);
}
```

VB

```
Private Async Sub RegisterPushNotifications()
    Dim channel = Await PushNotificationChannelManager
        .CreatePushNotificationChannelForApplicationAsync()
    AddHandler channel. PushNotificationReceived, AddressOf Me. OnPushNotificationReceived
    NotificationHelper.StoreNotificationChannel(channel.Uri)
End Sub
```

Server Side

On the server side, you'll write code that will accomplish the following objectives:

- Authenticate on WNS and get an access token.

- Prepare and send a request.

To authenticate on WNS, you'll create a class named WNSAuthToken that will contain the authentication token deserialized via the JSON deserializer inside the GetAccessToken method contained in WNSAuthHelper.

C#

```csharp
[DataContract]
public class WNSAuthToken
{
    [DataMember(Name = "access_token")]
    public string AccessToken { get; set; }
    [DataMember(Name = "token_type")]
    public string TokenType { get; set; }
}

public WNSAuthToken GetAccessToken(string secret, string sid)
{
    var urlEncodedSecret = HttpUtility.UrlEncode(secret);
    var urlEncodedSid = HttpUtility.UrlEncode(sid);
    var body = String
     .Format(
       "grant_type=client_credentials&client_id={0}&client_secret={1}&scope=notify.windows.com",
       urlEncodedSid,
       urlEncodedSecret);

    string response;
    using (var client = new WebClient())
    {
        client.Headers.Add("Content-Type", "application/x-www-form-urlencoded");
        response = client.UploadString("https://login.live.com/accesstoken.srf", body);
    }

    using (var ms = new MemoryStream(Encoding.Unicode.GetBytes(response)))
    {
        var ser = new DataContractJsonSerializer(typeof(WNSAuthToken));
        var wnsAuthToken = (WNSAuthToken)ser.ReadObject(ms);
        return wnsAuthToken;
    }
}
```

VB

```vb
<DataContract> _
Public Class WNSAuthToken
        <DataMember(Name := "access_token")> _
        Public Property AccessToken() As String
                Get
                        Return m_AccessToken
                End Get
                Set
                        m_AccessToken = Value
                End Set
        End Property
```

```
        Private m_AccessToken As String
        <DataMember(Name := "token_type")> _
        Public Property TokenType() As String
                Get
                        Return m_TokenType
                End Get
                Set
                        m_TokenType = Value
                End Set
        End Property
        Private m_TokenType As String
End Class

Public Function GetAccessToken(secret As String, sid As String) As WNSAuthToken
        Dim urlEncodedSecret = HttpUtility.UrlEncode(secret)
        Dim urlEncodedSid = HttpUtility.UrlEncode(sid)
        Dim body = [String].Format("grant_type=client_credentials&client_id={0}&client_
secret={1}&scope=notify.windows.com", urlEncodedSid, urlEncodedSecret)

        Dim response As String
        Using client = New WebClient()
                client.Headers.Add("Content-Type", "application/x-www-form-urlencoded")
                response = client.UploadString("https://login.live.com/accesstoken.srf", body)
        End Using

        Using ms = New MemoryStream(Encoding.Unicode.GetBytes(response))
                Dim ser = New DataContractJsonSerializer(GetType(WNSAuthToken))
                Dim wnsAuthToken = DirectCast(ser.ReadObject(ms), WNSAuthToken)
                Return wnsAuthToken
        End Using
End Function
```

These two classes are useful for the remaining part of the code, which is responsible for sending the notification to the device. You define a method named NotifyNextAppointment that uses GetAccessToken method to retrieve the access token to use WNS.

C#

```csharp
public void NotifyNextAppointment(object sender, RoutedEventArgs e)
    {
        try
        {
            SendWideTileAppointmentNotification();
        }
        catch (WebException webException)
        {
            string exceptionDetails = webException.Response.Headers["WWW-Authenticate"];
            if (exceptionDetails.Contains("Token expired"))
            {
                GetAccessToken();
                SendWideTileAppointmentNotification();
            }
        }
```

```
            else
            {
                // Log the response
            }
        }
        catch (Exception ex)
        {
            //manage the exception
        }

    }

    private void SendWideTileAppointmentNotification()
    {
        accessToken = GetAccessToken();
        string notificationType = "wns/tile";
        HttpWebRequest request = HttpWebRequest.Create(channelUri) as HttpWebRequest;
        request.Method = "POST";

        request.Headers.Add("X-WNS-Type", notificationType);
        request.Headers.Add("Authorization", String.Format("Bearer {0}",
accessToken.AccessToken));

        string xml = NotificationsHelper.PrepareWideTileNotification();
// THIS METHOD CREATES THE XML NOTIFICATION

        byte[] contentBytes = Encoding.UTF8.GetBytes(xml);

        using (Stream requestStream = request.GetRequestStream())
            requestStream.Write(contentBytes, 0, contentBytes.Length);
        string test = string.Empty;
        using (HttpWebResponse webResponse = (HttpWebResponse)request.GetResponse())
            test = webResponse.StatusCode.ToString();
    }

    private WNSAuthToken GetAccessToken()
    {
        var sid = WNSAuthHelper.GetAppSid();
        var secret = WNSAuthHelper.GetAppSecretKey();

        var urlEncodedSecret = HttpUtility.UrlEncode(secret);
        var urlEncodedSid = HttpUtility.UrlEncode(sid);

        var body = String.Format("grant_type=client_credentials&client_id={0}&client_
secret={1}&scope=notify.windows.com", urlEncodedSid, urlEncodedSecret);
```

```csharp
            string response;
            using (var client = new WebClient())
            {
                client.Headers.Add("Content-Type", "application/x-www-form-urlencoded");
                response = client.UploadString("https://login.live.com/accesstoken.srf", body);
            }

            using (var ms = new MemoryStream(Encoding.Unicode.GetBytes(response)))
            {
                var ser = new DataContractJsonSerializer(typeof(WNSAuthToken));
                var oAuthToken = (WNSAuthToken)ser.ReadObject(ms);
                return oAuthToken;
            }
}
```

VB

```vbnet
Public Sub NotifyNextAppointment(sender As Object, e As RoutedEventArgs)
        Try
                SendWideTileAppointmentNotification()
        Catch webException As WebException
                Dim exceptionDetails As String = webException.Response.Headers("WWW-Authenticate")
                If exceptionDetails.Contains("Token expired") Then
                        GetAccessToken()
                        SendWideTileAppointmentNotification()
                                ' Log the response
                Else
                End If
                        'manage the exception
        Catch ex As Exception
        End Try

End Sub

Private Sub SendWideTileAppointmentNotification()
        accessToken = GetAccessToken()
        Dim notificationType As String = "wns/tile"
        Dim request As HttpWebRequest = TryCast(HttpWebRequest.Create(channelUri), HttpWebRequest)
        request.Method = "POST"

        request.Headers.Add("X-WNS-Type", notificationType)
        request.Headers.Add("Authorization", [String].Format("Bearer {0}", accessToken.AccessToken))

        Dim xml As String = NotificationsHelper.PrepareWideTileNotification()

        Dim contentBytes As Byte() = Encoding.UTF8.GetBytes(xml)

        Using requestStream As Stream = request.GetRequestStream()
                requestStream.Write(contentBytes, 0, contentBytes.Length)
        End Using
```

```
            Dim test As String = String.Empty
            Using webResponse As HttpWebResponse = DirectCast(request.GetResponse(), HttpWebResponse)
                    test = webResponse.StatusCode.ToString()
            End Using
    End Sub

    Private Function GetAccessToken() As WNSAuthToken
            Dim sid = WNSAuthHelper.GetAppSid()
            Dim secret = WNSAuthHelper.GetAppSecretKey()

            Dim urlEncodedSecret = HttpUtility.UrlEncode(secret)
            Dim urlEncodedSid = HttpUtility.UrlEncode(sid)

            Dim body = [String].Format("grant_type=client_credentials&client_id={0}&client_
    secret={1}&scope=notify.windows.com", urlEncodedSid, urlEncodedSecret)

            Dim response As String
            Using client = New WebClient()
                    client.Headers.Add("Content-Type", "application/x-www-form-urlencoded")
                    response = client.UploadString("https://login.live.com/accesstoken.srf", body)
            End Using

            Using ms = New MemoryStream(Encoding.Unicode.GetBytes(response))
                    Dim ser = New DataContractJsonSerializer(GetType(WNSAuthToken))
                    Dim oAuthToken = DirectCast(ser.ReadObject(ms), WNSAuthToken)
                    Return oAuthToken
            End Using
    End Function
```

Sending Other Notifications

The code shown in the previous section is useful for all types of notification; you can simply change the value of notificationType accordingly to these values:

- wns/badge for badge notifications

- wns/tile (seen above) to send a tile notification

- wns/toast to send a toast notification

- wns/raw to trigger a background work item

This makes really simple to rapidly update the content in your application by choosing the appropriate template for the notificationType chosen. Of course, for every update you think to send, you must remember to extract the XML template from Windows 8.1 and send it from your cloud service.

Conclusion

In this chapter, we have introduced the code necessary to work with notifications. As you can see, the behavior of all notification types is quite similar; for this reason, when you learn to use one of them, you know how to use all of them, but you should never forget that every notification has its appropriate use.

CHAPTER 10

■ ■ ■

Accessibility and Globalization

Windows Store, discussed in the next chapter, is an online platform that allows developers to share and sell their apps. This platform offers your app global exposure to people of different cultures, languages, points of view, disabilities, and impediments. For this reason, if you are planning to expand your market to these people, you need to integrate into your apps specific features. Planning for accessibility and globalization is a mandatory step!

WinRT already provides basic support features for these aspects. In this chapter we will explain through a simple example how to integrate these features and prepare your apps for a global market.

Get Ready for Accessibility

The accessibility concept is directly linked to a user who suffers from a handicap or impediment that hinders everyday tasks such as using a PC. These limitations can include issues with mobility, vision, color perception, hearing, speech, cognition, and literacy. These limitations require using specific hardware or software linked to electronic devices like a PC. Therefore, when planning to provide accessibility in your Windows Store app, you must consider the following:

- Support for an interactive keyboard

- Support for screen readers

- Support for font customization, zooming (magnification), color, high-contrast settings

Luckily, XAML already has built-in support for these features, and they can be customized and extended.

Support for Assistive Technology

The medical equipment that helps people with disabilities accomplish everyday tasks usually tends to illustrate or read what is shown inside a user interface. For this reason, all of the items inside a UI must support interaction with the following:

- On-screen keyboard software

- Voice-recognition software

- Screen readers

As mentioned, Windows Store apps have built-in support for these hardware/software instruments. For example, every control inside a XAML page supports the Tab navigation or provides an "accessible name" that can be used from the screen reader. Usually the value of this name is the inner text for controls. Sometimes this value needs to be explicitly set using the `AutomationProperties.Name` field. Table 10-1 summarizes which controls have built-in support for the accessible name and in which controls this property needs to be set.

Table 10-1. *Built-In Support for WinRT Controls*

Element	Description
Static Text	Inner text (for example a TextBlock content property)
Images	AutomationProperties.Name or AutomationProperties.LabeledBy
Form	The accessible name must be linked to the Label associated to a specific control through AutomationProperties.LabeledBy
Buttons and links	If the button contains text, then the content is used. Otherwise, if the button contains an image, the AutomationProperties.Name must be specified

Listing 10-1 shows an example of how to use AutomationProperties.Name.

Listing 10-1. *AutomationProperties.Name*

```
XAML
<StackPanel>
  <!-- Content property is used as accessible name -->
  <TextBlock Name="BuiltInSupport">This is an accessible name</TextBlock>
  <!-- This is an example of AutomationProperties.Name -->
  <TextBox AutomationProperties.Name="MyAccessibleName" Name="AccessibleNameTextBox" Width="100"/>
  <!-- This is an example of AutomationProperties.LabeledBy -->
  <TextBox
      AutomationProperties.LabeledBy="{Binding ElementName=BuiltInSupport}"
      Name="LabeledByTextBox" Width="100"/>
</StackPanel>
```

To fully support keyboard capabilities, all the controls inside a user interface must provide navigation through the Tab key. Usually the navigation order is based on how the controls are added or listed in a XAML view, or how they are programmatically added to a container. It is possible to override this setting using the TabIndex attribute, assigning an incremental value corresponding to the order. If a control needs to be passed over the Tab key, IsEnabled or IsTabStop properties must be set to False. Listing 10-2 shows an example.

Listing 10-2. *TabIndex and IsTabStop Example*

```
XAML
<StackPanel>
  <!-- Content property is used as accessible name -->
  <TextBlock Name="BuiltInSupport" TabIndex="1">This is an accessible name</TextBlock>
  <!-- This is an example of AutomationProperties.Name -->
  <TextBox AutomationProperties.Name="MyAccessibleName" Name="AccessibleNameTextBox" Width="100"
TabIndex="2" />
  <!-- This is an example of AutomationProperties.LabeledBy -->
  <TextBox
      AutomationProperties.LabeledBy="{Binding ElementName=BuiltInSupport}"
      Name="LabeledByTextBox" Width="100" IsTabStop="False" />
</StackPanel>
```

In Listing 10-2, the third label won't ever take focus using Tab key.

`ItemsControls`, also a Tab navigation feature, provides built-in navigation between shown data. This is reached using directional arrows on the keyboard.

Sometimes is very helpful to provide **shortcuts** inside a user interface. There are two kinds of shortcuts:

- AccessKey, linked to a UI portion by a combination of Alt + letter key

- AcceleratorKey, linked to an app command by a combination of Ctrl + letter key

These shortcuts can be defined using the `AutomationProperties.AccessKey` and `AutomationProperties.AcceleratorKey` attached properties, as shown in Listing 10-3.

Listing 10-3. *AccessKey and AcceleratorKey Example*

```XAML
<StackPanel>
  <!-- This is an example of AutomationProperties.AccessKey -->
  <TextBox AutomationProperties.Name="MyAccessibleName"    Name="AccessibleNameTextBox" Width="100"
TabIndex="2"   ToolTipService.ToolTip="Shortcut key: Alt+P"
AutomationProperties.AccessKey="Alt P"
 />
  <Button x:Name="SubmitButton" Click="SubmitButton_Click"
      ToolTipService.ToolTip="Shortcut key: Ctrl+A"
      AutomationProperties.AcceleratorKey="Control A">
      <TextBlock>Submit</TextBlock>
    </Button>
</StackPanel>
```

Supporting High-Contrast Themes

High-contrast themes allow people with lower vision to identify controls on a user interface. Windows Store apps have a built-in support for high-contrast themes because the default theme has the high-contrast support in it. If you need to customize a theme, remember to check if support for high-contrast themes is present. If you use Blend to customize a theme, it automatically generates a cloned theme for high-contrast support. You can also check programmatically if a high-contrast theme is enabling by using the `AccessibilitySettings` class (Figure 10-1).

Figure 10-1. *AccessibilitySettingsClass*

There are two properties available in this class: **HighContrast**, which contains a value that indicates if high-contrast feature is enabled, and **HighContrastScheme**, which contain the name of the high-contrast scheme.

Testing a Windows Store App for Accessibility

After your app provides all the features related to accessibility, you can take advantage of some tools to verify if these functionalities are correctly implemented. Windows Software Development Kit for Windows 8.1 includes two tools named **Inspect** and **UI Accessibility Checker** that can be found in `<install_dir>\<Program Files>\Windows Kits\8.1\bin\<version>`.

Inspect allows you to verify accessible data in a UI element, reading available `AutomationProperties` (Figure 10-2).

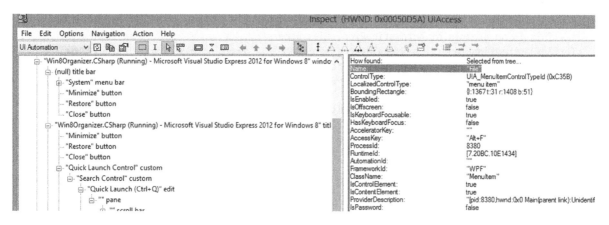

Figure 10-2. *Inspect accessibility tool*

UI Accessibility Checker (AccChecker) can be used to check if the app generates accessibility problems at runtime. Once started, select the name of the application in the "Choose window from list" field, then select on the right side what kind of verification routines need to be executed, and then click the Run Verification button. The results will be display in a series of tabbed windows inside the tool (Figure 10-3).

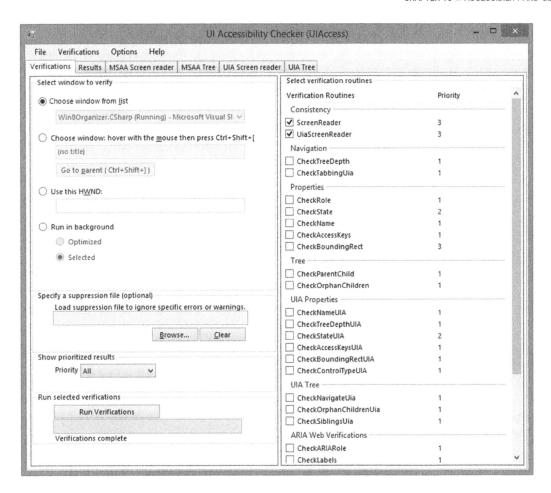

Figure 10-3. *UI Accessibility Checker window*

Get Ready for Localization

Again, if you are planning to distribute your application to users in different cultures and languages, it is necessary to provide localization for UI controls. There are few steps to follow.

- Translate the UI resources

- Convert the date and time format

- Convert the number and currency format

- Adapt layout and fonts for different languages

- Use the Multilingual App Toolkit

The localization process is not simple, so it is best to use a global-ready format to simplify the process (if you decide to distribute to a global market your app in the development stage).

Let's start from resources.

Using UI Resources in Windows Store Apps

It's a good practice to put strings shown in the user interface inside the resource file: this makes editing very simple. Then the strings are ready to be referenced in the code or markup.

The first step is to set the **Default Language** property of a Windows Store app: double-click package. appxmanifest in Visual Studio 2013 and find the **Application UI** tab. Type into the Default Language box **en-US** (using the BCP-47 language tag, more info at tools.ietf.org/html/bcp47). This setting is used when no user language or display language on the user machine is available inside the application (Figure 10-4).

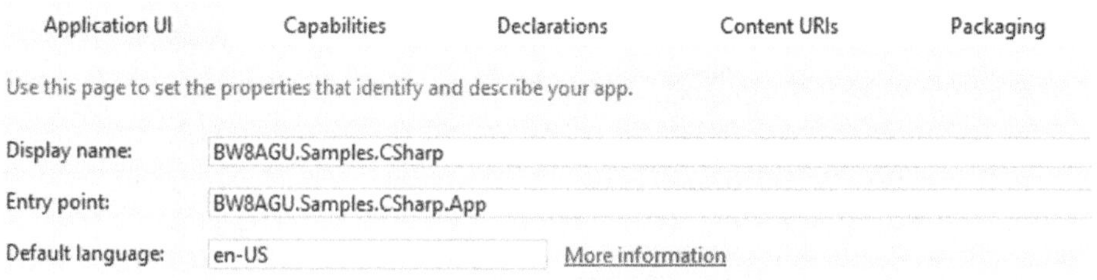

Application UI	Capabilities	Declarations	Content URIs	Packaging

Use this page to set the properties that identify and describe your app.

Display name: BW8AGU.Samples.CSharp

Entry point: BW8AGU.Samples.CSharp.App

Default language: en-US   More information

Figure 10-4. *How to set the default language in a Windows Store app*

All the string resources are contained inside a resource file: to create an English-localized resource file these steps need to be followed.

1. Localize the Strings folder in the project root, and then add a subfolder named as the BCP-47 language tag. Note that the project already has an en-US folder because it's the default language (Figure 10-5).

▷   obj
◢   Strings
   ◢   en-US
     Resources.resw
◢   App.xaml
   ▷   App.xaml.cs
     BW8AGU.Samples.CSharp.csproj.vspscc

Figure 10-5. *Resources folder structure*

2. Add a new item, selecting the "Resources File (.resw)" template from the list (Figure 10-6). It is suggested to use the default name for the resource file (Resources.resw).

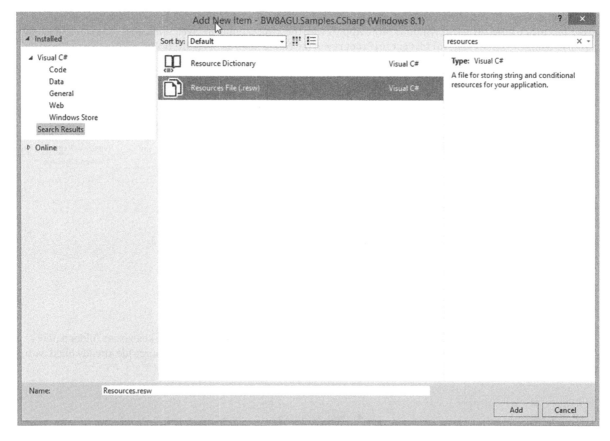

Figure 10-6. *Resource File (.resw) item template*

Finally, each localized string needs to be added to this file. After double-clicking `Resources.resw`, Visual Studio 2013 opens the Resource Editor. For each localized string, the following fields must be filled:

- *Name*: A unique name for the resource
- *Value*: The value for the resource
- *Comment*: A comment for the resource

It's a good practice to always fill the comment field to simplify the translation process to other languages by other people then the resource can be used inside the code (see Listing 10-4).

Listing 10-4. *Use Resources Inside the Code*

```
C#
var loader = new Windows.ApplicationModel.Resources.ResourceLoader();
var message = loader.GetString("WelcomeMessage");
VB
Dim loader = New Windows.ApplicationModel.Resources.ResourceLoader()
Dim message = loader.GetString("WelcomeMessage")
```

Another way to link a resource to a control is to use a pointed notation in the resource file. For example, to insert text inside a `TextBlock` in Windows Store App UI with the `x:Name` equal to "WelcomeLabel", you can add a new resource using the syntax `ControlId.ControlProperty` in the Name field, as in Figure 10-7.

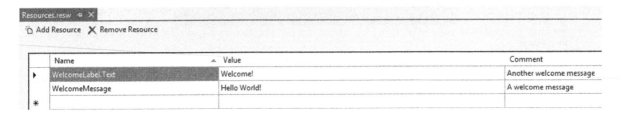

	Name	▲ Value	Comment
▶	WelcomeLabel.Text	Welcome!	Another welcome message
	WelcomeMessage	Hello World!	A welcome message
✱			

Figure 10-7. *How to define a resource for a control*

Then you can set the **x:UID** field with the value of the `x:Name`, as shown in Listing 10-5.

Listing 10-5. *Use Resources Inside Markup*

XAML
```xaml
<TextBlock x:Name="WelcomeLabel" x:Uid="WelcomeLabel"></TextBlock>
```

Now it is possible to add other languages to your Windows Store app by adding to the Resources folder a new subfolder for the specific language. Figures 10-8 and 10-9 show the adding of another resource file already filled with the value for the it-IT language.

Figure 10-8. *New localized resource file*

	Name	▲ Value	Comment
	WelcomeLabel.Text	Salve mondo dall'etichetta di benvenuto!	A message for a welcome label
▶	WelcomeMessage	Salve mondo!	A welcome message
✱			

Figure 10-9. *Localized resource strings*

To test the application in a different language, it is possible to change the display language on the development machine in the Clock, Language and Region section of the Control Panel, as shown in Figure 10-10.

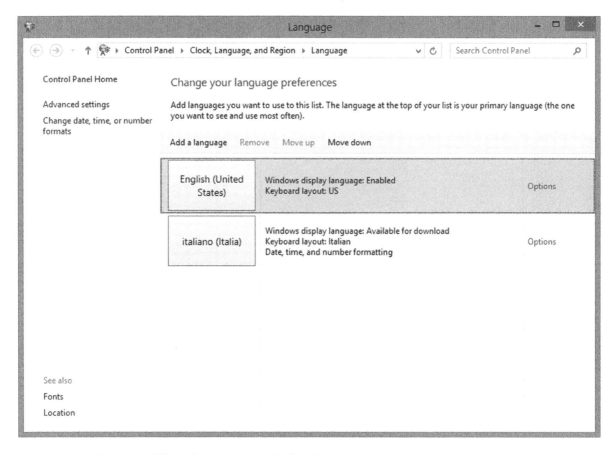

Figure 10-10. *How to test different languages in a Windows Store app*

Note that the listed order is important: if the first language is not available in the application, the following language is chosen as a display language replacement.

You can create more resource files for specific languages inside a language subfolder by using the same filename in different available language subfolders. Figure 10-11 shows how to create a new resource file and Listing 10-6 shows how to retrieve stored values using the syntax /ResourceFileName/StringName. In this case you use GetCurrentView, passing in the name of the resource file.

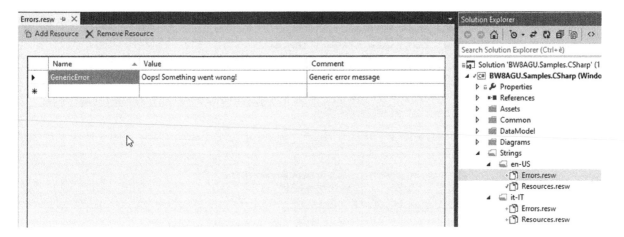

Figure 10-11. *Multiple resource files in a Windows Store app*

Listing 10-6. *Use Multiple Resource Files*

```
XAML
<TextBlock x:Name="ErrorLabel" x:Uid="/Errors/GenericError"></TextBlock>
C#
var res = Windows.ApplicationModel.Resources.ResourceLoader.GetForCurrentView("Errors");
ErrorLabel.Text = res.GetString("GenericError");
VB
Dim res = Windows.ApplicationModel.Resources.ResourceLoader.GetForCurrentView("Errors")
ErrorLabel.Text = res.GetString("GenericError")
```

How To Set Available Languages for a Windows Store App

Available languages in your Windows Store app can be set inside the Package.appxmanifest file: by doing this, the Windows Store will show the same language in the app description. The following steps show how to set available languages.

1. Open the Package.appxmanifest with a right-click and then select View Code (Figure 10-12).

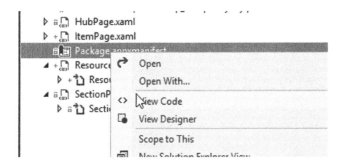

Figure 10-12. *Open the Package.appxmanifest code editor*

2. Localize the Resources node.

3. Comment the item <Resource Language="x-generate" />.

4. Type the code lines in Listing 10-7 containing the language tag available in the app.

Listing 10-7. *Manually Set Available Languages*

```
<Resources>
  <!-- <Resource Language="x-generate" /> -->
  <!-- Manually setting available languages -->
  <Resource Language="en-US" />
  <Resource Language="it-IT" />
</Resources>
```

How To Format Date and Time Properly

The date and time needs to be formatted using the current culture. If the date is provided by a user, it is possible to use a DatePicker control that has a built-in support for localization. On the other hand, WinRT include the Windows.Globalization.DateTimeFormatting namespace, which includes all the classes and enumeration to format the date and time programmatically. Figure 10-13 shows its objects.

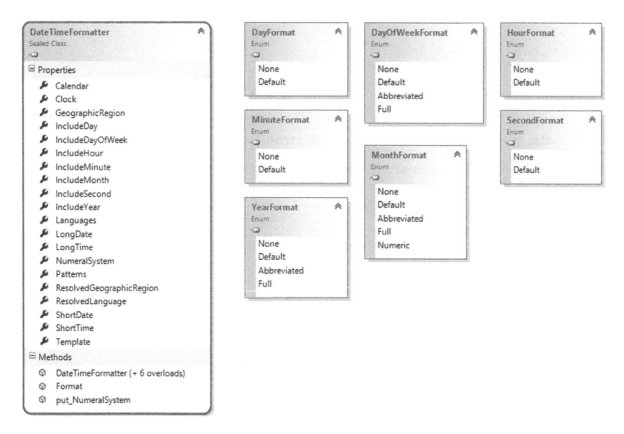

Figure 10-13. *DateTimeFormatting namespace elements*

The only available class is DateTimeFormatter, which allows you to format the date and time through its constructors. Let's see how to format a date inside a TextBlock using the display language. In this case, DateTimeFormatter needs to be created with the correct culture and then the date is passed to the Format() method of the current instance, as shown in Listing 10-8.

Listing 10-8. *Use DateTimeFormatter*

C#
```
DateTimeFormatter formatter =
    new DateTimeFormatter(HourFormat.Default, MinuteFormat.Default, SecondFormat.None);

DateNoSecondsTextblock.Text = formatter.Format(DateTime.Now);
```
VB
```
Dim formatter As New DateTimeFormatter(HourFormat.[Default], MinuteFormat.[Default],
SecondFormat.None)

DateNoSecondsTextblock.Text = formatter.Format(DateTime.Now)
```

In Listing 10-8, the output shows the date and the time without the seconds part. It is also possible to use templates to format the date. In Listing 10-9, you reach the same result as you do in Listing 10-8.

Listing 10-9. *Use DateTimeFormatter with Templates*

C#
```
DateTimeFormatter formatter =
    new DateTimeFormatter("longdate shorttime");

DateMaskFormatTextblock.Text = formatter.Format(DateTime.Now);
```
VB
```
Dim formatter As New DateTimeFormatter("longdate shorttime")

DateMaskFormatTextblock.Text = formatter.Format(DateTime.Now)
```

Table 10-2 summarizes the date format templates.

Table 10-2. *Date Format Templates*

longdate	shortdate	Longtime
shorttime	dayofweek	dayofweek.full
dayofweek.abbreviated	day	Month
month.full	month.abbreviated	month.numeric
year	year.full	year.abbreviated
dayofweek day month year	dayofweek day month	day month year
day month	month year	hour
minute	second	hour minute second
hour minute	minute second	

There are also available patterns to format dates: these are delimited by braces. Listing 10-10 shows how to use them.

Listing 10-10. *Use DateTimeFormatter with Patterns*

```
C#
formatter = new DateTimeFormatter("{month.integer}/{day.integer}/{year.full}
  {hour.integer}:{minute.integer}");
DateTemplateTextblock.Text = formatter.Format(DateTime.Now);
VB

formatter = New DateTimeFormatter("{month.integer}/{day.integer}/{year.full}{hour.integer}:{minute.
integer}")
DateTemplateTextblock.Text = formatter.Format(DateTime.Now)
```

Table 10-3 lists the common date format patterns.

Table 10-3. *Date Format Patterns*

Type	Pattern
Year	{year.<type>} where <type> is full / abbreviated / abbreviated(n)
Month	{month.<type>} where <type> is full / abbreviated / abbreviated(n) / integer / integer(n)
Day	{day.<type>} where <type> is integer / integer(n)
Hour	{hour.<type>} where <type> is integer / integer(n)
Minute	{minute.<type>} where <type> is integer / integer(n)
Second	{second.<type>} where <type> is integer / integer(n)

Starting with Visual Studio 2013, you can also take advantage of IntelliSense in XAML markup for these patterns. A full list can be found at msdn.microsoft.com/en-us/library/windows/apps/windows.globalization. datetimeformatting.datetimeformatter.aspx.

How To Format Number and Currency Properly

Every language has a way to format numbers and currency. WinRT provides one namespace to simplify the task: Windows.Globalization.NumberFormatting. Figure 10-14 shows the included classes.

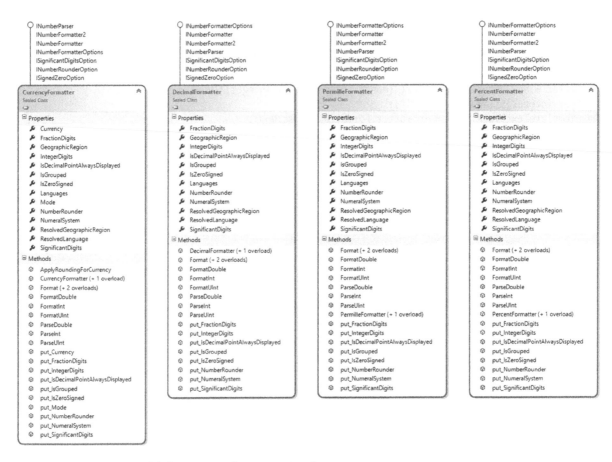

Figure 10-14. *Windows.Globalization.NumberFormatting classes*

Listing 10-11 shows a simple usage of DecimalFormatter that shows an integer part of the number grouped and always using a decimal point.

Listing 10-11. *Use DecimalFormatter*

```
C#
DecimalFormatter formatter = new DecimalFormatter();
formatter.IsGrouped = true;
formatter.IsDecimalPointAlwaysDisplayed = true;
DecimalFormatterTextblock.Text = formatter.Format(12345.00);
VB
Dim formatter As New DecimalFormatter()
formatter.IsGrouped = True
formatter.IsDecimalPointAlwaysDisplayed = True
DecimalFormatterTextblock.Text = formatter.Format(12345.0)
```

The same namespace also includes the CurrencyFormatter class that helps to format currencies. Usually the first step is to retrieve the default currency (linked to the default language in the app manifest) and use it as input to create a default formatter. Then it is possible to create a specific formatter based on an input string with the name of the currency (i.e. USD) or the name of the currency associated to the BCP code and the geographical region (i.e. EUR), as shown in Listing 10-12.

Listing 10-12. *Use CurrencyFormatter*

```csharp
C#
// Determine the current user's default currency.
string currency = GlobalizationPreferences.Currencies[0];

// Create currency formatter with current preferences
CurrencyFormatter defaultCurrencyFormatter = new CurrencyFormatter(currency);
DefaultCurrencyTextblock.Text = defaultCurrencyFormatter.Format(1234.56);

// Create currency formatter for USD
CurrencyFormatter usdCurrencyFormatter = new CurrencyFormatter("USD");
USDCurrencyTextblock.Text = usdCurrencyFormatter.Format(1234.56);

// Create currency formatter for EUR
CurrencyFormatter eurITCurrencyFormatter = new CurrencyFormatter("EUR", new[] { "it-IT" }, "IT");
EurItCurrencyTextblock.Text = eurITCurrencyFormatter.Format(1234.56);
```

```vbnet
VB
' Determine the current user's default currency.
Dim currency As String = GlobalizationPreferences.Currencies(0)

' Create currency formatter with current preferences
Dim defaultCurrencyFormatter As New CurrencyFormatter(currency)
DefaultCurrencyTextblock.Text = defaultCurrencyFormatter.Format(1234.56)

' Create currency formatter for USD
Dim usdCurrencyFormatter As New CurrencyFormatter("USD")
USDCurrencyTextblock.Text = usdCurrencyFormatter.Format(1234.56)

' Create currency formatter for EUR
Dim eurITCurrencyFormatter As New CurrencyFormatter("EUR", New () {"it-IT"}, "IT")
EurItCurrencyTextblock.Text = eurITCurrencyFormatter.Format(1234.56)
```

Layout and Font Adjustment, Bi-Directional Support

Different languages may occupy more space than others in a user interface. For this reason, you should avoid setting a fixed width to controls that show text; it's preferable to add a string resource in a localized resource file that contains the value. In Figure 10-15 you add a string named WelcomeLabel.Width with the value of 75 in the file Resources/en-US/Resources.resw. This value is used when the default language is used. Instead, if the current language is Italian, 80 is the value used in Resources/it-IT/Resources.resw (Figure 10-16). You don't need to add anything more to the markup or code!

Name	▲ Value	Comment
WelcomeLabel.Text	Hello World from Welcome Label	A message for a welcome label
WelcomeMessage	Hello World!	A welcome message
▶ WelcomeLabel.Width	75	Correct size of width
✳		

Figure 10-15. A localized width for a TextBlock in the English resource file

Name	▲ Value	Comment
▶ WelcomeLabel.Text	Salve mondo dall'etichetta di benvenuto!	A message for a welcome label
WelcomeMessage	Salve mondo!	A welcome message
WelcomeLabel.Width	80	Correct size of width
✳		

Figure 10-16. A localized width for a TextBlock in the Italian resource file

WinRT also provides built-in support for bi-directional text. In XAML it is possible to use the `FlowDirection` control property to `LeftToRight` (0) or `RightToLeft` (1). This value can be set directly inside the resource files (Figure 10-17).

Name	▲ Value	Comment
WelcomeLabel.Text	Salve mondo dall'etichetta di benvenuto!	A message for a welcome label
WelcomeMessage	Salve mondo!	A welcome message
WelcomeLabel.Width	80	Correct size of width
WelcomeLabel.FlowDirection	LeftToRight	Set the flow direction
✳		

Figure 10-17. How to set FlowDirection directly inside a resource file

The Multilingual App Toolkit

The translating process sometimes be very long and tedious. In these cases, the Multilingual App Toolkit may come in handy. This is a tool directly integrated inside Visual Studio 2013 that provides the following capabilities:

- Verify and track changes in resource files

- Provide a useful UI for choosing languages

- Support the XLIFF file format (more info at www.oasis-open.org/committees/tc_home. php?wg_abbrev=xliff)

- Help translate and identify translating issues (it supports also Microsoft Translator)

The Multilingual App Toolkit is a free tool and can be downloaded from msdn.microsoft.com/en-US/windows/apps/hh848309.aspx. Once installed, it needs to be enabled in Visual Studio in the Tools menu by clicking Enable Multilingual App Toolkit (Figure 10-18).

Figure 10-18. *Enabling Multilingual App Toolkit in Visual Studio 2013*

This step adds a new folder with a file in it called `Pseudo Language (Pseudo).xlf` (Figure 10-19).

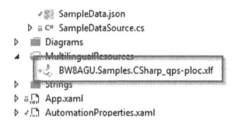

Figure 10-19. *Pseudo language file*

Now it is possible to add a new translation language inside your app by right-clicking the project name and choosing the "Add translation languages" item (Figure 10-20).

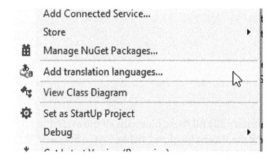

Figure 10-20. *Add a new translation to the project*

This opens a pop-up window where you can choose the desired language (Figure 10-21).

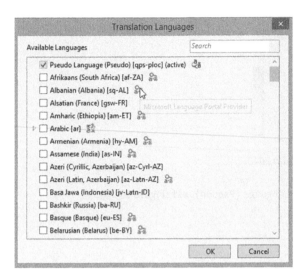

Figure 10-21. *Translation Languages pop-up window*

As you can see, some items offer the Microsoft Translator to automate the resource translation process, but the non-selectable Pseudo Language item is used during testing. After selecting the Italian [it] item, a new file is added to the MultilingualResources folder (Figure 10-22).

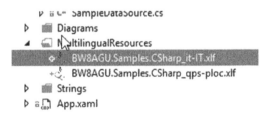

Figure 10-22. *Italian localized xlf file*

Now you can rebuild the project and Visual Studio 2013 will automatically fill these files with all the available resources in the project. To test if something went wrong, double-click the Italian localized xlf file. Visual Studio will open the Multilingual Editor (Figure 10-23).

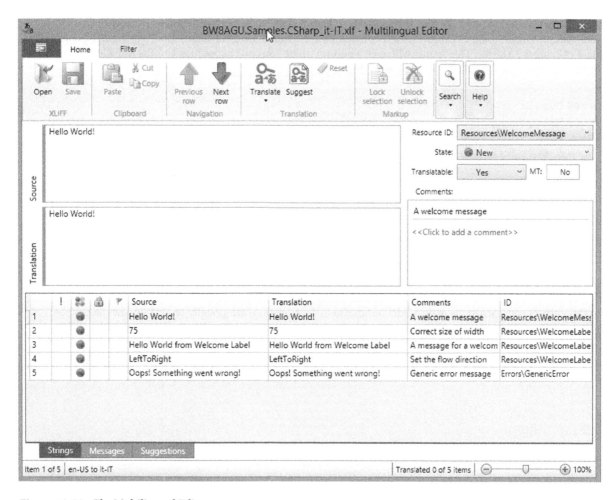

Figure 10-23. *The Multilingual Editor*

In this editor it is possible, using the Translate button, to automatically translate (through Microsoft Translator) all the resources (Figure 10-24).

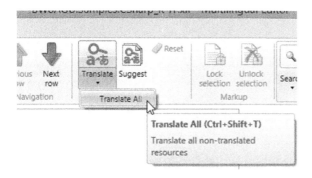

Figure 10-24. *Automated translations in the Multilingual Editor*

The main reason that XLIFF files are created is so that you can share them with others to create or check translations. Visual Studio 2013 provides a very helpful feature called Send For Translation, which can be reached by right-clicking the XLF file. This feature will open a pop-up where you can choose to export the XLF file inside a folder or attach it and send through e-mail to a friend (Figure 10-25).

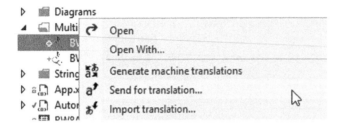

Figure 10-25. *Send For Translation feature in Visual Studio 2013*

Conclusion

In this chapter you learned the main guidelines that help developers create globally-ready Windows Store apps that can be installed without problems on devices used by people in different cultures or by people who suffer impediments. It is really important to clearly understand these concepts in order to create usable applications. The next and last chapter of this book will explain in detail the process of publishing your app to the Windows Store.

CHAPTER 11

Sell Your App

In your life as a developer, regardless of which methodology you choose for your application lifecycle management, you must deliver your app to the end user. In this chapter we are going to analyze what you need to do before you submit your app to the Windows Store, and why your app should appear in the Store.

We will start with a brief introduction to the Windows Store and the opportunities it offers economically and in terms of visibility for your application. Then we will show the entire process of app submission.

Windows Store

When we talk about the Windows Store we refer to the entire ecosystem that help us to distribute our apps to users all around the world, and allows them to buy and install the apps on their devices. There are many reasons you might choose to learn to develop Windows Store apps, but two popular reasons are the following:

- Get paid for your work (and passion!).

- Increase your visibility as a developer or company.

The Windows Store can be a good choice to accomplish these targets. We'll explain why.

Presenting the Windows Store

The Windows Store is simply the Windows Store app marketplace. Inside this marketplace are a great number of apps that can be installed on the Windows 8.x operating systems. Since Windows OSs are largely diffuse, it could be a good way to expose your apps to a large number of customers. The Windows Store is right now accessible from over 200 countries and supports more than 100 languages. This means that you can choose to sell your apps in countries other than your own, and you can enable different languages inside them (we will talk more about this later in the chapter).

Once your app is published, it can be found by potential customers directly on their PCs, using the Windows Store integrated app. This app can be launched on the Windows 8.x operating system directly from Start window (Figure 11-1).

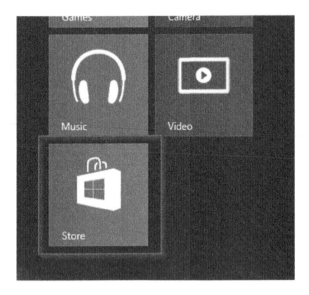

Figure 11-1. *The Windows Store integrated app tile*

Once opened, it shows different apps in the store, based on category or relevance; you can also search a specific app through the integrated search box (Figure 11-2).

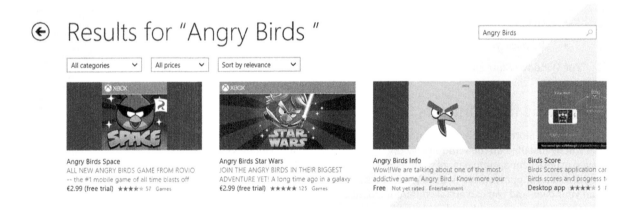

Figure 11-2. *Search feature using the Windows Store integrated app*

Inside the store, you can find free or paid apps. For this reasons you need to add a payment method in your account settings (Figure 11-3).

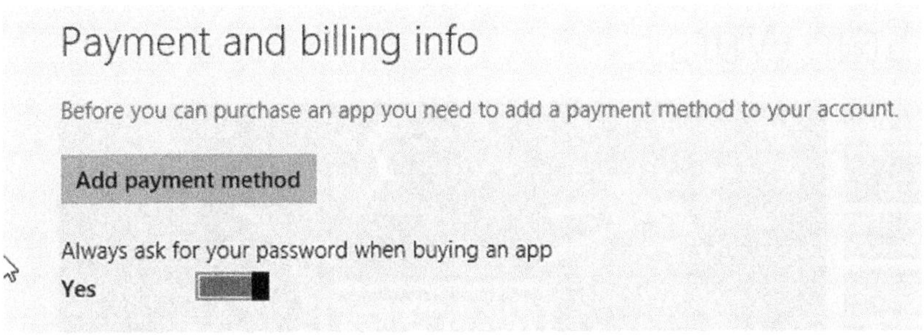

Payment and billing info

Before you can purchase an app you need to add a payment method to your account.

Add payment method

Always ask for your password when buying an app

Yes

Figure 11-3. *Payment method inside the Windows Store integrated app*

Inside the store, you can choose to install an app. Each app has a detail page, which shows the following information (also shown in Figure 11-4):

- Name
- Price
- Buttons to install, try, or buy the app
- Rating
- Terms of use and permissions
- Description text
- Rating certificate
- App's features
- App's screenshots
- Publisher name
- Copyright and trademark info
- App's category
- App's size (MB)
- Age rating
- Supported processor (x32, x64, ARM)
- Languages
- Keywords
- Release date
- Countries and regions

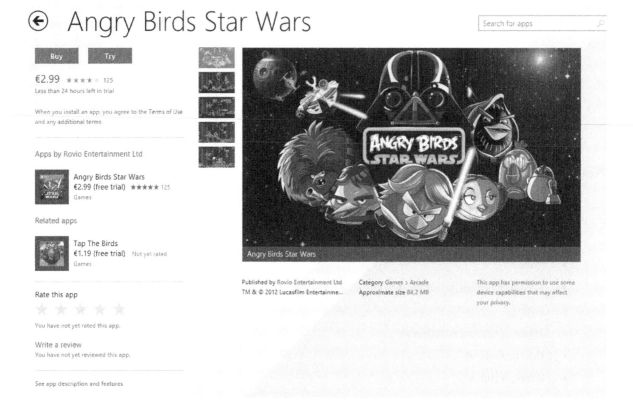

Figure 11-4. *Angry Birds Star Wars app detail page*

All of this information is filled in by the developer during the app's submission process.

The installation process is executed in the background so you can continue to work (Figure 11-5). At the end of the installation, a notification will appear (Figure 11-6).

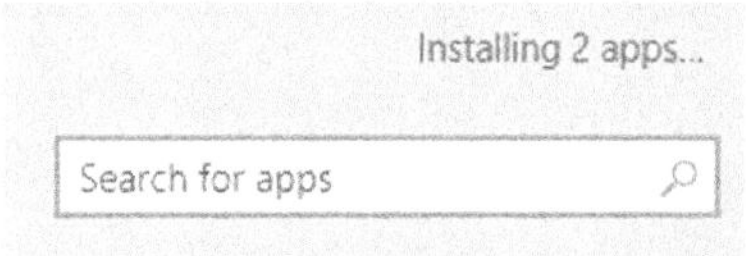

Figure 11-5. *App installation message*

Hill Climb Racing was installed.

Figure 11-6. *Notification after app installation*

A great feature of a Windows Store integrated app is the update management. It will automatically manage all updates of an installed app, notifying the user when an update is available on the tile in the Start window (Figure 11-7) and letting the user choose what update to install (Figure 11-8).

Figure 11-7. *Windows Store app tile update notification*

Figure 11-8. *Windows Store app tile update options*

Now that you understand the Windows Store, let's see how to submit an app.

■ **Note** Before submitting an app, you need a Windows Store App Developer Account. Appendix B fully explains the entire creation process.

Submit Your App

Once you have set all information related to your account, you are ready to submit the app. In the Dashboard of your profile, you can select the "Submit an app" item. The submission process consists of the following steps (Figure 11-9):

- App name
- Selling details
- Services
- Age rating and rating certificates
- Cryptography
- Packages
- Description
- Notes to testers

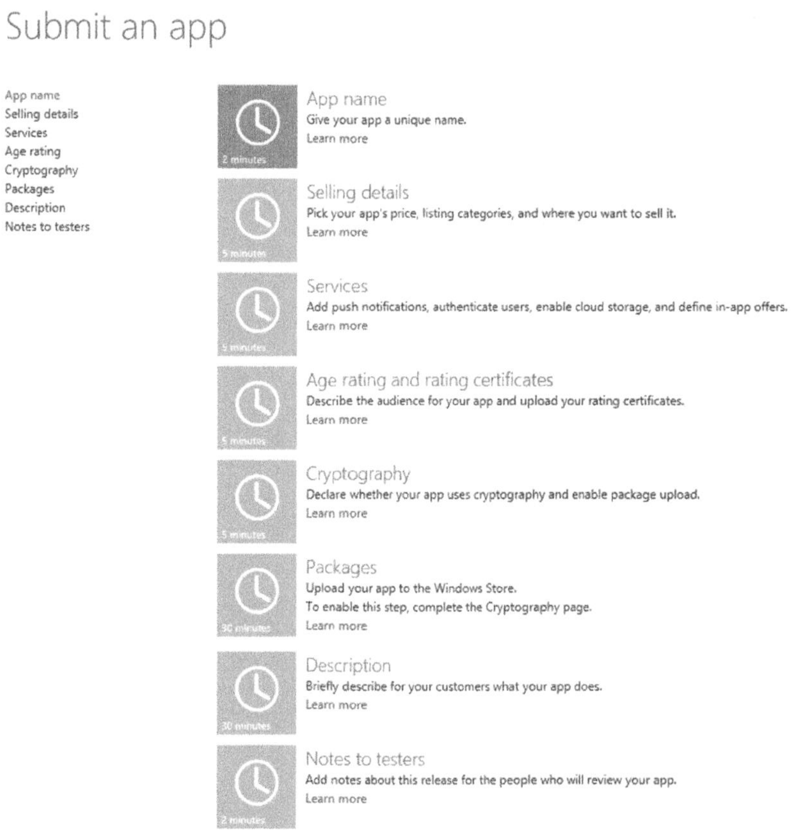

Figure 11-9. *App submission page*

Let's look at each one of these.

App Name

One of the most important choices about your app is the name. This can be a difficult decision to make. I would suggest that you make your app's name:

- *Short*: Your app name is listed in the store or in tiles. It is better to choose a short one, although it can have up to 256 characters.

- *Simple*: Just choose a simple, clear, and creative name. Avoid appending info at the end of the name. Try to use different images for different app editions.

- *Avoid trademarks*: Don't use trademarks. If you have chosen a trademarked name, your app will be removed from the store and will be not published until the trademarked word is completely removed from your app.

When you start to develop an app, you can decide to reserve a name. This can be realized through Visual Studio using the following steps.

1. Select the Store item in the menu and then select Reserve App Name (Figure 11-10). This step will open the page to submit an app.

Figure 11-10. *Reserve App Name menu item*

■ **Note**   You can reserve an app name using the contextual menu of your solution project. This is the path: select Store ➤ Associate App with the Store. This will open a window to manage your apps, and below you can find the "Reserve a new app name" textbox (Figure 11-11). If you use an edition of Visual Studio 2013 different from the Express version, you can use just this path.

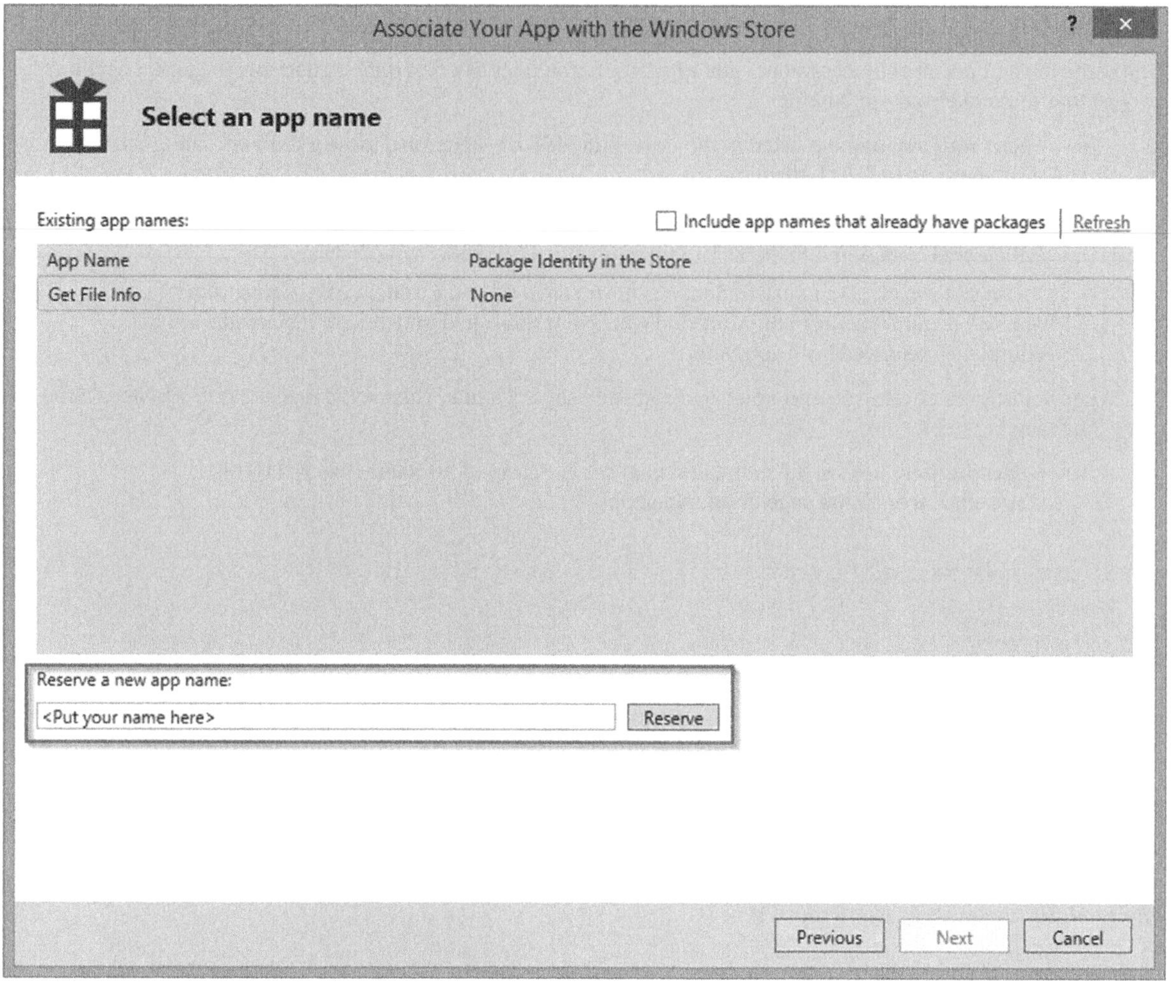

Figure 11-11. *Another way to reserve an app name*

2. Click the App Name option.

3. Type your app name in the App name textbox. If the name you have chosen for your app is not available, an error message will appear.

4. Click the "Reserve app name" button (Figure 11-12).

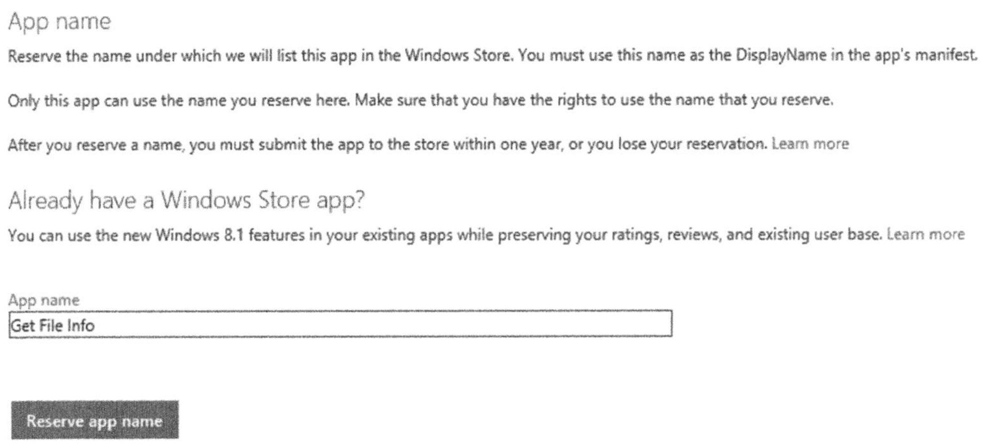

App name

Reserve the name under which we will list this app in the Windows Store. You must use this name as the DisplayName in the app's manifest.

Only this app can use the name you reserve here. Make sure that you have the rights to use the name that you reserve.

After you reserve a name, you must submit the app to the store within one year, or you lose your reservation. Learn more

Already have a Windows Store app?

You can use the new Windows 8.1 features in your existing apps while preserving your ratings, reviews, and existing user base. Learn more

App name

Get File Info

Reserve app name

Figure 11-12. *The process for reserving an app name*

> 5.   If the file name is not already taken, a confirmation will be shown. Click the Save button (Figure 11-13).

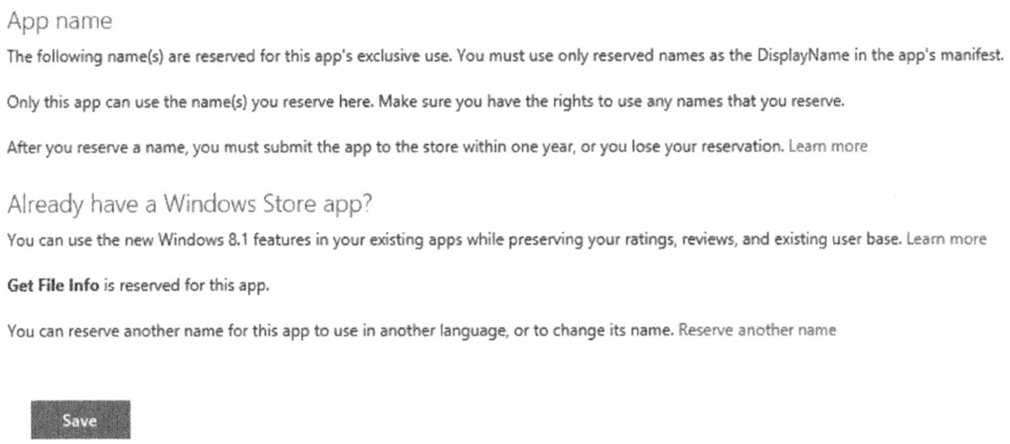

App name

The following name(s) are reserved for this app's exclusive use. You must use only reserved names as the DisplayName in the app's manifest.

Only this app can use the name(s) you reserve here. Make sure you have the rights to use any names that you reserve.

After you reserve a name, you must submit the app to the store within one year, or you lose your reservation. Learn more

Already have a Windows Store app?

You can use the new Windows 8.1 features in your existing apps while preserving your ratings, reviews, and existing user base. Learn more

Get File Info is reserved for this app.

You can reserve another name for this app to use in another language, or to change its name. Reserve another name

Save

Figure 11-13. *Saving app name information*

It is also possible to reserve an app name in another language, if you plan to submit an app for a different market. You can accomplish this by clicking "Reserve another name" on the App Name page in the Windows Dev Center (Figure 11-14).

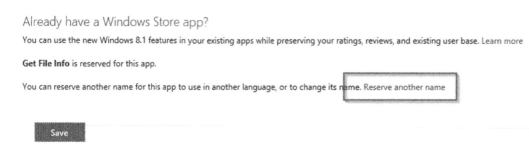

Already have a Windows Store app?

You can use the new Windows 8.1 features in your existing apps while preserving your ratings, reviews, and existing user base. Learn more

Get File Info is reserved for this app.

You can reserve another name for this app to use in another language, or to change its name. Reserve another name

Save

Figure 11-14. *Reserve another app name*

Once you have completed the app name reservation, you need to change a few settings in your `Package.appxmanifest`.

First, change the **Display Name** and **Description** properties in the Application section to match the name you chose and add some information about what the app does (Figure 11-15). Then you can make the same change to the **Name** property in the Packaging section (Figure 11-16).

Application	Visual Assets	Capabilities	Declarations	Content URIs	Packaging

Use this page to set the properties that identify and describe your app.

Display name: Get File Info

Entry point: BW8AGU.Samples.CSharp.App

Default language: en-US   More information

Description: This app retrieve information about a selected file

Figure 11-15. *Fill in the app info in the Application section*

Application	Visual Assets	Capabilities	Declarations	Content URIs	Packaging

Use this page to set the properties that identify and describe your package when it is deployed.

Package name: 49bfa645-f318-4b1e-b659-557ef3906dd2

Package display name: Get File Info

Version: Major: 1 Minor: 0 Build: 0 Revision: 0

Publisher: CN=AntonioTuribbio   Choose Certificate...

Publisher display name:

Package family name: 49bfa645-f318-4b1e-b659-557ef3906dd2_yxen3gkzcvs92

Generate app bundle: If needed ▼   What does an app bundle mean?

Figure 11-16. *Fill in the app info in the Packaging section*

Now you have completed the first step of the app submission process. Let's move to the next step.

Selling Details and Services

In this section, you can set all the information about app selling. The first subsection you need to select is if the app is free to download and use or if the user needs to pay money to buy it. If you choose to sell your app, you can offer a free trial period (Figure 11-17).

Figure 11-17. *Select a price and a free trial period for your app*

■ **Note**   Since the account is registered to a person that lives in Europe, the price is shown in EUR currency. Of course, a customer will see the price in their own currency inside the Windows Store.

Let's change the app price to "Free" and then move to the next subsection.

In-app purchase is a simple way to add new features to your apps and then let the users pay for them. So let's say that you want to submit an app for free, you can choose to add new features using the **Windows Store in-app purchase system** to manage them and sell them. You can also choose a third-party commerce system for in-app purchases (Figure 11-18).

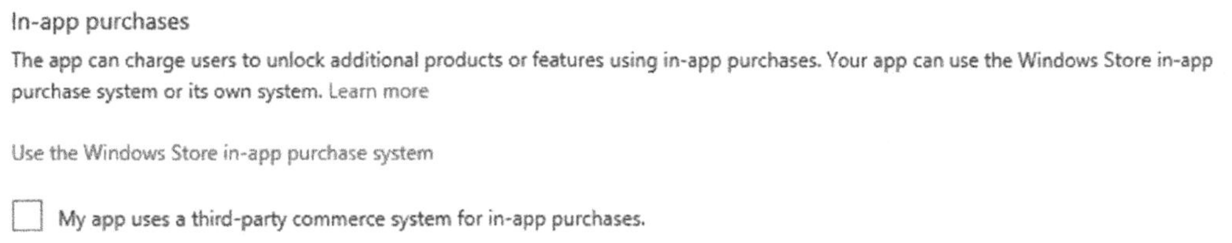

In-app purchases

The app can charge users to unlock additional products or features using in-app purchases. Your app can use the Windows Store in-app purchase system or its own system. Learn more

Use the Windows Store in-app purchase system

☐ My app uses a third-party commerce system for in-app purchases.

Figure 11-18. *In-app purchases feature*

If you select the link "Use the Windows Store in-app purchase system," a new page will open (Figure 11-19), which is the same page linked to the Services item you saw in Figure 11-9.

Services

Add services to bring connected, integrated experiences to your app and make it more engaging, dynamic, and appealing to your customers. You can also provide in-app offers to let customers make additional purchases from within your app.

Windows Azure Mobile Services

You can use Mobile Services to send push notifications, authenticate and manage app users, and store app data in the cloud. Learn more

Sign in to your Windows Azure account. Or sign up now to add services to up to ten apps for free.

If you have an existing WNS solution or need to update your current client secret, visit the Live Services site.

In-app offers

You can use in-app offers to sell additional features and products for this app through the Windows Store. Learn more

Enter a unique product ID for each offer. The product ID is the internal reference to the offer that you use in the app's program code. Your customers won't see the product ID, but they will see the offer's description that you enter on the Description page later.

You can't change or delete product IDs after you submit the app for certification.

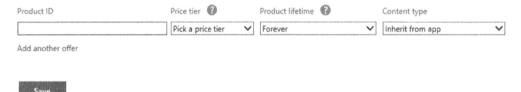

Add another offer

Save

Figure 11-19. *In-app purchase options*

In this page you can add up to 10 Windows Azure Mobile Services to integrate push notification, authentication, or to store app data, or you can add **In-app offers** that a user can buy. Each offer has the following information:

- *Product Id*: A unique id for your app that you can use inside your app to enable features. This key is not shown to the user, but could be linked to a description to show to the user.

- *Price Tier*: To set if the offer is free of charge or not.

- *Product Lifetime*: To set how long this offer is valid.

- *Content Type*: The category related to the offer.

Next subsection is **Markets** (Figure 11-20). Here you can choose all the markets in which your app will be available. Be careful in this step, considering that each market could have some restrictions. For example, there are few markets that only accept free apps (like Isle of Man) or that 18+ (minimal age for a user) apps are not allowed in countries like Australia or Germany. Information on various restrictions can be found at msdn.microsoft.com/en-us/library/windows/apps/hh694064.aspx.

Marksts ❓
Select all

☐ Algeria	☐ Argentina	☐ Australia
☐ Austria	☐ Bahrain	☐ Belgium
☐ Brazil	☐ Bulgaria	☐ Canada
☐ Chile	☐ China	☐ Colombia
☐ Costa Rica	☐ Croatia	☐ Cyprus
☐ Czech Republic	☐ Denmark	☐ Egypt
☐ Estonia	☐ Finland	☐ France
☐ Germany	☐ Greece	☐ Hong Kong SAR
☐ Hungary	☐ India	☐ Indonesia
☐ Iraq	☐ Ireland	☐ Israel

Figure 11-20. *List of available markets*

Also, when you select a different market than your own, you need to provide some globalization features to your app or it will not pass the submission tests. Some other things that need to be considered are the ethnic, cultural, and religious perspectives. For example, if your app includes some information that goes against a religion foundation of the country in your selected market, then the app will not pass the submission.

For a sample app, let's choose two markets: United States and Italy.

The **Release date** subsection allows you to postpone the app release date to a specific day. This could cause delay in the submission process (Figure 11-21).

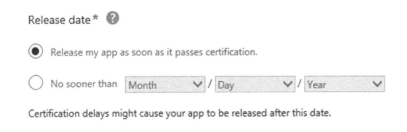

Figure 11-21. *Release date options*

App category and subcategories let you choose in what category of the Windows Store your app will appear (Figure 11-22). Subcategories are not are not always required. Always pick the correct category for the app. For this sample app, choose "Productivity."

App category and subcategories
The Category and Subcategory determine where the app will be listed in the Store. Learn more
Category *
Pick a category
Subcategory *

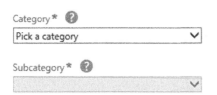

Figure 11-22. *Categories selection step*

The next subsection is **Hardware Requirements**. Here you can select DirectX and RAM requirements that a device needs to have to let the user download the app. For example, if you are submitting a game, you might need to choose one of the available options to let the user play the game on a required platform (Figure 11-23).

Hardware requirements
We want users to have the best experience possible when they install your app. Let us know if your app requires a minimum DirectX feature level, or if it needs a certain amount of RAM. Only users that meet these requirements can download your app. While this information might limit how many people can download your app, it also helps you avoid poor ratings caused by users who install your app on a system that falls below your minimum requirements.
If your app supports ARM, you must select the All Systems option for DirectX.
Minimum DirectX feature level
Available to all systems
Minimum system RAM
Available to all systems

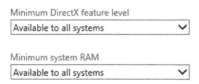

Figure 11-23. *Hardware Requirements selection*

Finally, the last option in Selling Details is **Accessibility**. Once selected, your app will be tested to verify if all the accessibility guidelines are met (Figure 11-24).

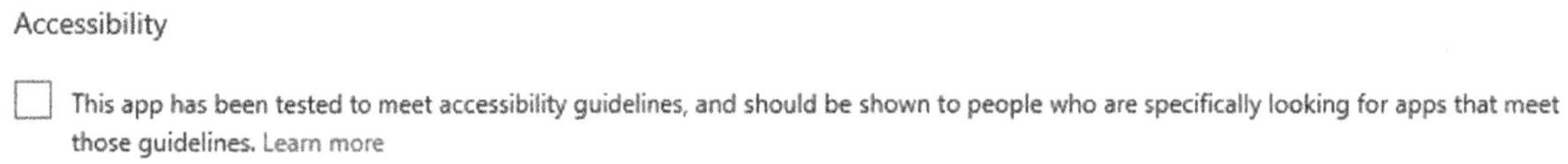

Accessibility
This app has been tested to meet accessibility guidelines, and should be shown to people who are specifically looking for apps that meet those guidelines. Learn more

Figure 11-24. *Accessibility subsection*

Age Rating and Rating Certificates

In this section you can choose the suitable age for the app's users and the rating certificates. The first option allows you to select the minimum age for users. There are several options:

- 3+ Suitable for young children

- 7+ Suitable for ages 7 and older

- 12+ Suitable for ages 12 and older

- 16+ Suitable for ages 16 and older

- 18+ Suitable for adults only

Apps for young children should meet basic requirements such as no violence or sexual references. The 18+ option is available only for games that are rated by a third-party ratings board and follow all Windows content policies. Usually the ratings board releases an approval to sell the game. These authorities check if the game is suitable for an appropriate age group, and are not available in all countries (you can find more at msdn.microsoft.com/en-us/library/windows/apps/hh694080.aspx). Once the game is rated, you can update a certificate (.GDF file) as a rating certificate inside the Age Rating and Rating Certificates page (Figure 11-25). For this sample app, let's select 3+ option for the user age.

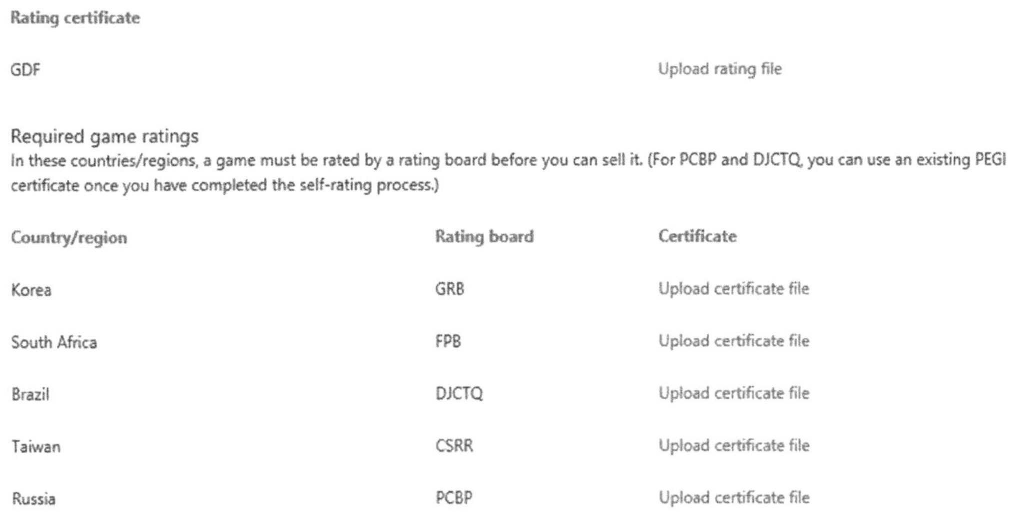

Rating certificate

GDF   Upload rating file

Required game ratings
In these countries/regions, a game must be rated by a rating board before you can sell it. (For PCBP and DJCTQ, you can use an existing PEGI certificate once you have completed the self-rating process.)

Country/region	Rating board	Certificate
Korea	GRB	Upload certificate file
South Africa	FPB	Upload certificate file
Brazil	DJCTQ	Upload certificate file
Taiwan	CSRR	Upload certificate file
Russia	PCBP	Upload certificate file

Figure 11-25. *Age rating certificate section*

Cryptography

In this page, you can report if your app uses cryptography or encryption (Figure 11-26). If yes, you need to be aware of the laws and regulations of the destination markets to avoid failing submission process. Some tasks are not considered in the cryptography category, such as the following:

- Password encryption
- Copy protection

- Authentication

- Digital rights management

- Using digital signatures

Cryptography

Describe how this app uses cryptography and encryption. Learn more

Here are some examples of how this app might apply cryptography or encryption. This list is a guide and not every possible example is listed.
- Any use of a digital signature such as authentication or integrity checking.
- Encryption of any data or files that your app uses or accesses.
- Key management, certificate management, or anything that interacts with a public key infrastructure.
- Using a secure communication channel such as NTLM, Kerberos, Secure Sockets Layer (SSL), or Transport Layer Security (TLS).
- Encrypting passwords or other forms of information security.
- Copy protection or digital rights management (DRM).
- Antivirus protection.

This app is considered to use encryption even if another entity performs the encryption, such as the operating system, an external library, a third-party product, or a cryptographic processor.

Does this app call, support, contain, or use cryptography or encryption? *
- ⦿ Yes
- ◯ No

Is the cryptography or encryption limited to one or more of the tasks listed here? *
- Password encryption
- Copy protection
- Authentication
- Digital rights management
- Using digital signatures

If this app calls, supports, or uses cryptography or encryption for any task that is not in this list your answer to this question is No.
- ⦿ Yes
- ◯ No

☐ I confirm that this app is widely distributable to all jurisdictions without government review, approval, license or technology-based restriction. *

For info about how to evaluate compliance with encryption controls, see the Bureau of Industry and Security website. The Windows Store uses the U.S. standards on encryption controls. Other jurisdictions have similar standards and requirements.

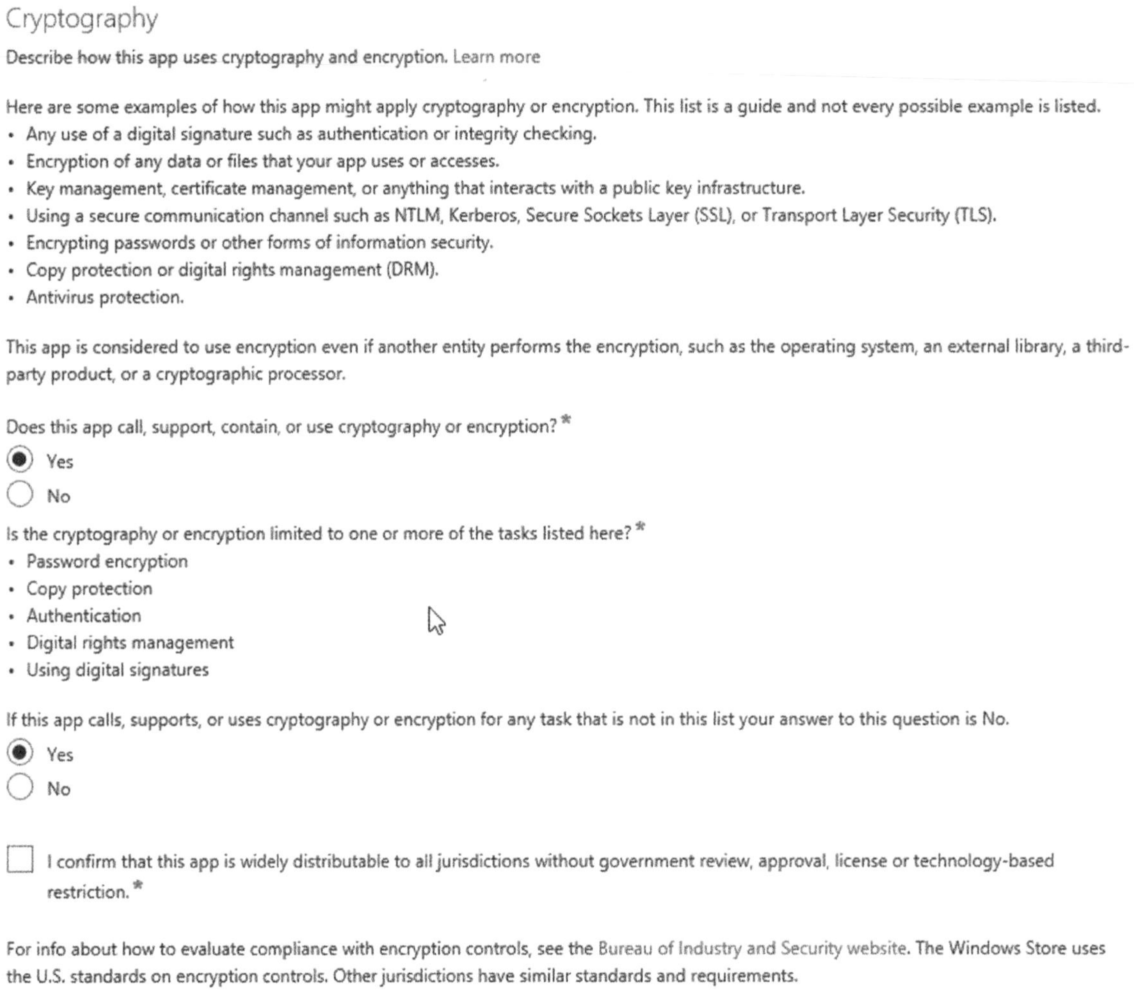

Figure 11-26. *Cryptography settings*

If in your app you use any cryptography or encryption process different from those listed, you need an **Export Commodity Classification Number (ECCN)**. In this sample app you do not use any cryptography.

Packages

In this step you submit your app packages to the Windows Store. This step is divided into three phases:

- Validate your app with the **Windows App Certification Kit**.

- Create app packages in Visual Studio 2013.

- Upload your app packages.

The Windows App Certification Kit is a tool that allows you to test the app before you submit it to the Store. This helps you avoid submitting an app that does not follows all of the requirements.

This tool executes different tests on your app to check if everything is ok. The following is a list of tests that are executed:

- Crashes and Hangs Test

- App Manifest Compliance Test

- Windows Security Features Test

- Supported Windows Store API Test

- Performance Test

- App Manifest Resources Test

- Debug Configuration Test

- Filed Encoding Test

- App Capabilities Test

- Windows Runtime Metadata Validation

- Package Sanity Check

- Resource Usage Test

The Windows App Certification Kit can be installed with the Windows 8.1 SDK here: `msdn.microsoft.com/en-us/windows/apps/bg127575`. Note that if you are planning to deploy your app for an ARM device, you also need to install the Windows App Certification Kit for Windows RT.

▮ **Note**   Visual Studio Express 2013 for Windows already installs the Windows App Certification Kit.

Let's see how to use it. When you open the Windows App Certification Kit, you can pick one of the three following items (Figure 11-27):

- Validate Windows Store App

- Validate Desktop App

- Validate Desktop Device App

Figure 11-27. *Windows App Certification Kit 3.1*

■ **Note**   Windows Store allows also you to submit a Windows Desktop app. Check this here:

blogs.msdn.com/b/windowsstore/archive/2012/06/08/listing-your-desktop-app-in-the-store.aspx

---

After choosing the first item, Validate Windows Store App, a list of apps is shown so you can choose the one you want to validate (Figure 11-28).

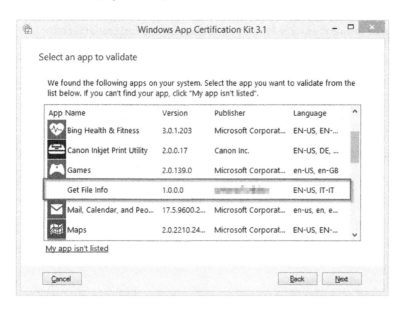

Figure 11-28. *App selection in Windows App Certification Kit*

In this case, choose the "Get File Info" app that you are ready to submit to the store.

■ **Note**   If you could not find your app on the list, you can go into Visual Studio Express 2013 for Windows, open your app project, select "Release" as a build configuration mode, and then click Build ➤ Deploy. After that deploy is completed, you can click the "My app isn't listed" link.

Next, you need to choose what tests are executed by the Windows App Certification Kit (Figure 11-29). Let's select all tests and then click the Next button. In the next step, the app will be tested. This means that the app will be open different times by the tool; it is suggested to let the tool work until it has finished (Figure 11-30). If the app did not pass a test, you will be prompted to save a report file and the message in Figure 11-31 will be shown.

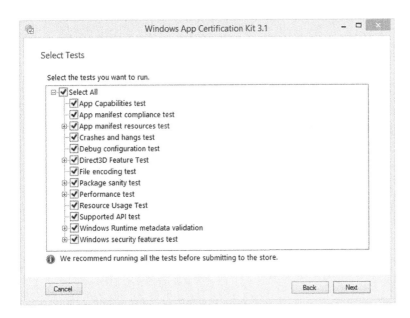

Figure 11-29. *List of selectable tests*

Figure 11-30. *Testing phase in Windows App Certification Kit*

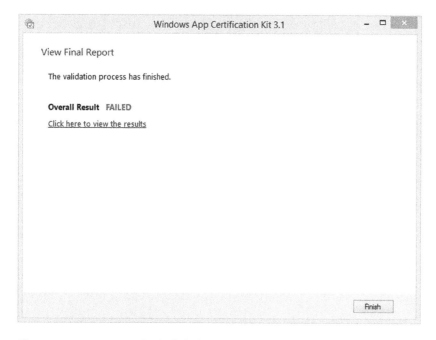

Figure 11-31. *An example of a failed process*

If you want to understand what happened, you just need to click the link "Click here to view the results," which will open a web page with all the information about the error and resolution (Figure 11-32).

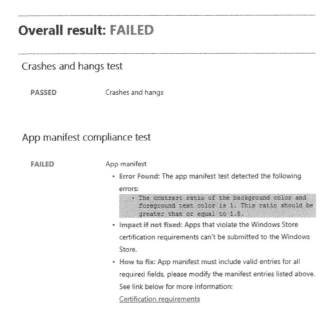

Figure 11-32. *An example of an error and a hint for resolution*

Once you have resolved all the issues, you can re-run the Windows App Certification Kit validation. If everything is ok (Figure 11-33), you are ready to create the packages. Remember that if the Windows App Certification Kit successfully validates your app, this does not mean that your app will pass app submission. It is just a tool to check basic settings and configuration of your app.

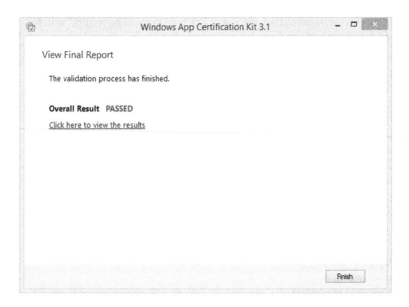

Figure 11-33. *Successful validation of a Windows Store app*

The process of creation of an app package is very simple. First, you need to go in the Solution Explorer, right-click the project, and then go to Store ➤ Associate app with the Store (Figure 11-34). In this way, the Packaging section of the Package.appxmanifest is updated with the information regarding the app name and author. A wizard is opened, so type your credentials for the Windows Store account, select the app name (Figure 11-35) you want to use, and then it will display all the updated information (Figure 11-36).

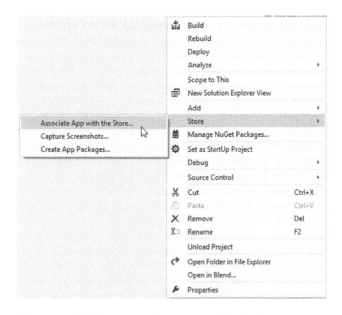

Figure 11-34. *How to associate an app with the Store*

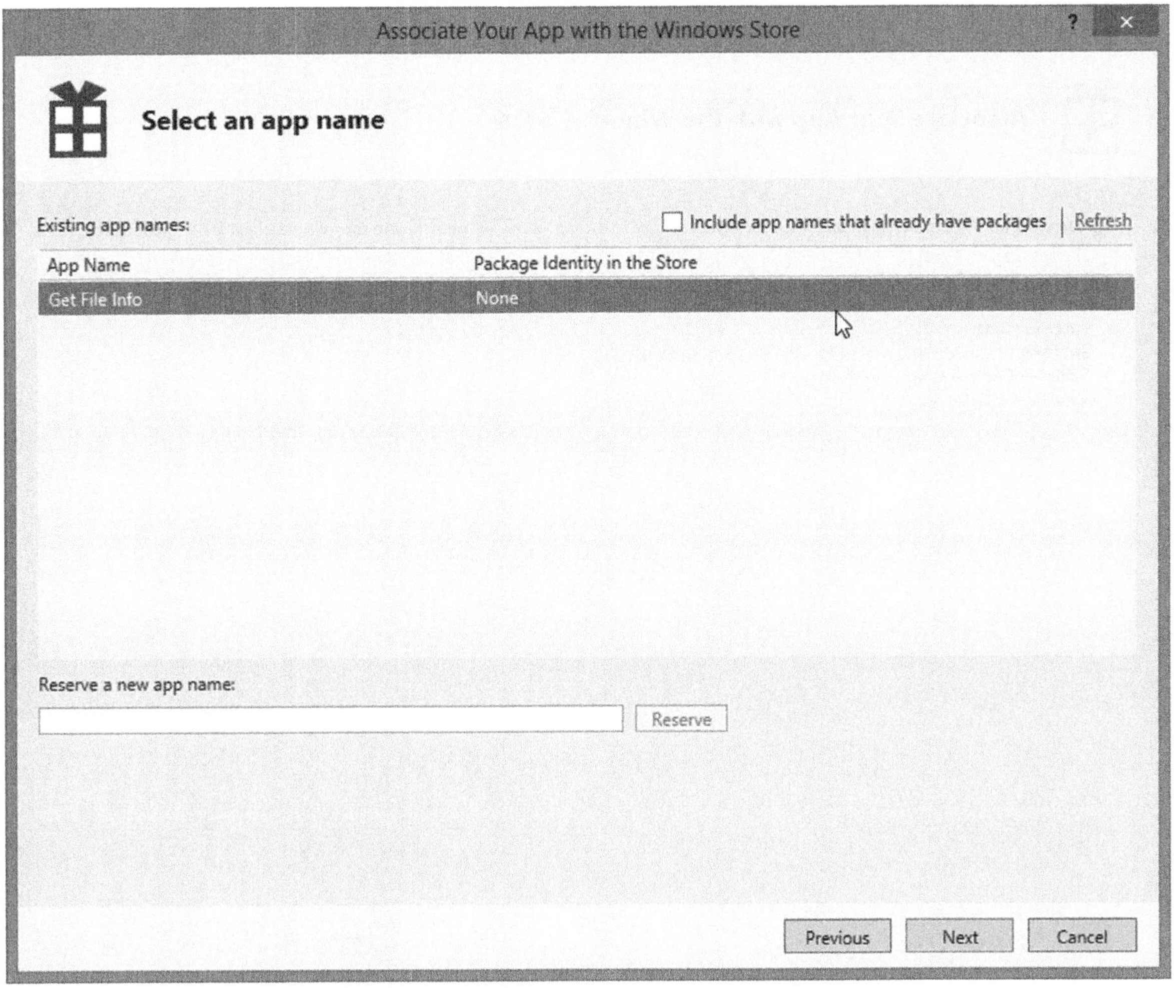

Figure 11-35. *Select a reserved app name from the Store*

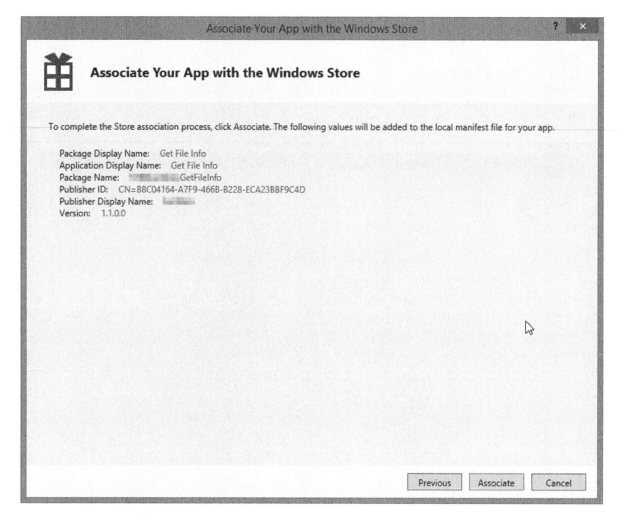

Figure 11-36. *Review of the app name Store association*

Now you need to create your app packages, which is a set of files with the .appxupload extension that you will upload on the Windows Store. You go again to the Solution Explorer, right-click the project, and then go to Store ➤ Create App Packages (Figure 11-37). Once again a wizard will open (Figure 11-37). In the first step you can choose to create an app package to upload it in the store, or choose to create a package to use for testing purposes on a device that has a developer license installed. Then you need to follow the same path as the app association until you arrive at the step in Figure 11-38.

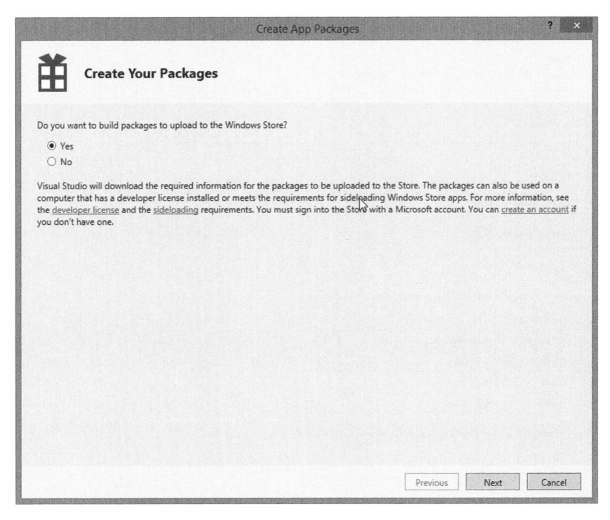

Figure 11-37. App package creation wizard

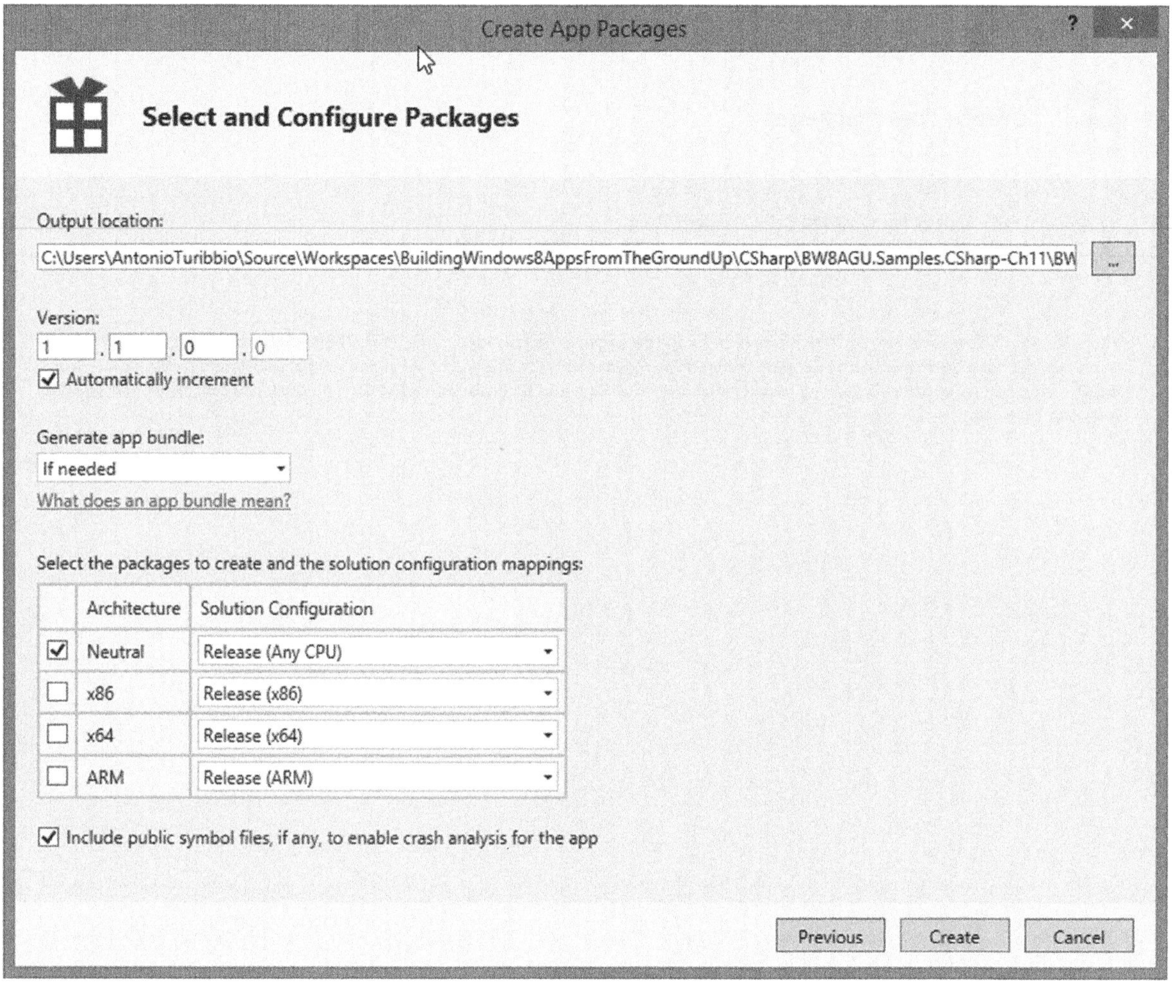

Figure 11-38. *Package configuration step*

In this step you need to configure the following options:

- *Output Location*: The drop folder for the package.

- *Version*: The app version number. It can be set manually or automatically.

- *Generate App Bundle*: This option can be useful if you have a localized app with many localized resources. This helps the customer to download only localized resources for his language instead of all the localized files. There are three options: If needed, Always, and Never.

- *Select the packages to create and the solution configuration mappings*: A package is created for different platforms, and different build configuration can be chosen.

- *Include public symbol files, if any, to enable crash analysis for the app*: These files can be used to collect information about bugs and crashes. If this option is selected, debug symbols are included inside the .appxupload file.

After you click the Create button and the package is correctly created, you can re-execute the validation process through Windows App Certification Kit (you can also choose a remote machine) or open the output location and check if a file with extension `.appxupload` is in it (Figure 11-39).

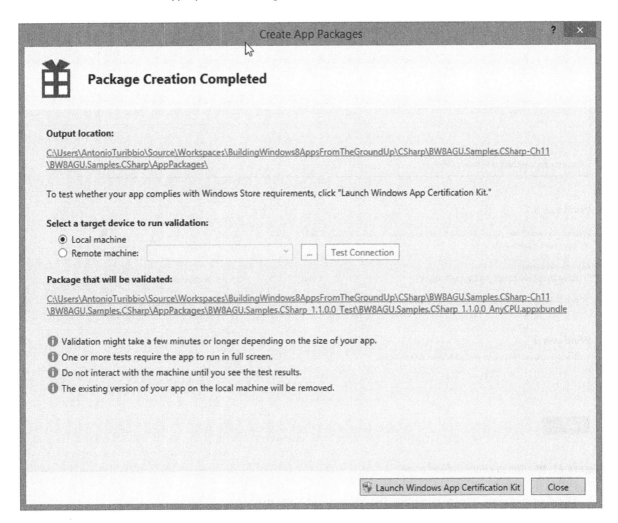

Figure 11-39. *Package creation completed*

Now you have to submit your package to the Store. Go to the Windows Store dashboard and in the app section select Edit ➤ Packages. On this page you can just drag and drop the package from the output location to the browser and the package will be uploaded. Then click Save (Figure 11-40).

Packages

Use the control to upload the packages (the .appxupload file) that you created with Create App Packages in Visual Studio. Some parts of the package are specific to your Windows Store developer account. To build the .appxupload package correctly in Visual Studio, sign in with the Microsoft account that you use with your Windows Store developer account. Learn more

Drag your packages here or browse to files.

Windows 8.1

BW8AGU.Samples.CSharp_1.1.0.0_AnyCPU_bundle.appxupload   v2013.1120.2216.5617   ✖
We uploaded the app bundle.

App bundle contains:

BW8AGU.Samples.CSharp_1.1.0.0_AnyCPU.appx   v1.1.0.0   Architecture: neutral

BW8AGU.Samples.CSharp_1.1.0.0_language-it.appx   v1.1.0.0   ResourceId: split.language-it

Windows 8

You haven't uploaded any packages for Windows 8. Learn more

Figure 11-40. *App package upload page*

There are two more steps to complete: Description and Notes to testers.

Description

In this step, you need to provide a description of your app based on supported languages and different platforms (Windows 8 and 8.1). This step consists of the following sections:

- *Description*: Your main app description. It's important to be very detailed to help customers understand what your app does and wisely choose words to grab attention.

- *App Features*: These are short descriptions in a bulleted list for your app.

- *Screenshot*: You can provide up to nine app screenshots. These can be created directly from Visual Studio 2013 using the Capture Screenshots menu item, as shown in Figure 11-34, that will start the Windows Store App simulator. You can also choose a few settings using the Screenshot Settings button (the default location is Windows Simulator folder in the Pictures library).

You need to click the Copy Screenshot icon to create images (Figure 11-41). Each screenshot must be in .png format with a size less than 2MB and a resolution of 1366x768 or 768x1366 and must have a description.

Figure 11-41. *Copy Screenshot button in the Windows Store App Simulator*

- *Notes*: You can add few notes like the features in this release version.

- *Recommended Hardware*: Minimal hardware requirements for your app.

- *Keywords*: A list of tags that can improve your app searchability.

- *Copyright and Trademark Info*: Provide your copyright information.

- *Additional License Terms*: In this field you can provide more information about license terms that are different from the Standard Application License Terms (more details at msdn.microsoft.com/en-us/library/windows/apps/hh694058.aspx).

- *Promotional Images*: A set of images that can be used in the store to promote your app.

- *App Web Site*: The link to the web site that is about your app.

- *Support Contact Info*: An e-mail address or a web site link to help customers get support.

- *Privacy Policy*: In this field, you need to provide a URL that declares if you collect or use personal info inside your app. For example, if you enable internet client capability, you must specify a privacy policy description here and inside the app settings pane.

Notes to Testers

In this step, you can provide any useful information to Microsoft testers to help them to understand and test your app (Figure 11-42). This can help to accelerate the app submission process. Some useful information could include the following:

- Login credentials for testing purposes

- Explain what feature your app provides that is visible or locked and how to test it

- If an update, explain what has changed

Figure 11-42. *Notes to testers page*

You have finally completed app submission process. In the detail page of your app you have two new buttons at the bottom: "Review release info" and "Submit for certification." The first one shows all the information provided; the second one sends your app for the submission process. After clicking the latter button, you need to wait about six business days to know if your app has passed the submission process (Figure 11-43).

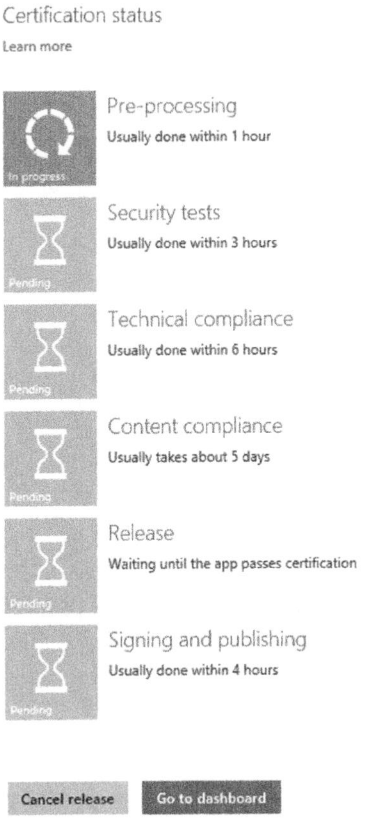
Certification status
Learn more
In progress
Pre-processing
Usually done within 1 hour
Pending
Security tests
Usually done within 3 hours
Pending
Technical compliance
Usually done within 6 hours
Pending
Content compliance
Usually takes about 5 days
Pending
Release
Waiting until the app passes certification
Pending
Signing and publishing
Usually done within 4 hours
Cancel release
Go to dashboard

Figure 11-43. *App certification status*

If your app did not pass the submission process, a failure notification will be shown on the dashboard. A full report about what went wrong is available, with notes from testers (see Figure 11-44).

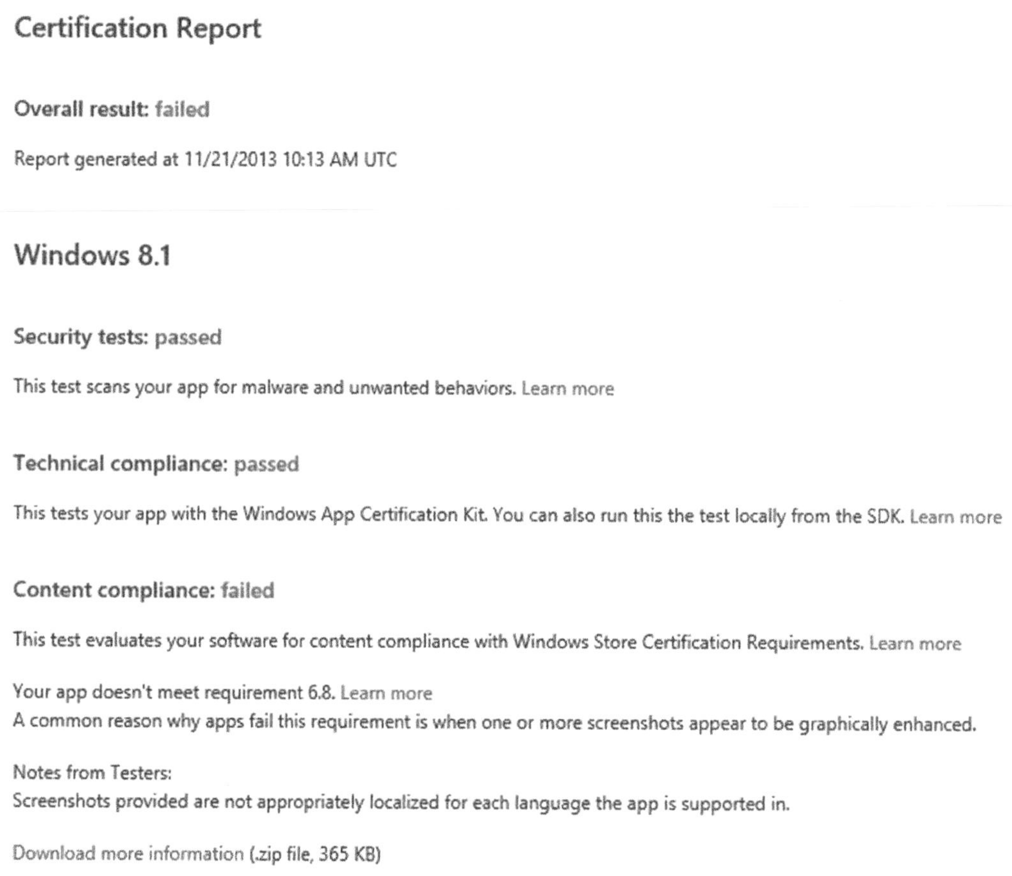

Certification Report

Overall result: failed

Report generated at 11/21/2013 10:13 AM UTC

Windows 8.1

Security tests: passed

This test scans your app for malware and unwanted behaviors. Learn more

Technical compliance: passed

This tests your app with the Windows App Certification Kit. You can also run this the test locally from the SDK. Learn more

Content compliance: failed

This test evaluates your software for content compliance with Windows Store Certification Requirements. Learn more

Your app doesn't meet requirement 6.8. Learn more
A common reason why apps fail this requirement is when one or more screenshots appear to be graphically enhanced.

Notes from Testers:
Screenshots provided are not appropriately localized for each language the app is supported in.

Download more information (.zip file, 365 KB)

Figure 11-44. *An example of failed certification*

After you have solved all certification errors, you can upload once again the package to restart the submission process. Finally, once your app passes the submission process, it will be available in the chosen markets using the search feature in the Windows Store.

Monitoring Your App

After your app is published in the store, you can check the number of downloads and the app usage. To check download history, go to the Windows Dev Center dashboard, click the Details option on your app tile, and then Downloads. This page shows a chart that lists all downloads over time (Figure 11-45). You can also export this information in CSV format.

Downloads

App downloads

☐ Subcategory benchmark

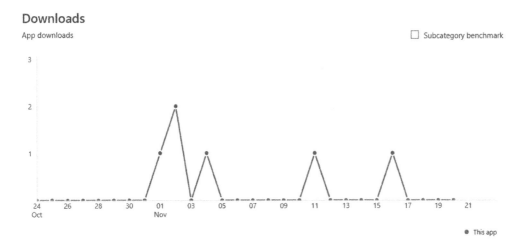

Figure 11-45. History download chart on the Download page

To show app usage, go to the Windows Dev Center dashboard, click Details ➤ Usage. Here, you can use filters to show app usage (Figure 11-46).

Average app usage per day

Average app usage in minutes per day

☐ Subcategory benchmark

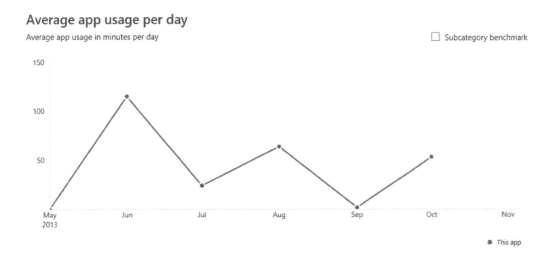

Figure 11-46. Usage chart on the Usage page

Another interesting feature is monitoring app quality on the Quality page. You can open this page in the Windows Dev Center dashboard, clicking Details ➤ Quality. In this section, you can find charts and useful information about app crashes, unresponsive events, and JavaScript exceptions. You can use all this information to fix bugs and improve your app. To use this feature you need to enable telemetry data collection in your account profile. Also, your .appxupload file needs to include public symbols.

Updating Your App

If you have found bugs or you want to add new features to your app, you need to upload it again to the store. To submit an app update, you just need to go to the Window Dev Center dashboard, and select Edit ➤ Packages. Here you just drag and drop a new package of your app with an assembly version number greater than the actual release. You also need to update the Notes section in the Description page and list new features. Then you can submit your app for certification.

Conclusion

In this final chapter, you took a deep dive into the Windows Store and the Windows Store app submission process. All this information will help you understand how to take advantage of the Store to improve your app downloads and increase your earnings. Now that you have read all of these chapters, you're finally ready to start creating a great number of quality apps!

■ ■ ■

Live Tile and Toast Templates

This appendix lists all the templates available in Windows 8.1. Table A-1shows the template name (and the fallback name where applicable), the XML of the template (which you manipulate to provide your content), and an image that shows how your tile will appear after your update.

Live Tile

Table A-1. *Template XML and Example*

Template Name	XML	Example
TileSquare150x150Image **TileSquareImage**	```<tile>` ` <visual version="2">` ` <binding template="TileSquare150x150Image"` ` fallback="TileSquareImage">` ` <image id="1" src="Assets\picture.png" />` ` </binding>` ` </visual>` `</tile>```	
TileSquare150x150Block **TileSquareBlock**	```<tile>` ` <visual version="2">` ` <binding template="TileSquare150x150Block"` ` fallback="TileSquareBlock">` ` <text id="1">text id="1"</text>` ` <text id="2">text id="2"</text>` ` </binding>` ` </visual>` `</tile>```	
TileSquare150x150Text01 **TileSquareText01**	```<tile>` ` <visual version="2">` ` <binding template="TileSquare150x150Text01"` ` fallback="TileSquareText01">` ` <text id="1">text id="1"</text>` ` <text id="2">text id="2"</text>` ` <text id="3">text id="3"</text>` ` <text id="4">text id="4"</text>` ` </binding>` ` </visual>` `</tile>```	

(continued)

Table A-1. (*continued*)

Template Name	XML	Example

TileSquare150x150Text02
TileSquareText02
	``xml
	<tile>
	  <visual version="2">
	    <binding template="TileSquare150x150Text02"
	    fallback="TileSquareText02">
	      <text id="1">text id="1"</text>
	      <text id="2">text id="2"</text>
	    </binding>
	  </visual>
	</tile>
	``
		text id=...
		text id="2"

TileSquare150x150Text03
TileSquareText03
	``xml
	<tile>
	  <visual version="2">
	    <binding template="TileSquare150x150Text03"
	    fallback="TileSquareText03">
	      <text id="1">text id="1"</text>
	      <text id="2">text id="2"</text>
	      <text id="3">text id="3"</text>
	      <text id="4">text id="4"</text>
	    </binding>
	  </visual>
	</tile>
	``
		text id="1"
		text id="2"
		text id="3"
		text id="4"

TileSquare150x150Text04
TileSquareText04
	``xml
	<tile>
	  <visual version="2">
	    <binding template="TileSquare150x150Text04"
	    fallback="TileSquareText04">
	      <text id="1">text id="1"</text>
	    </binding>
	  </visual>
	</tile>
	``
		text id="1"

TileSquare150x150PeekImage
AndText01
TileSquarePeekImageAndText01
	``xml
	<tile>
	  <visual version="2">
	    <binding template="TileSquare150x150PeekImage
	    AndText01" fallback="TileSquarePeekImageAndText01">
	      <image id="1" src="Assets\picture.png" />
	      <text id="1">text id="1"</text>
	      <text id="2">text id="2"</text>
	      <text id="3">text id="3"</text>
	      <text id="4">text id="4"</text>
	    </binding>
	  </visual>
	</tile>
	``
		text id=...
		text id="2"
		text id="3"
		text id="4"

(*continued*)

Table A-1. (*continued*)

Template Name	XML	Example
TileSquare150x150PeekImage AndText02 **TileSquarePeekImageAndText02**	```<tile> <visual version="2"> <binding template="TileSquare150x150PeekImage AndText02" fallback="TileSquarePeekImageAndText02"> <image id="1" src="Assets\picture.png" /> <text id="1">text id="1"</text> <text id="2">text id="2"</text> </binding> </visual></tile>```	
TileSquare150x150PeekImage AndText03 **TileSquarePeekImageAndText03**	```<tile> <visual version="2"> <binding template="TileSquare150x150PeekImage AndText03" fallback="TileSquarePeekImageAndText03"> <image id="1" src="Assets\picture.png" /> <text id="1">text id="1"</text> <text id="2">text id="2"</text> <text id="3">text id="3"</text> <text id="4">text id="4"</text> </binding> </visual></tile>```	
TileSquare150x150PeekImage AndText04 **TileSquarePeekImageAndText04**	```<tile> <visual version="2"> <binding template="TileSquare150x150PeekImage AndText04" fallback="TileSquarePeekImageAndText04"> <image id="1" src="Assets\picture.png" /> <text id="1">text id="1"</text> </binding> </visual></tile>```	

(*continued*)

Table A-1. (*continued*)

Template Name	XML	Example

TileWide310x150Image
TileWideImage
	```<tile>```
	``` <visual version="2">```
	``` <binding template="TileWide310x150Image"```
	``` fallback="TileWideImage">```
	``` <image id="1" src="Assets\picture.png" />```
	``` </binding>```
	``` </visual>```
	```</tile>```	

TileWide310x150ImageCollection
TileWideImageCollection
	```<tile>```
	``` <visual version="2">```
	``` <binding template="TileWide310x150ImageCollection"```
	``` fallback="TileWideImageCollection">```
	``` <image id="1" src="Assets\picture1.png" />```
	``` <image id="2" src="Assets\picture2.png" />```
	``` <image id="3" src="Assets\picture3.png" />```
	``` <image id="4" src="Assets\picture4.png" />```
	``` <image id="5" src="Assets\picture5.png" />```
	``` </binding>```
	``` </visual>```
	```</tile>```	

TileWide310x150ImageAndText01
TileWideImageAndText01
	```<tile>```
	``` <visual version="2">```
	``` <binding template="TileWide310x150ImageAndText01"```
	``` fallback="TileWideImageAndText01">```
	``` <image id="1" src="Assets\picture.png" />```
	``` <text id="1">text id="1"</text>```
	``` </binding>```
	``` </visual>```
	```</tile>```
		text id="1"

TileWide310x150ImageAndText02
TileWideImageAndText02
	```<tile>```
	``` <visual version="2">```
	``` <binding template="TileWide310x150ImageAndText02"```
	``` fallback="TileWideImageAndText02">```
	``` <image id="1" src="Assets\picture.png" />```
	``` <text id="1">text id="1"</text>```
	``` <text id="2">text id="2"</text>```
	``` </binding>```
	``` </visual>```
	```</tile>```
		text id="1"
		text id="2"

TileWide310x150BlockAndText01
TileWideBlockAndText01
	```<tile>```
	``` <visual version="2">```
	``` <binding template="TileWide310x150BlockAndText01"```
	``` fallback="TileWideBlockAndText01">```
	``` <text id="1">text id="1"</text>```
	``` <text id="2">text id="2"</text>```
	``` <text id="3">text id="3"</text>```
	``` <text id="4">text id="4"</text>```
	``` <text id="5">text id="5"</text>```
	``` <text id="6">text id="6"</text>```
	``` </binding>```
	``` </visual>```
	```</tile>```
		text id="1"
		text id="2"
		text id="3"
		text id="4" "5" text id="6"

(*continued*)

Table A-1. (*continued*)

Template Name	XML	Example

TileWide310x150Block AndText02
 TileWideBlockAndText02
	```<tile>```
	``` <visual version="2">```
	``` <binding template="TileWide310x150BlockAndText02"```
	``` fallback="TileWideBlockAndText02">```
	``` <text id="1">text id="1"</text>```
	``` <text id="2">text id="2"</text>```
	``` <text id="3">text id="3"</text>```
	``` </binding>```
	``` </visual>```
	```</tile>```	

TileWide310x150PeekImage Collection01
 TileWidePeekImageCollection01
	```<tile>```
	``` <visual version="2">```
	``` <binding template="TileWide310x150PeekImage```
	``` Collection01" fallback="TileWidePeekImageCollection01">```
	``` <image id="1" src="Assets\picture1.png" />```
	``` <image id="2" src="Assets\picture2.png" />```
	``` <image id="3" src="Assets\picture3.png" />```
	``` <image id="4" src="Assets\picture4.png" />```
	``` <image id="5" src="Assets\picture5.png" />```
	``` <text id="1">text id="1"</text>```
	``` <text id="2">text id="2"</text>```
	``` </binding>```
	``` </visual>```
	```</tile>```	

TileWide310x150PeekImage Collection02
 TileWidePeekImageCollection02
	```<tile>```
	``` <visual version="2">```
	``` <binding template="TileWide310x150PeekImage```
	``` Collection02" fallback="TileWidePeekImageCollection02">```
	``` <image id="1" src="Assets\picture.png" />```
	``` <image id="2" src="Assets\picture.png" />```
	``` <image id="3" src="Assets\picture.png" />```
	``` <image id="4" src="Assets\picture.png" />```
	``` <image id="5" src="Assets\picture.png" />```
	``` <text id="1">text id="1"</text>```
	``` <text id="2">text id="2"</text>```
	``` <text id="3">text id="3"</text>```
	``` <text id="4">text id="4"</text>```
	``` <text id="5">text id="5"</text>```
	``` </binding>```
	``` </visual>```
	```</tile>```	

TileWide310x150PeekImage Collection03
 TileWidePeekImageCollection03
	```<tile>```
	``` <visual version="2">```
	``` <binding template="TileWide310x150PeekImage```
	``` Collection03" fallback="TileWidePeekImageCollection03">```
	``` <image id="1" src="Assets\picture.png" />```
	``` <image id="2" src="Assets\picture.png" />```
	``` <image id="3" src="Assets\picture.png" />```
	``` <image id="4" src="Assets\picture.png" />```
	``` <image id="5" src="Assets\picture.png" />```
	``` <text id="1">text id="1"</text>```
	``` </binding>```
	``` </visual>```
	```</tile>```	

(*continued*)

Table A-1. (*continued*)

Template Name	XML	Example

TileWide310x150PeekImage Collection04
 TileWidePeekImageCollection04
	<pre><tile>
	  <visual version="2">
	    <binding template="TileWide310x150PeekImage
	    Collection04" fallback="TileWidePeekImageCollection04">
	      <image id="1" src="Assets\picture.png" />
	      <image id="2" src="Assets\picture.png" />
	      <image id="3" src="Assets\picture.png" />
	      <image id="4" src="Assets\picture.png" />
	      <image id="5" src="Assets\picture.png" />
	      <text id="1">text id="1"</text>
	    </binding>
	  </visual>
	</tile></pre>	

TileWide310x150PeekImage Collection05
 TileWidePeekImageCollection05
	<pre><tile>
	  <visual version="2">
	    <binding template="TileWide310x150PeekImage
	    Collection05" fallback="TileWidePeekImageCollection05">
	      <image id="1" src="Assets\picture.png" />
	      <image id="2" src="Assets\picture.png" />
	      <image id="3" src="Assets\picture.png" />
	      <image id="4" src="Assets\picture.png" />
	      <image id="5" src="Assets\picture.png" />
	      <image id="6" src="Assets\picture.png" />
	      <text id="1">text id="1"</text>
	      <text id="2">text id="2"</text>
	    </binding>
	  </visual>
	</tile></pre>	

TileWide310x150PeekImage Collection06
 TileWidePeekImageCollection06
	<pre><tile>
	  <visual version="2">
	    <binding template="TileWide310x150PeekImage
	    Collection06" fallback="TileWidePeekImageCollection06">
	      <image id="1" src="Assets\picture.png" />
	      <image id="2" src="Assets\picture.png" />
	      <image id="3" src="Assets\picture.png" />
	      <image id="4" src="Assets\picture.png" />
	      <image id="5" src="Assets\picture.png" />
	      <image id="6" src="Assets\picture.png" />
	      <text id="1">text id="1"</text>
	    </binding>
	  </visual>
	</tile></pre>	

TileWide310x150PeekImage AndText01
 TileWidePeekImageAndText01
	<pre><tile>
	  <visual version="2">
	    <binding template="TileWide310x150PeekImage
	    AndText01" fallback="TileWidePeekImageAndText01">
	      <image id="1" src="Assets\picture.png" />
	      <text id="1">text id="1"</text>
	    </binding>
	  </visual>
	</tile></pre>	

(*continued*)

Table A-1. (*continued*)

Template Name	XML	Example

TileWide310x150PeekImage AndText02
TileWidePeekImageAndText02
	``xml
	<tile>
	  <visual version="2">
	    <binding template="TileWide310x150PeekImage
	    AndText02" fallback="TileWidePeekImageAndText02">
	      <image id="1" src="Assets\picture.png" />
	      <text id="1">text id="1"</text>
	      <text id="2">text id="2"</text>
	      <text id="3">text id="3"</text>
	      <text id="4">text id="4"</text>
	      <text id="5">text id="5"</text>
	    </binding>
	  </visual>
	</tile>
	``	

TileWide310x150PeekImage01
TileWidePeekImage01
	``xml
	<tile>
	  <visual version="2">
	    <binding template="TileWide310x150PeekImage01"
	    fallback="TileWidePeekImage01">
	      <image id="1" src="Assets\picture.png" />
	      <text id="1">text id="1"</text>
	      <text id="2">text id="2"</text>
	    </binding>
	  </visual>
	</tile>
	``	

TileWide310x150PeekImage02
TileWidePeekImage02
	``xml
	<tile>
	  <visual version="2">
	    <binding template="TileWide310x150PeekImage02"
	    fallback="TileWidePeekImage02">
	      <image id="1" src="Assets\picture.png" />
	      <text id="1">text id="1"</text>
	      <text id="2">text id="2"</text>
	      <text id="3">text id="3"</text>
	      <text id="4">text id="4"</text>
	      <text id="5">text id="5"</text>
	    </binding>
	  </visual>
	</tile>
	``	

TileWide310x150PeekImage03
TileWidePeekImage03
	``xml
	<tile>
	  <visual version="2">
	    <binding template="TileWide310x150PeekImage03"
	    fallback="TileWidePeekImage03">
	      <image id="1" src="Assets\picture.png" />
	      <text id="1">text id="1"</text>
	    </binding>
	  </visual>
	</tile>
	``	

(*continued*)

Table A-1. (*continued*)

Template Name	XML	Example

TileWide310x150PeekImage04
TileWidePeekImage04
	```<tile>```
	`  <visual version="2">`
	`    <binding template="TileWide310x150PeekImage04"`
	`    fallback="TileWidePeekImage04">`
	`      <image id="1" src="Assets\picture.png" />`
	`      <text id="1">text id="1"</text>`
	`    </binding>`
	`  </visual>`
	`</tile>`	

TileWide310x150PeekImage05
TileWidePeekImage05
	```<tile>```
	`  <visual version="2">`
	`    <binding template="TileWide310x150PeekImage05"`
	`    fallback="TileWidePeekImage05">`
	`      <image id="1" src="Assets\picture.png" />`
	`      <image id="2" src="Assets\picture.png" />`
	`      <text id="1">text id="1"</text>`
	`      <text id="2">text id="2"</text>`
	`    </binding>`
	`  </visual>`
	`</tile>`	

TileWide310x150PeekImage06
TileWidePeekImage06
	```<tile>```
	`  <visual version="2">`
	`    <binding template="TileWide310x150PeekImage06"`
	`    fallback="TileWidePeekImage06">`
	`      <image id="1" src="Assets\picture.png" />`
	`      <image id="2" src="Assets\picture.png" />`
	`      <text id="1">text id="1"</text>`
	`    </binding>`
	`  </visual>`
	`</tile>`	

TileWide310x150SmallImage
AndText01
TileWideSmallImageAndText01
	```<tile>```
	`  <visual version="2">`
	`    <binding template="TileWide310x150SmallImage`
	`    AndText01" fallback="TileWideSmallImageAndText01">`
	`      <image id="1" src="Assets\picture.png" />`
	`      <text id="1">text id="1"</text>`
	`    </binding>`
	`  </visual>`
	`</tile>`	

(*continued*)

Table A-1. (*continued*)

Template Name	XML	Example
TileWide310x150SmallImage AndText02 **TileWideSmallImageAndText02**	```<tile>\n <visual version="2">\n <binding template="TileWide310x150SmallImage\n AndText02" fallback="TileWideSmallImageAndText02">\n <image id="1" src="Assets\picture.png" />\n <text id="1">text id="1"</text>\n <text id="2">text id="2"</text>\n <text id="3">text id="3"</text>\n <text id="4">text id="4"</text>\n <text id="5">text id="5"</text>\n </binding>\n </visual>\n</tile>```	text id="1" text id="2" text id="3" text id="4"
TileWide310x150SmallImage AndText03 **TileWideSmallImageAndText03**	```<tile>\n <visual version="2">\n <binding template="TileWide310x150SmallImage\n AndText03" fallback="TileWideSmallImageAndText03">\n <image id="1" src="Assets\picture.png" />\n <text id="1">text id="1"</text>\n </binding>\n </visual>\n</tile>```	text id="1"
TileWide310x150SmallImage AndText04 **TileWideSmallImageAndText04**	```<tile>\n <visual version="2">\n <binding template="TileWide310x150SmallImage\n AndText04" fallback="TileWideSmallImageAndText04">\n <image id="1" src="Assets\picture.png" />\n <text id="1">text id="1"</text>\n <text id="2">text id="2"</text>\n </binding>\n </visual>\n</tile>```	text id="1" text id="2"
TileWide310x150SmallImage AndText05 **TileWideSmallImageAndText05**	```<tile>\n <visual version="2">\n <binding template="TileWide310x150SmallImage\n AndText05" fallback="TileWideSmallImageAndText05">\n <image id="1" src="Assets\picture.png" />\n <text id="1">text id="1"</text>\n <text id="2">text id="2"</text>\n </binding>\n </visual>\n</tile>```	text id="1" text id="2"
TileWide310x150Text01 **TileWideText01**	```<tile>\n <visual version="2">\n <binding template="TileWide310x150Text01"\n fallback="TileWideText01">\n <text id="1">text id="1"</text>\n <text id="2">text id="2"</text>\n <text id="3">text id="3"</text>\n <text id="4">text id="4"</text>\n <text id="5">text id="5"</text>\n </binding>\n </visual>\n</tile>```	text id="1" text id="2" text id="3" text id="4"

(*continued*)

Table A-1. (*continued*)

Template Name	XML	Example

TileWide310x150Text02
TileWideText02
	``xml
	<tile>
	  <visual version="2">
	    <binding template="TileWide310x150Text02"
	    fallback="TileWideText02">
	      <text id="1">text id="1"</text>
	      <text id="2">text id="2"</text>
	      <text id="3">text id="3"</text>
	      <text id="4">text id="4"</text>
	      <text id="5">text id="5"</text>
	      <text id="6">text id="6"</text>
	      <text id="7">text id="7"</text>
	      <text id="8">text id="8"</text>
	      <text id="9">text id="9"</text>
	    </binding>
	  </visual>
	</tile>
	``
		text id="1"
		text id="2" text id="3"
		text id="4" text id="5"
		text id="6" text id="7"

TileWide310x150Text03
TileWideText03
	``xml
	<tile>
	  <visual version="2">
	    <binding template="TileWide310x150Text03"
	    fallback="TileWideText03">
	      <text id="1">text id="1"</text>
	    </binding>
	  </visual>
	</tile>
	``
		text id="1"

TileWide310x150Text04
TileWideText04
	``xml
	<tile>
	  <visual version="2">
	    <binding template="TileWide310x150Text04"
	    fallback="TileWideText04">
	      <text id="1">text id="1"</text>
	    </binding>
	  </visual>
	</tile>
	``
		text id="1"

TileWide310x150Text05
TileWideText05
	``xml
	<tile>
	  <visual version="2">
	    <binding template="TileWide310x150Text05"
	    fallback="TileWideText05">
	      <text id="1">text id="1"</text>
	      <text id="2">text id="2"</text>
	      <text id="3">text id="3"</text>
	      <text id="4">text id="4"</text>
	      <text id="5">text id="5"</text>
	    </binding>
	  </visual>
	</tile>
	``
		text id="1"
		text id="2"
		text id="3"
		text id="4"

(*continued*)

Table A-1. (*continued*)

Template Name	XML	Example

TileWide310x150Text06
TileWideText06
	```<tile>```
	``` <visual version="2">```
	``` <binding template="TileWide310x150Text06"```
	``` fallback="TileWideText06">```
	``` <text id="1">text id="1"</text>```
	``` <text id="2">text id="2"</text>```
	``` <text id="3">text id="3"</text>```
	``` <text id="4">text id="4"</text>```
	``` <text id="5">text id="5"</text>```
	``` <text id="6">text id="6"</text>```
	``` <text id="7">text id="7"</text>```
	``` <text id="8">text id="8"</text>```
	``` <text id="9">text id="9"</text>```
	``` <text id="10">text id="10"</text>```
	``` </binding>```
	``` </visual>```
	```</tile>```
		text id="1" text id="2"
		text id="3" text id="4"
		text id="5" text id="6"
		text id="7" text id="8"

TileWide310x150Text07
TileWideText07
	```<tile>```
	``` <visual version="2">```
	``` <binding template="TileWide310x150Text07"```
	``` fallback="TileWideText07">```
	``` <text id="1">text id="1"</text>```
	``` <text id="2">text id="2"</text>```
	``` <text id="3">text id="3"</text>```
	``` <text id="4">text id="4"</text>```
	``` <text id="5">text id="5"</text>```
	``` <text id="6">text id="6"</text>```
	``` <text id="7">text id="7"</text>```
	``` <text id="8">text id="8"</text>```
	``` <text id="9">text id="9"</text>```
	``` </binding>```
	``` </visual>```
	```</tile>```
		text id="1"
		text id="2" text id="3"
		text id="4" text id="5"
		text id="6" text id="7"

TileWide310x150Text08
TileWideText08
	```<tile>```
	``` <visual version="2">```
	``` <binding template="TileWide310x150Text08"```
	``` fallback="TileWideText08">```
	``` <text id="1">text id="1"</text>```
	``` <text id="2">text id="2"</text>```
	``` <text id="3">text id="3"</text>```
	``` <text id="4">text id="4"</text>```
	``` <text id="5">text id="5"</text>```
	``` <text id="6">text id="6"</text>```
	``` <text id="7">text id="7"</text>```
	``` <text id="8">text id="8"</text>```
	``` <text id="9">text id="9"</text>```
	``` <text id="10">text id="10"</text>```
	``` </binding>```
	``` </visual>```
	```</tile>```
		text id="1" text id="2"
		text id="3" text id="4"
		text id="5" text id="6"
		text id="7" text id="8"

(*continued*)

Table A-1. (*continued*)

Template Name	XML	Example

TileWide310x150Text09
TileWideText09
	```<tile>```
	``` <visual version="2">```
	``` <binding template="TileWide310x150Text09"```
	``` fallback="TileWideText09">```
	``` <text id="1">text id="1"</text>```
	``` <text id="2">text id="2"</text>```
	``` </binding>```
	``` </visual>```
	```</tile>```
		text id="1"
		text id="2"

TileWide310x150Text10
TileWideText10
	```<tile>```
	``` <visual version="2">```
	``` <binding template="TileWide310x150Text10"```
	``` fallback="TileWideText10">```
	``` <text id="1">text id="1"</text>```
	``` <text id="2">text id="2"</text>```
	``` <text id="3">text id="3"</text>```
	``` <text id="4">text id="4"</text>```
	``` <text id="5">text id="5"</text>```
	``` <text id="6">text id="6"</text>```
	``` <text id="7">text id="7"</text>```
	``` <text id="8">text id="8"</text>```
	``` <text id="9">text id="9"</text>```
	``` </binding>```
	``` </visual>```
	```</tile>```
		text id="1"
		te... text id="3"
		te... text id="5"
		te... text id="7"

TileWide310x150Text11
TileWideText11
	```<tile>```
	``` <visual version="2">```
	``` <binding template="TileWide310x150Text11"```
	``` fallback="TileWideText11">```
	``` <text id="1">text id="1"</text>```
	``` <text id="2">text id="2"</text>```
	``` <text id="3">text id="3"</text>```
	``` <text id="4">text id="4"</text>```
	``` <text id="5">text id="5"</text>```
	``` <text id="6">text id="6"</text>```
	``` <text id="7">text id="7"</text>```
	``` <text id="8">text id="8"</text>```
	``` <text id="9">text id="9"</text>```
	``` <text id="10">text id="10"</text>```
	``` </binding>```
	``` </visual>```
	```</tile>```
		te... text id="2"
		te... text id="4"
		te... text id="6"
		te... text id="8"

TileSquare310x310BlockAndText01	```<tile>```
	``` <visual version="2">```
	``` <binding template="TileSquare310x310BlockAndText01">```
	``` <text id="1">text id="1"</text>```
	``` <text id="2">text id="2"</text>```
	``` <text id="3">text id="3"</text>```
	``` <text id="4">text id="4"</text>```
	``` <text id="5">text id="5"</text>```
	``` <text id="6">text id="6"</text>```
	``` <text id="7">text id="7"</text>```
	``` <text id="8">text id="8"</text>```
	``` <text id="9">text id="9"</text>```
	``` </binding>```
	``` </visual>```
	```</tile>```
		text id="1"
		text id="2"
		text id="3"
		
		text id="4" "8"
		text id="5"
		text id="6"
		text id="7" text id="9"

(*continued*)

Table A-1. (*continued*)

Template Name	XML	Example

TileSquare310x310BlockAndText02	```xml
	<tile>
	  <visual version="2">
	    <binding template="TileSquare310x310BlockAndText02">
	      <image id="1" src="Assets\picture.png" />
	      <text id="1">text id="1"</text>
	      <text id="2">text id="2"</text>
	      <text id="3">text id="3"</text>
	      <text id="4">text id="4"</text>
	      <text id="5">text id="5"</text>
	      <text id="6">text id="6"</text>
	      <text id="7">text id="7"</text>
	    </binding>
	  </visual>
	</tile>
	``	

TileSquare310x310Image	```xml
	<tile>
	  <visual version="2">
	    <binding template="TileSquare310x310Image">
	      <image id="1" src="Assets\picture.png" />
	    </binding>
	  </visual>
	</tile>
	``	

TileSquare310x310ImageAndText01	```xml
	<tile>
	  <visual version="2">
	    <binding template="TileSquare310x310ImageAndText01">
	      <image id="1" src="Assets\picture.png" />
	      <text id="1">text id="1"</text>
	    </binding>
	  </visual>
	</tile>
	``	

TileSquare310x310ImageAndText02	```xml
	<tile>
	  <visual version="2">
	    <binding template="TileSquare310x310ImageAndText02">
	      <image id="1" src="Assets\picture.png" />
	      <text id="1">text id="1"</text>
	      <text id="2">text id="2"</text>
	    </binding>
	  </visual>
	</tile>
	``	

(*continued*)

Table A-1. (*continued*)

Template Name	XML	Example
| **TileSquare310x310Image AndTextOverlay01** | ```xml
<tile>
  <visual version="2">
    <binding template="TileSquare310x310Image
    AndTextOverlay01">
      <image id="1" src="Assets\picture.png" />
      <text id="1">text id="1"</text>
    </binding>
  </visual>
</tile>
``` | |
| **TileSquare310x310Image AndTextOverlay02** | ```xml
<tile>
  <visual version="2">
    <binding template="TileSquare310x310Image
    AndTextOverlay02">
      <image id="1" src="Assets\picture.png" />
      <text id="1">text id="1"</text>
      <text id="2">text id="2"</text>
    </binding>
  </visual>
</tile>
``` | |
| **TileSquare310x310Image AndTextOverlay03** | ```xml
<tile>
  <visual version="2">
    <binding template="TileSquare310x310Image
    AndTextOverlay03">
      <image id="1" src="Assets\picture.png" />
      <text id="1">text id="1"</text>
      <text id="2">text id="2"</text>
      <text id="3">text id="3"</text>
      <text id="4">text id="4"</text>
    </binding>
  </visual>
</tile>
``` | |
| **TileSquare310x310ImageCollection AndText01** | ```xml
<tile>
  <visual version="2">
    <binding template="TileSquare310x310ImageCollection
    AndText01">
      <image id="1" src="Assets\picture.png" />
      <image id="2" src="Assets\picture.png" />
      <image id="3" src="Assets\picture.png" />
      <image id="4" src="Assets\picture.png" />
      <image id="5" src="Assets\picture.png" />
      <text id="1">text id="1"</text>
    </binding>
  </visual>
</tile>
``` | |

(*continued*)

Table A-1. (*continued*)

Template Name	XML	Example
| **TileSquare310x310ImageCollection AndText02** | ```xml
<tile>
  <visual version="2">
    <binding template="TileSquare310x310ImageCollection
    AndText02">
      <image id="1" src="Assets\picture.png" />
      <image id="2" src="Assets\picture.png" />
      <image id="3" src="Assets\picture.png" />
      <image id="4" src="Assets\picture.png" />
      <image id="5" src="Assets\picture.png" />
      <text id="1">text id="1"</text>
      <text id="2">text id="2"</text>
    </binding>
  </visual>
</tile>
``` | |
| **TileSquare310x310ImageCollection** | ```xml
<tile>
  <visual version="2">
    <binding template="TileSquare310x310ImageCollection">
      <image id="1" src="Assets\picture.png" />
      <image id="2" src="Assets\picture.png" />
      <image id="3" src="Assets\picture.png" />
      <image id="4" src="Assets\picture.png" />
      <image id="5" src="Assets\picture.png" />
    </binding>
  </visual>
</tile>
``` | |
| **TileSquare310x310SmallImages AndTextList01** | ```xml
<tile>
  <visual version="2">
    <binding template="TileSquare310x310SmallImages
    AndTextList01">
      <image id="1" src="Assets\picture.png" />
      <image id="2" src="Assets\picture.png" />
      <image id="3" src="Assets\picture.png" />
      <text id="1">text id="1"</text>
      <text id="2">text id="2"</text>
      <text id="3">text id="3"</text>
      <text id="4">text id="4"</text>
      <text id="5">text id="5"</text>
      <text id="6">text id="6"</text>
      <text id="7">text id="7"</text>
      <text id="8">text id="8"</text>
      <text id="9">text id="9"</text>
    </binding>
  </visual>
</tile>
``` | |

(*continued*)
```

Table A-1. (*continued*)

Template Name	XML	Example
| **TileSquare310x310SmallImages AndTextList02** | ```xml
<tile>
  <visual version="2">
    <binding template="TileSquare310x310SmallImages
    AndTextList02">
      <image id="1" src="Assets\picture.png" />
      <image id="2" src="Assets\picture.png" />
      <image id="3" src="Assets\picture.png" />
      <text id="1">text id="1"</text>
      <text id="2">text id="2"</text>
      <text id="3">text id="3"</text>
    </binding>
  </visual>
</tile>
``` | text id="1" <br><br> text id="2" <br><br> text id="3" |
| **TileSquare310x310SmallImages AndTextList03** | ```xml
<tile>
  <visual version="2">
    <binding template="TileSquare310x310SmallImages
    AndTextList03">
      <image id="1" src="Assets\picture.png" />
      <image id="2" src="Assets\picture.png" />
      <image id="3" src="Assets\picture.png" />
      <text id="1">text id="1"</text>
      <text id="2">text id="2"</text>
      <text id="3">text id="3"</text>
      <text id="4">text id="4"</text>
      <text id="5">text id="5"</text>
      <text id="6">text id="6"</text>
    </binding>
  </visual>
</tile>
``` | text id="1" <br> text id="2" <br><br> text id="3" <br> text id="4" <br><br> text id="5" <br> text id="6" |
| **TileSquare310x310SmallImages AndTextList04** | ```xml
<tile>
  <visual version="2">
    <binding template="TileSquare310x310SmallImages
    AndTextList04">
      <image id="1" src="Assets\picture.png" />
      <image id="2" src="Assets\picture.png" />
      <image id="3" src="Assets\picture.png" />
      <text id="1">text id="1"</text>
      <text id="2">text id="2"</text>
      <text id="3">text id="3"</text>
      <text id="4">text id="4"</text>
      <text id="5">text id="5"</text>
      <text id="6">text id="6"</text>
    </binding>
  </visual>
</tile>
``` | text id="1" <br> text id="2" <br><br> text id="3" <br> text id="4" <br><br> text id="5" <br> text id="6" |

(*continued*)
```

Table A-1. (*continued*)

Template Name	XML	Example

TileSquare310x310Text01	```xml
	<tile>
	  <visual version="2">
	    <binding template="TileSquare310x310Text01">
	      <text id="1">text id="1"</text>
	      <text id="2">text id="2"</text>
	      <text id="3">text id="3"</text>
	      <text id="4">text id="4"</text>
	      <text id="5">text id="5"</text>
	      <text id="6">text id="6"</text>
	      <text id="7">text id="7"</text>
	      <text id="8">text id="8"</text>
	      <text id="9">text id="9"</text>
	      <text id="10">text id="10"</text>
	    </binding>
	  </visual>
	</tile>
	``
		text id="1"
		
		text id="2"
		text id="3"
		text id="4"
		text id="5"
		text id="6"
		text id="7"
		text id="8"
		text id="9"
		text id="10"

TileSquare310x310Text02	```xml
	<tile>
	  <visual version="2">
	    <binding template="TileSquare310x310Text02">
	      <text id="1">text id="1"</text>
	      <text id="2">text id="2"</text>
	      <text id="3">text id="3"</text>
	      <text id="4">text id="4"</text>
	      <text id="5">text id="5"</text>
	      <text id="6">text id="6"</text>
	      <text id="7">text id="7"</text>
	      <text id="8">text id="8"</text>
	      <text id="9">text id="9"</text>
	      <text id="10">text id="10"</text>
	      <text id="11">text id="11"</text>
	      <text id="12">text id="12"</text>
	      <text id="13">text id="13"</text>
	      <text id="14">text id="14"</text>
	      <text id="15">text id="15"</text>
	      <text id="16">text id="16"</text>
	      <text id="17">text id="17"</text>
	      <text id="18">text id="18"</text>
	      <text id="19">text id="19"</text>
	    </binding>
	  </visual>
	</tile>
	``
		text id="1"
		
		text id="2" text id="3"
		text id="4" text id="5"
		text id="6" text id="7"
		text id="8" text id="9"
		text id="10" text id="11"
		text id="12" text id="13"
		text id="14" text id="15"
		text id="16" text id="17"
		text id="18" text id="19"

TileSquare310x310Text03	```xml
	<tile>
	  <visual version="2">
	    <binding template="TileSquare310x310Text03">
	      <text id="1">text id="1"</text>
	      <text id="2">text id="2"</text>
	      <text id="3">text id="3"</text>
	      <text id="4">text id="4"</text>
	      <text id="5">text id="5"</text>
	      <text id="6">text id="6"</text>
	      <text id="7">text id="7"</text>
	      <text id="8">text id="8"</text>
	      <text id="9">text id="9"</text>
	      <text id="10">text id="10"</text>
	      <text id="11">text id="11"</text>
	    </binding>
	  </visual>
	</tile>
	``
		text id="1"
		text id="2"
		text id="3"
		text id="4"
		text id="5"
		text id="6"
		text id="7"
		text id="8"
		text id="9"
		text id="10"
		text id="11"

(*continued*)

Table A-1. (*continued*)

Template Name	XML	Example
TileSquare310x310Text04	``` <tile> <visual version="2"> <binding template="TileSquare310x310Text04"> <text id="1">text id="1"</text> <text id="2">text id="2"</text> <text id="3">text id="3"</text> <text id="4">text id="4"</text> <text id="5">text id="5"</text> <text id="6">text id="6"</text> <text id="7">text id="7"</text> <text id="8">text id="8"</text> <text id="9">text id="9"</text> <text id="10">text id="10"</text> <text id="11">text id="11"</text> <text id="12">text id="12"</text> <text id="13">text id="13"</text> <text id="14">text id="14"</text> <text id="15">text id="15"</text> <text id="16">text id="16"</text> <text id="17">text id="17"</text> <text id="18">text id="18"</text> <text id="19">text id="19"</text> <text id="20">text id="20"</text> <text id="21">text id="21"</text> <text id="22">text id="22"</text> </binding> </visual> </tile> ```	text id="1" text id="2" text id="3" text id="4" text id="5" text id="6" text id="7" text id="8" text id="9" text id="10" text id="11" text id="12" text id="13" text id="14" text id="15" text id="16" text id="17" text id="18" text id="19" text id="20" text id="21" text id="22"
TileSquare310x310Text05	``` <tile> <visual version="2"> <binding template="TileSquare310x310Text05"> <text id="1">text id="1"</text> <text id="2">text id="2"</text> <text id="3">text id="3"</text> <text id="4">text id="4"</text> <text id="5">text id="5"</text> <text id="6">text id="6"</text> <text id="7">text id="7"</text> <text id="8">text id="8"</text> <text id="9">text id="9"</text> <text id="10">text id="10"</text> <text id="11">text id="11"</text> <text id="12">text id="12"</text> <text id="13">text id="13"</text> <text id="14">text id="14"</text> <text id="15">text id="15"</text> <text id="16">text id="16"</text> <text id="17">text id="17"</text> <text id="18">text id="18"</text> <text id="19">text id="19"</text> </binding> </visual> </tile> ```	text id="1" text id="2" text id="3" text id="4" text id="5" text id="6" text id="7" text id="8" text id="9" text id="10" text id="11" text id="12" text id="13" text id="1... text id="15" text id="16" text id="17" text id="18" text id="19"

(*continued*)

Table A-1. (*continued*)

Template Name	XML	Example
TileSquare310x310Text06	```<tile>```	

<tile>
  <visual version="2">
    <binding template="TileSquare310x310Text06">
      <text id="1">text id="1"</text>
      <text id="2">text id="2"</text>
      <text id="3">text id="3"</text>
      <text id="4">text id="4"</text>
      <text id="5">text id="5"</text>
      <text id="6">text id="6"</text>
      <text id="7">text id="7"</text>
      <text id="8">text id="8"</text>
      <text id="9">text id="9"</text>
      <text id="10">text id="10"</text>
      <text id="11">text id="11"</text>
      <text id="12">text id="12"</text>
      <text id="13">text id="13"</text>
      <text id="14">text id="14"</text>
      <text id="15">text id="15"</text>
      <text id="16">text id="16"</text>
      <text id="17">text id="17"</text>
      <text id="18">text id="18"</text>
      <text id="19">text id="19"</text>
      <text id="20">text id="20"</text>
      <text id="21">text id="21"</text>
      <text id="22">text id="22"</text>
    </binding>
  </visual>
</tile>

TileSquare310x310Text07

<tile>
  <visual version="2">
    <binding template="TileSquare310x310Text07">
      <text id="1">text id="1"</text>
      <text id="2">text id="2"</text>
      <text id="3">text id="3"</text>
      <text id="4">text id="4"</text>
      <text id="5">text id="5"</text>
      <text id="6">text id="6"</text>
      <text id="7">text id="7"</text>
      <text id="8">text id="8"</text>
      <text id="9">text id="9"</text>
      <text id="10">text id="10"</text>
      <text id="11">text id="11"</text>
      <text id="12">text id="12"</text>
      <text id="13">text id="13"</text>
      <text id="14">text id="14"</text>
      <text id="15">text id="15"</text>
      <text id="16">text id="16"</text>
      <text id="17">text id="17"</text>
      <text id="18">text id="18"</text>
      <text id="19">text id="19"</text>
    </binding>
  </visual>
</tile>

(*continued*)

Table A-1. (*continued*)

Template Name	XML	Example
TileSquare310x310Text08	```<tile>``` ``` <visual version="2">``` ``` <binding template="TileSquare310x310Text08">``` ``` <text id="1">text id="1"</text>``` ``` <text id="2">text id="2"</text>``` ``` <text id="3">text id="3"</text>``` ``` <text id="4">text id="4"</text>``` ``` <text id="5">text id="5"</text>``` ``` <text id="6">text id="6"</text>``` ``` <text id="7">text id="7"</text>``` ``` <text id="8">text id="8"</text>``` ``` <text id="9">text id="9"</text>``` ``` <text id="10">text id="10"</text>``` ``` <text id="11">text id="11"</text>``` ``` <text id="12">text id="12"</text>``` ``` <text id="13">text id="13"</text>``` ``` <text id="14">text id="14"</text>``` ``` <text id="15">text id="15"</text>``` ``` <text id="16">text id="16"</text>``` ``` <text id="17">text id="17"</text>``` ``` <text id="18">text id="18"</text>``` ``` <text id="19">text id="19"</text>``` ``` <text id="20">text id="20"</text>``` ``` <text id="21">text id="21"</text>``` ``` <text id="22">text id="22"</text>``` ``` </binding>``` ``` </visual>``` ```</tile>```	te... text id="2" / te... text id="4" / te... text id="6" / te... text id="8" / te... text id="10" / te... text id="12" / te... text id="14" / te... text id="16" / te... text id="18" / te... text id="20" / te... text id="22"
TileSquare310x310TextList01	```<tile>``` ``` <visual version="2">``` ``` <binding template="TileSquare310x310TextList01">``` ``` <text id="1">text id="1"</text>``` ``` <text id="2">text id="2"</text>``` ``` <text id="3">text id="3"</text>``` ``` <text id="4">text id="4"</text>``` ``` <text id="5">text id="5"</text>``` ``` <text id="6">text id="6"</text>``` ``` <text id="7">text id="7"</text>``` ``` <text id="8">text id="8"</text>``` ``` <text id="9">text id="9"</text>``` ``` </binding>``` ``` </visual>``` ```</tile>```	text id="1" / text id="2" / text id="3" / text id="4" / text id="5" / text id="6" / text id="7" / text id="8" / text id="9"
TileSquare310x310TextList02	```<tile>``` ``` <visual version="2">``` ``` <binding template="TileSquare310x310TextList02">``` ``` <text id="1">text id="1"</text>``` ``` <text id="2">text id="2"</text>``` ``` <text id="3">text id="3"</text>``` ``` </binding>``` ``` </visual>``` ```</tile>```	text id="1" / text id="2" / text id="3"

(*continued*)

Table A-1. (*continued*)

Template Name	XML	Example
TileSquare310x310TextList03	```\n<tile>\n <visual version="2">\n <binding template="TileSquare310x310TextList03">\n <text id="1">text id="1"</text>\n <text id="2">text id="2"</text>\n <text id="3">text id="3"</text>\n <text id="4">text id="4"</text>\n <text id="5">text id="5"</text>\n <text id="6">text id="6"</text>\n </binding>\n </visual>\n</tile>\n```	text id="1" text id="2" text id="3" text id="4" text id="5" text id="6"
TileSquare310x310SmallImage AndText01	```\n<tile>\n <visual version="2">\n <binding template="TileSquare310x310SmallImage\n AndText01">\n <image id="1" src="Assets\picture.png" />\n <text id="1">text id="1"</text>\n <text id="2">text id="2"</text>\n <text id="3">text id="3"</text>\n </binding>\n </visual>\n</tile>\n```	text id="1" text id="2" text id="3"
TileSquare310x310SmallImages AndTextList05	```\n<tile>\n <visual version="2">\n <binding template="TileSquare310x310SmallImages\n AndTextList05">\n <image id="1" src="Assets\picture.png" />\n <image id="2" src="Assets\picture.png" />\n <image id="3" src="Assets\picture.png" />\n <text id="1">text id="1"</text>\n <text id="2">text id="2"</text>\n <text id="3">text id="3"</text>\n <text id="4">text id="4"</text>\n <text id="5">text id="5"</text>\n <text id="6">text id="6"</text>\n <text id="7">text id="7"</text>\n </binding>\n </visual>\n</tile>\n```	text id="1" text id="2" text id="3" text id="4" text id="5" text id="6" text id="7"
TileSquare310x310Text09	```\n<tile>\n <visual version="2">\n <binding template="TileSquare310x310Text09">\n <text id="1">text id="1"</text>\n <text id="2">text id="2"</text>\n <text id="3">text id="3"</text>\n <text id="4">text id="4"</text>\n <text id="5">text id="5"</text>\n </binding>\n </visual>\n</tile>\n```	text id="1" text id="2" text id="3" text id="4" text id="5"

Toast Templates

Table A-2 shows the various toast notification templates.

Table A-2. *Toast Notification Templates*

Enumeration Value (JavaScript Value)	XML Template	Example

ToastImageAndText01 (toastImageAndText01)	```<toast>```
	 ``` <visual>```
	 ``` <binding template="ToastImageAndText01">```
	 ``` <image id="1" src="images/draw.png" />```
	 ``` <text id="1">Lorem ipsum dolor sit amet, consectetur adipisicing elit, sed do eiusmod tempor incididunt ut labore et dolore magna aliqua. </text>```
	 ``` </binding>```
	 ``` </visual>```
	 ```</toast>```	

ToastImageAndText02 (toastImageAndText02)	```<toast>```
	 ``` <visual>```
	 ``` <binding template="ToastImageAndText02">```
	 ``` <image id="1" src="images/draw.png" />```
	 ``` <text id="1">Lorem ipsum dolor sit amet, consectetur adipisicing elit</text>```
	 ``` <text id="2">Lorem ipsum dolor sit amet, consectetur adipisicing elit, sed do eiusmod</text>```
	 ``` </binding>```
	 ``` </visual>```
	 ```</toast>```	

ToastImageAndText03 (toastImageAndText03)	```<toast>```
	 ``` <visual>```
	 ``` <binding template="ToastImageAndText03">```
	 ``` <image id="1" src="images/draw.png" />```
	 ``` <text id="1">Lorem ipsum dolor sit amet, consectetur adipisicing elit, sed do eiusmod.</text>```
	 ``` <text id="2">Lorem ipsum dolor sit amet, consectetur adipisicing elit.</text>```
	 ``` </binding>```
	 ``` </visual>```
	 ```</toast>```	

ToastImageAndText04 (toastImageAndText04)	```<toast>```
	 ``` <visual>```
	 ``` <binding template="ToastImageAndText04">```
	 ``` <image id="1" src="images/draw.png" />```
	 ``` <text id="1">Lorem ipsum dolor sit amet, consectetur adipisicing elit.</text>```
	 ``` <text id="2">Lorem ipsum dolor sit amet, consectetur adipisicing elit.</text>```
	 ``` <text id="3">Lorem ipsum dolor sit amet, consectetur adipisicing elit.</text>```
	 ``` </binding>```
	 ``` </visual>```
	 ```</toast>```	

(continued)

Table A-2. (*continued*)

Enumeration Value (JavaScript Value)	XML Template	Example
ToastText01 (toastText01)	```<toast>` ` <visual>` ` <binding template="ToastText01">` ` <text id="1">Lorem ipsum dolor sit amet, consectetur` ` adipisicing elit, sed do eiusmod tempor incididunt` ` ut labore et dolore magna aliqua. Ut enim ad minim` ` veniam.</text>` ` </binding>` ` </visual>` `</toast>```	Lorem ipsum dolor sit amet, consectetur adipisicing elit, sed do eiusmod tempor incididunt ut labore et dolore magna aliqua....
ToastText02 (toastText02)	```<toast>` ` <visual>` ` <binding template="ToastText02">` ` <text id="1">Lorem ipsum dolor sit amet, consectetur` ` adipisicing elit.</text>` ` <text id="2">Lorem ipsum dolor sit amet, consectetur` ` adipisicing elit, sed do eiusmod tempor incididunt.` ` </text>` ` </binding>` ` </visual>` `</toast>```	Lorem ipsum dolor sit amet, consectetur a... Lorem ipsum dolor sit amet, consectetur adipisicing elit, sed do eiusmod tempor...
ToastText03 (toastText03)	```<toast>` ` <visual>` ` <binding template="ToastText03">` ` <text id="1">Lorem ipsum dolor sit amet, consectetur` ` adipisicing elit, sed do eiusmod tempor incididunt ut` ` labore.</text>` ` <text id="2">Lorem ipsum dolor sit amet, consectetur` ` adipisicing elit.</text>` ` </binding>` ` </visual>` `</toast>```	Lorem ipsum dolor sit amet, consectetur adipisicing elit, sed do eiusmod tempor... Lorem ipsum dolor sit amet, consectetur adi...
ToastText04 (toastText04)	```<toast>` ` <visual>` ` <binding template="ToastText04">` ` <text id="1">Lorem ipsum dolor sit amet, consectetur` ` adipisicing elit.</text>` ` <text id="2">Lorem ipsum dolor sit amet, consectetur` ` adipisicing elit.</text>` ` <text id="3">Lorem ipsum dolor sit amet, consectetur` ` adipisicing elit.</text>` ` </binding>` ` </visual>` `</toast>```	Lorem ipsum dolor sit amet, consectetur a... Lorem ipsum dolor sit amet, consectetur adi... Lorem ipsum dolor sit amet, consectetur adi...

APPENDIX B

Windows Store Developer Account

Before you start selling your apps in the Windows Store, you must have a developer account, which means that you must register yourself at the Windows Developer Center. To do so, you must register with a Microsoft account at https://appdev.microsoft.com/StorePortals/. The procedure has a cost: $49 as individual or $99 as company. This will allow you to access the Windows Developer Center Dashboard. Optionally, if you are already registered as a Windows Phone developer you can link these two accounts in order to use the same publisher name for both platforms (see Figure B-1).

Account type

Things you need before you register

- Your tax info
- Your contact and identification info
- A valid credit card, so that we can verify your account. Sorry, we can't accept pre-paid cards.
- A registration code, if you have one

Country/region

Pick the country/region where you live or where your business is located.

[United States ▾]

Pick account type

If you want to link this to another Microsoft developer account so they both share the same publisher display name, you must go back and sign in with your other Microsoft account. Learn more

Individual	Company
- Develop apps as an individual or a small unincorporated group - Submit Windows Store apps	- Develop apps as a business - Submit Windows Store apps and desktop apps - Use additional app capabilities
Annual price: 49.00 USD	Annual price: 99.00 USD
Enroll now	Enroll now

Figure B-1. *Account type registration*

To create a developer account, you can log in with a Microsoft account. The process is simple. You choose the type of account (Individual or Company) and then you add your personal or company information, like the name of the publisher, country, phone, and e-mail. At the end, you will use a credit card to pay the registration fee (see Figure B-2).

Account info

Figure B-2. *Developer account steps*

The Individual account has also some limitations that company account does not have; this account type is for people who want to create apps for consumers, because one of the limitations is the ability to publish just Windows Store apps. If you plan to publish both Windows Store and desktop apps, you must opt for a Company account. Choosing a Company account type enables you to access special use capabilities like.

- Enterprise authentication (enterpriseAuthentication) for Windows domain credentials use

- Shared user certificates (sharedUserCertificates) to access software and hardware certificates such as digital signature

- Documents library (documentsLibrary) to gain access to the user's Documents library programmatically. You should use this capability only in particular scenarios where you cannot use the file picker.

Each account needs to be verified by confirming registrant identity and payment method before you can submit an app.

As mentioned, there are two reasons to start developing Windows Store apps, one of which is economic opportunity. Microsoft knows that to attract new developers on this new platform, besides the number of potential users, it must entice economically, providing an interesting revenue sharing rate. Initially, you make 70% of your app's price on each sale; when you reach $25,000 of sales, the percentage increases to 80% for the rest of your application's lifetime. Once your app has earned at least $200, you can get paid from the Windows Store by setting your bank account information in the Payout section of your profile (see Figure B-3).

Payout account

Dashboard
Submit an app
Explore Store trends
Financial summary

Profile
Account
Payout
Tax
Subscription

Your payout account is where we deposit the money you earn in the Store. We confirm with you any changes made to your account. If you add or change an account shortly before your next payment is due, we'll delay that payment and add it to the next one. This delay gives you time to confirm that the changes are correct. Learn more

Add a payout account

Figure B-3. *Setting a payout account*

You also need to fill a tax form in the Tax section of your profile. If you live in the United States, the tax form is the W-9; otherwise you need to fill out the W-8BEN form (see Figure B-4).

Tax profile

Dashboard
Submit an app
Explore Store trends
Financial summary

Profile
Account
Payout
Tax
Subscription

Set up your tax form

In order to establish your tax status, you must complete the information below and on the next page. Then you will be guided to complete applicable tax form.

🔵 **Please check here if any of the following apply to you:**
You are a US citizen
You were born in the US
You are a US resident (you have a "green card")
You file a joint tax return with a US taxpayer
You have been in the US more than 183 days in the past three years
You are a corporation that was incorporated in the US

⭕ **Please check here if none of the above apply to you.**

After clicking next, you will start to submit or re-submit your tax information. You won't be eligible for payments until this information is submitted and passed validation.

Back   Next

Microsoft is committed to helping protect your privacy. For more information, read the Privacy Statement

TRUSTe
CERTIFIED PRIVACY

Figure B-4. *Fill in the tax form*

Once you have set this information, you are ready to submit your first app.

Index

Get the eBook for only $10!

Now you can take the weightless companion with you anywhere, anytime. Your purchase of this book entitles you to 3 electronic versions for only $10.

This Apress title will prove so indispensible that you'll want to carry it with you everywhere, which is why we are offering the eBook in 3 formats for only $10 if you have already purchased the print book.

Convenient and fully searchable, the PDF version enables you to easily find and copy code—or perform examples by quickly toggling between instructions and applications. The MOBI format is ideal for your Kindle, while the ePUB can be utilized on a variety of mobile devices.

Go to www.apress.com/promo/tendollars to purchase your companion eBook.

Apress®
THE EXPERT'S VOICE™

CPSIA information can be obtained at www.ICGtesting.com
Printed in the USA
LVOW03s1815130514

385614LV00013B/623/P